PENGUIN BOOKS
THE BARCELONA COMPLEX

Simon Kuper is a journalist who writes for the *Financial Times* and whose work has appeared in newspapers and magazines around the world. He is one of the world's leading writers on soccer. His book *Soccer Against the Enemy* won the William Hill Sports Book of the Year award. His works are also widely read in translation. Born in Uganda, Kuper spent most of his childhood in the Netherlands and now lives in Paris.

Praise for *The Barcelona Complex*

"This is a masterfully written history of the world's greatest football club. Més Que un Book."
—Gary Lineker

"Readers need not follow the sport to enjoy [*The Barcelona Complex*]. . . . A smart, engaging look at soccer as both game and business."
—*Kirkus Reviews* (starred review)

"Brilliant. Simon Kuper is one of the smartest minds in soccer, and his three decades of covering Barça and his tremendous access produce a book that is clear-eyed about Barça's greatness and more recent decline."
—Grant Wahl, *Sports Illustrated* writer, author of
The Beckham Experiment and *Masters of Modern Soccer*

"This is a book worthy of the club it chronicles. With virtuosic reporting, joyous storytelling, and complete authority, Kuper has added another classic to the canon of great soccer books, a genre he practically invented. And by providing such a vivid behind-the-curtain view into the operations of one the world's most successful institutions, he's also written an unlikely guide to managing talent."
—Franklin Foer, bestselling author of *How Soccer Explains the World*

"What is the point of football, Simon Kuper asks? It makes our lives a little happier than they would be without it. And the point of this book? It makes our lives even happier. Kuper has written a great story, a history and a biography, a work of philosophy and gossip, that is the best book about sports, any sport, that I have read in a long time. An outright joy. An instant classic."
—Bill Buford, author of *Among the Thugs* and *Heat*

"Kuper writes with both awe and insight about one of the world's most fabled teams. This book is packed full of endearing details and stories and the characters are lovable, fallible, and honest. It feels like being let inside the dream. In an era where monstrous contracts and commercialization have killed off some of the game's innocence, it is good to immerse yourself in a Barcelona that was, in large part, the team we wish all professional teams were—a neighborhood team composed of boyhood friends who love to play and love their club."

—Gwen Oxenham, author of *Under the Lights* and *In the Dark*

"Simon's writing has been an indispensable part of football's landscape for the better part of the last three decades. His access to Barça has enabled him to tell a story that no one else can about the biggest club in the world and its biggest star. This book both chronicles and analyzes an era in football history that we're lucky to have witnessed, and that may never be matched."

—Billy Beane, legendary general manager of the Oakland A's and subject of Michael Lewis' *Moneyball*

"Simon Kuper is an incredible storyteller. He sees football as a mirror that reflects the world around it. In the same way as Barça claims to be 'more than a club,' this is more than a football book. It explores visionary creativity through Cruyff, the limitations of genius through Messi, and human decision-making lived out under conditions of hysterical pressure. A must read that is about football in the same way *Animal Farm* is a tale of horses and pigs."

—Roger Bennett, author of *Men in Blazers Present Encyclopedia Blazertannica*

"Founded in 1899, the FC Barcelona soccer club (also known as Barça) from Spain's Catalonia region is one of the sport's most famous franchises, with a rich history of dynamic coaches and managers, as well as superstars like Johan Cruyff and Lionel Messi. Who better to explore this legacy than veteran British sports journalist Kuper (*Soccernomics*, 2009). His account delivers an insider's view of FC Barcelona. . . . Kuper vividly captures the unique cultural phenomenon that is FC Barcelona. A must for soccer fans."

—*Booklist*

"Kuper translates his decades of coverage of the world's highest-grossing sports club into a fascinating record of its legacy. . . . Brilliantly captures the business of sports. [*The Barcelona Complex*] is likely to be the definitive account of the business side of the famous club." —*Publishers Weekly*

"Essential reading for anyone interested in innovation or high performance. . . . [*The Barcelona Complex*] is both a debunking and a restoration. . . . Kuper diverts our eye away from the dazzling but familiar skyline and instead takes us inside the cathedral close."   —*New Statesman*

"May be one of the most forensic books about the football industry ever written. Thoughtful and dramatic."
—*The Economist* (Books of the Year issue)

"The best football book of 2021 begins as a tribute and ends as an elegy. It is a celebration of one of the greatest glories in a lifetime of watching sport yet concludes as a cautionary tale. [*The Barcelona Complex*] by Simon Kuper is all the more compelling for that late twist of sadness, and failure. . . . Forensic."   —*The Times* (London)

"Gripping account . . . At its heart, this is an intimately told story about how to create a winning organizational culture—and how, by avoiding Barça's mistakes, not to lose it."   —*The Financial Times*

"Will interest both business theorists and football fans."
—*The Guardian* (Best Sports Books of 2021)

"2021's best book on soccer."   —*The Toronto Globe & Mail*

"Kuper has long been one of the most thoughtful and intelligent writers about football. The almost Shakespearean narrative of the rise and fall of the world's most exciting and inspirational club makes a suitably epic tapestry for his talents. . . . A compelling account, brilliantly told, of ambition, sublime ability, and political infighting."
—*The Daily Mail* (Sports Books of the Year list)

"Beyond its immediate appeal, Kuper's fine book has two other virtues. It educates readers like me about many of the game's subtleties. And it also offers leaders of any organization an abiding lesson about how not to manage for tomorrow."   —Michael Moritz, *Sunday Times*

ALSO BY SIMON KUPER

Soccernomics

Spies, Lies, and Exile

Ajax

Soccer Against the Enemy

THE BARCELONA COMPLEX

LIONEL MESSI AND THE MAKING—
AND UNMAKING—OF THE WORLD'S
GREATEST SOCCER CLUB

SIMON KUPER

PENGUIN BOOKS

PENGUIN BOOKS
An imprint of Penguin Random House LLC
penguinrandomhouse.com

First published in the United States of America by Penguin Press,
an imprint of Penguin Random House LLC, 2021
This updated edition published in Penguin Books 2022

Graphs by John Burn-Murdoch

ISBN 9780593297735 (paperback)

THE LIBRARY OF CONGRESS HAS CATALOGED THE HARDCOVER EDITION AS FOLLOWS:
Names: Kuper, Simon, author.
Title: The Barcelona complex : Lionel Messi and the making—and
unmaking—of the world's greatest soccer club / Simon Kuper.
Other titles: Barça complex
Description: New York : Penguin Press, 2021. |
Includes bibliographical references and index. |
Identifiers: LCCN 2021021665 (print) | LCCN 2021021666 (ebook) |
ISBN 9780593297711 (Hardcover) | ISBN 9780593297728 (eBook)
Subjects: LCSH: Futbol Club Barcelona—History. |
Soccer teams—Spain—Barcelona—History. |
Sports teams—Spain—Barcelona—Economic aspects. |
Michels, Rinus, 1928– | Cruyff, Johan, 1947–2016. | Messi,
Lionel, 1987– | Nationalism—Spain—Catalonia—History. |
Catalonia (Spain)—Politics and government. |
Nationalism and sports—Spain—Catalonia—History.
Classification: LCC GV943.6.B3 K87 2021 (print) |
LCC GV943.6.B3 (ebook) | DDC 796.33409467/2—dc23
LC record available at https://lccn.loc.gov/2021021665
LC ebook record available at https://lccn.loc.gov/2021021666

Printed in the United States of America
1st Printing

DESIGNED BY MEIGHAN CAVANAUGH

To Pamela, Leila, Joey, and Leo,

for letting me write this book in our Paris

living room during the months of the lockdown,

and for falling in love with Spain and

Catalonia with me. It wouldn't have been

worth it without you.

Before he came we didn't have a cathedral of football, this beautiful church, at Barcelona. We needed something new. And now it is something that has lasted. It was built by one man, by Johan Cruyff, stone by stone.

—PEP GUARDIOLA

The truth is that there has been no project or anything for a long time. They juggle and cover holes as things go by.

—LIONEL MESSI, SEPTEMBER 2020

I suspect that if journalists really understood football they wouldn't be journalists.

—JOHAN CRUYFF

CONTENTS

CAST OF CHARACTERS

Eric Abidal (1979–): Club legend since he lifted the 2011 Champions League months after surviving cancer. Served Barcelona successfully as left-back of Pep Guardiola's great team, and then unsuccessfully as sporting director, buying the wrong players from 2018 to 2020.

Jordi Alba (1989–): A Masia boy, who left Barcelona to launch his career and returned in 2012. Left-back. Good friend and holiday companion of Messi's.

Thiago Alcântara (1991–): Midfielder. Son of the Brazilian world champion Mazinho. Came through the Masia but couldn't break into the first team, left for Bayern, and starred in their 8–2 thrashing of Barça in 2020. Now at Liverpool.

Josep Maria Bartomeu (1963–): As Barça's president from 2014 until his resignation in 2020, he bought the wrong players for too much money. Runs a family business. Nice chap.

Tonny Bruins Slot (1947–2020): Johan Cruyff's trusted assistant, a working-class Amsterdammer born the same year as Cruyff, and one of the few people he never fell out with. Did the tactical analyses of opponents that Cruyff didn't have the patience for.

Sergio Busquets (1988–): A brilliant *pivote*, as long as he doesn't have to run. A Masia boy, he went from the bench of Barcelona's B team in 2008 to winning all the biggest prizes in football by 2011. Son of Cruyff's not-so-brilliant reserve goalkeeper Carles Busquets.

Albert Capellas (1967–): Spent much of his early coaching career in Barça's Masia academy, ending up as its coordinator. In June 2021, he returned to the Masia after a decade coaching abroad. Disseminates Cruyffian ideas at Possessionfootball.com. Example of Barcelona's brain drain, and an essential adviser to the author of this book.

Manus Cruijff (1913–1959): Johan's father. An Ajax fan, and a grocer in the neighborhood opposite the club's old stadium. His early death from a heart attack was the most formative moment of Johan's life. Manus never put a *y* in his name.

Danny Cruyff (1949–): Johan's widow. Treated Cruyff as just a regular guy from Amsterdam. Doesn't like publicity or football.

Johan Cruyff (1947–2016): Father of the modern club. Born Cruijff, but realized that the *y* worked better internationally. Most interesting man in modern football history. A brilliant player from 1964 to 1984, then an entirely original coach. As manager of Barcelona from 1988 to 1996, he created the "Dream Team," then let it decay. Invented much of contemporary football, including the Barcelona style (though other clubs now play it better). Quite batty.

Jordi Cruyff (1974–): Johan's son, which can't have been easy. Played (and sat on the bench) for Barcelona, Manchester United, and Holland. In June 2021, he returned home from Shenzhen FC in China and became Barça's powerful director of international soccer.

Ousmane Dembélé (1997–) : Nippy French winger, but did not have a spartan lifestyle in his first seasons with Barcelona and was often injured and/or in conflict with the club. Barça surely regrets paying Borussia Dortmund €140-million-plus for him.

Robert Enke (1977–2009): German goalkeeper. During his disastrous spell at Barcelona from 2002 to 2004, he was scapegoated for a Cup defeat to a third-division side. After this, he fell into a depression, which may have been a step on the path to his suicide in 2009.

Samuel Eto'o (1981–): A difficult man and a brilliant striker. Guardiola will have been relieved that he decided not to sell him after all in 2008. Cameroonian.

Cesc Fàbregas (1987–): A Masia boy who played with Messi and Piqué on the adolescent "Baby Dream Team." Joined Arsenal at sixteen, then returned home at twenty-four, just in time for Barcelona's last glory years.

Francisco Franco (1892–1975): A Galician who became an army general, Nationalist leader in Spain's civil war (1936–1939), and then dictator of Spain from 1939 until 1975. His White Terror during and after the war killed an estimated two hundred thousand Spaniards, and drove many others into exile. Brutally suppressed Catalan nationalism.

Louis van Gaal (1951–): A Cruyffian who was hated by Cruyff. Coached Barcelona from 1997 to 2000 and again in 2002–2003. Won two Spanish league titles but is remembered in town more for his very un-Catalan rude directness, and for his Amsterdam-accented Spanish.

Joan Gaspart (1944–): Hotelier, former waiter at the Connaught in London, and from 2000 to 2003, unsuccessful president of Barcelona. Played a hotel receptionist in Antonioni's 1975 Barcelona-based movie *The Passenger*.

Antoni Gaudí (1852–1926): Catalan architect. Started the still-unfinished Sagrada Família cathedral. The author draws possibly overambitious parallels between him and another mad genius, Johan Cruyff.

Antoine Griezmann (1991–): A star of the French world champions of 2018. A brilliant player, but not during his two years at Barcelona. A mini-Messi, which may have been the problem.

Pep Guardiola (1971–): Johan Cruyff's best pupil, who joined Barcelona at age thirteen. A Cruyffian who renovated the cathedral that is Barça. Since his departure as coach in 2012, the club has never been quite the same. Catalan nationalist.

Thierry Henry (1977–): French striker who spent his best years at Arsenal, but from 2007 through 2010 enjoyed a late heyday at Barcelona. Played with and observed Messi.

Zlatan Ibrahimović (1981–): Swedish striker whose sole season at Barcelona (2009/10) went wrong because Messi decided he didn't want a massive Swede blocking his runs into the middle. Not a fan of Guardiola.

Andrés Iniesta (1984–): Pale-faced genius. Came through the Masia, won everything with Barcelona, overcame some sort of depression, and left for Vissel Kobe in Japan in 2018. A great footballer who was happy to play in the service of an even greater one, Messi.

Frenkie de Jong (1997–): Dutch midfielder who gives his coaches anxiety dreams by dribbling out of his own defense. Joined Barcelona in 2019, not the best possible moment.

Ronald Koeman (1963–): A hero of Barcelona as a goal-scoring center-back from 1989 to 1995. Scored the winner in the 1992 Champions League final at Wembley. Lived next door to Cruyff. Unhappy coach of Barcelona from August 2020 through October 2021.

Joan Laporta (1962–): President of FC Barcelona from 2003 to 2010, and then again from March 2021. A handsome lawyer, the most charismatic man in Catalonia, but more opportunist than organizer.

Michael Laudrup (1964–): Upper-middle-class Danish "shadow striker" (or "false nine") of Cruyff's Dream Team from 1989 to 1994. Fell out with Cruyff and moved to Real Madrid. A season after helping Barça beat Madrid 5–0, he helped Madrid beat Barça 5–0. Now coaches football and imports Spanish wine to Denmark.

Gary Lineker (1960–): English striker who played for Barcelona from 1986 to 1989, loved the place, and even learned Spanish. Unfortunately, Cruyff didn't want him. Now presents the *Match of the Day* TV program in the UK.

Antonia Lizárraga (unknown–): Nutritionist. Hired by the health fanatic Guardiola in 2010 to teach Barcelona's footballers how to eat. Still trying.

Diego Maradona (1960–2020): Played for Barcelona from 1982 to 1984, but the city was too bourgeois for him, and

Andoni Goikoetxea, the "Butcher of Bilbao," destroyed his ankle. Still managed to fit in some orgies.

Lieke Martens (1992–): A forward on Barcelona's women's team who has continued the club's tradition of Dutch imports. Named Best FIFA Women's Player in 2017, but still earns too little to bring over an entourage.

Jorge Messi (1958–): Father and agent of Lionel. Former manager in a steel factory in Rosario, Argentina. Fancies himself a brilliant businessman. Convicted with his son of tax fraud in 2016, but escaped with a fine. A prime culprit of Barça's financial collapse.

Lionel Messi (1987–): The single most powerful person inside the club until he was suddenly forced to leave in August 2021. Arrived at age thirteen, scored more than six hundred goals for the first team, but ended up turning FC Barcelona into FC Messi. His salary (well over $150 million a year by the end) helped bring down the club.

Rinus Michels (1928–2005): Former gym teacher for deaf children. Spent most of his coaching career—with Ajax, Barcelona, Holland, and the Los Angeles Aztecs—locked in a maddening yet fertile Lennon-and-McCartneyseque relationship with Johan Cruyff. Coinventor of "total football" and therefore of twenty-first-century football. Grandfather of the modern Barcelona.

José Mourinho (1963–): Portuguese coach. Longtime nemesis of Barcelona who was shaped at Barcelona between 1996 and 2000, working as a translator,

tactical analyst, and assistant coach. Absorbed the Cruyffian idea that football is a dance in space, but prefers to shut down space rather than open it.

Neymar (1992–): Joined Barcelona in 2013 and then, disastrously, left for Paris Saint-Germain in 2017, never to be replaced. The most momentous football transfer of the 2010s. Messi wanted to be reunited with him in Barcelona. It happened in Paris instead.

Josep Lluís Núñez (1931–2018): Went from real estate magnate to president, in his case of FC Barcelona from 1978 to 2000. Hired Cruyff but never liked him. Hasn't received any credit for overseeing the club's rise to greatness. Barça's last non-Catalan president.

Pedro (1987–): A Masia boy who went from Barcelona's C team in 2007 to winning pretty much everything in football by 2011. Not a genius, which means that his rise is even more of a credit to the Masia than Messi's was.

Gerard Piqué (1987–): Member of the Catalan merchant elite, entrepreneur, husband of the singer Shakira, and FC Barcelona center-back. Played with Messi for twenty years. Touted as a future club president. Has the genes for it.

Inma Puig (unknown–): Sports psychologist who worked at FC Barcelona for fifteen years until 2018. Helped Iniesta through his personal crisis. Advises companies as a "chief emotional officer."

Carles Puyol (1978–): Hairy central defender of Guardiola's great Barcelona team, and world champion with Spain in 2010. After graduating from the Masia to the first team, he bequeathed his mattress to Iniesta.

Mino Raiola (1967–2022): Dutch-Italian "superagent" who learned his trade in his father's pizza restaurants. Agent of Ibrahimović, and therefore enemy of Guardiola.

Carles Rexach (1947–): Has spent his life within the square kilometer around the Camp Nou. A fragile, gifted, and cowardly winger for FC Barcelona, who later held almost every job in the club, including assistant and friend to Cruyff. Inevitably fell out with him.

Frank Rijkaard (1962–): A brilliant Dutch footballer, and Barcelona's head coach from 2003 to 2008. Universally regarded as a gentleman. Won the Champions League in 2006, but drifted out of coaching early because he didn't feel like it anymore.

Rivaldo (1972–): Barcelona's most creative player from 1997 to 2002. Told the team he wouldn't play on the wing anymore. That was probably a mistake. On the upside, was named European Footballer of the Year in 1999 (as witnessed by the author) and won the 2002 World Cup with Brazil.

Sergi Roberto (1992–): Local boy, a rare Catalan speaker on the first team, and at the time of writing one of Barcelona's four club captains. Possibly more of a presence in the changing room than on the field.

Romário (1966–): Brilliant if frequently motionless goal scorer of Cruyff's

Dream Team from 1993 to 1995. Didn't like: training, running, defensive work. Liked: sleeping, sex. Now a Brazilian senator for the left-wing Podemos party. Won the World Cup with Brazil in 1994.

Ronaldinho (1980–): Brazilian creator. Bought by Barcelona in 2003 because they couldn't get David Beckham. Won the Champions League with Barça in 2006, when he was briefly the world's best player, but almost immediately lost interest in football. Messi's hero and mentor. Briefly jailed in Paraguay in 2020 after allegedly entering the country on a false passport.

Cristiano Ronaldo (1985–): Brilliant Portuguese forward. Second-best footballer of his era. Nearly joined Barcelona as a teenager. Star of Barça's archrivals Real Madrid from 2009 to 2018, then joined Juventus before moving to Manchester United.

Sandro Rosell (1964–): Member of the Barcelona *burgesia*. Club president from 2010 to 2014 after ousting his old ally Joan Laporta. Resigned amid legal troubles over the purchase of Neymar from Santos. Spent nearly two years in prison but was then fully acquitted. Celebrated with the best-ever beer in a hotel bar.

Eusebio Sacristán (1964–): Little midfielder who found his home at Barcelona from 1988 to 1995. Cruyff showed him the essence of an orderly, passing football that Eusebio had had in his head since childhood. Later Rijkaard's assistant coach.

Paco Seirul·lo (1945–): Guardian of Barça's Cruyffian tradition. A physical trainer who started out in the club's handball wing, served as Cruyff's right-hand man, teaches at the University of Barcelona, speaks like a Parisian philosopher, has a magnificent mane of white hair, and is a sort of walking USB stick containing the club's institutional memory. Known inside the Camp Nou as "El Druida," "the Druid."

Ferran Soriano (1967–): Local boy with an MBA. Barça's chief executive from 2003 to 2008. Now does the same job at Manchester City, where he hired Guardiola. His little-known book, *Goal: The Ball Doesn't Go In by Chance*, is a surprisingly rich source on modern Barça.

Hristo Stoichkov (1966–): Bulgarian striker of Barcelona's Dream Team from 1990 to 1995. Cruyff liked his *mala leche* ("bad milk," or nasty streak). Stoichkov liked partying with Romário, until they fell out. There's a great YouTube video of Cruyff showing him how to skip rope.

Luis Suárez (1987–): Uruguayan striker, and neighbor and best friend of Messi. Played for Barcelona from 2014 to 2020, until Ronald Koeman told him in a forty-second phone call that he was no longer needed. Nobody from the board rang to thank him for his 198 goals for the club. Immediately began banging in more for Atlético Madrid.

Lilian Thuram (1972–): French intellectual and defender. When he joined Barcelona at age thirty-four and discovered the club's Cruyffian principles, he felt for the first time that he was fully a footballer. He wondered what sport he had been playing until then. Now an antiracism campaigner.

Oriol Tort (1929–1999): Barcelona's longtime unpaid chief scout. A pharmaceutical representative in civilian life. Sometimes watched fifteen to twenty boys' matches in a day, recording every promising name on his typewriter. He decided Barça needed a residence to house talented kids from out of town. In 1979, the Masia opened its doors. Brought Iniesta to Barcelona.

Jorge Valdano (1955–): World champion footballer with Maradona's Argentina, former coach and technical director of Real Madrid, lovely writer, charmer, and nice guy—pretty much the author's idea of the ideal man. Moved from military dictatorship in Argentina to Spain in 1975, just in time to see Franco die and the country change. A Cruyffian, but also a critical observer of Cruyff and Barcelona.

Victor Valdés (1982–): A Masia boy who became goalkeeper of Guardiola's great team. Too stressed out to enjoy football until Guardiola taught him to analyze the game coldly. True friend of Iniesta's.

Ernesto Valverde (1964–): A bit-part forward with Barcelona under Cruyff from 1988 to 1990. Won two league titles in two completed seasons as coach from 2017 to January 2020, until Barça sacked him. They had no idea how good they had had it. Modest little man, good sense of humor.

Tito Vilanova (1968–2014): Teenage friend of Guardiola's in the Masia in the 1980s, and his assistant coach with the first team from 2008 to 2012. Played good cop to Guardiola's bad cop. When Guardiola resigned, Vilanova agreed to take over as head coach. Guardiola wasn't pleased. While head coach, Vilanova got terminal cancer. His widow banned Guardiola from the funeral.

Arsène Wenger (1949–): Arsenal's manager from 1996 to 2018. Admirer of Cruyffian football. Features in this book as a veteran observer of the modern game, largely because the author was lucky enough to nab an interview with him in the crucial final months of writing. Now works for FIFA. Alsatian.

Xavi (1980–): The midfielder who defined Barcelona's passing game: look, pass, look, pass, repeat. So faultless that his teammates nicknamed him La Maquina, "the Machine." Came through the Masia and played for the first team from 1998 to 2015. Returned from Qatar in November 2021 to become Barça's head coach.

Boudewijn Zenden (1976–): Much-traveled, multilingual Dutch former winger who played for Barcelona from 1998 to 2001, and later for Chelsea, Liverpool, Marseille, and others. An anthropological observer of football mores, and occasional interviewee of the author since 1997.

Andoni Zubizarreta (1961–): Basque and wise man. Goalkeeper of Barcelona from 1986 to 1994, and sporting director from 2010 to 2015. Signed Neymar and Suárez. Bartomeu shouldn't have sacked him. Played nearly a thousand professional football matches.

A BARCELONA LEXICON

burgesia: The Catalan merchant class, the local version of the bourgeoisie. Members of the *burgesia* fill Barça's boardroom and usually provide the club president. Almost all of them speak Catalan at home.

Can Barça: "The House of Barça." An elevated moniker for the club as an institution.

Clásico: The Barça–Real Madrid game, the biggest match in the Spanish calendar—though only since February 1974, when Cruyff's Barcelona won 0–5 at the Bernabeu. Before then Real Madrid–Atlético Madrid was the big game. The Clásico has become a forum for expressing the centuries-old tension between Catalonia and Madrid.

culer (*culé* in Spanish): Barcelona fan, though the literal meaning is "backside." The nickname supposedly dates from the days of Barça's old stadium a century ago, when people on the street outside could see spectators' behinds jutting out over a wall.

en un momento dado: "At a given moment." Cruyff's favorite stalling phrase when he ran out of words in Spanish.

entorno: Literally, "surroundings" or "environment." Cruyff repurposed it to mean the specific surroundings of Barça: the *socis*, the *ultra* fans who'd come round the president's house to threaten him, the journalists who lived off the club, the interfering local politicians, sponsors, current directors, former directors, and staffers who were trying to get back into the club, and the opposition plotting to unseat the board.

indepe: Short for *independentiste*: a supporter of Catalan independence, i.e., about half the population of Catalonia. *Indepes* tend to be native Catalan-speakers.

madriditis: An anxious obsession with Real Madrid, and with the Spanish capital more broadly.

Masia: Literally, "farmhouse." Barcelona's Masia—originally based in an old farmhouse—is the club's no-longer-quite-so-famed youth academy.

Més que un club: "More than a club," FC Barcelona's motto. The phrase stands for Catalan nationalism, Cruyffian football, homegrown players, and a general sense of dignity and *valors* ("values"). *Més que un club* is genuinely all those things, as well as a self-congratulatory and now somewhat outdated marketing slogan.

pa amb tomàquet: Bread smeared with tomato, an everyday Catalan specialty.

rondo: Essentially, a piggy-in-the-middle game. Barça's favorite training exercise since Cruyff became coach here. A few players pass the ball to each other in a limited space, while defenders try to intercept. The rondo captures the Cruyffian essence of football: time, space, passing, and geometry.

soci: A dues-paying club member (*socio* in Spanish). Barcelona's 150,000 or so *socis*—almost all of whom live in Catalonia—are considered the owners of the club.

A NOTE ON THE TEXT

When talking about Barça, I have favored Catalan terms over Spanish ones, because Catalan is the club's main language. For instance, I call the club's dues-paying members *socis*, rather than using the Spanish word *socios*. Even when Spanish and Catalan words are the same, Catalan usually dispenses with accents: "methodology" is *metodología* in Spanish, but plain *metodologia* in Catalan. La Masia (the name of Barça's youth academy) has an accent on the *i* in Spanish but not in Catalan.

PART ONE

INSIDE THE
CATHEDRAL

INTRODUCTION

BARÇA AND ME

now see that I began researching this book in 1992, when I walked into the Camp Nou as a twenty-two-year-old in a torn jacket. I was traveling around the world on about $9,000, with a typewriter in my rucksack, writing my first book, *Football Against the Enemy*. I stayed in the Hostel Kabul on the mugger-rich Plaça Reial, eked out my money by skipping lunch, and dined every night on a falafel from a stall. Barcelona, long considered a shabby provincial backwater, had been freshly renovated for that summer's Olympics. I had never known it was such a beautiful city. I played bad chess in the sun at Kasparo bar, and decided I wanted to return here one day.

I had come because I was fascinated by the local football club. I grew up in the Netherlands (which may show here and there in this book), so my childhood hero was Johan Cruyff, the Dutchman who first came to Barcelona as a player in 1973. By 1992, he was the club's head coach and spiritual leader. Cruyff was both a great footballer and a great thinker about football, as if he were the light bulb and Edison in one. He is the father of Barcelona's style, which is a thrilling one-touch high-pressing game of constant attack. In this book I'll argue that he is also the father of modern football itself.

One day in 1992, I took the metro to the Camp Nou to see if I could interview him for *Football Against the Enemy*. The kindly press officer, Ana, took in my dubious journalistic credentials and torn jacket and suggested I interview Barça's elderly first vice president, Nicolau Casaus. In hindsight, he probably needed to be kept occupied. Ana told me he had no English, but waiting outside his office I heard him repeat several times, in an American accent, the word "siddown." He seemed to be practicing for me. When I went in, Casaus was smoking a large cigar. I asked whether the club's motto—*Més que un club*, "More than a club"—referred to FC Barcelona's political significance in Spain. Speaking Spanish, he replied that it didn't. He said people of different parties and religions supported Barça. So why the motto? "Barcelonism is a great passion," he answered vaguely. Politics seemed to be too sensitive a topic for him. I didn't know then that he had spent five years in jail under the Franco dictatorship as a Catalan activist, after initially being condemned to death.

I nagged Ana to produce Cruyff, but she fobbed me off with his assistant, Tonny Bruins Slot. I was secretly relieved: the thought of meeting my hero was overwhelming.

Football in 1992 was a more intimate business. Barça in those days trained on a pitch beside the Camp Nou. One morning before training began, I was given a seat outside the changing-room door to wait for Bruins Slot. At this point I think I'd met one professional footballer in my life. Michael Laudrup emerged from the changing room and glanced at me. Then Cruyff came out, with a football in his arms, walking at top speed ("If they time normally with me, they're always just too late"). He was bantering simultaneously with a changing-room attendant and a Colombian journalist hoping for an audience. It was a beautiful morning, he was about to train the European champions, and he wanted to let the kid in the torn jacket share in his happiness. I'm fairly sure he beamed at me from a range of two yards, but by the time I managed to get out "Hello" in Dutch, he was gone. Bruins Slot came out and asked how long I needed. He was in a hurry to get to training. I said twenty minutes.

Bruins Slot was unmistakably a working-class Amsterdammer like Cruyff. He took me to a lounge, found me black coffee in a paper cup, wandered around looking for an ashtray, used another paper cup instead, and then engaged me in a two-hour argument about football. He never did get to training that day. "We have a copyright, a patent," he said. "You can imitate every patent, but there is a finishing touch which only one man has."

Cruyff created the great Barça. In the words of his chief disciple, Pep Guardiola, he built the cathedral. More than that, Cruyff arguably created modern football itself. He is the Freud or Gaudí of the game, the most interesting, original, and infuriating man in football's history. The cathedral of Barça was later updated by Guardiola and perfected by Lionel Messi, before it fell into decay.

Messi is the other person who prompted me to write this book. I have always wanted to understand how he does what he does on the field. Once I began sniffing around Barça, I became interested in something else: his power. The quiet Argentinian might seem like Cruyff's polar opposite, but in fact he inherited the Dutchman's role as the most influential character inside the club. For years, outsiders mistook his blank gaze and public muteness for a lack of personality. Barça people had long known him as a domineering and scary figure. Over time, FC Barcelona morphed into FC Messi.

That did not end well. It turned out that I was studying Barça as it unraveled. I had first come here at the start of the club's glory days, in

1992, and I finished as they seemed to be ending, in 2021 with Messi's departure. It felt a bit like writing a book about Rome in AD 400 while the barbarians were pouring through the gates. I began my research thinking I was going to be explaining Barça's rise to greatness, and I have, but I've also ended up charting the decline and fall.

OVER THE DECADES, I got to know Barcelona as a journalist visiting for stories. When you reach middle age, you fall asleep after lunch, but there are upsides, too: you have built up a contacts book, some sense of how things change, and a back catalog. Beside me in my office in Paris as I write is a bookcase containing two-hundred-plus notebooks filled with all my research since 1998. There are interviews with Barça players and coaches past and present such as Rivaldo, Lilian Thuram, Neymar, and Gerard Piqué, and my one encounter with Cruyff, an amiable evening in the living room of his mansion in 2000 (after which we fell out traumatically).

I have even played in the Camp Nou. In 2007, I won FC Barcelona's annual sportswriting prize, and a crew from the club's TV channel wanted to film me kicking a ball around the pitch in my street clothes. When I ran onto the grass, it was so thick, short, and perfect that I actually laughed. The field has the maximum dimensions for a football pitch, to create space for Barça's attacks, and I felt I was gamboling on a vast lawn. There was even a small crowd: a few dozen tourists doing the Barça tour.

I dribbled around trying to imagine what it was like playing here in a match. Looking up at the stands of Europe's biggest stadium, I thought: This is strangely familiar. Strip away the fancy packaging and it's just a football field, like every other you've ever played on. That thought must have reassured some debutants down the decades.

In the center of the field it was almost possible to forget that anyone was watching, but when I dribbled down the wing, I was excruciatingly aware of the tourists. The spectators there stare straight at you. Near the touchline, a player is closer to them than to the action in the goalmouth. I could pick out individual faces. It was possible to feel, for a moment, a relationship with this or that person in the stands.

I took some shots at the empty goal, and each time the ball went in, the tourists cheered ironically. Lord knows what they thought was going on.

When I placed the ball to take a corner and looked up toward goal, my glance took in the entire stadium. It was a theatrical moment: for a second or two, the game was at my feet, and I had a sense of myself as an actor, performing for an audience. I would later learn from a psychologist at Barça that top-class footballers shut out these impressions. During a game they hear the shouted instructions of their teammates, but not the chants of the fans.

My final prompt to start writing the book was a visit to Barcelona in 2019. I had come to research an article for my newspaper, the *Financial Times*, and I happened to arrive on the day that the club awarded the sportswriting prize. Club officials insisted I come to the awards ceremony and to lunch afterward. I ended up sitting for hours at a table in a nook of the Camp Nou, drinking wine and chatting with President Josep Maria Bartomeu and various club *directius* (literally "directors," but really more like counselors to the president). That was when I realized that Barça regarded me as an alumnus, or even a club member. The media department cheerfully set up interviews for me with Bartomeu, with the then head coach Ernesto Valverde, and with many of Barça's ordinary employees: doctors, data analysts, and brand managers.

Access is the hardest thing in football writing. Around the same time that I started this book, I asked a lower-division club for an interview with a youth coach, got no response, phoned and emailed for weeks to press my case, and was finally told no. Most big clubs now offer journalists little more than a seat at a press conference to hear the managers' self-justifications, some off-the-record "briefings," and, every few months, a fifteen-minute "sit-down" with a player determined to say nothing.

I published my newspaper article, but thought: there's loads more to say. I wanted to understand Cruyff and Messi as people, not as demigods. And I wanted to study Barça not as a theater of dreams but as a workplace. This is a club created by fallible humans who went to work every day and quarreled with each other, tried things and made mistakes, and ended up creating something Catalan and international, brilliant and flawed, of its time and eternal. What is office life at Barça like day to day? Who are the people who run the club? How much power do they actually have over the players? How does Barça manage talent? How do the players live? What should they eat, and can anybody persuade them to eat it?

I asked my contacts at the club whether they were willing to open their doors to me for a book. They were. Nobody at Barça then or since tried to interfere with what I was writing. No favors were exchanged in the making of this book.

From spring 2019 until a last snatched visit during the pandemic in September 2020, I visited Barcelona regularly for research. I dredged up my shaky Spanish, became part of the city's Airbnb problem, and learned to have lunch at three p.m. (Absolutely no skipped meals this time.) My day job at the *Financial Times* is writing a sociopolitical column. It was a joy to switch from the coronavirus, climate change, Trump, and Brexit to writing about the greatest in human achievement. I used to worry that football was a lower subject than politics. I don't anymore.

Football in Barcelona turned out to be deliciously intertwined with food. Barça people really do use wineglasses and sugar packets to explain formations. Over a four-hour lunch of paella and white rioja, Albert Capellas, former coordinator of Barcelona's Masia youth academy and by then coach of Denmark under-21s, used a pepper pot, saltshaker, and bottle of olive oil first to set up a midfield and then to teach me how to make *pa amb tomàquet*, the classic Catalan delicacy of bread smeared with tomato. Capellas became one of my best informants, not just on food.

I like my life in Paris, but I would move to Barcelona like a shot if the family would let me. The Born neighborhood of the city, or Gràcia, or the bourgeois streets on the lower slopes of the Tibidabo mountain, or nearby beach towns like Gavà Mar and Sitges exemplify the European dream: that perfect blend of beauty, good weather, cuisine, wealth, a manageable pace, friendliness, mountains, and sea.

Before each visit, I sent press officers a list of interview requests. Interviews with first-team players were hardest to arrange. Sometimes the club itself struggles to contact a player directly, and is blocked by his agent or press representative or some random member of his entourage. I interviewed three club presidents (one of them freshly released from jail) and midfielder Frenkie de Jong, but I learned the most from my conversations with dozens of mid-ranking club employees: everyone from nutritionists to video analysts to social media experts. Many of them seemed delighted at the chance to explain the thing they spend their lives doing, whether that is coaching kids, setting up the new professional women's team, or running the club's business office in some distant metropole. The club wouldn't allow most of these staffers to be quoted by name. The book is in my voice, but it channels what they told me. In short, though I have had some access to the players, I've had more to the people who run the club day to day.

All the while, I was doing my best to understand this parochial Catalan workplace with a global reach. How does Barcelona the club sit within Barcelona the city? How did Barça transform itself, in thirty years, from Catalan to European to global club? What was gained and lost along the way? How did Barcelona create arguably the best youth academy and best football team in history, and why did they fade? Why is the latest version of Cruyffian football played not in Barcelona but in Liverpool, Manchester, and Munich?

I found out that the Barça Innovation Hub, a kind of in-house think tank quietly launched in 2017, was asking just these questions. The Hub's job is to reimagine professional football. Its staffers think about everything in the game, from virtual reality to beetroot juice. They admitted to me that they didn't know how football worked (nobody does), but they were at least starting to figure out which questions to ask. Barça's urgent attempts to understand how exactly it did what it did—something it had almost taken for granted in good times—made my quest all the more interesting, at least to me.

Several interviews ended with pre-coronavirus hugs. José Mourinho, himself an alumnus of Barça, once scoffed, "Barcelona draw you into the trap of thinking they are all likable, nice, friendly people from a perfect world."[1] It's true that smiles at Barça can conceal oceans, but (and I hope I'm not being naive) my experience is that people here actually are likable, or at least friendly. For nearly thirty years, they've always treated me nicely, and my rule of thumb for football people is that if they are even nice to journalists, they're probably nice to everybody.

Many excellent writers and documentary filmmakers from around the world have studied the club before me. I spent much of the Parisian lockdowns of spring and autumn 2020 devouring their work.

There is always a risk of being seduced by a glamorous institution, but I have tried to keep my head. This book isn't an official account. It's my view of Barça: generally admiring, often critical, always curious, and, I hope, without illusions.

Much of it is about Barcelona as a regular workplace. Much else, though, is about extraordinary talent: Cruyff, Messi, and the young winger who sacked four private chefs in a row. The tension between the everyday and the exceptional is what makes Barça.

I

WHO'S WHO IN THE HOUSE
OF BARÇA

For days at a time during my visits, the Camp Nou became my workplace. I got used to wandering around the giant empty concrete husk, going to meet someone in an adjoining tapas bar or inside the club's offices of power behind Gate 11. One day, just opposite Barça's museum, I discovered the soul of the club: the ice-rink café with its cheap wooden tables, where Barça staffers meet for coffee and intrigue. Next door is the clubroom for *socis* (the dues-paying club members—*socios* in Spanish), a place where old men play cards and a poster advertises the Christmas lottery.

I came to see that Can Barça, the House of Barça, is inhabited by four overlapping castes: *directius*, *socis*, employees, and players. For such a big club, these castes are surprisingly local. Barça people have often known each other since childhood. The former president Sandro Rosell, Pep Guardiola, Carles Puyol, and Andrés Iniesta were all once ball boys in the Camp Nou. The club is run by and for people who expect to hang around the club until they die.

Certain things follow from that. First, personal relations inside Barça are often lifelong and intense. Second, Barça people instinctively take the long view. The staffers in the ice-rink café care about the under-13s team, because they expect still to be around when the kids are old enough to play on the first team.

In short, Barça is very different from English football clubs, which are limited companies run by highly paid interim executives. Barcelona is a genuine club: a local voluntary association of members. That's a very Catalan beast. Catalonia has strong trade unions, cooperatives, and the Real Automóvil Club de Cataluña, the biggest car club in Spain, with about a million *socis*. In a region where the Spanish state has historically been weak, people have learned to organize themselves.

The club directors constitute Barça's ruling caste. They are drawn from the Catalan merchant class, the *burgesia*, or bourgeoisie. Catalonia (population 7.6 million) doesn't have its own state, or much of an aristocracy, so the *burgesia* sits at the top of society. Barcelona has had the most functional economy on the Mediterranean for centuries, and the merchants are its main beneficiaries. For generations they have done their business looking outward from Spain toward the sea. Their caste traditionally considers itself more cosmopolitan, modern, and European than supposedly primitive, savage Spain.

The most prestigious powerbase in Catalonia is probably the boardroom (and de facto government) of FC Barcelona. The club emphatically isn't a working-class institution; merchants have run it since 1899, when the Swiss immigrant accountant Hans Gamper placed a sixty-three-word ad in a local sports newspaper inviting anyone who wanted to arrange football matches to show up at the newspaper offices.[1]

Gamper founded Barça in the middle of the *tancament de caixes*, the "closing of the cash boxes," in 1899, when hundreds of local businesses in Catalonia shut down in a tax strike against the Spanish government. Madrid responded by declaring war on Catalonia, though no troops were ever sent.[2] Even then, the conflict between the rebellious region and Madrid went back centuries. *Catalanisme*, Catalan nationalism, infused Barça from the start. Hans Gamper himself went native and catalanised his first name to Joan.

The Catalan merchants sat out both world wars. Their big twentieth-century trauma was the Spanish Civil War of 1936 to 1939, and the post-war reprisals by the winner, the Fascist general Francisco Franco. The historian Paul Preston has estimated that Franco's White Terror killed two hundred thousand Spaniards. One of them was Barça's thirty-eight-year-old president, Josep Sunyol, who was on his way to visit Republican troops near Madrid in 1936 when his chauffeur unknowingly crossed the front line into Nationalist territory. Stopped by troops at a checkpoint, Sunyol and his two companions innocently called out the standard greeting, "¡Viva la república!" not realizing that the soldiers who had stopped them were Fascists. He was shot in the back of the head even before being identified.[3] Almost forgotten for decades, he finally entered Barça's mythology as the "martyr president" in the 1990s.

When Franco's troops approached Barcelona in January 1939, hundreds of thousands of locals fled to France, often on foot, recounts Preston. "Women gave birth at the roadside. Babies died of the cold, children were trampled to death."[4] Families were torn apart or destroyed. Many exiles would never return home.

After the Fascists took Barcelona, they conducted open-air executions at the Camp de la Bota in the Poblenou district.[5] In later decades, fifty-four mass graves containing four thousand corpses would be unearthed in the city.[6] Franco banned the Catalan language. Signs urged the population to "speak Christian," meaning Spanish.[7] Certainly initially, the Fascists ruled Catalonia as if it were occupied enemy territory.

Some Catalan merchants, like Nicolau Casaus, suffered under Franco, but most made their peace with "El Caudillo." In fact, many merchants welcomed him as an antidote to the anarchists and communists in Barcelona who had been plundering their mansions, seizing their factories, and lining the owners up against the wall. The left had probably executed more people in Catalonia before and during the war than Franco did afterward.[8]

By summer 1945, Franco was the most murderous dictator left standing in Europe west of the Soviet Union. By then his rule had softened, but the memory of his killings—hardly ever mentioned in Spain in his lifetime—would silence almost all Catalans for decades to come.

The local author Manuel Vázquez Montalbán (himself jailed under Franco) said that "in the fourth place of the organizations that were persecuted, after the Communists, anarchists and separatists, was Football Club Barcelona."[9] "Persecuted" is probably too strong, but the Fascists did keep close tabs on Barça. In 1940, they forced it to replace the English "Football Club" in its name with the Spanish *Club de Fútbol*.[10] At first, the regime selected the club's presidents. Gradually, though, CF Barcelona's ruling *burgesia* and the *franquistas* learned to live with each other. In 1949, the club was even allowed to restore the Catalan flag to its crest.[11]

The merchants of Barcelona turned inward under Franco, devoting themselves to their families, their businesses, and their football club. Only in the waning years of his regime did some of them start bucking his will. When he finally died, in 1975, they drank the city's stores of cava dry.[12] Once he was safely buried, everybody joined the anti-Franco resistance. Many Catalans came to buy into a false historical myth that their region had been uniformly anti-Franco, and that the city of Madrid had been pro-regime.

The truth was much less black and white. In fact, Madrid, like Barcelona, had fought against Franco's troops in the civil war, while Real

Madrid was briefly run by revolutionary communists.[13] Franco's regime had executed thousands in Madrid as well as in Barcelona. Each city had also contained its fair share of *franquistas*. The civil war wasn't Catalonia versus Spain, but that's the way some modern Catalan nationalists have chosen to retell it.[14]

The sense of Catalonia versus Madrid still underlies El Clásico, the Barça–Real Madrid game. When the match is played in the Camp Nou, fans visit the adjoining cemetery beforehand to ask dead family, friends, and footballers for good luck.[15] For them, Real Madrid is the archrival. The people who run Can Barça take a gentler view: they see Real Madrid as a sort of twin brother. The directors of the two clubs generally get on, with lots of hugging at pre-match banquets. The relationship is a mixture of complicity and jealousy, with constant paranoia in Barcelona that the other sibling is being unfairly favored, and suspicion in Madrid that Barça is overpraised.

Still, a club is what it means to its fans not its directors, and especially during Clásicos, Barça becomes what Vázquez Montalbán called "the unarmed army of Catalonia," fighting the eternal battle against Madrid. For much of the past century, the main outlet for *catalanisme* has been the Camp Nou on Sundays. Instead of a nation-state, Catalonia built a nation-club. Catalans poured so much love and money into Barça that the second city of a midsize, economically struggling European country was able to boast (in 2018) the world's highest-grossing sports club.[16]

Barça's motto, "More than a club," is more than a self-congratulatory marketing slogan (though it is that as well). The *franquista* club president Narcís de Carreras seems to have coined the phrase in January 1968, saying, "Barcelona is something more than a football club. It is a spirit that is deep inside us, colors that we love above all else." Under Franco, he wasn't free to be more specific, but what he was talking about (in Spanish, of course) was the spirit of *catalanisme*.

The meaning of the phrase "More than a club" has expanded over the decades. It now also stands for Cruyffian football, for homegrown players, and for a general sense of dignity and *valors* ("values"), exemplified by Barça's charitable foundation and by President Joan Laporta's decision in 2006 to put UNICEF on the team shirt rather than a sponsor's name. Laporta summed up "More than a club" as "Cruyff, Catalonia, Masia, UNICEF."[17]

Barça changes, but the *burgesia* always remains in charge. Today's ruling merchants are *Catalans de tota la vida*, lifelong Catalans. (When I asked one senior former Barça director to define the *burgesia*, his own class, the first thing he said was: "to be Catalan—two generations at least.") Their families belong to the Reial Club de Tennis Barcelona, go on holiday in Cerdanya in the Pyrenees mountains, listen to music at the Liceo opera, and watch Barça from the *tribuna*, the grandstand. The poshest seats at the Camp Nou are filled by directors' relatives and local notables; the ones at the Bernabéu in Madrid, by ministers, corporate tycoons, and judges.

Members of the Catalan *burgesia* aren't all very rich—they include architects and professors—and they certainly don't flash their cash. Their understated outfits in quiet colors exude rather than scream wealth. Most of them live in beautiful apartments (ideally built by Gaudí), often handed down by their grandparents. They spend summers in their second homes in the Catalan countryside. They are cosmopolitans who send their children to English- or French- or German-language schools, and later to American-influenced business schools. So prestigious is foreign schooling here that Messi drove his children to his local Colegio Británico every morning.

The language of Barça's boardroom is Catalan. That's a class marker: the city's proletariat mostly speaks Spanish at home. Historically, Barcelona's working classes have been imported from poorer Spanish regions such as Andalusia. Some of them display a disconcerting tendency to support Real Madrid. Migrants can integrate by learning Catalan at school, eating *pa amb tomàquet,* and supporting Barça, but they almost never ascend to the boardroom.

A typical specimen of the *burgesia* is the family of Barcelona's center-back Gerard Piqué. His grandfather was a Barça *directiu.* Piqué's mother is a neuroscientist. His father, a debonair figure in an impeccably wound scarf, introduced himself to me in English as "a fellow writer": he dabbles as a novelist, while running a family company that exports construction materials.

Gerard Piqué himself is a born merchant. He bought control of tennis's Davis Cup and is chummy with Mark Zuckerberg. Over dinner in San Francisco in 2015, he helped persuade another business pal, Hiroshi Mikitani, founder of Rakuten, the "Japanese Amazon," to become Barça's chief sponsor.[18] At times, Piqué gives the impression of treating football as a side hustle. A *soci* from birth, he registered his son, Milan, at birth, too. Piqué used to sing Milan the Barça anthem at night (though as Milan got older, he came to prefer Disney's Mickey Mouse song). Piqué is touted as a future club president. He certainly has the genes for it.

You need money to be a Barça *directiu.* A seat on the board is unpaid, and you generally have to take years off work (often in the family company) and put up a personal guarantee worth millions of euros against the club's potential losses. As of spring 2022, a new Spanish law was in the works that intended to scrap the need for a guarantee, but until then, if the club lost €100 million during a board's tenure, then each of the fifteen directors was on the hook for nearly €7 million. If Barça hit bad financial times, a *directiu* could lose his home. Several *directius* joked to me that their wives were furious that they'd joined the board. (Almost all board members are men.)

Barça's *directius* often come from intertwined families and have known each other forever. The population of the Barcelona metropolitan area is 3.2 million, but that of the city itself, where the *burgesia* clusters, is only 1.6 million. When locals describe Barça or their city, they often use the word *endogàmic*, which means, roughly, "inbred." While interviewing the vice president, Jordi Cardoner, in 2020, I discovered that he was the grandson of Casaus, the cigar-puffing first vice president whom I had interviewed in 1992. Cardoner was registered as a *soci* by Casaus on the day he was born. He also just happened to be a school friend of the club's president, Bartomeu. And Cardoner's sister had sat on the board before him.

On nights when everyone is singing the Barça hymn together in the directors' bus after a win in Madrid, these ties feel deep. But personal connections don't prevent incessant boardroom infighting. Whereas Real Madrid under Florentino Pérez resembles an autocracy, Manchester United has come to operate like a corporation, and Manchester City functions like a family office, Barça is a democratically elected oligarchy. Barcelona prides itself on being the only true democracy among the world's biggest football clubs. (Barça people are often privately snooty about English clubs selling themselves to foreigners.)

But presidential elections every six years create inbuilt instability. First, the previous directors leave with all their hard-earned knowledge, while the new president installs his team of newbies. The executive committee of twelve to fifteen people—day to day, the club's top decision-making body—can suddenly find itself with just a couple of old-timers. Imagine trying to negotiate with the hardened industry veterans of Real Madrid or Manchester City. To make things even more complicated, many of the president's board members aspire to become president themselves one day. The small-town squabbles at this global club are traditionally fought on the endless post-midnight sports broadcasts on local radio, or in the city's newspapers. (The *burgesia* still reads newspapers.) Prowl the overlit offices in club headquarters and you'll see copies of *Mundo Deportivo* or *La Vanguardia* (the Catalan edition) overflowing on desks. The club will sometimes take out a bulk subscription to a newspaper, or invite journalists on a cushy foreign trip, in hopes of buying gentler coverage. (Declaration of interest: The only presents I've received from Barça other than cups of coffee are two club shirts with my name on them. For the second one, I remembered to donate the equivalent of the shirt's price to UNICEF.) More than one past president paid newspapers a secret stipend in exchange for kinder coverage. Under Josep Lluís Núñez, president from 1978 to 2000, recalcitrant journalists reported receiving warnings or even thumps.[19]

Barça's blandishments don't always work. Leaks from club people to old friends in local media frequently turn the club upside down. Sometimes local journalists know more than the head coach about what's going on. When I asked Rosell whether being president had been a happy time for him, he said, "A lot of people want to be president of Barça, and they do everything to destroy you. So every day when you wake up in the morning, you expect a bomb—normally fake news."

All club presidents in the post-Franco era have been panned in the media, even though they ruled during the period when Barça ascended from mediocrity to top rank. The job is simply too big for whichever local merchant happens to inhabit it. Catalans discuss the Barça president with the same contemptuous fascination that Americans tend to reserve for the U.S. president.

Ferran Soriano, who was Barça's chief executive before moving to Manchester City, wrote that *directius* and footballers in Barcelona read all the local sports coverage every day. "Whether their name appears in the corner of page 7 or not, whether or not they are words of praise or criticism, or whether they are mentioned more or less than others—this is important and affects their mood for the whole day."[20]

Gary Lineker, the English striker brought to Barcelona by manager Terry Venables in 1986, recalled for me, "There's two local newspapers that just covered sport. You'd get thirty, forty pages every day of stuff about . . . everything. I remember the news was so short one day, the front-page headline was: 'Venables has diarrhea.' When they say it's *més que un club*, it's not just the fact that it's an enormous football club. It's also a football club that is occasionally bonkers." The joke inside the club is that the pressure from what Cruyff named the *entorno*, the surroundings, drives every Barça head coach a little bit crazy.

The *entorno* weighs on all sports at Barça. The club's handball coach, Xavi Pascual, grumbled to me, "Some people put on pressure thinking they aren't putting on pressure, thinking they are helping."

I asked, "But surely the pressure in the handball team is less than in the football team?"

"The budget is, too," he replied.

The directors know that no matter how much money they make in a lifetime in business, their name will be made or broken during their nerve-shredding few years on the Barça board. *Directius* live under daily pressure, not just from the crowd in the stadium and the newspapers and radio but also from their children at home, their business partners, and even the people who serve them their morning coffee. Directors might spend €100 million on a footballer, then sit in the *tribuna* biting their nails every week watching him flop, while everyone else says, "Told you so." One director told me, "When the club wins, the players win. When the club loses, the board loses." A businessman on one of the slates campaigning for the presidency in 2021 told me, "All Barça presidents end up in failure or in prison. And most board members. So you have to know that." He was exaggerating, slightly.

Anxious *directius* can make unpredictable interventions in club management. For instance, if a footballer's agent asks the sporting director for a new contract and the sporting director says no, the agent might try his luck with the club president. The sense that personal reputations are on the line encourages rule stretching: unaccounted payments in the purchase of Neymar in 2013; illegal signings of underage foreign players, punished by FIFA in 2014; and the allegations in 2020 that Barça's board had made secret payments to the Uruguayan company I3 Ventures to attack the president's opponents, including the club's own players, on social media. (Barça said I3 was merely monitoring social media.)

THE LARGEST CASTE WITHIN BARÇA are the 150,000 *socis*.

About half of them hold season tickets. In the days before television rights, it was their subscriptions that made Barça into one of Europe's richest clubs: more than 60 percent of the club's revenues in the late 1970s came from season tickets. By 2020, that proportion had fallen below 5 percent. The *socis* don't care: they still consider themselves the club's owners.

The *socis* elect the *directius*, though their choice is limited to rival members of the city's upper class. Like the *directius*, the *socis* are overwhelmingly local, conservative, and Catalan. For all the marveling about official fan clubs from Los Angeles to Shanghai, 92 percent of *socis* live in Catalonia and 60 percent in the metropolitan area of Barcelona. Ten percent are in Les Corts, the middle-class neighborhood around the Camp Nou.

The parochialism is deliberate. When Rosell was president, he stopped an international drive by the club to reach a million *socis*; he feared that one day a majority of Chinese *socis* might elect a president who lived in Beijing. Immigrants from Latin America, North Africa, or Pakistan rarely become *socis* even if they've lived in Barcelona for decades. In this newly global city, where 26 percent of inhabitants are now born abroad, Barça remains a native concern.[21]

Being a *soci* is a family affair. Rosell said it was a misconception to think that 150,000 *socis* elect the president. No, 20,000 families vote. A family will generally unite behind one candidate after discussing the matter over a traditional Catalan multigenerational Sunday lunch, he said.

Many *socis* have inherited a specific, treasured seat in the ground from parents or grandparents. If a *soci* dies without assigning his seat in his will, his children might go to court to dispute it among one another.[22] Your *soci* number shrinks each year with seniority; the longest-serving *soci* (or their heir) is number one. The lower your number, the higher your status.

Very few *socis* are diehards who insist on seeing every second of every game. Some will pop into the ground twenty minutes after kick-off, dressed to the nines, there just to show their face and make sure the team is still playing the right kind of football, watch in silence, and leave early. They routinely skip games, especially on school nights, renting out their seats online to visiting foreigners. There are *socis* who don't even like football; they just love Barça. A couple thousand hardly ever turn up to games at all.[23] Only for the Clásico is everyone there, as raucous and anxious as football fans anywhere on earth. Yet being a *soci,* or *culer* (*culé* in Spanish, meaning a Barça fan, literally "backside"), is always part of who they are. The 550 Barça *penyas* (fan clubs) in Catalonia alone are hubs of social life for a big chunk of the region's population.

The *socis'* representatives sit in the Assemblea, the club parliament, so their wishes constrain the *directius*. The Assemblea tends to be skeptical of exciting new commercial schemes. *Socis* don't like anything that feels vulgar, and they don't care much about profits. Their priority is cheap season tickets. Barça aims to have the cheapest in all of top-class football. In 2017–2018, season tickets in the Camp Nou started at the equivalent of about $115; Arsenal's cheapest cost more than ten times as much.[24] Barcelona froze real prices for ten years in a row through 2020, which goes a little bit of the way toward explaining the club's gargantuan gross debt (about $1.7 billion by early 2022).[25]

. . .

THE THIRD CASTE inside the club consists of the regular, or nonplay-ing, employees. In 2003, just before the Messi era, Barça had about 150 nonplaying staffers, almost all of whom knew each other. But from then until 2019, as the club became a global business, its revenues jumped sixfold to €841 million. By the time the coronavirus shut down football in 2020, Barça employed about five hundred full-timers, and approxi-mately as many occasional workers (match stewards, security staff, and the like). The club had become overstaffed, with perhaps a third more employees than autocratic Real Madrid, because it's always nicer to hire someone new than sack a lifer.

Whenever a new merchant faction takes over the board, new execu-tives come in, but they're always drawn from much the same local pool. Barça's *directius* attended the city's most prestigious universities and schools, where they got to know fellow students who became local psy-chologists, data analysts, and brand managers. They hire these people as senior executives. When done well, this creates a melding of the local knowledge economy and the club that you'll rarely find in English football.

But often *directius* appoint their pals rather than the best candidates. One ex-president told me that he had continued to employ a semi-competent old friend because he was worried about him. A local advertising man, a *soci* himself, remarked that competence among Barça executives was so iffy that he wouldn't work at the club for fear of damaging his pro-fessional reputation. Taking a job there was "a career elevator that only goes downwards," he told me.

The club's employees include a hard core of lifers, some of them *socis*. One ex-staffer explained to me that the lifers are the unseen power brokers who really run things at Barça, the equivalent of the senior civil servants in the TV series *Yes, Prime Minister*. They form a kind of priestly caste that stores traditional knowledge in-house, like the gnarled old coaches in Liverpool's now demolished Boot Room. The lifers have even learned to find their way around the labyrinthine Camp Nou, a task that can take decades. Most of them are Catalans who will fight for their positions with everything they have. They know they wouldn't get hired at another big club.

Only at the very top of Barça's staffing pyramid do you find many foreigners. By football standards, Barça has a decent record of hiring black ex-players in big jobs: Frank Rijkaard was head coach here, Eric Abidal sporting director, and Patrick Kluivert ran the Masia.

The embodiment of Barça's culture is the septuagenarian thinker on sport, Paco "El Druida" Seirul·lo, possibly the club's most influential employee, even if hardly anyone outside the Camp Nou has ever heard of him. Seirul·lo (yes, he really does have a floating full stop in his name) started out in Barça's handball wing, coached the thirteen-year-old Guardiola, became Cruyff's right-hand man, is a professor at the University of Barcelona, speaks like a Parisian Rive Gauche philosopher, sports a magnificent mane of white hair, and is a sort of walking USB stick containing the club's portable memory. "I am the only one remaining—the others have gone!" he chuckles. When I met him, he was running the *metodologia* department, which trains Barça's coaches in Barça's own traditions.

I interviewed Seirul·lo and a few other employees in Spanish, but most staffers of the newer generation (unusually for Spain) speak excellent English. They need it to do business and absorb best practices from around the world. Many of them have MBAs or PhDs. Older employees sometimes refer to them by the disparaging English nickname "clusters," a word that connoted high-tech modernity before it became associated with the coronavirus. (Soriano, the club's former general manager, cofounded a company called Cluster Consulting and brought some of its bright young sparks to Barça.) In the Camp Nou's cafés, the clusters favor energy drinks, whereas older staffers eat bocatas, the heavy baguette sandwiches served in working-class Spanish bars.

In certain offices, Barça looks like a multinational knowledge company, where young people with MacBooks chase monthly revenue targets. Mostly, though, it doesn't. Barça's rise to the top was not propelled by a brilliant, dynamic front office. One former employee said of his time at the club: "It didn't feel like a corporation at all. It felt like you were a functionary working for a local council." He said staffers would show up at about ten a.m., fetch coffee and swap gossip, then settle down to work at about eleven. Salaries were relatively low, because working for Barça was a privilege that enhanced staffers' status in town. This man said the main question informing every internal decision was not "How much money will this make the club?" but "How will this affect the president's standing with the *socis*?"

THE HIGHEST-STATUS CASTE in Can Barça are the athletes in the various sports. They spend most of their working lives fifteen minutes' drive from the Camp Nou, at the closely guarded Joan Gamper training complex just outside town. The Gamper lies in a dip, sandwiched between an industrial area and the highway, and is accordingly polluted, but because it's sealed to the outside world, it's an intimate place. One morning, I interviewed a club psychologist in the Gamper café over a breakfast of coffee and two mini-croissants (total bill €2.20) while the handball general manager and staffers and coaches in different sports chatted at the neighboring tables. Outside, an older bald employee known as "the mayor" of the Gamper was doing his daily round, hugging colleagues.

The Gamper is a place of exchange between coaches and players from the various sports. Barça has long-standing basketball, handball, futsal, and other nonfootball wings. These generally lose money, and every now and then a decision-maker will propose closing one of them down. (Conversely, a staffer in indoor sports jokes that if he ever becomes Barça president, he'll shut down the football team.) Still, I saw how much Barça benefits from the cross-pollination of different sports. Cruyff and Guardiola, who each chose a former water polo player as right-hand man, were always getting ideas from Barça's other sports. Cruyff would often go for coffee in the ice-rink café with the club's all-conquering handball coach, Valero Rivera. Guardiola as a young footballer even trained with the handball team. I came to understand FC Barcelona as a "multisports" rather than a football club.

Many of the players are lifers, too. Sergio Busquets's dad, Carles, kept goal for Cruyff's Barça, not always reliably. Several other first-teamers have been here since entering the Masia as children, and remain dutiful Catalan sons. Even after Piqué had reached his thirties, his dad sometimes drove him to games. Jordi Alba's father drove him to training sessions, as if the left-back were still a ten-year-old in the Masia's "Benjamin" team. Alba grumbles that Real Madrid's center-back Raphaël Varane once teased him during a Clásico, "Rat boy, you don't have a driver's license." It's possible to remain a Barça footballer in spirit all your life, or even longer. Local ex-players meet at the Gamper for weekly kick-arounds. Some foreign stars, like Ladislao Kubala, Cruyff, and Kluivert, settled in the city after retiring. Kubala now lies in the graveyard behind the Camp Nou.

The lifers in Barça's football squad tend to feel a connection with the club and its ordinary employees (though not with the board). That helps explain why the first team, under Messi's leadership, agreed to protect the salaries of nonplaying staffers by taking a pay cut during the sport's shutdown in spring 2020. One staffer said Messi joked to him afterward, "You haven't thanked me yet, have you?"

Still, the first-team footballers exist at a remove from the club, like a world-class department grafted onto city hall. The working language of Barça's changing room is Spanish, not Catalan—and not even the Catalan-accented variety. New signings are often urged by the *directius* to learn some Catalan, but few bother.

This is not one of those business self-help books that will reveal "How you and your company can win the Barcelona way!" I don't believe a normal company can learn much from a great football club, because there is one unbridgeable difference: the outsize role of the talent in football. In most normal companies, when a senior executive leaves, a new one comes in, and hardly anybody notices the difference. But top-class footballers who can function within the Barça system are almost irreplaceable. The logic is that they and not the directors can end up running the club.

For decades the four castes of Can Barça fought their battles with Real Madrid and with each other, mostly ignored by the world outside Catalonia. For the first seventy-odd years of its history, Barça was a big club that didn't even entirely aspire to be a great one. It was a bastion of local pride, like Newcastle United or the Buffalo Bills of the NFL, rather than a winner of trophies. Then Cruyff came along and turned it into a great club. He played here from 1973 to 1978, was head coach from 1988 to 1996, and hung around as a kind of godfather until his death in 2016. He shaped Barça's playing style, its academy, and even its attitude of mind. Xavi called him "the most influential person in FC Barcelona's history."[26] But his influence has spread far beyond the club. Cruyff, says Guardiola, is "the most important person in the history of football."[27]

PART TWO

THE ARCHITECT

II

THE MAN WHO TALKED
ON THE BALL

When his death was announced in March 2016, videos of the "Cruyff Turn" filled social media. Playing for the Netherlands against Sweden at the 1974 World Cup, Cruyff back-heeled the ball so suddenly past his own leg that the Swedish defender Jan Olsson almost fell over. Olsson told me decades later: "I thought, 'Now I have the ball,' and then I thought, 'Where is the ball?' I didn't understand. I think many people laughed about it. It is very interesting."

It is, but Cruyff did much more interesting things than that. In the full span of his oeuvre, the Cruyff Turn barely registers. There's nothing surprising about it for Dutch or Catalan fans, who saw him (at least in brief TV highlights) every week. Nor is there for a rootless cosmopolitan like me who happened to spend a decade of his childhood in the Netherlands, or for Michel Platini, who grew up in Lorraine in eastern

France and so was one of the few French people able to watch Cruyff's great Ajax of the early 1970s. "We, the lucky ones, received Radio Télé Luxembourg,"[1] gloated Platini. We lucky ones also have years of Cruyff's moves and decades of his interviews stored in our brains. The total Cruyff is our secret. Whereas Messi belongs to global culture, Cruyff belonged only to Dutch and Catalan culture.

It's hard now to recapture how little international football used to be shown on TV. Nick Hornby writes in *Fever Pitch* that until the World Cup of 1970, "a good three quarters of the population of England had about as clear a picture of Pelé as we'd had of Napoleon one hundred and fifty years before."[2] Cruyff was equally elusive until the World Cup 1974. Most of the planet's football fans of his day only saw him at that one tournament—the only month of his career that was televised worldwide. Angela Merkel, a football-mad nineteen-year-old East German in 1974, said decades later, "Cruyff impressed me. I don't think I was the only one in Europe."[3] But she probably never saw him play again. Sadder still, foreign fans never heard Cruyff either. Few foreign journalists visited the canteen of the old Ajax stadium to grab him for a lunchtime interview over cigarettes.

Anyone trying to discover Cruyff from YouTube will be disappointed. The supreme footballer of his day, he could pass like Messi, but he wasn't in Messi's class as a dribbler, and his shot was weak. Physically, he was a stick-thin chain-smoker. To appreciate his genius, you had to watch him for a whole match, and in the stadium rather than on TV, so that you could see him change his team's tactics and point teammates where to go even while he was dribbling past people.

In most of the world, where he was consumed without the soundtrack, Cruyff was little more than a picture. He belonged, with people like Richard Nixon and David Bowie, to the wallpaper of the 1970s. Even the globalized version of his name, "Cruyff," creates distance. (I wanted to use his real name, Cruijff, in this book, but eventually gave up: it would have been too confusing given that "Cruyff" is ubiquitous everywhere outside the Netherlands.)

When he died, many reimagined the grocer's son as a long-haired left-wing hippie idealist. "L'icône des 70's: L'aura d'une rock star" was the headline over the tribute in French sports newspaper *L'Équipe*. Yet even his image wasn't instantly recognizable. The cover portrait on *The Guardian* newspaper's memorial supplement was of his stick-thin, long-haired Dutch teammate Rob Rensenbrink.

Cruyff's most enduring creation is Barça. Much of the club's style and approach today derives from his brain waves and personal quirks. Any understanding of today's Barcelona starts with Cruyff, the player, the coach, the teacher, and the person. But to understand him, it's necessary first to understand his formative decades at Ajax.

HENDRIK JOHANNES CRUIJFF WAS BORN in 1947 in Betondorp ("Cement Village"), a neighborhood of model working-class homes in Amsterdam East, a few hundred meters from the old Ajax stadium. His parents, both descendants of Amsterdam market traders and shopkeepers,[4] ran a grocery shop that supplied Ajax with fruit and vegetables. His father, Manus, even had business cards printed with borders in red and white, Ajax's colors, proclaiming himself "court purveyor" to his beloved club.[5]

Johan and his older brother, Hennie, were always playing football and baseball on the almost car-free cobblestone streets of Betondorp. They would play one-twos off the pavement edge, and dodge tackles so as not to fall and ruin their trousers.[6] "I had the elegance of the street," Cruyff said in old age. "My whole philosophy of coaching rests on the memories of the techniques of the street."[7]

From about age four, he would toddle across the road to the Ajax stadium. On match days he helped the groundsman raise the flag and draw the white lines. He'd sit in the first-team changing room before the match and at halftime, listening to players talk tactics or money. "I was part of the household, like a child in a family,"[8] he recalled shortly before he died.

People at Ajax called him Jopie (a diminutive of Johan) or Kleine (Little One)—nicknames that would follow him all the way into the Dutch national team. At age six, he'd come and watch Ajax's ten-year-olds play, hoping someone wouldn't show so that he could get a game.[9] During school holidays he'd sweep the stands. (Looking back from the peak of his stardom, he'd complain that he had only been paid twenty-five cents per shift.)[10] When he was ten, the board enrolled him as a club member. He hadn't even applied.[11]

The Ajax of Cruyff's childhood was a genuine club like Barça, a local voluntary association that offered multiple sports. The young Cruyff occasionally played cricket for Ajax, and became a renowned catcher and stealer of bases[12] in the club's baseball section. He treated all sports as variants of each other. As a catcher, he recalled later, "You had to know where you were going to throw the ball before you received it, which meant that you had to have an idea of all the space around you and where each player was before you made the throw. . . . You're always busy making decisions between space and risk in fractions of a second."[13] He later captured this need for anticipation in one of his aphorisms: "Before I make a mistake, I don't make that mistake."[14]

Little Jopie was a brilliant footballer, always playing in older age groups. Manus once joked to an Ajax director, "One day, that *Kleine* will cost you 50.000 guilders!"[15] But one summer evening when Johan was twelve, Manus died of a heart attack, at age forty-five. He was buried on the stadium side of the cemetery so that he could hear the crowd cheer Ajax's goals.[16] Each time Johan cycled past, he'd talk to his dead father. Well into adulthood, he continued to hold conversations with Manus's spirit.

The father's death plunged the family into precarity. The grocery closed, and the boys' mother, Nel, had to clean Ajax's changing rooms. (She later married the Ajax groundsman whom her toddler son used to help.) Johan, bereft without Manus, dropped out of school in early adolescence. Looking back, he said his father's death left him with the feeling: "I must have security. I later want to be able to give my children everything I want."[17]

It didn't look then as if football could provide. Ajax at the start of the 1960s was merely the neighborhood club of Amsterdam East, and Dutch football was a part-time affair. Players earned little more than match bonuses. When I interviewed Cruyff in 2000, he recalled his childhood worship of English clubs like Manchester United and Liverpool: "English football, in the time I was growing up, was three houses above everything else. They were already pros when we didn't even know the ball was round, in a manner of speaking."

A small boy in a world of men, he had to find ways to cope. He discovered that his physical weakness was a strength: it forced him to think. Being little, he had to react faster than anyone else.

From childhood on, Cruyff had complete control of the ball so he didn't need to look down at it. He played with his head up, scanning the field. He always believed that the one thing he had over other players was his reading of the game. "Football is a game you play with your head,"[18] he said.

At age seventeen, in November 1964, Cruyff made his official debut for Ajax's first team. Already he was irritating veteran internationals by telling them where to run. He never just let his feet do the talking. He felt entitled to say what he thought, partly because he saw more than other players did, and partly because he had the characteristically Dutch Calvinist belief that anyone of any status could possess the truth.

Ajax in 1964–1965 were fighting relegation. Two months after Cruyff's debut, they sacked their English manager, Vic Buckingham.

His replacement was a thirty-six-year-old former Ajax forward named Rinus Michels, who worked as a gym teacher for deaf children. Ajax had hired him to give three evening training sessions a week. Michels pulled up at the little stadium in a secondhand Škoda and told a journalist, "We have to start at zero."[19]

The new manager had a crazy plan: the struggling neighborhood club was going to conquer Europe.[20] Michels and his eighteen-year-old forward got talking tactics. They discovered a shared desire to innovate that Cruyff would describe with hindsight as typically 1960s.[21]

Michels could be a witty and cheery fellow, who liked to sing arias at parties, but he rarely showed that side to his players. They called him "the Bull" at first, because he looked and behaved like one, and later "De Generaal." (He once said that "top-level football is something like war."[22])

"Michels was the father and we his children, whom he raised with a hard hand," analyzed the fatherless Cruyff. The coach thought his players were softies. He often accused them of having "a typical Dutch mentality," meaning that they were unambitious and unwilling to suffer, and they didn't kick opponents enough. Every preseason, he put them through three training sessions a day, followed by an evening friendly match. De Generaal wanted to speed up the slow Dutch game. The ball needed to move much faster, and so did the players. In case extra energy was required, the team doctor John Rolink, an amphetamine user himself, provided a variety of nameless pills. (There were no drug tests in Dutch football at the time.)[23]

Many Ajax players in the 1960s worked as shopkeepers, teachers, or driving instructors.[24] Cruyff for a time hauled bales of textiles in a warehouse. Michels wanted his men to become full-time professional footballers, so they could train more often. The transition was financed partly by the club's motley crew of financiers: a few Jewish businessmen who had survived the war and found a kind of ersatz family at

Ajax, and the two Van der Meijden brothers, contractors known as the "bunker builders" who had made a bundle working for the German occupiers during the war, and were now laundering their reputations through football.

Most Dutch coaches in those days were sentimental in their dealings with players, many of whom were lifelong club members. Even in 1973, after Michels had moved to Barcelona, nobody at Ajax dared tell the aging outside-right Sjaak Swart that he needed to cede his place to Johnny Rep. Eventually a typically Dutch compromise was found: Swart would play the first half of matches, and Rep the second. Ajax at that point were European and world champions.

Michels, though, was unsentimental. Each season after Ajax were knocked out of European competition, he got rid of the weakest players, though usually without daring to tell them in person. Cruyff was tougher still. For six-a-side games in training, he and the other captain would take turns picking players, like in street football. That way every player got a daily reminder of his place in the hierarchy.

As with Lennon and McCartney, the Michels-Cruyff relationship was equal parts inspiration and irritation. Cruyff drove Michels mad. The kid was always disobeying his tactical orders, shouting at teammates, smoking to excess, going out late, and, in those first years, frequently failing in big matches. Michels also suspected him of faking injuries.[25] But none of that stopped Cruyff and Michels from creating something extraordinary at Ajax. By 1970, they had developed a revolutionary new brand of football, one that would help shape the sport for the next fifty years, especially in the Netherlands and Barcelona. Ajax people didn't really have a name for the style, but foreigners called it "total football."

"Total football" meant that every player attacked and everyone defended. Ajax's players changed position so fluidly that it became hard even to speak about positions. Ajax's game evolved into what Cruyff called "a controlled chaos."[26] Every player had to think for himself non-stop, adapting his position second by second depending on where every other player was. The ideal of a totally fluid football team went back to the "Danubian Whirl" of the 1930s' Austrian Wunderteam. Ajax had reinvented it for a new era.[27]

The dominant style of the 1960s had been defensive Italian *catenaccio*. Ajax took the opposite approach: they played in the opponents' half, passing one-touch at top speed, with players changing positions all the time. They positioned themselves so the man on the ball always had at least two diagonal passes to choose from. A pass that goes straight ahead is easy for an opponent to read, while a square ball is usually pointless, and can be fatal if intercepted. But no single opposition player can block two diagonals simultaneously. So Ajax made triangles, prefiguring the great Barcelona teams of Cruyff himself and Pep Guardiola.

Cruyff saw football as geometry, a question of space. When Ajax had the ball, they made the pitch wide: he said wingers had to have "chalk on their boots." When Ajax lost possession, they shrank space: several players would "press" the opponent on the ball, aiming to win it back at once. That was the perfect moment, because a team that had just won the ball was usually disorganized, with players out of position. If you could rob them, you could have a clear run on goal. And if your opponents never got a chance to build, they grew demoralized.

Pressing, or "hunting," as Ajax called it, required almost military coordination. Each player had to occupy exactly the right spot, and everyone had to join the press. Ajax's attackers were the first defenders. Conversely, the goalkeeper was the first attacker, starting moves with incisive passes. He played like a "fly keeper" in street football, patrolling his entire half as if he were a defender in gloves. This meant that Ajax used all eleven players, whereas other teams played with just ten.

"Nobody had overturned the codes of football like we did,"[28] Cruyff said later. Arrigo Sacchi, coach of "il Grande Milan" of 1987–1990, would comment, "There has only been one real tactical revolution, and it happened when football shifted from an individual to a collective game. It happened with Ajax."[29]

Cruyff marshaled the collective. He could pass in any direction because he was, in the phrase of his great biographer, Nico Scheepmaker, "four-footed":[30] he used the insides and outsides of both feet, curling the ball like a snooker player. He clocked at a glance which foot a defender had planted in the ground, and accelerated past him on that side. He always said that speed wasn't about running fast, but about knowing when to run—a claim that denied his own astonishing acceleration.

On the field, Cruyff was everywhere. Ajax's trademark changes of position were in part an adaptation to his penchant for roaming. He was an extreme version of what we now call a "false nine": a center-forward who constantly abandoned his position, dropping back into midfield or the wing or even central defense, losing his markers to find space and opportunity. He once explained, "If they don't follow me, I'm free. If they follow me, they're one man short in defense."[31] Ajax's midfielders would burst into the space he vacated. His trademark shirt number, fourteen, encapsulated his unclassifiable role, even though he had taken it almost randomly after a return from injury.[32]

Michels chose the players and wrote the tactics on the blackboard. On the field, minute by minute, it was Cruyff who ran the show. Sometimes he'd turn to the bench and demand a substitution: "Rep must come on!"[33] Football was like Hollywood, Cruyff explained: there were stars (Pelé and Eusebio, Richard Burton and Brigitte Bardot) and there were supporting roles. He added, "Often the supporting roles are much better acted, in football as in film."[34] He himself always played the lead, and also directed the movie. He later said, "Generally, if you see great teams, you know they're all good footballers, but at most there's one who sees something."[35]

But seeing was a terrible responsibility. Cruyff reflected later, "That was the worst thing about my career: that you see everything, and so you always have to keep talking."[36] On the field and off it, he was always talking (ungrammatically) with his mouth, his hands, his shoulders, his whole frail body. Even while he evaded the flailing boots of opponents, he was telling teammates where to run.

Arsène Wenger, an admirer of 1970s' Ajax, told me the team's system was impossible to replicate because it required having Cruyff on the field, coaching dynamically the way a manager on the bench never could. A good footballer controls his zone of the field; Cruyff controlled the entire field. He would order two midfielders to switch positions, then fifteen minutes later tell them to switch back. He was always working out which Ajax player wasn't functioning on the day and needed to be "hidden," and which opposing player was the weakest link, the man who had to be left unmarked to receive the ball—and then pressed. Anyone could play well if given time on the ball. You had to let bad players play badly.[37]

Sometimes Michels would scream at him for changing his tactics, "Well, goddammit, Cruyff, who asked you to meddle?"[38] In retirement, Michels would admit, "I sometimes deliberately used a strategy of confrontation. My objective was to create a field of tension, and improve the team spirit."[39] Cruyff would end up copying the *conflictmodel*, turning the dial up to eleven. Asked years later to describe his relationship with Michels, Cruyff held two fists against each other.[40]

The neighborhood club kept getting better. In 1971, they beat Panathinaikos 2–0 at Wembley to win the European Cup. Ajax's ambitions began to expand. For the first few years, winning had been their only aim. Beauty was an unintended by-product.[41] But Cruyff began to notice that outsiders perceived beauty. He was flattered when artists interpreted his feints as artistic creations: "That's so nice. It's funny, really funny."[42] The French mime artist Jacques Tati told him, "You are an artist. Your way of playing greatly resembles mine. We are two people who try to react instantaneously to situations that we haven't initiated ourselves."[43] The ballet dancer Rudolf Nureyev told Cruyff he should have been a dancer. (In real life, as his wife, Danny, pointed out, Cruyff was an appalling dancer.)[44]

One of the things he liked best about Ajax's system was that he never had to run long distances. He spent most of each game within twenty-five yards of the opposing goal, and when Ajax lost possession, he didn't have to track back; the forwards held their lines and pressed. The trick was to take the one or two steps that snuffed out an opponent's passing line, or that gave your team a new passing diagonal. "The difference between right and wrong is often no more than five meters,"[45] he said. Running was good only if you ran in the right direction.

This game suited Cruyff partly because he could see the right steps, and partly because he was a chain-smoker who couldn't run far. In the biographical documentary *Nummer 14*, made in 1972, there's a scene of the Ajax squad jogging up a hill in the woods. Each player is wearing a tracksuit of a different brand or color. Cruyff, in a camel-colored Puma tracksuit, grumbles to a camera, "There is no play element in it. At this moment I see it as a profession, not at all as a hobby." Reaching the top of the hill at the back of the pack, he walks the last steps, exclaims, "Jesus," and bends over, hands on his knees, panting and coughing. You can feel his lungs burning. Other players sprawl over each other on benches, speechless. It's like a punishment scene in a prison movie.

They performed this ritual multiple times a week.[46] Sometimes Cruyff hid in the woods and joined his teammates on the last lap. If Michels caught him, he had to get up early the next morning and run alone.[47] Left to his own devices, Cruyff moved as little as possible. An

English tailor who often made clothes for footballers, and once measured Cruyff after training, reports that he was the only player he'd ever seen come off the field without a drop of sweat.[48]

But playing like Cruyff in the 1960s and 1970s took courage. At the time, fouling was considered an integral, even an admirable, manly part of football. Here is the BBC's Kenneth Wolstenholme commenting on the Milan–Ajax European Cup final of 1969, when an Italian foul spoils a Cruyff dribble: "Oooh, and he was beautifully tripped by Malatrasi, the sweeper! Really caught his ankle . . . Just caught him, just in full stride! Takes a genius to do that." A year later the former Ajax defender Frits Soetekouw, who had moved within Amsterdam to DWS, injured Cruyff by sliding in on him with a raised leg, then told Dutch TV, "I also blame it a bit on him. [Beats] three, four men, a slalom. He's asking for it a bit, isn't he?"[49]

By this time Michels had moved to Barcelona. Ajax's players were postwar baby boomers impatient with old people telling them what to do, and De Generaal had become too strict for them.[50] Barça had offered good money, and he had never spat on banknotes, Michels recalled decades later.[51]

His replacement in Amsterdam was Ştefan Kovács, former coach of the Romanian army team. Cruyff, who had been transformed by his wife, Danny, from buttoned-up grocer's son with slicked-back hair into a 1970s fashion plate, asked Kovács what he thought of long hair. The man from behind the Iron Curtain replied, "You could grow it even longer as far as I'm concerned, but I'm not here to be your hairdresser."[52]

Under Kovács, an Amsterdam spring blossomed. The kindly Romanian gave the players freedom on the field, and by this time, they had the maturity to know what to do with it. In 1972, they won the European Cup again. In the footage of their homecoming, the players ride in open cars down the tram lines of Amsterdam East, Cruyff's old neighborhood, where a couple of rows of people line the suburban streets.[53]

Watching the video of Ajax beating Independiente in that year's Club World Cup final, there's a shock: half a century on, their game doesn't look embarrassingly ancient. It has something of the pace, and the sprints off the ball, and the fullbacks powering down the wings of modern football. Michels and Cruyff had invented the future. In 1973, Ajax won a third straight European Cup.

Even then, the players were still treated in Amsterdam as local boys. The egalitarian Netherlands didn't have a category for superheroes. Stars were expected to act *normaal*. Many Amsterdammers felt they had the right to stop "Cruijffie" on the street and debate football with him for half an hour. He himself shared that expectation. "People from Betondorp don't have airs," he explained. His wife complained that if a kid called and asked to interview Cruyff for the school magazine, Cruyff would give him the whole afternoon.[54] Much as he welcomed almost any opportunity to talk, it was draining. He had grown too big for the Netherlands.

Nor was he paid like a superhero. Ajax's league games often drew just 10,000 people, most of them arriving on Tram 9 or by bike. Cruyff, then considered the best footballer on earth, was earning 95,000 guilders a year gross (worth about $180,000 in today's money, adjusted for inflation). The Dutch state took 72 percent. Once at a reception Cruyff tried to lobby Queen Juliana for lower taxes—the only political position he ever seems to have held. "You're the queen and maybe you can arrange something for us," he suggested, while Michels sidled off trying to stifle his laughter. "Mr. Cruyff," replied Juliana, "you should speak to my minister of finance."[55]

Cruyff's conflicts with teammates and Ajax's club directors ground him down, too. Leading a bunch of antiauthoritarian Calvinist baby boomers was exhausting. Cruyff had a knack for arousing irritation and jealousy in others, and over the years Ajax's players spent too much time together.

In July 1973, things got out of hand. In training camp in a rural hotel in the eastern Netherlands, the players decided to hold an election for the captaincy. At a meeting in the hotel's recreation room, Cruyff, the incumbent, received seven votes. His old friend and mentor Piet Keizer got eight. Cruyff walked out of the room. Ajax's midfielder Gerrie Mühren would compare the moment to the breakup of the Beatles three years earlier.[56]

Cruyff picked up a phone on the wall of the hotel corridor, rang Coster, the father-in-law-*cum*-agent, and told him, "Call Barcelona."[57] The vote had changed the future of two great clubs.

III

FC BARCELONA—FROM
AN ORIGINAL IDEA BY
JOHAN CRUYFF

Cruyff and Barça had been flirting for years. England was his childhood idyll, but it didn't admit foreign footballers, and the money was in Spanish football. He and Danny had begun vacationing on the Costa Brava and in Mallorca in the late 1960s, as Spain became fashionable among northern European tourists. New to holidays, he found the Spanish weather enchanting.[1] In June 1970, *Revista Barcelona* magazine published a ten-page exclusive on the couple's visit to the city. The coup de grâce was a photograph of Cruyff posing on the grass of the Camp Nou in Barcelona kit. Danny told the magazine, "A wonderful city, really everything that we've seen. And we especially like that it's on the sea."[2]

Spain was then still ruled by Franco, but Cruyff saw no issues with moving to a dictatorship. He told an Amsterdam newspaper, "I'll be rich within two years in Spain, a millionaire within four."[3] His tax rate would drop to 10 percent in Spain, wrote his biographer, Scheepmaker.[4]

Michels was still in Barcelona, and despite everything, he was desperate to be reunited with his bossy former pupil.[5] After Spain's borders were opened to foreign footballers in May 1973 and Cruyff lost the Ajax captaincy in July, Barcelona jumped.

Real Madrid tried to hijack the deal, just as they had pinched Alfredo Di Stéfano from under Barça's nose twenty years earlier. However, Cruyff refused Madrid's offer, in part to spite Ajax's board, which had already accepted it. The *socis'* membership fees gave Barça an income unmatched in northern European football, and the club raised them by 25 percent for two years to help cover Cruyff's world-record $2.3 million transfer fee.[6] So high was the sum that to get around import regulations, Barcelona registered him as a *bien semimoviente*—livestock.[7] The salary they paid him remains a mystery. When his business adviser Harrie van Mens checked years later, "I found three or four different versions of Johan's contract: one for the taxes, one for the press, one for Johan himself, and so on."[8]

AT 3:05 P.M. ON AUGUST 22, 1973, Cruyff landed at Barcelona's ramshackle little airport on KLM flight 254, unaware that he would be spending most of the rest of his life in Catalonia. At the time he may not even have known what Catalonia was.

In the bus to the terminal, Danny pointed at a crowd of people inside: "What's going on?" she asked him. "No idea," he replied.

They were waiting for him. *"Cruf!"* they cried, with a very un-Dutch awe, reaching through his protective cordon of policemen to try to touch him.[9] Watching the video of the scene, it's as if an emissary from the 1970s—long hair, bony smoker's face, necklaces, and wide-lapel shirt (undoubtedly chosen by Danny)—has landed in the 1950s. Cruyff came from what the author Vázquez Montalbán called "northern Europe, first-class Europe"[10]—the modern, wealthy, democratic continent that Catalans aspired to join.

In footballing terms, too, Cruyff was taking a step backward: the world's best player was exchanging the world's best team for a club of losers in a decrepit provincial city, in a backward league, in an impoverished dictatorship.

Compared with Ajax, Cruyff's new teammates were refreshingly pleased to have him around, but they were anachronisms who gave slow square passes. Michels was amazed that such a rich club had such a tactically ignorant and undisciplined team. Nor did it have a proper training ground; he had to requisition a local golf course.[11]

Franco's Spain lacked even a language to analyze football. "There was only one word, 'furia' [rage, aggression], which isn't a football concept but a state of mind,"[12] recalled the Argentinian Jorge Valdano, who arrived in Spain to play for second-division Alavés in 1975. (Valdano would later become a world champion alongside Maradona, then a coach, technical director of Real Madrid, and a wonderful writer on football.) Spaniards were expected to play with furia, and anything else was considered overintellectualizing. The international performances of Spanish teams suggested that it wasn't enough.

Barça was perennially out of favor with Franco. In the 1950s, its wonderful team starring Ladislao Kubala frequently outdid Real Madrid in the Spanish league, yet was overshadowed by Madrid's five consecutive European Cups. In the 1960s, Barça went into decline. When Cruyff landed, the club hadn't won a Spanish title in thirteen years. The culers, schooled in defeatist victimhood by decades under the Caudillo, would take their seats in the stadium muttering, "Avui patirem" ("Today we will suffer").[13] The club's animating spirit was madriditis, an anxious obsession with Madrid.

But by 1973, Franco was eighty and dying. While Catalans awaited "the biological fact," they prepared for self-rule. That October, 113 members of the new Catalan Council—trade unionists, members of political parties, students, and merchants—were arrested. Many of them listened to Cruyff's debut against Granada on October 28 clustered around a radio set in prison, and even those who didn't like football cheered Barça's four goals.[14]

In these final Franco years, the Camp Nou had become a political arena, full of forbidden *Senyeras* (Catalan flags), with announcements made in Catalan.[15] In 1971, Franco had summoned Barça's president, Agustí Montal, and board members to his palace, El Pardo, to tell them to tone down the *catalanisme*.[16] Yet Catalans were no longer so obedient. In 1973, Montal was reelected on the slogan "More than a club."

This ferment mostly passed Cruyff by. His first priority was househunting. Barcelona at the time was a run-down and dirty city with slums that stretched to the seafront, and no beaches. It was known as *la Barcelona grisa*, "gray Barcelona."[17] Property developers such as the future Barça president Josep Lluís Núñez had got rich replacing ancient buildings with cheap, ugly, new ones.[18] Cruyff and Danny had dreamed of living in Castelldefels near the coast, but were told that the village was full of pesky Dutch holidaymakers in summer. So the couple and their two young daughters ended up in Barcelona, in a large apartment with a swimming pool and a price tag that shocked them. The Michels also lived in Pedralbes, having moved from their first apartment on the Avenida Generalísimo Franco (which today is called the Diagonal).[19] When Cruyff traveled to away matches, Michels's wife, Wil, came to stay with Danny to keep her company.[20]

In Barcelona, the Cruyffs remained egalitarian Hollanders: the Spanish maid ate meals with the family.[21] Still, Cruyff quickly learned that Spaniards accorded privileges to superheroes. Here he didn't have to be *normaal*. People on the street treated him with more respect than in Amsterdam. He discovered that if he ever needed a car, he could ask the nearest starstruck local to borrow theirs. Barça soon got him a private phone number, which ended the incessant calls from fans, and from the stalker who always introduced herself to Danny as "your husband's fiancée."[22]

Cruyff treasured family life, having learned at the age of twelve that it could shatter in a day. At Barça, he resumed his old role as Michels's representative on turf, more harmoniously than in their Ajax days. The coach, keen to preserve his distance, insisted that Cruyff call him Mr. Michels.[23] Together they taught the other players that football was a game you played with your head. Cruyff spent the rest of his time advertising liquors, sunglasses, jeans, television sets, and Puma boots.[24] Commercially, he was a generation ahead of Spanish football. He more or less replaced his family name, Cruijff, with an international brand name, Cruyff, because the "y" worked better outside the Netherlands.

He learned Spanish in months. "Spanish is a simple language, because you write it like you pronounce it. Although I don't know how to write it," he reflected decades later.[25] His Dutch "logisch" (the word he used to clinch arguments, usually emphasized by a shrug of the shoulders) became "lógicamente," still pronounced in an Amsterdam accent. He never mastered Spanish genders, or many other grammatical rules, but then he hadn't in Dutch either.[26] "Talking," he once mused, without irony, "if only I could do everything as well as I talk."[27]

He initially seemed to assume that Barcelona was a regular Spanish city, without regional particularities. "I don't want to get involved with their politics," he said in March 1974. "I didn't do that in Holland either."[28] In those early months, he fondly described Barça fans as "Spanish," and neither then nor later made the slightest effort to learn any Catalan. The story goes that asked once to say something in Catalan, he replied, "Hola." Even while coaching Catalonia's unofficial national team a few years before his death, he delivered his dressing-room talk in Spanish.[29] When Catalan nationalists in the post-Franco years complained, he said, "I too come from a small country and I don't demand that the whole world speaks Dutch."[30]

Franco's dictatorship didn't bother him. "What is fascist?" he asked in his memoir, *Boem*, published in the final months of Franco's reign.

> What is unfree . . . I've been told that there are more than a hundred countries where there is no press freedom. Why then the constant moaning about me in connection with Spain? . . . One thing is for sure: the people here in Spain are much more cheerful, less complaining, less unhappy than in the Netherlands.[31]

For all his political apathy, his personality made him the poster boy for an assertive, new, anti-Fascist Catalonia. He was a walking advertisement for European modernity and free speech, a born antiauthoritarian who argued with referees even in a dictatorship. The Catalan opera singer and Barça fan Josep Carreras (who under the Spanish name José would gain fame as one of the Three Tenors) said, "He had the good luck to come from a democracy, and he showed it, too. . . . Thanks to him we believe in ourselves."[32]

"He was the least spontaneous of the great geniuses," said Valdano, who revered Cruyff the footballer.[33] "He governed games. He had influence over teammates, opponents, the referee, the journalists, the crowd, the ball, the corner flags and the Coca-Cola sellers."[34] If a player from either team went down injured, Cruyff would inspect him, and if he deemed it necessary, he'd summon the physio, as if the referee didn't exist. Once, when a muddy pitch was hampering Barça's efforts to give him the ball, Cruyff moved himself to libero (free-ranging sweeper) and restructured the team without asking the coach's permission. "Incidentally, he was the best libero I have seen in my life," said Valdano, who diagnosed him as "a quasi-pathological case of self-confidence."[35]

During Cruyff's first season with Barça, Danny was pregnant with their third child. Because the birth was to be by cesarean in Amsterdam, Michels scheduled it for February 9, eight days before the Real Madrid–Barcelona match. (February 9 also just happened to be Michels's own birthday.)

The Cruyffs named the baby Jordi, the Catalan version of George, in honor of their new home. They had no idea that Jordi was the patron saint of Catalonia, a nationalist symbol, and a forbidden name under Franco. "We just thought it was a beautiful name," Cruyff admitted afterward.[36] On the family's return to Barcelona the newborn was greeted by another crowd at the airport, and then briefly went missing, until the childless Michels was discovered dandling him on his knee in the car.[37] (De Generaal would retain a lifelong affection for Cruyff's children—more so than for their father—and followed Jordi's playing career like a fan.)[38]

When Cruyff went to register Jordi at Barcelona's town hall, the clerk told him to name the boy Jorge, the Spanish version of George. Only Castilian names were permitted. Cruyff refused. He didn't particularly care what the Spanish state called his son, as he had already registered Jordi in the Netherlands. Eventually the clerk gave in.[39] "My son was the first Jordi registered as such in Catalonia," Cruyff later claimed.[40] Jordi would grow up to play football for Barcelona, Manchester United, and Oranje, and to consider himself a Catalan.[41]

The story of his naming was rapidly distorted into a Catalan myth, with Cruyff in the role of nationalist hero. Cruyff reflected decades later, "Things like that change the course of your life, they make your luck. That's why I was so popular here at first. And it's still that way."[42]

On February 17, 1974, at the Bernabéu, Cruyff played the best match of his Spanish years, and Barça hammered the team of Franco's capital 0–5. Vázquez Montalbán wrote, "1–0 for Barcelona—2–0 for Catalonia—3–0 for Saint Jordi—4–0 for democracy—5–0 against Madrid."[43] The pro-Franco daily *Solidaridad* unhappily shared that analysis: Barça's goals, it said, "represented far more than five goals. They imply a disquieting triumph over centralism."[44]

Until that day, Real Madrid–Atlético Madrid had been the biggest game in the Spanish calendar. From then on, Madrid–Barça became known in Spain as El Clásico.[45] That spring, Barcelona—who had been fourth from bottom when Cruyff made his debut—won their first title since 1960. Playing a version of Dutch pressing football, they were so good that even the referees couldn't stop them, Michels later recalled.[46]

"I'd never seen Barça win anything," remembered the club's future president Joan Laporta, eleven years old at the time.[47] A generation of Catalan children who would later run the club, or work for it, fell for Cruyffian football and Cruyffian long hair. In the 1974 song "Botifarra de Pagès" ("Catalan Sausage"), the local comedy band La Trinca croaked its eulogy like an army of frogs:

> *Cruyff,*
> *Cruyff, Cruyff, Cruyff,*
> *Cruyff, Cruyff, Cruyff,*
> *Cruyff, Cruyff, Cruyff,*
> *Like a vulgar frog choir*
> *we'll eulogize your feet*

Cruyff then headed to West Germany for the World Cup. Oranje, the Dutch team, had only ever played two matches in the tournament: one in 1934 and one in 1938, both defeats. Little was expected of them this time either.

Michels was managing Oranje, but he spent much of the tournament flying back and forth to Barcelona, where the team was preparing for the Spanish cup semifinal and final. That left Cruyff, at the height of his powers, with an outsize role in instructing and picking the team.

Before a warm-up match, he told Arie Haan, who had always been a midfielder, that he'd be playing sweeper in West Germany. "Are you crazy? Is this a joke?" asked Haan.

The Netherlands possessed a wonderful keeper in Jan van Beveren. However, he was un-Cruyffian in style, rarely leaving his goal line to join in play. Equally important, he and Cruyff didn't get along. Cruyff's fellow Amsterdammer Jan Jongbloed, a cigar-shop proprietor who was a classic fly keeper, was given the job instead. "I had the impression that the choice for me was mostly Johan's idea," said Jongbloed.[48]

In Germany, even the Dutch were surprised to discover how good they were. So was the Uruguayan defender who had been taking a leisurely stroll with the ball when he was suddenly stormed by five orange shirts. For TV viewers around the world, it was like watching the dodo go extinct in real time. Cruyff later remarked that almost all their opponents had seemed clueless: "They were doing things we'd given up doing five or six years ago."[49]

Fueled by multipacks of unfiltered Camel cigarettes,[50] he excelled through the semifinal. But the day before the final against West Germany in Munich, the German tabloid *Bild* published a story headlined "Cruyff, Champagne and Naked Girls." In it, an undercover reporter recounted his infiltration of a late-night skinny-dip involving Cruyff, several other Dutch players, and their groupies at their training camp in Hiltrup. (Disappointingly, the accompanying photograph showed an empty swimming pool.)[51] Cruyff spent much of the buildup to the final in the hotel's only phone booth, promising an irate Danny in Spain that *Bild* had made it all up. His longtime double life of discreet adulterer[52] and devoted family man came close to breaking down.

He started the final with a forty-yard solo that won the Dutch a first-minute penalty (though in fact the foul on him was just outside the box). Johan Neeskens hammered home a thunderous spot kick. But after that, noted his brother, Hennie, Cruyff "played like a dishrag," hanging about listlessly in midfield. His German marker, Berti Vogts, created more chances than he did. Gerd Müller's equalizing goal rolled past a motionless Jongbloed, and West Germany won 2–1.

Cruyff was just happy the whole thing was over. He always regarded family as more important than football, and he managed to stay married to Danny all his life. Her rage was probably the main reason why he skipped the World Cup of 1978 in Argentina. It's certainly a myth that he boycotted the tournament in protest against the Argentinian military regime. He once said, accurately, "People have always associated me with concepts of liberty and rebellion, but I've never sought either the one or the other."[53]

The German journalist Ulfert Schröder called Munich "the melancholy zenith" of Cruyff's career.[54] In fact, though, the Dutch defeat wasn't particularly tragic. The little Netherlands was proud to have come second in the world (and would be again in 1978 and 2010).

Cruyff eventually rationalized the defeat as a moral victory.[55] This was a new category for a man who cheated at dominos and Monopoly to beat his kids,[56] but the notion of moral victory would mark his thinking forever after. He came to argue that the Dutch had really won the World Cup, because they played beautiful football that people remembered. "Imagine—that defeat made us more famous than a victory could have."[57]

It turned out that beauty in football wasn't just a by-product, but a way to win even when you lost. The beauty that Cruyff cared about was collective: football as choreography, rather than individual tricks on the ball. He wasn't by nature a "one for all and all for one" kind of guy, like Liverpool's Bill Shankly. He just believed that the fullest expression of football was team play. From 1974 onward, he morphed into an "idealistic professional"[58] intent on winning beautifully.

Like so many of Cruyff's idiosyncratic beliefs, the idea of moral victory later took root in Barcelona. Laporta recalled telling Platini and Franz Beckenbauer during his first presidency, "I think winning is important, but mainly with Barça I want to be the best, like the Netherlands in 1974."[59]

That World Cup was the last time Cruyff ever played on a great side. His Barcelona didn't win another league title, and he kept picking up white cards (in Spain they weren't yellow yet). The countless cigarettes took their toll. He smoked discreetly in the changing room at halftime, and would have smoked on the pitch if he could. An Amsterdam friend who came to stay once persuaded him out for a jog: "After 50 meters Johan says, 'You're sick in your head.' And he stopped at once."[60] By his late twenties, Cruyff was in physical decline.

The biggest event of his last four seasons with Barça occurred on November 20, 1975. A concierge walked into club headquarters, interrupting a meeting of senior officials, and announced, "Gentlemen, the Caudillo is dead." Jaume Rosell, the club secretary (and father of Barça's future president Sandro), recalled later, "There were two reactions: those who said, 'Let's open a bottle of cava,' and the others who stayed silent and were evidently scared shitless." Later that day, Barça's chief secretary grabbed the bust of Franco that usually sat in Montal's office and chucked it at Rosell. The bust missed him and broke into pieces. "Fuck me," said Rosell (quoted in Jimmy Burns's *Barça: A People's Passion*). "We thought this was so solid that it could never break, and now it turns out it's nothing but shitty plaster!" Nonetheless, Montal cannily dispatched a batch of loyalist telegrams, declaring the club "filled with sadness at the irreplaceable loss of the Head of State."[61]

A month later, when Real Madrid visited Barcelona, hundreds of Catalan flags were smuggled into the Camp Nou.[62] Soon policemen on the city's streets were truncheoning protesters demanding Catalan autonomy. Spain's future hung in the balance. If you had asked people in the mid-1970s which of Spain and Yugoslavia would become a prosperous European democracy, and which would be destroyed by civil war between hostile regions, plenty would have given the wrong answer.

The ban on the Catalan language had been softening in the latter Franco decades. After his death it collapsed. In 1976, local newspapers and radio stations began covering Barça in Catalan. Since the language had almost no football vocabulary, they invented one.[63] Cruyff became Barça's first captain to wear the Catalan flag on his armband. However, he had his mind on other matters. He spent the months after Franco's death leading the resistance against Barcelona's new coach, Hennes Weisweiler. The German wanted him to spend more time at center-forward even in away games, when referees gave opponents license to assault him; Cruyff preferred to sit in midfield and protect his legs.[64] Franco's death was Catalonia's liberation, but Weisweiler's departure four months later was Cruyff's. Weisweiler concluded that training Barcelona wasn't that hard, but "working with Cruyff was impossible."[65] Michels returned to replace the German for two not very successful years.

Cruyff stayed at Barça long enough to help Josep Lluís Núñez win the club's first post-Franco democratic presidential elections, in 1978: the Dutchman threatened to leave if Ferran Ariño, one of his enemies, became president. In fact, he had already decided by then to stop playing, aged just thirty-one. "I had no more pleasure in it," he explained later.[66] Cruyff found football exhausting, because for him it was always conflictual. He also feared failure on the field: he knew that as his game declined, his enemies would pounce.

And his family had been shaken by an attempted kidnapping. In 1977, a man had broken into their apartment, held a gun to Cruyff's head, and made him lie on the floor. Cruyff, characteristically, tried to talk to him, asking if he wanted money. When the intruder tied him up,

Danny ran outside to call for help. The man followed her out and was caught. But the family lived in fear afterward.[67]

Cruyff left Barça at the same time as Michels, in summer 1978. With empty decades looming, he wanted to prove that he could excel at something else. He decided he was "first of all a businessman," like his father and his forebears in Amsterdam street markets.[68] Around this time, Cruyff and Danny met a French fantasist of Russian descent named Michel-Georges Basilevitch, a former model who drove around Barcelona in a leased Rolls-Royce. Danny called him "the handsomest man in the world." Cruyff was then still represented in business by his father-in-law, Coster. "The only thing Cruyff can do without me is go piss," Coster once said.[69] Now, in an Oedipal revolt, Cruyff ditched Coster for the couple's new friend.

Basilevitch persuaded Cruyff to let him invest his hard-earned money in a variety of ventures, the most disastrous of which was a pig farm.[70] Looking back in 2015, the victim laughed at himself: "Who could imagine that Johan Cruyff had gone into pig-rearing? I ended up saying to myself, 'Ditch the pigs. Your thing is football.'"[71]

CRUYFF RETIRED AND WENT BANKRUPT almost simultaneously, so he had to start playing again. He left Spain without paying all his taxes and debts[72] to join Michels at the Los Angeles Aztecs in 1979, and later migrated to the Washington Diplomats.

The American years are often dismissed as a parenthesis in Cruyff's story, but they were momentous in one regard, notes Pieter van Os, who wrote a book about them: in the U.S. Cruyff realized that he was not a born businessman, but a born teacher. He rediscovered the pleasures of football, and found a new one: explaining it to others.

The North American Soccer League was on a mission to sell soccer to Americans. Unlike most of the aging European stars eking out a final payday, Cruyff took this seriously. He spent hours giving soccer clinics to children and appearing on TV shows. He loved the work: "Every time speaking and showing, speaking and showing."[73]

About the only soccer people in America who wouldn't listen to him were his teammates at the Diplomats. Washington was the one time in his life that he was immersed in British football culture, and it was a shock. The Diplomats' coach, Gordon Bradley, and most of the players had come from the lower reaches of the English league. They liked beer, and they didn't like Cruyff rabbiting on about tactics.[74] Once, after Bradley gave a pre-match talk and then left the room, Cruyff got up, rubbed out the tactics that the manager had written on the board, and said, "Obviously we're going to do it completely differently."[75] This offended the British players' sense of hierarchy. At one point Cruyff grew so despairing of his teammates that he announced he would quit organizing and limit himself to scoring goals, which he did.[76]

Aged thirty-four, in 1981, he returned with his family to the Netherlands. This is when I discovered him. I was then a football-mad twelve-year-old living in Leiden, a small town south of Amsterdam, just after Dutch football's golden age. On weekends when the games at my amateur club were rained out—a time of deep despair in the Kuper home—we were shown videos of the 1974 and 1978 World Cups in the clubhouse. This was a national ritual: one friend told me that when his boys' team watched Neeskens's penalty hit the net yet again in the first minute of the 1974 final, they all jumped up cheering even though they knew how the game ended.

The knowledge of total football had been lost, like the knowledge of how to get clean water into cities after the fall of Rome. Then, in 1981, Cruyff signed for Ajax, with his pay linked once again to attendances. I nagged my father into taking my brother and me to see Cruyff's homecoming match, against Haarlem on December 6. Dutch fans were excited, but also skeptical. Cruyff was thirty-four, with a broken body. Surely "the Moneywolf" was a wreck looking for a final payday?

I phoned Ajax and asked if the match would be sold out. "It's never sold out," a woman assured me. When we got to the stadium that Sunday, it was sold out. I cried. We watched the highlights on the ritual Sunday-evening *Studio Sport* program. Twenty-two minutes in, Cruyff commandeered the ball from a teammate, jinked past two defenders, and from outside the box lobbed Haarlem's keeper Edward Metgod. That ended the argument. In the little stadium across the road from Cruyff's childhood home, the years had fallen away, and it was 1972 again.

On *Studio Sport* that evening, Cruyff explained his calculations. He had known that his former teammate Jongbloed was Metgod's goalkeeping coach, and that Jongbloed believed a keeper should advance from the near post. Cruyff had checked early on to make sure Metgod was doing it, then aimed his lob at the far post.[77]

From then on, stadiums filled around the country to see "Cruijffie" one last time. Referees and opposing defenders tacitly anointed him a national treasure, too precious to kick.

Cruyff always said there were players who were more skillful than him,[78] but since childhood he had seen things a fraction earlier than other footballers, and nobody saw things earlier than the mature Cruyff.[79] He once said that before he was thirty, he had done everything on instinct. After thirty he began to understand why he did the things he did.

He could put a teammate in front of goal with an outside-of-the-boot pass so unexpected that the TV cameras of the day sometimes couldn't keep up. He could now also explain football at length, to any journalist who would bring him a pack of cigarettes. It was as if you could read an interview with Edison in *Voetbal International* magazine every week.

Cruyff was often incomprehensible. His intelligence exceeded his vocabulary, and he'd skip crucial stages in his arguments. But as Scheepmaker said, "Even when Cruyff talked nonsense, it was always interesting nonsense."[80] Eventually he was given his own TV show[81]—quite a prize in a country with just two channels.

Cruyff taught the whole of the Netherlands football. He created the language of the Dutch game: football as geometry. "The other [countries] always have more money, more space, and more people," he said. "Holland has to get it from its intelligence."[82]

He said things that you could use even on a bumpy field in Leiden. Always pass to the farthest teammate forward. Never give a square pass, because if an opponent intercepts it, he has already beaten two players: you and the person you were passing to. Don't pass into a teammate's feet, but a meter or two ahead of him, because that forces him to run onto it, which raises the pace. Always pass to his good foot. Receive the ball facing the opponent's goal. If you have two or three opponents on you, pass to the other wing, because logic suggests they'll be a man or two short there. Leave the opposition's worst player unmarked, so that he gets the ball, and then press him. If your team is losing focus, commit a nasty foul to wake everyone up. If you're playing badly, just pass the ball to the nearest teammate a couple of times, and your confidence will return. Play simple one-touch football ("but the hardest thing is playing simply"[83]—Cruyff loved the apparent paradox). He could talk forever about "the third man": if player one is about to pass to player two, how exactly should the third man move into the space? Almost everything I know about football, I learned from Cruyff.

On December 5, 1982, he stepped up to take a penalty against Helmond Sport, and instead of shooting at goal, suddenly passed it to his left. Jesper Olsen popped up to pass back to Cruyff (they'd spent hours secretly rehearsing) and Cruyff tapped it into the empty net. Helmond's goalkeeper and defenders watched the whole sequence flat-footed, too surprised to move. Cruyff had deconstructed the penalty kick. His message: rethink every convention in football from scratch.

After our matches, my teammates and I would sit in the local snack bar having Cruyffian debates about what had gone wrong: "You were playing ten meters too far forward." When I returned to live in England at age sixteen, I learned that English footballers didn't debate football. They just urged each other on: "Win those fucking headers!" "Come on, Blues!" Ruud Gullit told me in 1997, when he was at Chelsea: "In a Dutch changing room everyone thinks he knows best. In an Italian changing room everybody probably also thinks he knows best, but nobody dares to tell the manager." "And in an English changing room?" I asked. "In an English changing room, they just have a laugh."

The Dutchmen who learned most from Cruyff were the budding talents, aged between seventeen and twenty, who played alongside him after his return to Ajax: Frank Rijkaard, Ronald Koeman, Gerald Vanenburg, and Marco van Basten. On the training field, in the changing room, and during matches, Cruyff would pester them with advice. He was informal, unhierarchical, delighted to spend an hour arguing with a teenager, but his pedagogical method relied excessively on abuse—*kankeren*, or "cancering," as he called it, in Dutch slang. The worst victims were the kids in whom he saw promise; he didn't waste time "cancering" mediocrities. He almost never offered praise, and disagreed compulsively with almost everything everyone said. He treated debate as a competitive sport like football. He thought he knew everything better, from the correct locations for traffic lights in Amsterdam to the right way to open a fizzy drink.[84] He once had Van Basten in tears.[85] He said in an interview that Vanenburg would never be a leader because his voice was squeaky. Vanenburg told me years later that what he'd learned from Cruyff was "how not to do it."

Cruyff didn't care. He had begun assembling his lifelong personal guard of loyal journalists (a couple of them practically stenographers) who acted as his attack dogs against erring teammates or directors. He always believed in the *conflictmodel* that he'd absorbed from Michels: a conflict was productive because it gave both parties something to prove. In truth, this argument was probably just a rationale for his own personality.

He won the league with Ajax in 1982 and 1983. His boyhood club then refused to extend his expensive contract, so at the age of thirty-six he made a shocking switch to their archrivals, Feyenoord, where he encountered another promising pupil, the twenty-two-year-old Gullit, but marveled at his teammates' tactical ignorance. Sometimes he'd have to shout instructions to six players within two seconds.[86] They were like children: the moment they won the ball, they'd all run forward, each one of them expecting to score a goal. Only Cruyff would stay back, dragging his middle-aged body around to fill the defensive holes in anticipation of the counterattack. You had to organize your defense before you lost the ball, because afterward was too late. This was the invisible game, the positions you occupied in the eighty-eight minutes when you didn't have the ball. Nobody would praise you for it, but it won matches. A footballer could play a brilliant match without touching the ball, Cruyff taught. Feyenoord defender Sjaak Troost said he learned more in his one season with Cruyff than in his first five years as a pro.[87]

The arc of a career was like driving a car, Cruyff explained in 1984. "In the beginning you think very concentrated about everything you do. . . . Then comes the period of automatism. And then there is the third phase: looking ahead, two or three cars in front of you."[88] It wasn't that he could see three moves ahead on the field, as the cliché about great footballers has it. Rather, he understood that every attack is a house of cards, always about to collapse, and he could intuit the probabilities of where the cards might fall.

He sat out Feyenoord's forest runs ("except the coffee and cake afterward"[89]), but in his only season there he won the Dutch double of league and cup. At age thirty-seven, he was voted Dutch player of the year. At 4:06 p.m. on May 13, 1984, in the last match of his career, against PEC Zwolle, he was substituted. He sighed with resignation when two teammates insisted on lifting him up and carrying him off on their shoulders. Luckily it didn't last long, and soon a club official in sagging jeans was walking him down the tunnel to unlock the changing room. Cruyff's biographer, Nico Scheepmaker, watched the final exit from the press stand. "I folded down my writing table," he recorded in his phenomenal *Cruijff, Hendrik Johannes, fenomeen*, "so that I could stand up and briefly applaud the man who in the past twenty years had undoubtedly made my life more agreeable and richer than it would have been without him."[90] It was the same for me.

IV

THE CHOREOGRAPHER

Cruyff's coaching career at Ajax and Barcelona lasted just eleven years, and ended in 1996 with him smashing up his own office in the Camp Nou. He never enjoyed coaching as much as playing. "The further from the field, the worse it is," he later told Xavi.[1] He probably wasn't as good a coach as Pep Guardiola or Louis van Gaal. But they were Cruyffians (though Van Gaal would never admit it) and Cruyff was the original. Without Cruyff there would have been no Guardiola, and possibly no Messi, Xavi, or Iniesta.

After retiring as a player, he took a year's break, and then in 1985 became manager of Ajax. Dutch football at the time had lost its identity. "Total football" of the 1970s had been forgotten by the 1980s. Cruyff revived it. It was here, in Amsterdam in the mid-1980s, that he rolled out the style that would later become the hallmark of Barcelona. His Ajax was going to attack, because he didn't want to be bored on the bench. Spectators ought to leave the stadium laughing and whistling.[2]

He wasn't going to compromise, not even in defeat: "You must die with your own ideas."[3]

The first thing he did was to make every team at Ajax from the under-8s to the firsts play the same formation: 4-3-3. He explained that 4-3-3 created passing triangles all over the field, whereas 4-4-2 created squares and rectangles.

But he didn't need four men in defense the whole time. Cruyff's rule was that you only had to have one more defender than the opposition had strikers. Since most Dutch teams at the time fielded two strikers, three defenders were enough. That freed up one central defender (usually Ronald Koeman) to advance into midfield whenever possible, turning the formation into 3-4-3. This retained the triangles on the field, and gave Ajax a majority in midfield—a requirement of Cruyffian dogma, because the team that dominated midfield dominated possession.

As if playing with three defenders for long stretches wasn't scary enough, Cruyff stationed them on the halfway line. He aimed to keep ten men camped permanently in the other team's half. Just like in the 1970s, when Ajax lost the ball, the whole team would press to recover it. If the distance between Ajax's last defender and most advanced attacker was thirty-five meters at most, the opposition would have no space in which to play. A dense formation also saved Ajax's forwards the effort of tracking back. "With me, a forward only has to cover 15 meters, unless he's stupid or asleep," said Cruyff.[4]

Ajax's keeper, Stanley Menzo, was expected to patrol his entire half alone, operating from in front of his penalty area like a fly goalkeeper in street football. "What if someone lobs me from the halfway line?" asked Menzo. "Then you applaud," said Cruyff.

None of the Ajax players had ever played a system like it. He wasn't going to make their on-field decisions for them, so he instituted a "learning process" to create autonomous, thinking, Cruyffian footballers. In one early match, when things weren't going well, a defender ran to the bench to ask for instructions. "Work it out yourself," Cruyff told him. He was forcing his players to be free. He welcomed their initiatives, even bad ones.[5] "Everyone says a tactic comes from the coach," he said. "At most he starts it. But the rest is the players, and they map it out."[6] Cruyff cared about winning, but he cared more about teaching. Sometimes on the bench he'd forget the score.

He was an intuitive coach, without a rule book. When he tried to lay out a grand theory, he'd often stumble over his limited vocabulary, or get distracted by the conflict du jour. He wasn't long on training methods either. He didn't have a single practice drill written down.[7] Since he found fitness work distasteful, he let an assistant handle it. Often Cruyff would make up that morning's session on his walk from changing room to pitch.

Everything he taught was drawn from his own experience. His training sessions were short, but required total concentration of his players. He spent much of the time drilling them in an exercise that has since become the staple of training at FC Barcelona, and at clubs around the world: the "rondo." Cruyff didn't invent the rondo, but he made it great.

A rondo is essentially piggy-in-the-middle. A few players pass the ball to each other, while defenders try to intercept it. Often it's four or five passers against two defenders, but you can vary the numbers. You can shrink the passing area to make the game more difficult. You can have "joker" players who join whichever team has the ball. You can even play the rondo with rugby balls, to teach players how to respond to unpredictability. You can add any rules you like. The rondo took Cruyff back to his childhood games on the street. For him, the exercise captured the essence of his sport: time, space, and passing, football as geometry.

Cruyff believed that a player who was good at rondos was good at football. In both games, you won by taking up positions in which a teammate could reach you with a diagonal pass. You had to position your body so that you could see as much space as possible. You never moved the ball aimlessly; behind every pass there had to be a thought. Best of all was the through ball, "the pass down the street," which cut through a defensive line. And if you alternated short and long passes, and switched from one side of the playing area to the other, the opponents had to chase back and forth and lost their structure.

In rondos as in real matches, the defensive team won possession by outnumbering the attacking team around the ball. If it could cut off every passing line but one, it knew where the ball was going. Even if it didn't win possession with the first tackle, it would derail the passing and probably win the second ball.

Best of all, rondos didn't require running, so that even in retirement Cruyff could join in. Sometimes he'd deliberately stand in the wrong position, and wait to see if anyone would correct him.[8] "I never felt like a coach. I always felt like a footballer," he said.[9] More precisely, he had played football like a coach, and now he coached like a footballer.

Of course, Cruyff turned Ajax into a debating society. His endless barrage of quasi-logical dogmas (he seldom did anecdote) exhausted the players, many of whom had previously suffered the torment of playing with him. Koeman recalled, "I burned with desire to tell him, 'Shut your mouth!'" But every day Cruyff opened new vistas for them. Rijkaard, a midfielder, diagnosed in him "this incessant need to create."[10] Cruyff brought in an opera singer to teach the players how to breathe. He introduced strategies that remain part of the Cruyffian repertoire today: for instance, if your team is under pressure, don't bring in an extra defender, but send on an attacker, as that will force the opposition to pull somebody back.

All the while he was looking for a Cruyff on the field: somebody who would take responsibility for running the game minute by minute, as he himself had for Michels. He eventually assigned the role to Rijkaard,

Ajax's best player. He couldn't see that Rijkaard—a gentle soul, an observer, and psychologist at heart—had no desire to be Cruyff.

Cruyff used his standard pedagogical methods—bullying, "cancering," exhortations to take control—until one day Rijkaard had had enough. Throwing off his training bib, he shouted, "Get cholera with your constant nagging."[11] (Most traditional Dutch swear words invoke ghastly diseases.) Then he walked out. Cruyff, who hadn't seen it coming, had to send him on loan to Real Zaragoza.

Cruyff sensed his own temperamental unsuitability to daily man management. He sometimes mused that a club should be run by a duo of a genius and an organizer.[12] It was a dilemma he never resolved: the structures he ran were always heavier on genius than organization.

But longer term, his cancering worked. In 1987, his young Ajax team won the European Cup Winners' Cup, the first continental trophy for any Dutch team since the 1970s.

In 1988, his prodigies Van Basten, Rijkaard, Ronald Koeman, Gullit, Vanenburg, and Jan Wouters, coached by Michels, lifted Oranje's only prize to this day, the European Championship. Almost all these players also won European Cups with their clubs. Without Cruyff, they would never have got so good. Koeman said, "He helped me understand the millions of details that determine why some games are lost and others are won."[13]

Rijkaard, who played regularly against Maradona in Italy, reflected later that Maradona could win a game by himself with a dribble, but that only Cruyff could win it by moving two teammates to new positions. Rijkaard told me in 2000, "I grew up with the footballers of the 1970s. And later I also played at a certain level, with many top players around me, and yet you always keep worshipping the 1970s . . . I can really enjoy that, those football truths, that logical reasoning . . . Reading a game: 'if you stand there, and I'm here'—the thinking."

Cruyff told me, triumphantly, about Rijkaard, "I had gigantic quarrels with him, because you wanted to give him that sharpness. In Milan he picked it up in the right way." Cruyff rarely bore grudges against players he'd fought with, perhaps because he enjoyed the fights.

During his final months at Ajax, in 1987, he recorded a remarkable television documentary.[14] The concept was simple: Cruyff and Rudi van Dantzig, artistic leader of the Dutch national ballet company, visited each other's workplaces and discussed their métiers. Cruyff was impressed by how hard ballet dancers trained: "Blood, sweat and tears."

When Van Dantzig made the return visit to Ajax, the two men stood in the sun in the empty stadium watching the players train. Cruyff said he imagined that top-class dance was about details:

CRUYFF: Look, at your level everyone can stand on their toes, that's obvious.

VAN DANTZIG: Yes.

CRUYFF: But that's just not what it's about. It's about: where do you do it, are you standing straight or just turned 90 degrees [he turns his knees toward Van Dantzig], so that you can do the next action too?

VAN DANTZIG: You have those kinds of details, too?

CRUYFF: Yes! That's what you talk about.

He then acts out on the grass some of the details of Cruyffian football. If a teammate has the ball on his weak foot, you have to stand near him so that he can pass to you. If you're passing to the third man, you must be facing him. Cruyff gives an imaginary no-look side-footed pass: "That doesn't work, because you don't have vision." If you couldn't see the third man, you had to lay the ball off to a teammate who could, he said. "Then you go a phase further, that you force somebody to run in your field of vision."

Van Dantzig asks, "So it's really a kind of choreography?"

"Yes, that's it," says Cruyff.

Asked at the end of the documentary what he had learned, he said, "Guys, whatever you do, it's all the same thing. Here and there a difference of detail, but mostly not."[15] He always saw cycle racing, horse riding, and all ball games as versions of the problem set of football.[16]

IN JANUARY 1988, Cruyff landed at Barcelona airport again, and took the Iberia bus to the terminal with all the other passengers. He had walked out of Ajax after yet another row. Barça's president was then still the tiny Josep Lluís Núñez, the man Cruyff had helped into office a decade before. Born with the Castillian name José Luis Núñez, the last non-Catalan to run the club, he had migrated to Barcelona with his family at age seven, later joined his father-in-law's construction business, and then struck out on his own.[17] Núñez disliked Cruyff, but hired him before his opponents in the next year's presidential elections could make the Dutchman's arrival their campaign promise.[18] Cruyff later said he was signed as "the photo to win the election."[19] Núñez agreed to pay off Cruyff's debts from his previous Spanish spell.[20] Cruyff's right-hand man, Tonny Bruins Slot, later recalled, "We were going to try it at Barça for a year . . . 'We'll see,' said Johan."[21]

At Cruyff's unveiling at the Camp Nou, he told the press that he was returning to "my second home." He promised "only spectacle,"[22] not titles, and noted that he alone would be making the lineup—not a given in the Byzantine political institution that was Barça.

He said during his first season, "I never take well thought-through and considered decisions, because otherwise I probably wouldn't have started this adventure in Barcelona."[23] It helped that in Barcelona his family could live near the stadium and the beach, and eat outside even in January.[24] His daughter Chantal's boyfriend, Danny Muller, an Ajax youth-team player, had come along with them, and Cruyff found him a spot in Barça's B team.

Looking back years later on the club he took over, Cruyff said, "There was nothing."[25] He was exaggerating only a little. Barça before Cruyff (BC) "never had a consistent or distinctive playing style," noted Guardiola later.[26] The club had won just two Spanish titles in twenty-five years (one of them, in 1974, thanks to Cruyff). In 1986, Barça had been so confident of winning the European Cup final against Steaua Bucharest in Sevilla that they had prepared a post-match banquet for three hundred people, but when the game went to penalties, all their penalty takers missed. (The banquet went ahead anyway, but wasn't much fun.)

Barça's fans had been embittered by habitual disappointment. The season before Cruyff's arrival, some home matches had drawn just twenty thousand spectators.[27] At one point the players had gathered in the city's Hesperia hotel to write a manifesto calling for Núñez to resign: "We have lost all confidence in the president. We feel totally cheated by the president." Núñez responded by clearing out fourteen players that summer.[28]

The English striker Gary Lineker, one of the few survivors, chuckled decades later, "I was kind of slightly pleased I wasn't around when they all signed the letter. I was back in England at the time." What were Lineker's first impressions of Cruyff? "I would describe him as a bit of a know-it-all. Actually not 'a bit of a know-it-all.' I would describe him as a know-it-all. He was the type of bloke to sit behind the bus driver when he was driving to games and tell him when to turn left, when to put his foot down a bit, et cetera."

Cruyff hadn't come merely to coach Barça. He was going to revolutionize it, from first team to the under-8s. He took it for granted that any club he ran was going to be a great club. His lifetime at Ajax—from toddler assistant groundsman to child prodigy and cleaning lady's son to European champion—had also left him with the sense of a club as a universe. Every time he walked into the changing room at the Camp Nou, he was aware that there were people who cleaned it.[29]

He meddled in every aspect of the club. He decided that Barça's red-and-blue shirts were hard for players to see against the backdrop of the stands, especially late in games when the shirts darkened with sweat. He told me in 2000, "The first thing I did when I got here was choose a material [not that I know about materials] that you said, 'Hey, if someone sweats, I want to *see* him.' And I wanted the second shirt to be orange, so that when we went somewhere, nobody could think, 'Who are these guys?' That's us." Orange also happened to be the Dutch national color.

He hired his former teammate Charly Rexach, a Catalan merchant's son born a few hundred meters from the stadium, as his assistant and navigator through Barça's political swamps. (Rexach liked to say he had "spent [his] whole life in one square kilometer."[30]) Cruyff found his fitness coach, Seirul·lo, in Barça's handball wing.

He thought Barça had too many *directius*, especially given that they didn't understand football and dropped into the changing room at will.[31] Cruyff banned them all from the players' "secret garden," except Núñez and his two vice presidents, whose presence was merely discouraged.[32] He didn't mind offending the people with the power to sack him: he thought a coach had to have the independence of mind and personal wealth to do what he wanted. The "unpleasant" job of coaching,[33] with its "thousand and one problems a day,"[34] wasn't worth it otherwise.

He also set himself the task of ridding Barça, and indeed Catalonia itself, of its defeatist self-image. He would recall much later that in 1988,

the Catalan mentality was still very marked by franquismo. You had to be discreet and hardworking, not be noticed. . . .

The fashionable color in Barcelona at the time was navy blue. A neutral color so that you couldn't be distinguished from others, you wouldn't be seen . . . Sport allows a very rapid change in the image that people have of themselves. It changed the mentality of Catalans. I was just a catalyst.[35]

To erase Barça's culture of victimhood, he imported a freightload of Basque players, notably Ernesto Valverde, Txiki Begiristain, and José Maria Bakero. Cruyff had concluded during his playing years in Spain that Basques were "fearless." He explained, "It's somehow psychology mixed with anthropology, but that's part of the coach's job."[36]

He explained his revolution to packed halls of journalists in the almost daily press conferences that Barça staged in those days. His Spanish remained Amsterdam-accented but fluent, and when he couldn't think of the right words, he used a favorite stalling phrase, *"en un momento dado,"* "at a given moment."

He was still frequently incomprehensible, which suited him. "If I'd have wanted you to understand, I would have explained it better,"[37] he told a journalist. His analysis after a match against Deportivo la Coruña was, "That's logical, in principle. Them then have five and we have six, because there's always two free."[38]

But Xavier Sala-i-Martin, economics professor at Columbia University in New York and for a while treasurer of Barça, remarked: "His press conferences were like lectures. He didn't just teach football to his players, but above all to the media and the people."[39] Cruyff was running the same national educational project that he had previously carried out in the Netherlands.

He shifted the focus of Catalan football from physique to possession, saying, "You can't be a victim and be the best, so you have to be in command. And to do that in football, you need the ball."[40]

Rondos became a daily ritual. They were warm-up and match practice in one, so Barça didn't waste time jogging and stretching. Training sessions in those days were held on a field next to the Camp Nou that was too narrow even to practice corner kicks. People passing by on the street would shout comments through the fence. There were always journalists watching the training sessions, as well as some fans, and aspiring coaches like Albert Capellas, who used to ride down on his motorbike from the university. Capellas learned that you could tell if a rondo was going well just from the sound: you turned your back to the training field and closed your eyes and listened to the rhythmic "poom, poom" of the ball flying from player to player. When Capellas began coaching teenagers at a local school, he discovered that Cruyff's exercises worked at every level of football.

Any player who joined Barcelona had to start in the middle of the rondo. Cruyff, Rexach, and a couple of senior players would pass the ball around so fast that the newcomer might not touch it for minutes. "Welcome to Barça," was the message.[41] Even the keeper, Andoni Zubizarreta, had to participate in rondos, and Cruyff sometimes put him in midfield in friendly games to sharpen his passing.

The rondo defined life at Barcelona. Outsiders judge football teams on matches, but inside a club, the daily training sessions can shape the atmosphere. Starting each day with rondos was more fun than wind sprints. After training, the players would sometimes go and get coffee together in a nearby café, and chat to the old men playing dominoes.

There was sneering from other Spanish clubs: "At Barça they don't train properly. They just play little games."[42] Cruyff didn't care. "The training sessions are lovely," he said. "Kicking a ball myself, that's really what I do it for. Sometimes I'm jealous of the players: I'm sitting in the dugout while they're having fun playing football." He threatened to quit coaching once he got too old to train with them.[43]

But joining in the rondo was also his best didactic tool. He was modeling positioning. He liked to say that he was practically the only coach who told footballers to run less.[44] Happily, he observed, Barça's players let him teach them: "They're not Dutchmen, who start saying, 'Yes, but . . .' the moment you breathe."[45]

Lineker recalled:

> He was always the best player in training. He did it in his cocky way, but what he said made sense. He did a lot of possession football, seven against five, nine against seven, four against two. It was all about keeping possession, and when you've got possession, making the pitch as large as possible. And you see that in the modern game now it's been taken on by many coaches, particularly Pep Guardiola.

For one player who arrived in summer 1988 and stayed seven years, Eusebio Sacristán, discovering Cruyff was the biggest joy of his career. Drinking tea with shy, tubby little middle-aged Eusebio at the Princesa Sofia hotel, you wouldn't peg him as a winner of the Champions League. As a player he was neither strong nor fast, and he rarely scored. The one thing he had done well since childhood was pass. But before Barcelona, he had always played in "disorderly systems."

Cruyff created order on the field. "The multiple possibilities became visible," Eusebio told me. "It was new for me, for my teammates, for all of Spanish football—and I think for all of football. We saw a bit of the essence that I had had in my head since I was a kid: how to enjoy football through technique, through passing."

Cruyff got every team in the Masia, the club's academy, playing and training the same way as the senior side. The story of his unearthing of Guardiola takes various forms, even in Cruyff's own telling, but in the most common version, Cruyff needed a central midfielder and asked,

"Who is the best in the Masia?" "Guardiola," replied the youth coaches. Cruyff went to the Miniestadi next to the Camp Nou, where the youth teams played in those days, and tried to take his seat unnoticed. Scanning the field, he realized that the boy wasn't even playing.

"Why isn't he here?" Cruyff asked.

"Too physically weak," came the reply.

It was true that Guardiola was slow and stick-thin and couldn't tackle. Cruyff promoted him to the senior B team. Decades later, over lunch in a restaurant with Xavi, he explained how he taught Guardiola to hide his shortcomings: "You have to know what you can't do. If I have to defend this restaurant, I'm lost. But if I just have to defend this table, I'm the best of all. It's a question of distance, nothing more."[46] Guardiola later said, "I knew nothing about football until I met Cruyff."[47]

Pep ("Pepe" on the field) found his berth just in front of defense, in a position that Cruyff named "number four." He didn't need to tackle, because he understood how to align the midfield to shrink space when the opposition had possession. And when Barça attacked, the slowest man on the field moved the ball fastest.

The fitness coach, Seirul·lo, once asked a conference:

> If I tell you that the fastest player at FC Barcelona is no one other than Guardiola, do you believe me or not? I organize a "speed" session every week, and Pep is the fastest player taking into account the specific constraints I impose. Look, over five or twenty meters, Sergi [Barjuán] is much faster. But if in this space I create a situation that demands a calculation in decision-making, such as evaluating the positioning of several teammates before changing direction, Guardiola is first.[48]

In Cruyffian football, speed was an intellectual quality. Guardiola became what Cruyff would call "a binder": a midfielder who bound the team together by closing gaps between lines and never losing the ball. Albert Capellas says there are three kinds of footballers. The irresponsible ones create problems for their own team, with passes that bounce or go behind their teammates' backs. Responsible players, like Javier Mascherano, can solve these problems.

But the ideal footballer foresees problems. When Cruyff was young, Michels had told him, "If a teammate makes a mistake, you should have prevented it." Guardiola was a player who prevented mistakes. Like Cruyff playing for Michels, he coached dynamically on the field the way a manager on the bench could not. He joined a long line of unspectacular Cruyffian "binders" (later known in Barcelona as *pivotes*) stretching from Gerrie Mühren in the 1970s through Jan Wouters in the 1980s to Sergio Busquets in the 2010s.

Perhaps Guardiola could only have succeeded in Cruyffian football. At age thirty, after a seventeen-year stint at Barça, he stood in Arsène Wenger's kitchen in north London lobbying to join Arsenal, but Wenger didn't need him.[49] Guardiola went to warm the bench at Roma, descended to little Brescia, then petered out as a player in Qatar and Mexico.

Cruyff said Guardiola was the most reasonable, farsighted man he'd ever coached, along with Dennis Bergkamp: "You could ask them for advice, because they could think about the problems of other people."[50] Certainly Guardiola understood Cruyff's own problems: "If there aren't any conflicts, he'll go and find them. There really are people who have their clearest insights in a controlled chaos."[51] The one bit of the Cruyffian inheritance that all his disciples have ditched is the *conflictmodel*.

At Barça, Lineker soon grew frustrated with Cruyff. A goal-scoring center-forward, he felt the 4-3-3 was made for him to play in the center. Instead Cruyff played him outside right.

I asked Lineker whether Cruyff might have been trying to be counterintuitive: showing the world that the Englishman who everyone thought was a center-forward was really a winger?

Lineker replied, "He did things in games—and I see the same thing with Pep sometimes, that he does tactics that you could almost have the opinion that he was doing it to look clever." Yet he thinks the reason Cruyff put him on the wing was to force him out. Spanish clubs at the time were only allowed two foreign players each, and Cruyff wanted to choose his own. Lineker believes Cruyff was afraid to play him center-forward:

> In case I did too well, and then it would be difficult to get rid of me, because there's no question in my mind that I would've scored a hatful of goals and assists.
>
> So we didn't have the most cordial relationship, but I totally respected him. I just wish he had come and spoken to me man to man about it and said: "Listen, I want my own players, we'll get you a good move," and I would've been absolutely fine. But he just kind of messed me about all season. As a person, I've met more impressive people.

In that first season under Cruyff, Barça beat Sampdoria in Bern to win the not-very-prestigious European Cup Winners' Cup. Burned by the upset against Steaua three years earlier, the club hadn't dared plan a post-match meal. By the time the players found this out, said Lineker, "it was after 10 p.m. and everything was shut. There was nowhere to go, so we all went to bed. Switzerland, folks."[52]

That season and the next, Real Madrid won the Spanish title. Núñez could have sacked Cruyff, but saw advantage in keeping him on. The Dutchman attracted so much attention that bad results were pinned on him rather than on the president.

Still, Cruyff always suspected that Núñez would eventually get him: "Every chairman has a black book. Everything's in there. The chairmen of clubs like Barcelona are special people. They're used to everyone doing what they say. In that black book they write down all the things you do to them."[53] Cruyff, of course, kept his own black book.

Meanwhile, his new team was taking shape. He offloaded Lineker to Tottenham, and supplemented his Basque-Catalan backbone by importing Ronald Koeman, Michael Laudrup (a Cruyffian false nine), and Hristo Stoichkov. The Bulgarian striker had made only one nonnegotiable demand in his contract talks: he had to have a red sports car.[54]

In an era of defensive football, Cruyff was building a startlingly attacking side. His son, Jordi, said, "I'd look at the line-ups and ask myself if he'd gone crazy. So daring."[55] Koeman and Guardiola, neither of them defenders, formed football's slowest central defensive pairing. Moreover, they'd take turns advancing into midfield. Koeman would often take the field terrified of being shown up,[56] especially as Barcelona's fullbacks were forwards at heart. But one of Cruyff's dictums was, "There is only one ball. If we have it, they don't." With Koeman and Guardiola in central defense, Barça usually had it. Cruyff had invented a new concept: defending with the ball.

He got bored of people asking, "What if it goes wrong?" "What difference does it make?" he'd reply.[57] Anyway, he argued, his way of defending might be safest. If you could keep twenty-one players in the opposition's half, you were a long way from your own danger area. And he didn't believe in trying to mark opponents out of games. If an opposition striker was too good to mark, then it was best not to mark him at all, and try to cut off his supply lines instead.

The truth was that Cruyff was radicalizing. By this point in his career, in his early forties, he had to keep thinking up new challenges to stay interested in coaching. His fellow former great Michel Platini sympathized: "A kid who becomes a footballer, his only real vocation, is a footballer until he's 32. And afterward . . . it will never be the same again."[58] Usually swathed in his oversize beige raincoat, Cruyff radiated zen indifference in the dugout. He even sat impassively through a mass player brawl that broke out a couple of yards in front of him during a Clásico: "Why intervene when absolutely nothing of interest is happening?"[59] There was little a coach could do during a game anyway. Cruyff never wrote anything down on the bench. Once when Barça came in 2–0 down at halftime, he simply got himself a coffee and nursed it in silence for ten minutes. Only when the bell rang for the second half did he speak: "Now go out there and fix what you screwed up."[60]

His players nicknamed him "Dios," "God." Certainly, his ways were unknowable. He encouraged Koeman to move into the house next door to him, sometimes looked after the player's infant children,[61] then dropped him. He told Stoichkov in front of the whole squad that he was "a disaster," then went for a meal with him.[62] Before one game he promised the Bulgarian a hundred thousand pesetas if he scored twice in the first half. When Stoickhov scored his first, a laughing Cruyff immediately substituted him.[63] His directness, extreme even by Dutch standards, was shocking to Spaniards.

In February 1991, the story nearly ended early. Cruyff began feeling pains in his stomach, chest, and back. He was forty-three; his father had died at forty-five. Danny made him go to the hospital, where he was diagnosed with coronary heart disease and prescribed a double bypass. A doctor told him, "If you'd breathed three more times, you'd have been dead."[64]

Cruyff's request for a pre-op coffee and cigarette was refused. During the nearly three-hour operation, his heart was stopped for thirty minutes. The surgeon, Josep Oriol Bonin, joked later that Cruyff would have preferred to have had the procedure without an anesthetic, so that he could have watched it himself. Cruyff had to settle for interrogating Bonin in detail beforehand. The Dutchman was an aficionado of surgery, who liked attending his players' knee operations, and once watched a brain operation.[65]

The bypasses changed him. In the dugout, the eternal cigarette was replaced by a lollipop. (The raincoat remained.) He even starred in an anti-smoking advertisement for Catalan TV. He also came to realize that he wouldn't work forever—Danny and his children would forbid it—and he began thinking more about his legacy. Football was no longer just about winning the next prize and shutting up his enemies. He wanted to leave behind a style of play that would outlive him. Jordi said, "My father never looked at the end-product of 90 minutes. My father looked at the end-product of many years to come."[66]

On April 10, 1991, after two months of convalescence, Cruyff returned to the bench. A month later, his team finally won the Spanish title.

The pressures inside Barça never subside, though. On April 1, 1992, Cruyff launched a word that is used inside the club to this day: *entorno*. Literally it translates as "surroundings" or "environment." Cruyff, as was his habit with language, repurposed it. By *entorno*, he meant the specific surroundings of Barça: the *socis*; the *ultra* fans who'd come round the president's house to threaten him; the journalists who lived off the club; the interfering local politicians, sponsors, current *directius*, former *directius*, and staffers who were trying to get back into the club; and the opposition plotting to unseat the board.

"There is an *entorno* that influences, and if it wasn't like that, Barcelona would have won many more titles," he told a press conference. He mimicked the questions that the *entorno* was always asking: "'Why didn't the system function? Why don't the players know more? Why didn't the ball go in?' The *entorno* affects my men . . . If things go on like this, it will be difficult for this club to have successes in future."[67]

He swiftly disproved his own prediction. Six weeks later, Barça played the European Cup final against Sampdoria at Wembley. Before kickoff, his players sat crammed in their tiny changing room, dressed in the headache-inducing orange kit that he had chosen, their heads filled with the defeat in Sevilla six years earlier. They felt they were playing for a trophy that Barça was doomed never to win. That's when Cruyff spoke the words that remain associated with him in Catalonia: "Salid y disfrutad," "Go out and enjoy it."

The players didn't particularly. After a tense, scrappy game, the score was still 0–0 in extra time when Koeman stepped up to take a free kick. The Dutchman had a kick like a horse. Cruyff always told him to blast the first free kick of the match straight at the wall. That would teach opponents not to charge out at him trying to block his shots.[68] This time, three valiant Italians sprinted out of the wall regardless, but Koeman put his shot through the hole they left. Cruyff, his face impassive, hurried out of his dugout, and—in an image that all Barça fans of a certain age can recall—climbed awkwardly in his suit over an advertising board, apparently so as to direct play. Fifteen minutes later, Barça had won its first European Cup. Seirul·lo, uniquely, had become champion of Europe in both football and handball.

In 1992, almost all the club's supporters still lived in Catalonia. The day after the final, they gathered to greet their heroes in Barcelona's Plaça Sant Jaume. Watching the video, you sense that Cruyff has shown up only out of politeness. Uninterested in basking or celebrating, he always switched off immediately after victory. He would say little to the media, melt away quietly, and let his players take all credit. "He closed the door and everything was gone," said Koeman admiringly.[69] What interested Cruyff was the journey.

But when he stepped to the microphone on the balcony of the Generalitat, the Catalonian government building, the crowd began chanting his trademark phrase: "Un momento dado!" Jordi Pujol, the Generalitat's president, standing by his side, told him the people wouldn't stop until he said the magic words. Cruyff obliged—"We have, en un momento *dado . . ."*—and the medieval square erupted.[70] A couple of weeks later, on the last day of the season, Real Madrid lost at Tenerife and Barcelona were champions by one point.

Nineteen ninety-two was Barcelona's annus mirabilis, the year the city went from caterpillar to butterfly. Cleaned up and "opened to the sea" with new beaches, the Catalan capital staged its global coming-out party: the Olympic Games. The Generalitat funded a worldwide advertising campaign with the slogan "Where is Barcelona?" (Answer: "In Catalonia, of course.") The American basketball team, "the Dream Team," became the face of the Olympics. Cruyff's Barça side stole their nickname.

His Dream Team was brilliant, fallible, and lucky. It won through individual genius as much as through Cruyffian method. It might have won more with proper defending—a subject rarely discussed inside the team, recalled Eusebio Sacristán: "Football hadn't evolved defensively as much as it has today."[71]

The Dream Team won four straight Spanish championships for the first time in Barça's history. As if by some Cruyffian magic, three of those four titles were clinched on the last day of the season, in a *final de infarto*, a "heart-attack finish."[72] At last, Barcelona had become Real Madrid's rivals rather than their victims.

The goals came from the Bulgarian-Brazilian duo of Stoichkov and Romário. Both were impossible people, who liked to welcome in the dawn on nights out together. Stoichkov was practically the only person in the squad whom Romário ever spoke to,[73] until they fell out. Cruyff praised Stoichkov's *mala leche* (literally: "bad milk"),[74] meaning his nasty streak, and called Romário "a negative character" but also the best player he'd ever coached.[75] The little Brazilian never trained hard, even when he deigned to show up, but Cruyff believed that great footballers made their own rules.

Romário would spend long stretches of games standing still, apparently indulging in his daytime hobby of napping. When he dipped his shoulder and turned toward the opposing goal, his teammates knew he had spotted the moment and was signaling for an instant pass.[76] It was an example of what Seirul·lo was always saying: passing is communication, a kind of language.

Nonetheless, Cruyff's era was ending. George Orwell said that "in many cases the creative impulse seems to last for about 15 years: in a prose writer these 15 years would probably be between the ages of 30 and 45, or thereabouts."[77] He might have been talking about Cruyff, who was forty-five years old in 1992. After victory at Wembley, he stopped thinking.

His luck ran out on May 18, 1994, against AC Milan in the Champions League final in Athens. A slow central defense of Koeman and Miguel Ángel Nadal (uncle of the tennis player Rafael), supplemented by the slow Guardiola in central midfield, succumbed to Milanese pressing and went down 4–0. Cruyff said, "It is not that we played badly. It was that we didn't play at all."[78] In a Cruyffian team, when things go wrong, they sometimes go very wrong, because there are so few defensive safeguards. Cruyff was a genius, explained Guardiola. "And if a genius does it right, and that's nearly always, the result is perfect. But if a genius does something wrong, it goes so incredibly wrong that you want to murder him. Only geniuses take those risks."[79]

The 4–0 was no accident. Milan's coaches, first Arrigo Sacchi and then Fabio Capello, had created a more organized update of Cruyffian pressing football. Ominously, the Milanese looked not just faster than Barça, but fitter. Barcelona had become a city of beach clubs and proliferating temptation. Rondos alone couldn't compensate. Like every innovator in football, Cruyff had eventually been overtaken.

That summer of 1994, he should have finally coached the Netherlands at a World Cup. The Dutch FA made him an offer. Its chairman, Jos Staatsen, later said something interesting about the unending negotiations: he felt that Cruyff the person wanted to do it, but Cruyff the company didn't. When Cruyff appeared on TV to explain his refusal, he bored on about money until his old teammate Piet Keizer, sitting beside him, interrupted with a football question: "Say, Johan, you suddenly started playing with the outside of your foot. Why?"

Cruyff ought to have left Barcelona after the thrashing in Athens. Unfortunately, he hung on for another two years. With Laudrup he reenacted the conflict he'd had with Rijkaard: Cruyff wanted him to be Cruyff on the field, running the show, but the mild-mannered Laudrup wasn't keen, telling him, "You were Cruyff and I am me."[80] Cruyff complained that the upper-middle-class Dane fell short of greatness because he lacked the "ghetto instinct."[81] Eventually Cruyff sold him to Real Madrid. In 1995, Laudrup starred in Madrid's 5–0 hammering of Barça.[82]

Cruyff also began treating the club as an expansion of his family mansion. He promoted his son, Jordi, to the first-team squad, explaining that he wanted to protect the boy: "There are more bad than good people in football. He's a good player, so I thought it might be better for him to stay with us."[83] His assistant Rexach had warned him against it, pointing out that the boy would become a proxy target for Cruyff's enemies in the *entorno*. Cruyff responded, "If somebody one day uses Jordi to attack me . . . I'll come with two guns, because two knives wouldn't be enough."[84] Cruyff was determined to be the father in the football jungle that he himself had never had. But Jordi—unready understudy to the great Romário and Stoichkov—did become a target of criticism.

Worse still, Barça's dubiously qualified reserve goalkeeper was Cruyff's son-in-law Jesús Angoy. The regular keeper, Carles Busquets, only five feet, ten inches (1.78 meters) tall, was just as contested. He was the ultimate Cruyffian fly keeper, a sort of Spanish Jongbloed, good with his feet, but as even Cruyff admitted, not so much with his hands.[85] Cruyff persisted with him after each blunder, perhaps precisely because everyone else was telling him not to. Radicalizing even further, he thought of putting a defender in goal. His family had to talk him out of it. Busquets's greatest contribution to the club would prove to be his son, the midfielder Sergio, also good with his feet.

With President Núñez always looking to get him, Cruyff needed to keep winning. Yet he no longer seemed to care much about winning. Before the Champions League quarterfinal at Paris Saint-Germain in 1995, he stood gazing at the stands with the Parisian coach Luis Fernández, then remarked, "They are 50,000 and we will give them pleasure. That's what football is."[86] After Barça lost 2–1 and were eliminated, Cruyff said, "The cycle is over."[87]

He still loved teaching. (Just watch the video of him demonstrating advanced jump rope to a befuddled Stoichkov in 1995. Even at forty-seven, Cruyff skipped like the best girl on the playground.[88]) But by 1996 he had finally failed long enough that Núñez could safely sack him. On the morning of May 18, Cruyff's old friend Joan Gaspart, Barça's vice president, visited him in the changing room. Cruyff knew what was coming. The sports pages that day had led with the news that Gaspart had met Cruyff's successor, Bobby Robson.

"Why are you trying to shake my hand, Judas?" Cruyff asked Gaspart.[89]

When Gaspart confirmed his sacking, Cruyff smashed a chair and screamed, "God is just, and there is a day when you will pay for this! He has already started to punish."[90] He seems to have been referring to the death of Núñez's grandchild; Cruyff had a tendency to think of God as his personal hit man.

Cruyff assumed his friend Rexach would leave Barça in solidarity with him. Rexach didn't, and Cruyff never spoke to him again.

Cruyff told the players, "If I have hurt you, forgive me." Some of them cried.[91] According to Dutch TV commentator Sierd de Vos, he went straight from the Camp Nou to the Port Olímpic, where he was due to participate in a sailing regatta. Spain's King Juan Carlos saw him, and called out in his deep voice, "Joan! ¿Cómo estás?" "Well," Cruyff replied, "I've been sacked."

"Have they gone completely crazy?" asked the king. They sailed and then had dinner in the port restaurant La Barca del Salamanca.[92]

(A word about Gaspart: he went on to become an unsuccessful president of Barça from 2000 to 2003. On the upside, he had a cameo role as a hotel receptionist in Antonioni's 1975 Barcelona-based movie, *The Passenger*. Gaspart was a hotelier in real life, too. As a young waiter in London's Connaught Hotel, he was once serving poached salmon in boiling water to Princess Grace of Monaco when the plate overbalanced. He tipped it so that the water fell on him rather than her, fainted from pain, spent three days in the hospital, and as a reward was named the Connaught's Employee of the Month.[93])

V

CRUYFF: MY PART IN HIS DOWNFALL

Cruyff's summary of his reign as Barça's head coach was, "When I started here, I was three times more famous than Barcelona. Now we're about even."[1] Though only forty-nine when he was sacked, he would never coach a club again. His eight years as head coach—still a club record—had drained him. "You don't have to start something new," he reflected later. "After you have triumphed at Ajax and Barcelona, what are you going to do?"[2]

Many Dutch baby boomers of Cruyff's generation took the earliest retirements in history, quitting in their early fifties to do "fun things." Cruyff, who had already outlived his father and grandfather, took nothing for granted, especially after being briefly hospitalized for obstructed arteries in 1997. He began playing more golf and football, taking his grandchildren to the zoo, and hosting Christmas dinners at his mansion for his children, their spouses, and their ex-spouses. In short, he morphed into a retired member of the Barcelona *burgesia*.

He continued to shape Dutch thinking on football, as a newspaper columnist and a pundit on public TV. In France in 1998, he watched Oranje's games at the World Cup standing on a TV platform in the corner of each stadium. His slight figure, silhouetted against the sky, had an allegorical effect: the father of Dutch football watching his creation from above. On Dutch TV, his perfectly preserved 1950s working-class Amsterdam diction—an anachronistic curiosity in an ever more educated country—turned him into a cult figure. A small industry of Cruyff impersonators arose.

In retirement he'd go to watch the local gridiron football team, the Barcelona Dragons, where his son-in-law Angoy (who had struggled to find another soccer team after Barça) had become a successful placekicker. Cruyff noticed that placekickers kicked with their heads down. That was the wrong way, he told a Dragons staffer. The staffer replied that kickers in gridiron football had been keeping their heads down for a hundred years. It was still wrong, said Cruyff.

He also devoted himself to his Johan Cruyff Foundation, which helped children, able-bodied and disabled. He founded Johan Cruyff Institutes, Cruyff Academies, and Cruyff Colleges, mostly in the Netherlands, where athletes could catch up on the formal education they had missed when young.[3] He lived to see thousands of his students graduate each year. He himself never bothered. Late in life, he said, "The only certificate I have is a swimming diploma I got aged eight."[4]

On visits to Amsterdam, he joined the ranks of old men who filled their days hanging around at Ajax. One day around 2000, Sjaak Swart, outside-right of the 1970s team, walked into the canteen at the recently built space-age Ajax stadium outside Amsterdam to find the former false nine, Cruyff, and outside-left Keizer at a table. "They're back again, the great forward line!" whooped Swart.

· · ·

AT THE START OF THE millennium, I was writing a football column for the *Observer* newspaper. The sports editor, Brian Oliver, told me he was looking for a Dutch pundit to write a guest column during Euro 2000 in the Netherlands and Belgium. "Who is the most interesting person in Dutch football?" he asked.

So the *Observer* contacted the Cruyff Foundation. One evening, Brian phoned me: "Can you fly to Barcelona tomorrow morning to interview Johan Cruyff?"

All my life had been a preparation for this moment.

"OK," I said.

The *Observer* and the Cruyff Foundation had agreed to a deal: I would have a half-hour phone call with Cruyff every week during Euro 2000 and ghost-write his column. In return, the Observer pledged to raise a massive sum from its readers for the foundation. If the paper couldn't raise the full amount, it would pay the difference itself. When the *Observer*'s editor was briefed on the deal he didn't sleep for a week, only sweated, but finally he said yes. My task in Barcelona was to do a long opening interview with Cruyff, to introduce him to our less enlightened readers.

"What time am I meeting him?" I asked Brian.

"You'll find out when you get there," said Brian. "Just catch the first flight."

I arrived at the Iberia counter at Heathrow Airport at six a.m. There were still tickets. At about ten a.m., overdosed on coffee, I landed in Barcelona and phoned Cruyff's daughter Chantal. "Can you call me back in a moment?" she asked. After calling her back for several hours, during which time her number was permanently engaged, I got through.

"My father is in Murcia today," she said. "He'll call you when he gets back. What's your number?"

I took a taxi to a café where I met my Catalan photographer, Txema. I put my mobile phone—a cheap, heavy thing with a tendency to run out of battery—in the middle of the table. It rang within minutes. I coughed a couple of times, picked up, and said a clear yet civilized hello in Dutch.

"Philippe here," said a friend of mine from the Netherlands. "Ask Cruyff if he remembers me."

I hung up instantly. Every time my phone rang that afternoon, Txema and I jumped, but it was always just some time waster trying to use up my battery.

At about six p.m. my phone rang again. A British number appeared. Not Cruyff, then. I picked up and yelled impatiently, "Hello?"

"Simon," said an Amsterdam voice. And then, in that unmistakable twisted double-Dutch syntax: "With Johan Cruyff speaking." He explained that he had just returned from Murcia and had to go to his physio. "But," he said logically, "that can never take more than half an hour." He told me that I was in a café five minutes from his house, in the Bonanova neighborhood. He'd ring as soon as he was done with the physio, and I could come round. He had portrayed everything so calmly and clearly, as if this weren't some great event in his and my life but a straightforward encounter between reasonable people of goodwill, that I calmed down.

"Yes," I said. My mobile still didn't die. Cruyff checked once more to make sure I'd understood the plan, then said goodbye.

He called again an hour later: "Simon, with Johan Cruyff speaking."

Five minutes later we were knocking on the wooden door of a square, white-pillared mansion near the foot of the Tibidabo mountain. Chantal opened the door. Suddenly ("if they time normally with me, they're always just too late") she disappeared and a black-clad figure dressed like an Italian fashion designer materialized at the top of the stairs. Cruyff shook our hands cheerfully.

He said he'd been planning to watch the Champions League that evening. "Which match?" I asked. All of them simultaneously, using his remote control. He pointed me to a little sofa, and took an armchair opposite, while Txema crawled around the floor as photographers do. Between us was a glass coffee table with books on Rembrandt and Vermeer. On the walls were contemporary paintings of children.

I felt a little high. I had been drinking coffee all day, I hadn't slept, and now I found myself in a dreamlike situation. Cruyff knew almost nothing about his deal with the *Observer*, and asked me to explain it. I would later discover that the march of technology had left him chronically underinformed: he had never acquired a mobile phone or an email address, or learned how to use the internet, so when everyone else shifted online, he dropped out of the loop.

The focus of my interview was England and English football. I'd noticed over the years that Cruyff was an Anglophile who always spoke about the English with love, not with the condescension of many Dutch people. He'd learned English as a child at the lunch tables of Ajax's British coaches Vic Buckingham and Keith Spurgeon. He reminisced to me about the first foreign holiday of his life, in his late teens, when he and the future Ajax chairman Michael van Praag drove a little car to England.

"You went to Norwich, didn't you?" I asked. But it turned out I knew the details of his life better than he did. Cruyff couldn't remember. "Even if you knocked me dead," he said.

In his mansion he watched English football on British Sky TV, which he received using an opaque trick I wasn't allowed to share with my readers. In retirement he loved touring bed-and-breakfasts in English villages.

He remained a born teacher. At one point he rose from his chair to show me how to kick with one's wrong foot: "Look, whether you kick with your right or left, the point is that you are standing on one leg. And if you stand on one leg, you fall over. So you need to adjust your balance, and the only way to do that is with your arm." He kicked an imaginary ball with his left foot, throwing out his right arm. (I swear that in my five-a-side match in London the next week, my left foot improved.)

He kept trying to bring the conversation round to his foundation, and I kept deflecting him back to football. After two enjoyable hours, I thanked him. He said, "I'm going to watch the second half. Real Madrid," and began accelerating out of the room. Txema blocked him. Uncomplaining, Cruyff jumped into position and began posing, while I snooped around the living room in a way that I could see he found irritating.

He escorted us back to the entrance hall and got our jackets out of the closet. I saw that he was trying to put my coat on me, as if he were a maître d'. This was too much. I grabbed the coat from him, we shook hands, he disappeared, and two seconds later Txema and I were out in the wide, empty street. I was delighted: Cruyff had been nice, and I hadn't come off as a complete idiot. But thinking about it afterward, I realized: he hadn't been brilliant or original, a man who changed the way you saw everything. The guy I'd met was more like your friendly, intelligent, well-traveled neighbor. Like many semiretired people, Cruyff had stopped thinking hard.

I took an early flight out of Barcelona the next morning. When I landed, there was one new message on my phone: "Simon, with Johan Cruyff speaking again. After we talked yesterday about what the foundation does, I've now found a letter about it, it has all those things." He then proceeded to read almost the entire letter into my answering machine. The foundation was doing something in Peru, "and in Bolivia, Tanzania, Brazil, ahem." He gave me the names of people to call at the foundation. He even read out their phone numbers. The most touching thing about it was that I had all that information already.

A couple of weeks later Brian Oliver called. "The deal with Cruyff is off," he said. It turned out that the foundation had said we had misunderstood the conditions: I would have to ghost-write Cruyff's column during the tournament without speaking to him every week. The *Observer* pulled out.

"It's a shame," said Brian. "You could have had regular interviews with your childhood hero."

"I don't really mind," I said truthfully.

The *Observer* published my interview with Cruyff, as we thought had been agreed. Immediately a letter arrived from the foundation claiming that we'd broken the deal and demanding more money. Some months after Euro 2000, I wrote a starstruck account of meeting my hero for the Dutch literary football magazine *Hard Gras*. When Cruyff saw it, he was furious. He thought I was getting rich off his back by writing about the interview a second time. (My fee from *Hard Gras* was about $500.) He said I should have paid the foundation again. (I'm now writing about the interview a third time.) His yes-men in the Dutch press wrote that I was a plagiarist who had accused Cruyff of fraud. (In my defense, these claims were false.) If anyone has had a more upsetting experience with their childhood hero, I can't bear to hear it.

Some months after the conflict, I met a former teammate of Cruyff's, a legend who had played two World Cup finals. I told him what had happened. The legend nodded sympathetically. He said he rarely saw Cruyff, who socialized more with his coterie of pet journalists than with former teammates. I thought it was an anodyne remark, but then a look of terror passed across the legend's face, and he pleaded, "Don't write that I said that! Johan can get me!"

I think my experience with Cruyff has helped me write about him with greater distance.

FROM HIS MANSION at the foot of the mountain, the father of modern Barça turned into the godfather of the *entorno* that he had once bemoaned. Cruyff became a kind of permanent offstage noise.[5] He used his newspaper columns in Catalonia and the Netherlands to attack his enemies, especially Núñez and Louis van Gaal, Barcelona's manager from 1997 to 2000, and again in 2002–2003. No matter that Van Gaal was practically his lost brother: four years younger than Cruyff, an obsessive thinker about football from Amsterdam East whose father had also died young. As a teenager in the 1960s, Van Gaal had stood on the sidelines watching Michels train the great Ajax. As a player, he was an inferior copy of Cruyff without pace (famously described as "running as if he'd swallowed an umbrella"). He spent years in Ajax's reserve team before making a long career in minor clubs. Barça appointed him precisely because it saw him (correctly) as a Cruyffian, albeit one who placed much tighter constraints on his players than Cruyff had. After Van Gaal took charge, Cruyff savaged him weekly.

In 2003, Cruyff's fanboy Joan Laporta, a lawyer and the most charismatic man in Catalonia, was elected Barça president. He asked Cruyff whom he should appoint as coach. Cruyff had no desire to work again, but he wanted to use his power to promote men in his image: former great players, not "schoolteachers" with laptops like Van Gaal. Cruyff endorsed Frank Rijkaard, the man who had walked out of Ajax after fighting with him, and who had just coached Sparta Rotterdam to relegation from the Dutch premier division. As the only candidate on Barça's short list willing to accept the salary on offer,[6] Rijkaard got the job. Cruyff also anointed Txiki Begiristain, an alumnus of his Dream Team, as technical director.

When Michels died in 2005 at age seventy-seven, Cruyff said, "I never met anybody who influenced me as much. I've often tried to be like him."[7] All that Cruyff had done, he said, was "follow Michels's principles."[8] He was overdoing the false modesty, but it's true that Michels—named best coach of the twentieth century by FIFA—deserves to be recognized as the grandfather of today's Barça.

Rijkaard succeeded in the Camp Nou, winning the Champions League in 2006, more of which in the next chapter. In December 2007, after he began to lose, Laporta asked Cruyff to return as manager for the rest of the season, assisted by Barça B's thirty-six-year-old coach, Guardiola. Once the season ended, Guardiola could take charge alone.

Cruyff replied, "Pep is ready. He doesn't need me. You should choose him."[9] In other words, Cruyff shaped and then anointed both the coaches who between 2003 and 2012 won three of the five Champions Leagues in Barcelona's history. "All our sporting decisions were validated by Cruyff," Laporta said later.

Laporta named Cruyff Barça's "honorary president" but always kept his hero under control. He never gave Cruyff an official job, explaining, "He would have polarized everything around him." It was better to have Cruyff as a genius outside the organization, and quietly discard his nuttiest ideas.[10]

Cruyff's link with Barça broke forever when one of his enemies, Sandro Rosell, became president in 2010. Cruyff diverted his energies to Ajax, where he led a coup in 2011 and brought in ex-players like Marc Overmars and Edwin van der Sar to run the club. A very 1960s belief— that the talent should run the business—deteriorated into a jobs-for-mates scheme.

But phoneless in Barcelona, Cruyff lost track of what his appointees were up to. It was worse when he did show up at Ajax. He told a fellow board member, the ex-player Edgar Davids, "You're only here because you're black," and told another, the lawyer Marjan Olfers, that she'd only been appointed because she was a woman.

Cruyff eventually broke with Ajax; with his brother, Hennie; and with Dutch TV, because he thought the anchormen were questioning his views. He became a retiree watching games at home with the sound off so that he could provide the commentary for friends. Núñez's jail sentence for tax fraud in 2014, at age eighty-three, was a late consolation.[11]

When there was nothing to fight about, Cruyff could be a lovely man. Then he took off what he called "his armor"[12] and strolled around his neighborhood in Barcelona or Amsterdam, patronizing little shops because he remembered his parents' struggle to compete with supermarkets. He'd chat to anyone he ran into, telling a woman smoking on a bicycle that cigarettes were unhealthy, or giving inaccurate advice to workmen fixing a street.[13] A Dutchwoman I know was sitting on her stoop in Amsterdam one morning when Cruyff cycled past. Spotting a familiar face, she automatically called out "Hello!" then realized that she knew him only from television. Cruyff instantly grasped what had happened, grinned, and said "Hello!" back. Fifteen minutes later, he returned from wherever he had been, and spotting her still on the stoop, called, "Here I am again!"

His foundation raised money to install "Cruyff Courts"—small artificial sports fields—in urban neighborhoods around the world. The idea was to replicate the lost street football of his childhood. Opening a court in his native Betondorp in 2014, he reportedly shed a rare tear.[14] He also spent many hours coaching disabled kids. In one video, he rolls a soft penalty at a keeper with Down syndrome. When the boy makes the save, Cruyff offers him a high five, but the boy races past him to celebrate with his equally ecstatic teammates. It's the best moment of everybody's day.

In February 2016, while Cruyff was being treated for lung cancer, Messi performed a tribute to his penalty of 1982 against Helmond Sport. Against Celta Vigo, the Argentinian passed the spot kick to his right, where Neymar was supposed to pop up. Luis Suárez got there first and slotted it home.[15]

Cruyff died on March 24, 2016, at age sixty-eight, surrounded by his family. His ashes are buried in the garden of his summer house in El Montanyà, in the Catalan mountains.[16] He had told me, "I'll always be a Dutchman, for a very simple reason: I have a Dutch mentality." But like the club's Swiss founder Joan Gamper and its Hungarian hero of the 1950s, Kubala, Cruyff made Catalonia his eternal home.

His old coaching raincoat—ugly, beige, and tattered—is now an exhibit in Barça's museum. You can imagine his wife's delight at finally getting rid of it. In 2019, the club unveiled a statue outside the Camp Nou of Cruyff pointing while dribbling (a much more characteristic pose than the Cruyff Turn) above those three famous words: *"Salid y disfrutad,"* "Go out and enjoy it."

AFTERLIFE

Once Cruyff had died and stopped being impossible, Ajax renamed its stadium after him. Barcelona's second stadium, where the youth teams, reserves, and women play, became the Estadi Johan Cruyff. The walls nearby are painted with Cruyffian sayings: "Football is a game that you play with your brains." "If you have the ball, the opponent doesn't." "In my teams the keeper is the first attacker and the striker the first defender."[17] Javier Fernández, when he was Barça's head of sports analytics, told me he often started and finished his talks with one of Cruyff's aphorisms: "He has an amazing ability to synthesize the essential with very short phrases." The Amsterdam school dropout had intuited the system that the club's data analysts with PhDs are still trying to understand fifty years later.

Cruyff had remade Barça in his image. He bequeathed it a language of triangles, "third men," "between the lines," and "numerical superiorities." Xavi said, "Here came someone called Johan Cruyff, who changed the method and the philosophy of football. Wanting to be the protagonist, keeping the ball, controlling the game, playing attacking attractive football. And we've been practicing that for the last twenty, thirty years."[18] Guardiola notes that few projects in football last that long.

Cruyff also overturned Spanish football's balance of power. Before his return in 1988, Barcelona had won ten Spanish titles and Real Madrid twenty-three; between 1989 and 2021, Barcelona won sixteen and Madrid eleven. It's also only under Cruyff that Barça became a leading European club: never continental champions until 1992, five times since. Attitudes changed accordingly. "From having been a victim club, Barça is now not far from arrogance," said Valdano.[19]

And Cruyff changed football itself. Fabio Capello once identified "the three great legacies in the modern history of football: the Dutch school, Sacchi's era [at Milan], and the era of [Guardiola's] Barça."[20] All these fast-passing high-pressing teams were inspired by Cruyff.[21] His crowning moment was the Cruyff versus Cruyff World Cup final of 2010, Spain versus the Netherlands. Seven of the Spaniards who played in the match had spent time in the Cruyffian Masia; seven of the Dutchmen had come from Ajax's Cruyffian academy. Cruyff supported Spain that night as being truer to his style.

Many once-revolutionary elements of Cruyffian "total football" have become commonplaces of today's game, writes German author Dietrich Schulze-Marmeling: attacking defenders, a defensive line that pushes forward, deep pressing in the opponents' half, rapid transitions from defense to attack, an emphasis on possession, and more.[22] Jürgen Klopp once had an assistant put together a video of great pressing teams: it starts with Cruyff's Oranje of 1974 and ends with Klopp's Liverpool.[23]

The position that Cruyff marked most of all is goalkeeper. Manuel Neuer and Marc-André ter Stegen are the footballers in gloves he had dreamed up before they were born. Passing goalkeepers have become the norm. In England, the website Stats Perform reports:

In 2000/01, no regular Premier League goalkeeper had a pass completion rate of more than 62% (and that was Chelsea's Ed De Goey, brought up in Cruyff's Netherlands). . . . in 2019/20,

13 goalkeepers have a higher pass completion rate than De Goey did 19 years ago.[24]

You even see teams in the English Championship passing in triangles from the goalkeeper now, notes Barcelona's former youth coach Capellas. They probably weren't influenced directly by Cruyff, but indirectly by coaches whom he influenced—a lineage that starts with the teenaged Van Gaal watching Ajax's training sessions in the 1960s. Van Gaal and Guardiola later shaped the Bayern Munich side that became the core of Germany's World Cup–winning team of 2014.

Even Mourinho is a black sheep in the Cruyffian flock. In his last four years before becoming a head coach, from 1996 to 2000, he assisted Bobby Robson and Van Gaal in Barcelona.[25] Barça were the first professional team he ever led in a training session, and he occasionally trained the B team and the under-19s. When Mourinho left Barcelona, he said he would "only ever coach Real Madrid to destroy them. I will never stop being a *culer*."[26] He absorbed the Cruyffian view of football as a dance for space. It's just that whereas Cruyff obsessed about creating space, Mourinho cared more about shutting down the opposition's space.

Men like Van Gaal, Guardiola, and Seirul·lo did what Cruyff never could, turning his intuitions into a system, then working out methods to train it. Football evolved in ways that left Cruyff behind: he died outraged that right-footers were playing left-wing and left-footers outside-right. But his principles became dominant. As Guardiola remarked, "In one way or another we are all his followers: coaches, technical directors, commentators."[27] Lineker said, "It's where the modern game has come from—from ideas set in motion by Johan Cruyff."[28]

PART THREE

THE GOLDEN AGE,
2008–2015

VI

SHORTIES AT BOARDING SCHOOL: MORE THAN A YOUTH ACADEMY

In the space of a few years around the turn of the century, Barcelona's academy, the Masia, produced the best homegrown generation in football's history: the core of the Spanish world champions of 2010, plus Lionel Messi. More than that, the Masia came up with revolutionary thinking on height and on the essence of football. Barça changed the way that clubs worldwide choose and coach young players.

WHEN CRUYFF WAS A CHILD in Ajax's youth teams, half the first-team players used to watch his games. "I felt that they came especially for me, because I'd known them so long."[1] Sometimes his boys' side played the curtain raiser in the stadium before the first team's match, and his mother in the stands would hear the spectators around her marvel, "That little footballer, he's going to be a footballer!"[2] Ajax people thought he might become one of the best players in all the Netherlands.

Looking back on his career, Cruyff once remarked, "The nicest time was of course at Ajax from age twelve to seventeen. . . . Maybe because it wasn't yet about anything. Maybe because everyone was still helping you."[3]

By 1973, when he arrived in Barcelona, he had begun thinking of new ways to coach kids. He wasn't the only one. Barça's youth coach Laureano Ruiz, who claimed to have invented the rondo in 1957,[4] was already trying to get the whole Masia to play "total football" in a 4-3-3 formation.

Barça's chief scout in those days was Oriol Tort, a pharmaceutical representative in civilian life. Tort would sometimes watch up to twenty boys' matches in a day, recording every promising name on his typewriter. His rule of scouting was, "It is the first impression that counts, because afterward, the more you see a player the more defects you see."[5]

Club directors such as Nicolau Casaus dreamed of a majority-Catalan first team.[6] However, Barça had always found its best talent abroad. Its *cantera* ("stone quarry," as an academy is known in Spanish football) didn't have much of a reputation. To expand the club's catchment area, Tort decided to create something that didn't yet exist in Spanish football: a residence to house talented kids from out of town. In 1979, the Masia opened its doors to young players.[7]

From the start, it was more than a football academy. Many of the boys recruited in Catalonia were sons of *socis*; a majority were probably Barça fans. The merchants who ran Barça aspired to remake these kids in their own class's bourgeois image.[8] Gratacós, who had been a youth player at Barça in the 1970s, even before the Masia opened, said the club paid for him to take two university degrees that his family could never have afforded. Later, a schoolteacher was attached to every youth team.[9] There is footage of one early pupil, the teenaged Pep Guardiola, who attended school a hundred meters from the Camp Nou, writing an elaborate algebraic equation on a schoolboard.[10] The small-town brick-layer's son would grow into a model member of the Catalan *burgesia*, a consumer of literature and serious cinema.

Guardiola had got into Tort's Masia only because he met the height requirement. One day in the Catalan village of Santpedor, he had come running home to tell his mother, "The doctor says I'm going to be 1.80 meters, so I can become a footballer!"[11] Ruiz recalled, presumably speak-ing metaphorically, "There used to be a note on the door of the coaches' room that said, 'If you are offering us a youth player who is under 1.80 meters tall, turn around and go home.'"[12] A bone scan, "the test of the wrist," weeded out kids unlikely to reach the magic height.[13] For de-cades, clubs everywhere made similar judgments. In 1960s Belfast, scouts from Glentoran, Wolves, and Manchester City passed up a consumptive-looking, five-foot-three-inch (1.6-meter) adolescent winger, before Man-chester United finally took a gamble on George Best.[14]

Around 1980, just as the Masia was getting going, Cruyff in the United States was unsuccessfully urging the Washington Diplomats to set up second and third teams for young American players.[15] Later he became a football dad in Amsterdam, ferrying Jordi to training ses-sions and matches with Ajax's youth teams, on the fields where he him-self had once played.[16]

As coach of Ajax from 1985, Cruyff remade the youth section. Youth coaches at Ajax had always boasted in the canteen about their teams' victories; this still happens at many big clubs. But Cruyff ordained that the point of an academy wasn't to win youth championships. It was to produce good footballers, and to do that you often had to lose. If a twelve-year-old boy was too good for his age category, Cruyff didn't let him stay there so as to win the league; he promoted the kid to the under-15s. That annoyed the coach of the twelve-year-olds, who lost his best player, and the coach of the under-15s, who was saddled with a shrimp, but the boy improved. Crunching tackles from older kids discouraged excessive dribbling. Cruyff himself as a child had made the same journey. "Good players have to develop through shame and getting things wrong," he said.[17]

Everything in Ajax's academy was a learning process. Cruyff sometimes put promising forwards in defense, so that they could understand how defenders thought. Dennis Bergkamp received that treatment, personally overseen by Cruyff: the head coach once trained his boys' team.[18] Into old age, Cruyff had a friend fax him the results of Ajax's youth teams.[19]

By the 1980s, Cruyff's beloved street football had been lost to cars. Thinking about how to replicate it, he suggested holding training sessions in Ajax's parking lot. He was told that the boys could hurt themselves if they fell on concrete. "Then you mustn't fall," he replied. Staying upright was one of the skills you learned on the street.[20]

After he took over Barça in 1988, he sent his assistant Tonny Bruins Slot to explain the new training methods to the youth coaches. Bruins Slot drew a few passing exercises on a blackboard, then said in tourist Spanish, "This is positional play. The essence is touching the ball once, at most twice." The youth coaches looked at each other. Finally somebody dared ask, "Is that it?" It was—bar the details.

The Masia became a university of the pass. Exchanging passes with teammates was a kind of conversation, just as a jazz combo in a jam session communicates without words. Depending on how a pass was weighted, the ball might, say, "move right," "let's do a one-two," or "raise the tempo." The speed of the ball sent its own message, explained Xavi:

"If you're setting up a shot, you need to hit the ball harder, so your team-mate can reuse the pace on the ball. . . . You must anticipate whether your teammate will play with one touch or if they have time to control the ball. If they're more likely to play first-time, I hit the pass more firmly."[21] Every player had to know how to read each pass.

Rondos taught kids the language of Barça: the diagonal pass, break-ing opponents' lines, and *buscar el tercero* ("looking for the third man"). "Rondo, rondo, rondo. Every. Single. Day," Xavi told the journalist Sid Lowe. "Pum-pum-pum-pum, always one touch. If you go in the middle, it's humiliating, the others applaud and laugh at you."[22]

Boys in the Masia learned that a series of passes was like a coherent sentence, not random words. The moment you passed, you had to take up the right position to create a new triangle and receive the next pass. "*Toco y me voy*," "I touch and go," they say at Barça.

Little of this was spelled out until children were in their early teens. It didn't need to be. If you misread the Cruyffian passing grammar, you'd end up the piggy in the middle. If you could master it in the tiny space of the rondo, or in a ten-against-ten match on a thirty-yard-long field, you'd find the wide-open spaces of a real football field easy. Ca-pellas compares it to Superman: because he was born into the much stronger gravity of his home planet Krypton, on Earth he can leap over skyscrapers.

Almost every training session in the Masia was with the ball. Cruyff abolished strength training and cross-country runs for players under sixteen.[23] Messi would later find the Masia's methods a "contrast to the experience I'd had in Argentina, where it was all much more physical." He was also surprised to find that the Masia prioritized improving over winning.[24]

But the secret of the Masia was never coaching. It was scouting. If you can find brilliant kids, there's a lot less coaching to do. Cruyff liked to recruit attacking players, because they were usually the most skillful footballers. You could always retrain them as defenders later, or just stick them at the back, as Cruyff did with Guardiola, and Guardiola would do with Mascherano. They'd quickly pick up the simpler craft. Seirul·lo said that in practice games in training, Iniesta was "the best defender on the team, much better than any of our defenders, because not only can he recover the ball but he also starts the move to create something."[25]

Masia scouts looked for kids who received the ball facing the right way, and who played with their heads up, scanning the field—the mark of all the best footballers, said Cruyff. It was like driving a car, he explained: you had to look at the road, not at your dashboard and gears. Xavi said, "The first lesson I learned at Barcelona was to play with your head up.... I've had wonderful advice in my career, but that first piece is still the most important."[26] Whatever level you play at, the quickest way to improve your game is by scanning more. On a football field, information is gold, and you gather it with your eyes. A player who's always running misses a lot of what's happening around him.

Cruyff's biggest innovation in scouting, though, was his attitude toward size. His policy was essentially "small is beautiful." He said, "Nine times out of ten, strange as it sounds, someone small is at an advantage in the end." He'd experienced it himself. At fifteen he hadn't had the power to lift a corner kick in front of goal. "So at every moment you had to adjust," he explained. "If you're small and not fast, you have to react faster. If you're fast you don't have to pay attention, because if you start running you'll be faster anyway."

He once remarked that Xavi, Iniesta, and Messi were "technically perfect, have enormous speed of action, just because they had to when they were small."[27] Xavi said his physical shortcomings had forced him to think at "200 kilometers an hour."[28] He always had to move the ball on before the big kid came flying in.

A small child could also accelerate, stop, and turn quicker than a boy with longer limbs and a higher center of gravity. By age eighteen, when size started to matter less, the little one would have learned more. In Cruyff's aphorism, which captures a general truth about life, "Every disadvantage has its advantage."[29] Sports scientists now call it (less elegantly) the "compensation phenomenon": an athlete who falls short in one area will develop compensatory strengths.[30]

During Cruyff's time as head coach, the youth teams still played next to the Camp Nou. He'd regularly pop into the *cantera*, partly to watch Jordi, but also to see what was cooking. In his eight years running Barça, about thirty boys went from Masia to Camp Nou. Skillful *canteranos* like Guillermo Amor (5'9"), Albert Ferrer (5'7"), and Sergi Barjuán (5'7") played in his Dream Team alongside signings like Romário (5'6") and Eusebio Sacristán (5'7").

If someone objected that small players were vulnerable against corners and free kicks, Cruyff would reply, "That's why we mustn't concede any."[31] Your team's height shaped your tactics.

Cruyff had identified a gap in football's talent market. Something similar was about to happen in American baseball. Billy Beane, general manager of the Oakland A's and hero of Michael Lewis's book *Moneyball*, discovered in the 1990s that baseball scouts had all sorts of "sight-based prejudices." They discriminated against fat guys or skinny little guys or "short right-handed pitchers," and they overvalued handsome strapping athletes of the type that Beane himself had been at age seventeen. The A's and Barcelona both exploited an almost identical market inefficiency.

Barça's *socis* liked to see *la gent de la casa* ("people from the house") in the first team. So did the staffers drinking coffee in the ice-rink café. For Masia coaches, a boy's debut might be their reward for a decade's unseen work. Cruyff himself felt the same way. He said, after Iván de la Peña (5'5") made his debut in 1995, "I think back to the eleven-year-old boy and his parents, with whom I had conversations myself."[32] It was also easier for a head coach to instill a complex revolutionary system in the first team if half his players had been reared in it from childhood.

CRUYFF'S SACKING IN MAY 1996 barely affected the Masia. The first generation of Barça footballers brought up on Cruyffism (el cruyffismo, Spaniards called it) was already taking shape.

Four months after Cruyff's departure, the Iniesta family got into their old Ford Orion without air-conditioning and drove five hundred kilometers from their village of Fuentealbilla to drop off their pale-faced little twelve-year-old at the Masia. Tort himself had recruited little Andrés. But when the time came to say goodbye, Iniesta's father, José Antonio, was seized by regrets and wanted to take Andresito straight back home, recounts the authorized biography The Artist: Being Iniesta. The father's football dream had broken the family.

Iniesta spent his first night in the Masia (and many subsequent ones) crying. He had exchanged the family home for a bunk bed with a little table, a safe, and a drawer, in a room full of giant basketball recruits. Happily, older boys in the Masia, such as eighteen-year-old Carles Puyol and the fourteen-year-old keeper, Victor Valdés, volunteered as big brothers. When Puyol later moved up to the first team, he bequeathed Iniesta his mattress. As at any boarding school, pupils in the Masia made friends for life.

The local Masia kids were luckier, because they could keep living at home. Geri Piqué (known as "El Jefe" even as a child center-back) grew up five minutes from the Masia. From age thirteen, he played on the "Baby Dream Team" of boys born in 1987, with another local named Cesc Fàbregas and a tiny Argentinian kid whose whole family had immigrated with him. The boys' coach for a while was Tito Vilanova.

Messi, Piqué, and Fàbregas didn't expect that they'd all eventually make the first team. After each season, eight to ten boys in every team would be cut, replaced by newcomers. The average kid lasts just three years in the Masia. Typically, at the meeting where Barcelona let him go, the dad demands to know why, while the mother and son just cry.[33] The players who survive are left to worry when their turn will come. Valdés, who joined Barça at age eight, recalled that up to the age of eighteen "there was so much pressure in my life that I couldn't find peace. The mere thought of next Sunday's game horrified me."[34]

Piqué saw so many teammates disappear that he didn't even allow himself to dream of the big time until he was seventeen. That was when he left Barcelona for Manchester United, while Fàbregas joined Arsenal because he couldn't see a route to Barça's first team. Foreign scouts have plagued the Masia ever since: one spectator filming an adolescent match with a video camera was found to be working for Liverpool.[35]

In Manchester, Piqué bought himself a rabbit for company. "I was more alone than the number one," he reminisced later.[36] The animal ate its way through his rented apartment, to the dismay of Piqué's landlord, Sir Alex Ferguson himself.

Loneliness in a foreign land has wrecked many young footballers' dreams, and sometimes their life chances, too. The Masia has learned that the hard way. In thirty years, only two of its graduates who came from outside Spain have become regulars on the first-team squad: Messi and Thiago Alcântara, and both of them lived with their parents. Thiago's father, Mazinho, a world champion with Brazil in 1994, retired as a player in Spain, and later closed his football school in the Galician city of Vigo to move to Barcelona and supervise his two sons' careers.[37] By 2022, Thiago was playing for Liverpool, and his brother, Rafinha, for Real Sociedad.

Iniesta's parents lived in Spain, but he still struggled to stick out the six years in the Masia without them. José Antonio would often drive up on weekends to watch him play. At age sixteen, Iniesta was promoted to train with the first team, partly because he behaved well and never skipped school. The Masia old boys in the side, Guardiola and Xavi, who were always interrogating their old coaches about rising talents, had heard about him a year earlier. "He'll send us both into retirement," Guardiola teased Xavi.[38] In *The Artist*, Barça's then youth coach Lorenzo Serra Ferrer recounts Iniesta's first training session with the first team: "If he had to speed the game up, he did. If he had to slow it down, he did. . . . He understood the game and the Barcelona philosophy. There was no way it could go wrong."[39] Soon the teenager was being picked as playmaker ahead of the expensive Argentinian signing Juan Román Riquelme. While on the first team, Iniesta—a bricklayer's son like Guardiola—also attended university.

Enough Masia boys came through at the same time in the early 2000s to form a power bloc. Around 2003, when the club hit a low, they sat down together and resolved to stop tolerating selfish stars. They would manage the changing room themselves. When Ronaldinho and Deco went off the rails a few years later, both were doomed.

It might seem inevitable that players as good as Xavi, Iniesta, and Messi should have made the first team. In fact, it wasn't: they might never have got there at another big club. Xavi has said he only made it at Barça because Cruyff had blessed shorties.[40] Before Cruyff, he had struggled even to get into the Masia: a Barça scout had wanted to recruit him at age six, in the era of the bone-scan policy, but concerns about Xavi's size delayed his arrival until he was eleven, when Cruyff was in charge.[41] For a long time after that, some people at Barça worried that Xavi was too small, and Iniesta took years to become a first-team regular. Even the Masia couldn't always quell its doubts about short players: in the early 2000s, it went through another brief phase of height discrimination.

Other clubs might even have turned down the tiny thirteen-year-old Messi, given his expensive hormone treatments and the cost of moving his family. Look at France, where the adolescent Antoine Griezmann was rejected by six professional youth academies as too small. In 2005, at age fourteen, the future star of the world champions had to emigrate to Spain for a chance in Real Sociedad's academy. Other little Frenchmen, like Franck Ribéry, Nabil Fekir, and Mathieu Valbuena, were also rejected or ditched by French academies. N'Golo Kanté (1.69 meters) was ignored entirely by professional clubs until he signed an amateur contract with little U.S. Boulogne at age nineteen. One marker of Barça's exceptionalism is that in the 2010s the team had the lowest average height of forty-two leading European sides.[42]

So many small footballers have been rejected, yet so many of the world's best footballers are small. If you combine those two facts, it suggests that a small player gifted enough to overcome height discrimination has a disproportionate shot at greatness. If this form of discrimination ever ends, short players could dominate football.

ONE DAY IN 2009, when Barcelona's first team were European champions, I walked into the Masia off the street. If there was a security guard, I didn't see him. The academy was then still headquartered in the old brick farmhouse (a *masia*, in Catalan) next to the Camp Nou. Engraved on the facade were the year 1702 and a sundial.

Inside the farmhouse, the spartan decor evoked a seminary. The two-story building was almost empty, because the boys were at school. A woman with a cooking cap set the wooden tables in the dining room, which was filling with the smells of home cooking. A delivery boy lugged a huge ham to the kitchen. When a friendly soul gave me coffee at the bar, I began to realize: Barça is actually a small club.

I had come to meet Albert Capellas, who was then the Masia's coordinator, chief scout Pep Boade, and youth coach-*cum*-schoolteacher Ruben Bonastre. They walked me past the photos of past Masia generations that adorned the whitewashed walls of the dining room. The grizzled Boade pointed out a teenager with long curly hair in the 1979 picture: that was him. "Nostalgia," he sighed. In the 1988 photo, a sea of mullets, we identified Barça's head coach, Guardiola. Two other boys in the picture, Tito Vilanova and Aureli Altimira, had become his assistants. As in a family, you belonged at Barça for life, even if your role kept changing.

A player in the academy of a big club will probably only get an extended chance in the first team if he's a genius, or if the head coach is personally invested in him. At most clubs, the head coach is an ex-pro recruited from elsewhere who doesn't have time during his brief tenure to get to know the academy; he has to win at once or get sacked, so he has every incentive to field mature, expensive pros. Luckily, in Barça's two great eras, under Cruyff and Guardiola, the links between Masia and first team were intimate.

Look at the career paths of the slow, gangling midfielder Sergio Busquets and the not-brilliant little striker Pedro, neither of them obvious bets for the top. When Guardiola took his first coaching job, as manager of Barça B in 2007, assisted by Vilanova, in the equivalent of Spain's regional fourth division, he inherited Busquets. Capellas briefed him, "'Busi' doesn't look like the best player, but as soon as you start coaching him you'll see he's a star." Busquets (like Xavi, Iniesta, and Fàbregas before him) had grown up modeling himself on the Dream Team's playmaker, Guardiola himself.[43]

Pedro, twenty years old in 2007, was playing one tier lower still, in Barça C. Capellas said later, "Everyone knew he was a fantastic player, but for some reason he couldn't perform in the C team's matches." The kid seemed destined for the exit. Capellas recommended him to his former club CF Gavà, which was playing fourth-division football in a beach town outside Barcelona. Guardiola said, "Pedro can go to Gavà, but he has to stay with Barça B for the first couple of weeks of preseason until we have enough players." During preseason, Capellas kept coming to ask if Pedro could leave, and Guardiola always told him to wait. In the end he decided to keep Pedro.

In 2007–2008, Guardiola's B team with Pedro and Busquets won promotion to the third division. In midseason, Pedro made his first-team debut as a late sub in a 4–0 thumping of Murcia. Each time he touched the ball, the Camp Nou, always delighted to welcome a Masia kid, gave him a long *"Oléééé!"* When Guardiola moved up to the first team in summer 2008, he took Pedro with him. Busquets initially stayed with the B team, but when its new coach, Luis Enrique, put him on the bench, Guardiola took him, too. Guardiola knew from personal experience that a suboptimal body sometimes camouflaged a brilliant footballer, and that a self-willed coach can make a player's career. Busquets and Pedro made their league debuts in a dispiriting 1–1 home draw with Santander in September 2008. Within twenty-two months they had won the Spanish title, the Champions League, and the World Cup.

Standing in the Masia's driveway in 2009, midway through that magical period, Capellas told me, "You have to have someone up there who says, 'Go in.'" With his shoe he drew a circle on the ground: Guardiola had come through the Masia, and had ended up coaching the first team, where he drew on the Masia. As head coach, he knew every promising kid in the club. He and his assistants were always asking youth coaches how this or that boy was doing, and which sixteen-year-old could fill an empty spot in first-team training the next day.

Guardiola in 2009 was already thinking about who would be ready for the Camp Nou in three years' time. Like Cruyff, he tried only to buy players who were in the global top ten, or who played in positions the Masia couldn't fill. Under Guardiola, the circle was round.

Andreu Cases Mundet joined the Masia in 2009 as a twelve-year-old goalkeeper. Eleven years later I reached him at Santa Clara University in Northern California, where he was studying on a soccer scholarship. "When I joined Barça," he recalled, "I could feel that everyone in the club, from top to bottom, believed in the Masia. It was what made us different from everyone else." In those days, when Barça was trying to recruit a kid, it might bring him to the first-team changing room, where Masia graduates like Puyol or Xavi would kick a ball with him, knowing that he would never forget the experience. Cases Mundet himself was given keepers' training by Valdés.

And the step to the first team back then was surprisingly small— easier, in some ways, for a boy from the Masia than for a veteran star from Brazil or Britain. The homegrown kid already knew some first-team players, had played Barça's system since childhood, and was unlikely to be intimidated by the giant stadium because he literally lived inside it, in a nook behind the stands. (The dormitories had quickly outgrown the farmhouse.) Of course, it was true even then that a head coach had no margin for error, nor time to teach players once they were on the first team, but the Masia coaches had invested that time when the players were young.

Bonastre, the youth coach, told me, "Masia players find the first team easy, because it's easier to play with Xavi and Iniesta than with players from the academy." Xavi always gave his teammates exactly the right pass at the right moment on their good foot.

The new boy would have to start in the middle of the first team's rondo, chasing around to intercept passes, but he could count on the Masia's old boys' network. When a new kid moved up, the youth coaches might tell Iniesta, "Andrés, watch out for him," and Iniesta would reply, "Don't worry, we give them the best treatment."

That doesn't happen at every club. When the South African youngster Mark Byrne went for a trial at Portsmouth decades ago, he marked the former England striker Paul Mariner in training. Byrne ended up with four stitches in his forehead and three in his shins. "What was that all about?" he asked Mariner, and Mariner said, "If you can't fucking take it, fucking fuck off." Byrne had found the response impressive, the mark of a true pro.[44]

Before I began writing this book, I thought that luck might determine whether a second-rate player gets a professional career, but I believed that every star would have made it under any circumstances. I no longer believe that. It seems that even the careers of some excellent players live or die depending on the time and place when they make the leap to senior football. Imagine what might have happened to Pedro and Busquets at a club where the first-team manager didn't know their names. Busquets in particular (like Guardiola himself) was built to succeed in Cruyffian football. He might have sunk at a gritty little club that chased the ball and booted it long.

Pedro without Guardiola might have spent his career in Spain's second division, said Capellas (just as Guardiola without Cruyff might have succeeded in a different profession). Only the bravest managers say, "Nobody believes in this boy, but I do. I'll put him in the team instead of a proven star who cost twenty million dollars."

How many Busquetses and Pedros have been lost over the years at Real Madrid? Capellas said that in youth Clásicos, Madrid's players were as good as Barça's, yet they never ended up on the first team. In Madrid, the circle didn't seem to be round.

The Masia understood its responsibilities as going beyond football. Some of the boys it recruited said they didn't want to study, they just wanted to play football. (Messi had been that way.) But by 2009, Barça no longer allowed that. Everyone had to learn something, even if it was only IT or English. Upstairs in the playroom the day I visited, the table football and the billiards were covered with cloths, because school came first. Daily training was at full intensity—every pass and positional choice counted—but it only lasted about ninety minutes.

The Masia didn't want adolescents thinking about football all day. In any case, most of them were never going to have careers in the game. Every academy recruits some kids just to make up the numbers: you need eighteen or so players to fill the under-16s squad, even if every coach can name several who are never going to get anywhere near the Camp Nou. (A case study prepared in 2015 by Harvard Business School quantifies the high failure rate. By that summer, more than 530 footballers had been through the Masia. Fourteen percent had made their debut for Barça's first team, while another 33 percent had played professionally elsewhere[45]—and many of them won't have lasted more than a season or two in the game.)

The Masia pushed kids to get a proper education. In 2015, the academy's then director Carles Folguera told Harvard, "Among other top European clubs, we have the highest rate—50 percent—of 18- and 19-year-old players studying at the university level. Unlike most other clubs, we are happy with more hours spent studying rather than in the gym."[46] Masia boys typically come across as more middle-class than their foreign teammates. Barça tried to prepare the boys for a life beyond football. They were encouraged to speak politely, and discouraged from getting tattoos or dyeing their hair or wearing shiny cleats, because they had to stand out only on the pitch. Even pouring too much milk on their cornflakes was frowned upon. Barça preferred to pay the kids modest salaries, partly out of miserliness, but also because big money made other kids jealous and poisoned the atmosphere. In 2009, the Masia had lost interest in the seventeen-year-old Danish prodigy Christian Eriksen due to his agent's demands.

The approach seemed to work. Most Masia players who became stars have behaved pretty modestly. Just look at how Messi dresses. Xavi said, "I am just a pupil of the Barça school. Otherwise I am nothing."[47] As for Iniesta, he was still living with his parents and sister at age twenty-four. Even Barça fans found him so dull that one local sports newspaper noticed slumps in sales when he appeared on the front page.

On the satirical TV show *Crackòvia*, he was always portrayed beside his peasant mother, who carried her shopping basket and chorizo.[48] These humble stars were held up as role models to boys in the Masia. If you achieved high status but behaved normally, people were always impressed.

Zlatan Ibrahimović didn't like Barça's ordinariness, but he confirmed that it was real. After his stint at the club, from 2009 to 2010, he marveled, "Barcelona was a little like school, or some sort of institution . . . none of the lads acted like superstars, which was strange. Messi, Xavi, Iniesta, the whole gang—they were like schoolboys. The best footballers in the world stood there with their heads bowed, and I didn't understand any of it. It was ridiculous." Ibrahimović wasn't pleased to be told by Guardiola, "Here in Barcelona we don't turn up to training sessions in Ferraris or Porsches."[49] Guardiola himself had stuck with his used VW Golf for years after breaking onto the first team. He remained a Masia boy at heart.[50]

Masia boys who became stars often remained close to former roommates who became ordinary civilians.

And the ones who survived at Barça into adulthood generally continued to help each other. In 2009, Iniesta was going through a months-long personal crisis that looked like a depression. At one point the twenty-five-year-old asked his parents if he could sleep in their bed with them.

Barça offered him unquestioning support. Guardiola encouraged him to walk out of training whenever he needed to: "Don't ask permission, just go. You are important: you and only you." Iniesta frequently took up the offer, disappearing wordlessly to the changing rooms. The coach expressed the club's respect for professional expertise: "I don't know how to treat this, but we need a specialist." Barça sent Iniesta to a psychologist, Inma Puig, whom he saw for months, arriving for each session ten to fifteen minutes early so he could prep.[51] He also had long conversations with Masia old boy Bojan Krkić, who had experienced panic attacks as a young pro.

Certainly at the time, there were football clubs that showed less understanding for mental illness. But Guardiola and his assistants had known Iniesta since childhood. They trusted him. More than that: they loved him.

In Johannesburg in July 2010, the Masia won the World Cup final. Amid the heap of Spaniards celebrating Iniesta's winning goal in the 116th minute, two were hugging each other in tears: the match winner and a reserve goalie in a tracksuit. Victor Valdés knew how much his Masia brother had been through to get there.

The people running Barça at the time understandably succumbed to hubris. They felt they had cracked the secret of raising footballers. "Madrid buy European Footballers of the Year. We make them," boasted the freshly departed club president Laporta.[52] Barça's internal target had been to get 50 percent of the first team from the Masia, but there were discussions about raising that to 60 percent. Around that time, I asked Joan Oliver, the club's chief executive, whether Barcelona had got lucky. Surely they couldn't produce a Messi, a Xavi, or an Iniesta in every generation? Oliver replied, "Yeah, good fortune exists always in the world. Perhaps you could not always get the best player of the world from your academy. But we get six, seven first-team players."

On November 25, 2012, Barça won 0–4 at Levante. When Martín Montoya replaced the injured Dani Alves after fourteen minutes, all Barcelona's eleven players on the pitch had come through the Masia (or in the cases of Puyol and Pedro, spent at least a year there). Even the coach that day, Tito Vilanova, was a Masia graduate. One of the academy's longtime coaches, Gratacós, told me: in football you're always looking back nostalgically, or hoping for a better future, but that game against Levante was the Masia's peak. It couldn't get better than that.

I came to understand life in the Masia better after I got talking to the mother of a fourteen-year-old boy there. Barça hadn't put us in touch; she was a friend of a friend. Over Zoom (this was in 2020, at the height of the coronavirus pandemic, and thousands were dying in Catalonia), she told me her story. When the family had moved to Barcelona for work, her son joined a local club. Barça keeps tabs on all youth football in Catalonia, and the family soon noticed coaches in Barça gear watching his games. She only discovered the depth of the club's interest in her son when people around her began offering congratulations. The boy joined Barça, but like most local players he continued to live at home, not in the Masia.

He returned from his first training sessions exhilarated. He didn't care how things went from here, he said; at least he had had this chance. Club staffers praised his game, but they never mentioned a possible professional career. Barça's message was, "This is a place to train and develop."

The boy got a red card on his Barcelona debut, for protesting to the referee after the final whistle. The coaches made a big deal of it, reprimanding him but also treating it as a teachable moment. He ended up apologizing to the referee. "It's a huge priority there: respect," the mother said. In 2016, after his Barça under-12s team beat a Japanese side in the World Challenge, he and his teammates comforted their weeping opponents.

Barça's parent-liaison staffers sent the family regular information on sleep, homework, nutrition, and study habits, and monitored the boy's schoolwork. Everyone the mother dealt with at the club was pleasant, she said. "Anytime I ask a question I get a response right away, and it's usually thoughtful."

The boy initially trained three days a week, then four days from age fourteen. He played one or two games a week. "They don't overpractice," the mother commented. "Practice is an hour and a half, and they don't have any expectations of training beyond that. I feel like it's totally reasonable. That kind of surprised me: it feels like a family-run operation."

"So winning's not that important?" I asked.

She laughed. "It is important. They might say, 'Not your best game,' but they choose the moments to say it. They might not tell you when you're playing really well, but when you are not, they pick you up."

She said Barça made sure the parents behaved well, too. They weren't allowed to watch training or shout at referees. "What I love," she added, "is that parents give their kids a big hug and kiss after the game, and then maybe it's lunch with the grandparents." Sometimes people gave someone else's kid a hug, too: there was little overt competition between families. Some kids had been in the Masia for years, so the parents had grown tight.

She'd heard parents whose sons had been cut say they were glad their kids had had an opportunity to play at Barça. In any case, the cut rarely came as a shock: the usual warning signal was that the child's game time decreased.

Her son has done well. She feels he's playing with joy, and he has occasionally captained his team. When he was eleven or twelve, the family began getting approaches from sports apparel companies, from other clubs, and from agents in Britain, Spain, and the United States. The family hasn't yet hired an agent, though many of his teammates in the Masia have one. She told me, "We frankly are mystified by it." Her son has blocked agents who contacted him on Instagram.

Someone advised her, "Don't let an agent sit with you at games," so she tries not to. Still, she has become friendly with some agents. One Spanish agency, a small shop, sent the family feedback after matches, and kept them posted about the goings-on with the Catalan national team in his age group. About six agencies check in with them regularly, for "respectful" monthly contacts. "They have been great," she says. When we spoke, the family was considering getting an agent after the boy turned fifteen. She tells her son, "Keep dreaming. Your dreams are coming true."

Agents have told her that sixteen is the turning point. At that age, some boys progress to the *Juvenil* levels of the Masia, while others might leave to play in another country.

I asked, "What if he gets injured?"

She replied, "If he gets injured, he'd had an amazing experience and then he goes and does other amazing things in life."

It's worth pausing a moment to compare the approach of football's most prestigious academy with almost any selective youth team in any sport in the United States. Some American sporting parents hire $225-an-hour sports therapists, scream at their kids during games, harass umpires afterward, and when the child reaches high school, if she hasn't yet succumbed to overuse injuries, pay "body brokers" to market her to college athletics programs.[53] Some of these kids aren't particularly athletic, have no chance of turning pro, yet are chronically tired from playing seven days a week. The happy few teenagers who do win athletics scholarships to college usually only get partial ones, which can rarely repay the debts their families have racked up along the way.

Take Jennifer Sey, who became the U.S. national gymnastics champion in 1986, and all it took was most of her childhood, frequent broken bones, "untold boxes of laxatives," semi-starvation, and a dysfunctional relationship with her mother, who derived her identity from her child's career. When Sey wanted to quit the sport, her mother said, "I won't let you eat! I'll lock the cabinets! You're not going to throw this away after all the time and money we've spent."[54]

Michael Lewis remarked while writing a book on the professionalization of youth sports:

> If you want to see people get really crazy, go to some place
> where they're watching their kids play something. It makes the

problems between Democrats and Republicans seem trivial . . .
Youth sports, the business, is bigger than all the professional
sports combined, in terms of the dollars spent by American
consumers.[55]

Lewis's own daughter, who played youth softball, spent thirty-seven
nights in hotels in 2019. Her itinerary looked like that of a traveling
salesman for a major company, he said.[56]

By contrast, most people at Barça really do seem to treat young footballers as children. They don't do this purely out of altruism. Humanity
in football also offers competitive advantages. One, parents are happier
to send their kids to an academy whose friendly scout comes to dinner
at the family home, behaves like a human being, and stays in touch afterward. Two, altruism reduces the risk of losing talented kids to bullying. Three, if you can remind children that they are human beings and
not stars, they might avoid the temptations of fame.

Lastly—and this may sound like cant—humanity is essential because
a player at Barcelona has to bring his whole personality onto the field
with him. What people call the "Barça system" isn't really a system, but
a game of autonomous, thinking individuals. Players cannot simply
follow their coach's orders. Football is too dynamic for that. In fact,
good Barcelona players end up scarcely needing a coach, because
they learn to make their own passing and positioning decisions.
Seirul·lo told me, "The player is social, affective, emotional, coordi-
nated, and finally expressive, creative. It's about human beings with
free intentions."

VII

HOW DOES HE DO IT?
UNDERSTANDING LIONEL MESSI

One night in 2015, I sat beside a club official watching a Barça–Atlético Madrid game in the Camp Nou. When the game began, he said, "Watch Messi."

It was a bizarre sight. From kickoff, Messi went on a stroll around the opposition defense, apparently ignoring the ball. "In the first few minutes he just walks across the field," explained the official. "He is looking at each opponent, where the guy positions himself, and how their defense fits together."

Messi was storing his observations in his visual memory. At one point in the opening minutes, Barça's center-back Javier Mascherano passed to him, and Messi just let the ball roll into touch. He wasn't ready to play yet. He performs the same routine every match. His old coach Guardiola explains, "After five, ten minutes, he has the map in his eyes and in his brain, to know exactly where is the space and what is the panorama."[1]

Messi is a curiously overlooked footballer. He has been predictably brilliant for so long that we have come to take his brilliance for granted, something to be dismissed in a phrase. He's a "PlayStation footballer," said Arsène Wenger; "Like a cartoon," said Samuel Eto'o; "A magician!" shout commentators. I want to try to let daylight in on the magic.

One sun-drenched February morning at the Joan Gamper training complex, when it felt unfair that anyone was allowed to have a stimulating job in such a paradisial city, I watched Messi cruise past me into the players' parking lot: a little man in a baseball cap, perched high in his luxury crossover SUV sponsor's car, reporting for another day at the office. It got me thinking about how Barça managed him day to day, and how he did what he did week in, week out, ever since his debut for the first team in 2004. How did Barcelona transform a soloist into a team player? And how did the club keep him on board for so long? Barça's Messi strategy—which entailed shaping the entire workplace around employee number one—was for fifteen years possibly the most successful long-term man-management project in football history. But it worked also because Messi's career has coincided with the most star-friendly era of the game. This chapter takes his story up to about 2015. The period after that, during which FC Barcelona degenerated into FC Messi, culminating in his departure, comes in the final chapters of the book.

I didn't interview Messi. I was careful not to use up my bank of favors with Barça, and I understood that requesting fifteen minutes with him would have taken me over the limit, even presuming the club was able to produce him. (Nobody at Barcelona tells Messi what to do.)

It also probably wouldn't have been worth it. Messi reached the age of thirty without ever saying an interesting sentence in public. My colleague John Carlin, who interviewed him twice, said that if offered a third opportunity he'd decline it. Even after Messi grew older and began to talk, he showed almost no inclination to explain either his art or his power within Barça. It's not clear that he is able to. Instead, I've tried to understand Messi by watching him closely, and by listening to people who have watched him even more closely.

THE COMING OF MESSI WAS foretold to me by a man from his hometown of Rosario. In October 2000, I had coffee in Buenos Aires with a cheery little football nut called Roberto Fontanarrosa, a cartoonist and novelist. He explained to me the Argentinian belief that Maradona could only have come from Argentina. Maradona, in Fontanarrosa's telling, was an Argentinian type that dates back to the 1920s, or even earlier: the *pibe* (boy) from the *potrero* (bumpy urban space) who wins games with dribbles. Fontanarrosa admitted that he himself cherished the absurd belief that Argentina would produce another Maradona. Fontanarrosa lived just long enough to see it happen. He died in 2007, his funeral procession pausing beside the home ground of his beloved Rosario Central.

While Fontanarrosa and I were having coffee, a thirteen-year-old from Rosario and his dad were waiting impatiently in Barcelona for the club to sign him. Lionel Andrés Messi Cuccittini was then just 4'7", the height of a nine-year-old, but he had needed only about five minutes in a training session with bigger boys to get Barça's technical director Charly Rexach exclaiming, "Who's that?" and then, "Christ, we need to sign him right now." When someone remarked that the kid looked like a table-football player, Rexach said, "Then bring me all the table-football players because I want them in my team."[2]

Only months later, in December 2000, did Rexach finally scrawl an agreement in principle on a now-legendary paper napkin.[3] Barça agreed to fund Messi's growth-hormone treatments. Without those, he wouldn't have attained even his modest adult height of 1.69 meters, and like so many people from poorer countries, would probably have ended up physically unsuited to top-level sport. Small may be beautiful in football, but tiny is not.

His club in childhood, Newell's Old Boys, had the foresight to film his games.[4] Watching videos of him from the age of five, you see that he arrived at Barcelona as almost a perfect *pibe*, a dribbler who could see opponents coming as if in slow motion. In one video, a tiny kid with slicked-back hair, cooler than you'd expect, smiles into the camera and says, "My name is Lionel Messi, I'm thirteen years old. I'd like to play for Barcelona. I think it's the best football team in the world."[5] (It wasn't then.)

Very unusually, Barça paid for Messi's parents and siblings to move with him. The child's salary of €120,000 a year—probably unprecedented in the Masia—was meant to support them all.[6] The Messis retained their family structure at the price of inverting it: the thirteen-year-old youngest son became the migrant breadwinner. Like the twelve-year-old Cruyff after the death of his father, Messi experienced the sudden end of childhood, and the onset of responsibility. All the Messis cried in the taxi to Rosario airport, he would recall,[7] yet taking the family with him may have made the difference. His mother and siblings lasted only a few months before returning homesick to Argentina for a while, but his father stayed throughout. Living in a dorm room across the ocean away from his entire family having to inject himself with growth hormones every day, might have been beyond even Leo Messi. Once the hormones had helped him beat nature, he felt he could overcome anything.

Unlike many Masia families, the Messis held together and resisted chasing quick money. They waited patiently for their boy to mature in

Barcelona. A club staffer who is close to the player told me, "Messi had a structure. Good or bad, he had one." Protected by his father, Messi never needed to find a father figure in football, which helps explain his lack of interest in coaches. But his older brother Rodrigo later admitted, "We didn't adapt very well. We were united, but one person did something and the others did nothing. So we all suffered in different ways."[8]

Messi is a more limited and disciplined figure than past greats largely because he has been a professional athlete since adolescence. Whereas Maradona and Cruyff are products of Argentina and the Calvinist Netherlands, Messi grew up almost outside society, the joint creation of a family and a football academy.

Until he broke into Barcelona's first team at age seventeen and encountered teammates who demanded the ball, he didn't need to pass, recalled Pere Gratacós, who coached him in the Masia. As Messi recalled it, he kept "forgetting" to pass, adding, "Gradually I managed to play more for the team but I didn't make it easy for them, because I have always been very stubborn."[9]

Barça had to try to teach a natural to play collective football. Twice coaches benched him for holding on to the ball too much, but the Masia never quite turned him into a Cruyffian ensemble player. On the Baby Dream Team, Messi scored his goals alone. That wasn't a good omen. None of the Argentinian *pibes* who were supposed to become the next Maradona—not Pablo Aimar or Ariel Ortega or Marcelo Gallardo or Javier Saviola, who signed for Barça's first team in 2001—ever fully transitioned from *el fútbol de la calle*, street football, to the collective European game.

There was also something worryingly childlike about Messi, recounts the German writer Ronald Reng. When Guardiola first spotted the tiny shy kid with his father in the Nike shop at the airport, he wondered, "Is this one as good as they say?" Messi practically lived in tracksuits, didn't seem to own a pair of jeans, had only ever attempted to read one book, a biography of Maradona (which he didn't finish), and was assumed by his teammates to be mute until one day he suddenly burst into speech during an emotional game of PlayStation.[10] "The game was his means of communication," Gratacós told me.

Still, by the time Messi was sixteen and on the verge of the first team, the club was desperate. "There is a curse on us," sighed Radomir Antić, briefly Barça's first-team coach during the 2002–2003 season, which they finished sixth in the Spanish league playing boring football. "In 2003 I was 'the cancer of Barcelona,'" recalled Xavi. His style of play seemed to have become outdated: most other big clubs were fielding giants in central midfield. Barça's debts were estimated at €186 million, well above its annual revenues. Even the players' wage bill exceeded total revenues. Barça was a "money-losing machine" that risked "remaining a small local brand," more a Valencia than a Real Madrid, said Ferran Soriano, who became the club's chief executive in 2003.[11] The club had then won just one Champions League in its history; Madrid had won nine.

Laporta had been elected club president that summer on the promise of signing David Beckham. The Englishman was to be Barça's very own *galáctico*. But Beckham understandably preferred to join his fellow *galácticos* at Real Madrid. Barça also failed to sign an eighteen-year-old Portuguese winger named Cristiano Ronaldo, who went to Manchester United instead. "We thought €18 million was too high a price," Soriano admitted later.[12] Imagine football history had they put Ronaldo and Messi together as teenagers.

Instead Barça hurriedly bought Brazilian playmaker Ronaldinho from Paris Saint-Germain, where he'd had an up-and-down time, with spells on the bench and others being used as an old-fashioned English-style target-man center-forward.

Club officials initially struggled to convince Barça's new coach,

Frank Rijkaard, to let a tiny sixteen-year-old train with the first team. When the Dutchman finally gave permission, a staffer collected Messi from his brother Rodrigo's apartment a few streets from the stadium. "Nervous?" the staffer asked kindly as the boy got into the car. "No," replied Messi. After the session, the staffer asked Ronaldinho if the Argentinian child with a flowerpot haircut was good enough to train with the team. "He should be playing for the team already," replied the Brazilian.

In November 2003, in a friendly match against FC Porto (who were managed by a young Barça alumnus, José Mourinho), Messi made his debut for the first team. He "had absolutely no trouble with nerves,"[13] recalled Rijkaard's assistant Henk ten Cate. The boy, who rarely bothered watching football on TV, didn't know the names of his opponents or much football history.[14] None of it interested him. He knew he belonged on Barça's first team. But he quickly learned to play down his talents so as not to offend his famous teammates, who were having a hard enough time as it was. In December 2003, after a 5–1 defeat in the rain at Malaga, *Mundo Deportivo* struggled to choose its front-page headline: "Shame" or "Intolerable"? "Ridiculous" had already been rejected as "too strong."[15] Only in early 2004 did Barça's turnaround begin.

After each training session, the squad went to the gym. Other players lifted weights, but Messi didn't see the point. He played tennis football with the Brazilian fullback Sylvinho. Ten Cate said, "I saw little Messi playing with Sylvinho, and Sylvinho was beating the crap out of him every time, and soon Messi was beating Sylvinho, and then he was beating Ronaldinho." When Rijkaard's other assistant, Eusebio Sacristán, played tennis football with Messi, he noticed that the boy always tried to beat him 11–0. "He had a winner's mentality," said Eusebio. "Other players weren't like that."

There is a democracy of greats in which age and status melt away. Ronaldinho offered Messi the locker next to his in the stars' corner of the changing room. (The room was divided by columns into separate sections—a shape that naturally created cliques. Guardiola found this so damaging that when he later designed the changing room for Manchester City's training ground, he made it oval.)[16]

On October 16, 2004, Messi made his official debut as a sub against Espanyol. A little over six months later, the seventeen-year-old became Barcelona's youngest ever goal scorer, against Albacete, with a lob after a lobbed pass from his mentor, Ronaldinho. The Brazilian celebrated by giving him a piggyback. "Watch this player. He will outdo us all," Ronaldinho said afterward.[17]

The first time I saw Messi was just after his eighteen birthday, on June 28, 2005, in the semifinal of the under-20s World Cup: Brazil versus Argentina in the Dutch town of Utrecht. I'd gone in hopes of making notes on stars of the future that I could drop into articles in the years ahead.

The shortest and youngest member of the Argentinian squad had started the tournament on the bench, but had been promoted after Argentina's opening defeat to the United States. Going into the semifinal, he had scored three goals in four matches, and Laporta had raced to the Netherlands to deter potential bidders by raising his salary, reportedly thirtyfold.[18] No other player in the semifinal was even under contract to a European club. Leafing through my notebook of the time, I see that I focused on Messi from kickoff:

"Playing as the lone striker. Not very active in moving off the ball, hangs around motionless a lot, with his head down," is my first note. But then:

In the 7th min, Messi does something for the first time: is given the ball about 30 yards from goal, accelerates past his man and curls it into the top corner with his left foot from outside the box. Brilliant.

Messi is the one man on the pitch who frequently dribbles past opponents; the crowd loves it when he has the ball . . .

V consistent, concentrated; doesn't waste the ball, always an intelligent pass > more mature than the older kids around him . . .

I wish Messi would involve himself w/the game just a bit more, as he's no mere goalscorer, but Argentina's best passer. . . .

Messi has nothing in the air; barely even tries.

Four days later I returned to Utrecht for the final, Argentina versus Nigeria. I sat in the stands next to Piet de Visser, a birdlike septuagenarian Dutch scout who had overcome various cancers and had essentially lost his stomach. He was working for Chelsea, something he tried ineffectually to keep secret. De Visser spent his life crossing the planet watching youth tournaments and knew every talented teenaged footballer on earth, referring to each one by his shirt number. When Nigeria made a substitution, he remarked, "Yes, they will be even stronger with eleven. Eleven is better than fifteen."

De Visser opened the match with a long eulogy to Argentina's number seven (the midfielder Fernando Gago): "He is the best. Never a ball wrong, that seven. Never a wrong pass, and in one minute, he has given six to eight passes. He is the boss of Boca, eh? A graceful player."

De Visser was less impressed with Argentina's captain Pablo Zabaleta: "That's what he can do: control. But you mustn't give him the ball."

Then Messi was fouled for a penalty. He waited for the keeper to move before softly rolling the ball into the other corner. "Yes, he's so good," purred De Visser. He mentioned that at the World Cup under-17s in Finland a couple of years before, Messi had been the best player, too.

The quality of the match was remarkably high. At one point in the second half, the Dutch spectators, sensing that they were witnessing something special, began clapping to the beat of the action. But had anyone asked them which player would go on to become the best in the world, many would probably have named the Nigerian midfielder Jon Obi Mikel. When Mikel beat three men in Argentina's penalty area, De Visser exclaimed, "Look, boy! Not normal, eh? Ruler of the midfield. Outclasses even Gago."

Still, when Gago was substituted for Lucas Biglia with twenty minutes to go, De Visser yelled, "That bastard coach! Boooooooo! That's never allowed."

Late in the final, Argentina got another penalty. Messi took it again. De Visser's commentary: "Such a cool frog. He waits for what the keeper does. If the keeper just stands there, [Messi] has a problem." The keeper did stay standing, but the moment he merely shifted his weight onto his right leg, Messi put the ball in the other corner. Argentina were youth world champions. Messi won the Golden Boot for highest scorer and was named player of the tournament. Mikel was runner-up. Six of the Argentinians who played that day—Gago, Biglia, Zabaleta, Messi, Ezequiel Garay, and the fifty-seventh-minute substitute Sergio Agüero—would feature nine years later in the senior World Cup final against Germany in Rio de Janeiro.

Within a few months of Utrecht, Messi had become Barcelona's starting outside-right. He loathed the position at first, as he had always wanted to play centrally, but this was the new fashion in football: left-footers on the right wing, right-footers on the left, cutting inside. The position set the template for the rest of Messi's career. In his first start for Barça, against Osasuna in October 2005, he completed eleven dribbles.

He also began playing for Argentina, starting at the bottom of the team's hierarchy: after a friendly match against Croatia in Basel, the Argentinian federation returned him to Barcelona on EasyJet.[19]

In those early months on Barcelona's first team, he would walk to the stadium from his brother's apartment. He drank Coke, played computer games, helped look after his baby nephew, and starred at the Camp Nou.[20] A club medic told me that Messi at this stage still felt invincible, absolved by his genius from the need to live an athlete's life. Soon he bought a house in Castelldefels (the beach town rejected by the Cruyffs in 1973).[21]

At the time Ronaldinho, who could pass with his back, was considered the world's best player. Messi said in 2005, "He's got an ability to control the ball that makes me jealous."[22] Ronaldinho talked of spending his whole life in Barcelona: "There isn't a place on earth where I could be better off."[23] But people at Barça were already worrying that he wouldn't last. The club knew the scenario: great player comes to the Camp Nou, shines briefly, then fades. That had been the story of Cruyff, of Diego Maradona (at Barça from 1982 to 1984), and the German Bernd Schuster. "All stars leave Barcelona through the back door," said Schuster.[24] The Brazilian Ronaldo had left for Inter Milan in 1997, aged just twenty, the move arranged by his agents on the very afternoon that Barça's directors were in a restaurant with the player celebrating the impending renewal of his contract. By the time they returned to the club offices after lunch to sign the contract, it was too late.[25]

In May 2006, Barça beat Arsenal 2–1 in the Champions League final in Paris. Messi was recovering from injury, and Rijkaard kept him on the bench all game. Afterward, while the team celebrated in a nightclub on the Champs-Elysées, the boy sat alone on a sofa in a corner, sulking. It's common for substitutes to resent collective triumphs in which they had no part, but it's rare for an eighteen-year-old to be brazen enough to show it.

That night felt like the beginning of the Ronaldinho hegemony, but it turned out to be the end. The Brazilian, then just twenty-five, would hardly play another great match in his career. Around this time, a journalist friend of mine was summoned to Barcelona to discuss ghost-writing Ronaldinho's autobiography. He checked into his hotel, and waited. At about two a.m., the phone rang: the Brazilian and his entourage were waiting for him in a nightclub. My friend went to meet them, and realized within minutes that Ronaldinho would never find the concentration to sit down and describe his life.

Soon enough, Ronaldinho grew a belly and began turning up late for training. Worryingly, Messi sometimes accompanied him on nights out. The Brazilian's bad habits infected the rest of the squad, too. Soriano, Barça's chief executive, reports a player telling him in 2007:

> At my last club, the players used to arrive an hour before we started training, and the coach was already there. Here, if the training session starts at eleven o'clock, some of them arrive five minutes before that, and even later. In the beginning I would also come in quite early, but now I just come five minutes early, like most of the others do.[26]

Cruyff once said that the most dangerous moment in a great player's career is when he's about twenty and suddenly fame and money arrive, especially if he isn't yet married with kids. That's when he runs the highest risk of going off the rails.

Messi at that age had the advantage over Ronaldinho of being an introvert who lived in a family, not an entourage. He was also more interested in football than Ronaldinho was. In 2007, he finished second behind the Brazilian Kaká in the vote for the world's best player. Third in the voting was a young Portuguese winger also making his first appearance on the podium. But when Cristiano Ronaldo and Messi walked onstage in their dinner jackets, the Portuguese was accidentally handed the prize for second place. Sepp Blatter, president of FIFA, acting as joint master of ceremonies, spotted the error, whereupon

Cristiano unsmilingly handed his trophy to Messi—a public humiliation at what was probably their first ever encounter.

Messi at this stage of his career was still an almost unreconstructed soloist. In his first three seasons, he averaged seven to eight completed dribbles per match, marveled the website StatsBomb in 2019. "All of these volumes are greater than *any player* in the big European leagues across the last two seasons . . . frequently teams go entire games recording fewer dribbles than young Messi did."[27] In January 2008, he beat one unfortunate defender, Clemente Rodríguez of Espanyol, six times in a single match.[28] That season, 2007–2008, he hit a new record of 8.6 completed dribbles per ninety minutes. But dribbling wasn't enough. Early opponents discovered the way to stop him: kick him. In a Champions League game in 2006, Chelsea's captain John Terry simply dived on top of Messi in the penalty area, pinioning him to the ground under his body. The referee, perhaps confused by the blatancy of the foul, didn't give a penalty. Some Barcelona players suspected Messi was too selfish ever to learn team play. Given his tiny body and unprofessional lifestyle, a long career appeared unlikely. Back then, the most probable outcome for him seemed to be brilliant cameos followed by an early flameout.

Rijkaard was concerned, too. In March 2008, I interviewed him in "the Cave," the head coach's windowless office in the bowels of the Camp Nou. Smoking cigarettes, his long, jeans-clad legs slung over his desk, he looked like the hero of a 1970s movie. Messi at the time was on the sidelines, dealing with yet another muscular injury. Rijkaard said, "He really has to realize that when the match ends, another match starts for him, and that's prevention, taking his rest, taking care of his body. With this recurring injury, he is going to have to learn to live with it, to exclude as much as possible the possibility of a repeat."

Rijkaard went into a critique of Messi's play. "I've seen games where for ninety minutes it looked as if it was one against eleven, and he got a lot of kicks, but we only won 1–0, or drew 0–0, or lost 1–0." He praised Messi for seeking variety in his game—not dribbling every time anymore—but the school report was very much "Has potential but must do better."

When I made the ritual comparison with Maradona, Rijkaard demurred: "We judge Maradona over his whole career. Messi's only twenty. Let's hope he gets fit again, but there is a possibility, that's the development of a player, that he says after two years, 'I've done it all, and now I want this.'" Rijkaard was presumably thinking of Ronaldinho.

With hindsight, Messi was going through a teething problem that is specific to geniuses in any sport. Not all of them get through it. With apologies for the name-dropping, I grasped this when I interviewed Roger Federer on his private jet in 2019. The Swiss is arguably the Messi of tennis, even if his global status is much lower: when the Argentinian joined Facebook in 2011, he overtook Federer's then total of 6.7 million followers within seven hours.[29]

Federer loves football, and when I mentioned Messi, he asked excitedly if I'd met him. Federer himself, he admitted regretfully, had only ever met Messi's parents, at a tennis tournament in Argentina. Then he said:

> Funnily enough, I haven't spoken about Messi nearly enough.
> What I love about Messi probably the most is when he gets the
> ball and is able to turn the body toward the goal, and then he's
> got full vision. Then you know he's going to play a good pass,
> or dribble, or just shoot. There's always three options for him,
> and he's one of the few who's got that.

It's similar for Federer—it has been estimated that he has twelve different forehands. Having such a range of choices, said Federer, "is definitely an advantage, if you get there. The problem when you're younger is knowing to use what when." He explained that life is simpler for a limited player, "who's just very good at doing forehands and backhands across courts, and can do that all day, all night." (The footballing equivalent would be the guy who wins the ball and delivers it to the nearest teammate.) Limited players don't have the problem of choice. Messi does. Federer continued:

> For us [i.e., for multifaceted geniuses] it's more challenging: "Which club shall I take out of the bag for this shot or this pass?" I think it's incredibly exciting, and maybe this is why my love for the game is so big nowadays. Geometry, angles, when to hit which shot, should I serve and volley? Should I stay back? Should I chip and charge? Should I hit big?

Like tennis, football is a game of decisions. When you dribble past someone, Cruyff explained in 1972, "You get the principle of: I've beaten a man, a hole has been created, now I have to do something. Well, what do you do? Do you beat another, or do you pass first? Yes: what do you do?"[30] Guardiola said that if you watched Messi on the ball and pressed the pause button, he always chose the best possible option.[31] Yet Messi took years to get to that point. Between 2005 and 2008, his percentage of through balls, passes into the box, and assists kept rising. After that, he began completing a higher proportion of his dribbles, while slightly reducing their frequency. Looking back, at age thirty-two, he said, "I've learned to read the games better, at which moment and where I have to be effective and decisive."[32]

He learned partly because he happened to have landed up at Barça, the Cruyffian school of the pass. Cruyff's son, Jordi, says, "I think Barcelona and Messi, it was destined. He came to the best club he could have."[33] On Barcelona's first team, Messi encountered players like Ronaldinho, Deco, and Eto'o, who wanted to get the ball from him, and to give it back, communicating through passing. And Messi was willing to learn, because his ambition was not to be a soloist but a winner. Even in training he had to win every exercise. When he didn't, he'd quarrel with teammates, and sometimes kick them. Thierry Henry, who joined Barça from Arsenal in 2007, recounted:

> In training, if the boss doesn't call a foul, or whatever, he used to go, "Oh! That's not a foul? OK," and then he'd get the ball, run past everyone, score. Now you get the ball. He runs after you, gets the ball back, scores, until he gets in a normal state again, and relaxes, and next thing you know you are 3–1 down.[34]

By summer 2008, nearly four years after his debut, Messi had scored just forty-two goals for Barcelona. That summer he turned twenty-one, the age at which Federer won his first Grand Slam, and matured into the world's best footballer. Over the next four seasons, he would add 211 goals and become the club's highest all-time scorer.[35]

IN SUMMER 2008, Barcelona entered the Messi era. The appointment of thirty-seven-year-old Guardiola as head coach was important, but it has been overrated. More significantly, this was the point when Barça adopted its Messi strategy: the club's priority became to please him. In Guardiola's words: "Coaching Barcelona consists principally in making Leo Messi happy."[36] The club staffer Pepe Costa, a former professional player, had already taken on the role of Messi's full-time confidant, body man, and "shadow."[37] The player at this stage still barely spoke. Juanjo Brau, his physiotherapist at Barça, said the key to gaining his confidence was "to respect his space and his silence."[38] But that left the coaching staff trying to divine what was going on under that flowerpot. Guardiola understood that Messi didn't care much who coached him, but the player had to believe at all times that none of Europe's other giant clubs could offer him a better environment. From this point on, Barça was willing to sacrifice any other player and coach in Messi's interest. For the first time, a great footballer was going to remain great at Barcelona.

Awkwardly, step one in the Messi strategy was to sell his hero. Guardiola publicly announced that Ronaldinho had to go, which inevitably suppressed the likely transfer fee. Though Barcelona understood that the Brazilian had become a bad influence, Messi didn't. Soon after Ronaldinho's departure, the boy got into a fight at training with the Mexican Rafael Márquez, whom he suspected of conspiring against the Brazilian. Fortunately, Guardiola and his staff had been raised in the Barcelona tradition of treating players—and especially Masia players—as humans. "Leo," said Guardiola after a training session, as if the two of them were still coach and child in the academy, "if someone doesn't like something, they should say so." In a five-minute conversation, he gave Messi the feeling that Barça would always love him.[39]

Guardiola also delivered a pastoral lecture on clean living.[40] One club official told me that Messi at this point had reached a fork in the road; Guardiola sent him down the right fork. Messi began eating better. An adult athlete in peak physical condition at last, he stopped getting injured. He had always been able to fool defenders. Now he had the power to accelerate away from them afterward. Opponents struggled even to foul him—if they dared. Pep Boade, Barcelona's chief scout at the time, told me that Guardiola had "structured a Messi strategy. If John Terry kicks Messi, the whole team will protect him."

Barça embarked on a deliberate project of pandering to one man. In 2007, it signed the Argentinian defender Gabriel Milito partly because he got on with Messi.[41] A year later, with the Beijing Olympics coming up, Barcelona obtained a court ruling that it had no obligation to release Messi to play for Argentina—only to discover that he had flown to China anyway.[42] What to do? Guardiola phoned to tell him to win gold.[43] Of course, Messi did—alongside Agüero and Ángel Di María and Juan Román Riquelme in a terrifying Argentinian attack that would never be replicated in a senior tournament.

The young Messi communicated chiefly through sulky silences, and Guardiola became an expert in interpreting them. He figured out that Messi always wanted to play the full ninety minutes even when Barça was winning 5–0, in part because the player was ceaselessly pursuing personal scoring records. Messi consciously constructed his lifetime oeuvre from the start. The unspoken agreement—which held until he reached late career—was that he would never be substituted.

Soon after Barça signed Ibrahimović in 2009, Messi conveyed to Guardiola that he didn't want a mammoth Swede blocking his runs into the middle. "Stick the others out wide,"[44] he told the coach. Messi's view of football—which would hardly change over time—was that the coach should pick the best players and not worry too much about tactics.[45]

When Ibrahimović realized that he was doomed, he was outraged, and fair enough: he had scored in all the first five matches of the season. At any other club, a teammate objecting to a top ten signing would have been told to live with it. Ibrahimović berated Guardiola, who in his Catalan way was too nonconfrontational to shout back. Ibrahimović misread the coach's courtesy for deficient masculinity. In fact, the Swede was overestimating his own status. Guardiola said years later, "It's as if the supporting actor wanted to take the main role."[46] Messi had become the Boss Baby.

Barcelona's deference to Messi goes against football's traditions. A club that caters to the desires of a mere footballer offends against the game's hierarchical thinking.

Authoritarians are right to think that player power has its downsides. Sometimes players will abuse it to laze about in training (as in the last two Ronaldinho years) or to get a mate picked. The same tension exists in any workplace: if you give the people on the work floor more power, they might make better decisions, or they might goof off more, or both.

But Barcelona had been shaped by Cruyff, and Cruyff had believed in player power since he was a fifteen-year-old at Ajax ordering veteran internationals about in training. Cruyff argued (even after he became a coach) that if you gave footballers power, you also gave them responsibility. That was particularly true for great footballers, he said. One of his dictums was that whereas an ordinary player is responsible only for his own performance, a great player is responsible for team performance.

That had been the story of Cruyff's own playing career. He found this extra burden so stressful that he coped with it by chain-smoking, but he always accepted it. So did Zinedine Zidane. One of his French teammates describes Zidane in the changing room before the game, quietly pulling on his kit, knowing that he was going to walk onto the field with twenty-one world-class footballers and decide the game. He felt he had to.

So did Messi. He found matches so stressful that he sometimes vomited in the changing-room toilet before kickoff.[47] Guardiola recalled that when Messi lost, "he was angry, even furious but he'd go home without ever complaining about the coach or anything else."[48] If you're the best player, the result is on you. On Barcelona's bad days, Messi would feel it was on him to change the match. To him, every league title felt like a task completed, a duty done.

If a great player is responsible for team performance, he also needs a say over process. If he is allowed to decide that Ibrahimović must go, then the onus is on him to prove the decision right. He "owns" future results. By contrast, if the club ignores his wishes, he has an excuse to shrug and say, "I only work here."

Joan Oliver, then Barça's chief executive, told me in 2009, "You have to, in some sense, build the team for him. But you have to make him conscious that he needs the team. You are offering him the best opportunity in the soccer world. As long as it remains this way, it's hard for him to leave."[49]

Barcelona merged the Cruyffian dogma of player power with a Spanish or Catalan spirit of nonconflictual rubbing along. It handed Messi the keys to the club. Whereas off the field he could be a ghostly presence, on the field he became himself, and there he did speak—rarely, but tellingly. If he told a teammate during a match to shift position or change his passing patterns, obedience was assumed. Oliver said, "He doesn't make explicit gestures, but he is saying to everyone what he expects from them on the field. It's not obvious—it's very subtle."[50]

Even off the field, he gradually began to speak more. One former Barça official told me: "He was very keen on knowing how the negotiations with other players were going. He wanted to know how strong we were going to be for the following year." Occasionally Messi would recommend transfer targets, such as his friends Sergio Agüero or Angel Di María. It's true that he wasn't given a veto over decision-making. There were too many other currents inside the club for that. In 2014, for instance, Barça signed Luis Suárez instead of Agüero. Still, Barça's decision-makers began taking Messi's wishes into account for every player transfer, major tactical choice, and coaching appointment. Often those wishes were made very clear. He has never seen the point of projecting his personality outside the club, but he does inside. Rosell, Barça's president from 2010 to 2014, told me, "He doesn't need to speak. His body language is the strongest I've seen in my life. I've seen him with a look in the locker room that everyone knows whether he agrees or not with a suggestion. And that's it. He is much more clever than people think—or what he transmits."

"And what does he want?" I asked.

"He wants football," replied Rosell, meaning that Messi wanted

Barça to play exactly the way he wanted it to. Cruyff explained, "If you have the possibility to be the best player in every match, you have to be a bit of a dictator, as Messi is, because your prestige is at stake."[51]

Professional football teams usually have a strict hierarchy. Often the oldest players, or the coolest, or the bullies, are at the top, but at the highest level of the game, quality trumps everything, and the best player rules. One of Messi's teammates said, "He's better than you with his right foot, his left foot and his head. He's better at defending and attacking. He's faster. Better at dribbling, and passing." The teammate holds out his hands in wordless disbelief.

"Keeper?" comes the question.

The teammate bursts out laughing: "Watch out if he tries that too!"[52]

What adds force to this encomium is that the teammate saying this is Xavi. Even he and Iniesta accepted that their role was to feed Messi. They forwent their fair share of glory.

Some teammates feared Messi. He once acknowledged, "I'm capable of getting angry about anything, usually stupid things. I heat up quite quickly, even if it's not visible on the field."[53] Real Madrid's former goalkeeper Jerzy Dudek recalled, "Nobody could have imagined from such a quiet, pleasant-looking guy the horrible things he said to Pepe and Sergio Ramos."[54] Referees know him as a serial complainer. Here is Dutch referee Björn Kuipers screaming at him in football English, "Hey, Messi, come on! Show some respect! Messi! Every time you do it! Why you do it? Go now!"[55]

Messi has admitted, "I should have gone to the psychologist, but I never went. Why? I don't know. It's hard for me to take that step, even though I know I need it. Antonela [his wife] has insisted a lot of times that I should go, but I'm someone who keeps everything to myself. I don't share things. I know it would do me good, but I haven't gone."[56]

No coach was allowed to get in his way. In past eras, Michels, Cruyff in 1988, Weisweiler, César Luis Menotti, and Van Gaal had each been greeted at the Camp Nou as a potential messiah. But after Guardiola left in 2012, Barça replaced him with lesser names: first with his assistant Tito Vilanova, who had been Messi's favorite youth coach, and when Vilanova succumbed to throat cancer, with an obscure Argentinian, Gerardo Daniel "Tata" Martino, from Messi's hometown of Rosario and a fellow old boy of Newell's Old Boys. At Barça, the coach was downgraded to a temporary member of Messi's support staff. In 2014, Martino's successor, Luis Enrique, took on Messi in a power struggle. First he tried to substitute him during a game against Eibar, but Messi refused to come off, issuing a thumbs-up from the field to show that all was well. Afterward, Luis Enrique was forced to fib to the media: "Before substitutions I always ask the players what they think." But he still wanted to show who was boss. He disallowed a Messi goal in training, and in January 2015 kept him on the bench till halftime for a game at Real Sociedad, which Barça lost. At this point Xavi, Mascherano, and other players intervened to explain to the coach that there was one rule for Messi and another for everyone else. Luis Enrique surrendered, and five months later Barça had won the treble. The coach had discovered who was boss.

With Argentina, too, Messi has helped pick the team and choose the tactics at least since 2008,[57] though in his early, mute years, his companions Agüero and Di María often had to interpret his wishes. (Similarly, at elementary school, a girl in his class had acted as his spokesperson.)[58] Argentina's coach at the 2014 World Cup, the inexperienced Alejandro Sabella, was appointed precisely for his willingness to obey Messi (though Sabella may not quite have realized this). Fernando Gago and Gonzalo Higuaín were brought into the team during the tournament on Messi's say-so.

Both Argentina and Barcelona molded themselves around what has proved to be Messi's improbably long peak. Federer marveled, "The consistency level . . . scoring his six hundredth goal just now. These are unheard-of numbers, and we see the same thing happening in basketball now, with all these records being broken. People are just more aware of them and I think they push harder, become more professional."

Messi also motivated himself by competing with Ronaldo for the status of world's best player. The French striker Kylian Mbappé told me that the best footballers keep tabs on one another, just as he imagined the best bakers do. He said, "I think Messi has done Ronaldo good, and Ronaldo has done Messi good. For me they are the two best players in history, but I think that one without the other might not have remained the best far ahead of the others for fifteen years. Maybe they would have let themselves go at some point. But to have an equally good player in the rival team of the same league, I think the motivation is at a maximum."

When Mbappé himself was in contention for highest scorer in Europe in the 2018–2019 season, he noticed that Messi kept outscoring him: "I'd score two, he'd score three; I'd score three, he'd score four. It was so crazy that I talked to Ousmane [Dembélé, Mbappé's friend at Barcelona]: 'It's not possible! Is he doing it on purpose? Does he check how many goals I score?'" And Dembélé replied: "Of course he's watching you!" Messi finished the season as Europe's leading scorer with thirty-six goals, three ahead of Mbappé.[59]

In 2008, Ronaldo won his first Ballon d'Or for the world's best footballer, and his agent, Jorge Mendes, hosted a sumptuous buffet. In 2009, Messi won his first, and the family served supermarket pizzas, recalls the delegate from *France Football*, the magazine that organizes the voting.[60] Of the thirteen Ballons d'Or awarded between 2008 and 2021, Messi won seven and Ronaldo five. No player before them had ever won more than three. Sitting beside Ronaldo in Monaco at the draw for the Champions League in 2019, Messi told an interviewer, "It was a beautiful rivalry, especially when he was at Madrid." Ronaldo listened to his words intently, then added: "I was curious, because we've shared this stage for fifteen years, me and him. I don't know if this has ever happened in football. And of course we have a good relationship. We've not had a dinner together yet, but I hope in the future—" and he trailed off, laughing.[61] There's a silly debate about who is better, Messi or Ronaldo. (For what it's worth, Messi is slightly better. They are the world's two best forwards, but Messi is also the world's best playmaker.) The real question, though, as Ronaldo suggests, is how they both remained supreme for longer than any previous great, except perhaps Alfredo Di Stéfano. One answer is that in the decade before they arrived on the scene, football was redesigned to favor the superhero.

The great player used to live like a rock star. He was pursued by groupies. He expected his body to give out by the age of thirty. He didn't make a fortune. And so he lived large. After all, being a genius meant you didn't have to work hard. Ferenc Puskás in the 1950s was fat, George Best in the 1960s an alcoholic, Cruyff chain-smoked, and Maradona took cocaine. The temptations of stardom were magnificent; succumbing was almost the point.

Best after 1968, and Maradona and Pelé for most of their club careers, played with many unremarkable teammates. Maradona at Napoli often received passes behind him (which he would kindly applaud). Both for his club and his country, he learned to play alone.

Few of these men aspired to weekly brilliance. Pelé was forever crossing the planet to play lucrative exhibition games. Maradona turned it on for World Cups but rarely in between. And they all got kicked a lot. In 1966, Pelé limped out of the World Cup. A few years later, before Cruyff joined Barça, Real Madrid's chairman Santiago Bernabéu warned that the Spanish league wouldn't suit the Dutchman, "because they'll break those little legs of his within three weeks."[62] Watching clips of Cruyff playing for Barcelona, it's noticeable that almost every opponent chops or trips or elbows him, or slides in with a two-footed challenge, or at least tries to. In his first match against Granada, his teammates wouldn't let him enter the opposition's penalty area for a corner: "You don't go into the box against these guys."[63]

In 1983, Maradona's spell with Barcelona effectively ended when his ankle was crushed by the defender Andoni Goikoetxea, the "Butcher of Bilbao." "Maradona has not died," Goikoetxea pointed out in mitigation. Sometimes, intimidation took baroque psychological forms. A month before Goikoetxea's assault, Barcelona hosted Nottingham Forest in a preseason friendly. Forest's manager Brian Clough went up to Maradona in the tunnel before the game, announced, "You might be able to play a bit, but I can still grab you by the balls," and proceeded to do just that, recalled Clough's midfielder Steve Hodge.[64]

What transformed the star's lot was TV. Before the 1990s, few matches were televised live. Then Rupert Murdoch and Silvio Berlusconi built TV channels on football. Suddenly clubs became content providers, and stars were premium content. The clubs offered the stars a new deal: we'll pay you fortunes if you'll live like professionals. Messi and Ronaldo accepted the offer.

Football's authorities protected stars by cracking down on fouls and banning the tackle from behind. Messi said in 2005, "In professional football nothing really happens because there are referees. At school was where kicks were real kicks."[65] Once he became recognized as an international treasure, from about 2008, he received extra protection. Even if a referee missed a foul, the culprit still had to worry about being caught on camera. Cruyff noted in retirement, "TV improved the skill level. Now the good players are protected."[66] Imagine what Cruyff himself could have done with that protection.

Perfect, telegenic fields have helped, too. Messi didn't have to navigate the muddy Dutch fields of Cruyff's youth, when simply not falling over was sometimes a feat. And Messi was never going to destroy his knee on a frozen pitch on Boxing Day, as Brian Clough did as a brilliant forward in 1962.

In the TV era, the best players have congregated at a handful of the richest clubs. Messi has spent his entire club career playing with world-class teammates, who enabled him to reach his best. Creativity is a property more of groups than of individuals. Just as John, Paul, George, and Ringo made better music together than later as solo artists, Barcelona had Xavi, Iniesta, and Messi, and from 2014 to 2017, the "MSN" attack of Messi, Suárez, and Neymar. (MSN, characteristically, found their own formation by experimenting in a match, without any apparent intervention from the coach.)[67]

Messi's need for a band became clear during all those tournaments struggling in front of mediocre midfielders and defenders with Argentina. He was unable to imagine the mindset of a player who couldn't see obvious one-twos or execute basic one-touch passes. At the World Cup 2010 I was transfixed by Newcastle United's ungainly winger, Jonás Gutiérrez, who performed a comic impersonation of a right-back for Argentina while often struggling to stay upright. The next World Cup it was center-back Federico Fernández, astute enough to know he had been promoted beyond his competence, so terrified of the ball that the moment he received it, he would try to shove it into the feet of the nearest teammate.

The manager of a leading national team explained to me the difference between the Messi of Barça and the Messi of Argentina. For his club, the manager said, Messi typically received the ball near the opposition's penalty area, after a series of short passes involving multiple players. He then had about five teammates within twenty meters of him, each one drawing away defenders. He could choose between multiple passes, or he could dribble. Often he was in a one-against-one situation, and as Mourinho said, "When Messi has the ball one-on-one, you're dead. There's no way to solve that problem."[68]

Argentina, by contrast, are a team without a system. They rarely manage to win the ball near the opposition's goal, and they give it to

Messi when they can find him rather than when he asks for it. Often that's in midfield, with no teammates near him, as if plan A is for him to re-create Maradona's solo goal against England. Opponents closing in on him know something useful: he'll probably dribble.

Argentina have forced Messi to play like a *pibe*. At the 2014 World Cup, he completed forty-six dribbles, seventeen more than his nearest rival, Holland's Arjen Robben; meanwhile, Messi completed only 242 passes, two fewer than Germany's keeper, Manuel Neuer. But Messi didn't want to be a *pibe* anymore. Whereas Maradona was the individual who wanted to beat the system, Barcelona had socialized Messi into a Cruyffian collective game. With Argentina, his frustrations often spilled over into quarrels with teammates and referees. After the defender Nicolás Burdisso was unable to get the ball to him during a match in 2011, he and Messi had to be separated in the changing room.[69] Cruyff in the 1970s had enjoyed playing for his national team because the standard was higher than at Barça;[70] for Messi it was the other way around.

Only at Barcelona did Messi find the ideal environment for greatness. One afternoon, a woman who lives in Castelldefels drove me past his home, and I realized: the essential underpinning of his routinely brilliant football was a boring life. High up in this unremarkable town, away from the beaches, he had bought the neighbor's house and constructed a compound complete with mini–football field. Palm trees, bougainvillea, and white walls provided privacy. He lived here for years without security cameras or alarms until eventually the club installed some. He later learned to make himself unpredictable to criminals by driving different routes to training in different cars.[71] But even with these precautions, his tranquil home life couldn't have been further from the overheated chaos of Argentina.

His wife, Antonela (whom he met in childhood in Rosario), has helped teach him to distance himself from football once work is done.

He has said that raising three young sons, he feels "destroyed" by evening, and goes to bed early.[72] He has a small circle of friends. His almost perfectly preserved Rosario accent shows his lack of outreach. So does his Cruyffian inability to speak any Catalan, after twenty years in the region. (Messi's children did learn the language, as children of migrants to Catalonia do.) Brau, his physio, said, "His center is his family, which is always with him."[73]

Messi experiences the outside world mostly as a mass of people holding up phones to film him. He has learned to ignore it. Far from the nightlife of Sitges, twenty minutes up the road, he ferried his sons to school, or to their training sessions at Barça's Gamper training complex. In the evening, the family sometimes ate at a secluded table in a local restaurant; the townspeople knew not to bother him.

Piqué, who played with Messi for nearly twenty years, told me, "When you're smaller, football is playing well on the field. When you get older, you see there are many other things, like looking after yourself, sleeping at night. I think that in this sense, Leo has grown a lot."

Messi's routine for fifteen years was to shine in the Camp Nou, and then commute twenty-five minutes home along the almost empty midnight highway. Three days later, he did it again.

BRILLIANCE ON DEMAND can become strangely boring. Whereas Maradona offered the spectacle of the footballer's struggle with the inner man, the greatness of Messi and Ronaldo has come to seem automatic. The Spanish journalist Santiago Segurola said, "Sometimes Maradona was Maradona. Messi is Maradona every day."[74] Years ahead of schedule, Messi completed the transition that Cruyff said the greats usually make at about twenty-four or twenty-five: from "footballer" to "bread footballer,"[75] meaning a professional who knows that he is playing for his team's daily bread and therefore always has to perform.

An "ordinary" great player does well to stay at the top for five years. Messi has remained there for over fifteen. He averaged more than a goal or an assist per game in eleven seasons up to 2019–2020, two more seasons than Ronaldo, calculates the data journalist John Burn-Murdoch, my colleague at the *Financial Times*. For comparison, forwards as great as Robben and Henry managed that four times; Eto'o and Didier Drogba did it twice.[76]

Messi offers a perfectly professional genius, as if Claude Monet had signed a contract to produce masterpieces twice a week and then delivered. But it's worth shaking off our numbness to ask, How does he do it? How do you regularly beat three men and put the ball in the top corner? Trying to answer these questions helps us understand football, because Messi is the supreme real-time analyst of the game. Here, aided by the insights of many knowledgeable people, is my interpretation of how he plays.

With both Barcelona and Argentina, he spends most of every match walking around. In the 2014 World Cup, for instance, he covered less ground per game than any other outfield player except Brazil's center-back Thiago Silva.[77] Seirul·lo remarked, "Every study of Leo shows he runs the least, he sprints the least, he participates the least in the game."[78]

This flies in the face of everything we know about modern football. As Guardiola told his players at Bayern Munich, "If we don't run, we're nothing. If we start asking teammates to send the ball to our feet instead of into the space in front of us, we'll lose much of our excellence."[79]

Yet Messi walks with unique purpose. Watching him on a laptop in James Erskine's eye-opening documentary about the player, *Wonder*, Guardiola comments, "He is walking about—that is what I like the most. He is moving his head, right, left, left, right," and Guardiola flicks his own shaven head from side to side in imitation.[80]

Messi's walks are reconnaissance missions. On the whole, the better the footballer, the more he scans the field, but Messi uses the time that he is exempted from defensive running to scan more than anyone else. He is drawing maps of his next moves. Lieke Martens, a star of Barcelona's women's team who studied him to improve her own decision-making, told me, "Messi knows what he is going to do before he gets the ball."

I learned more from David Sumpter, math professor at Uppsala University in Sweden, author of *Soccermatics*, and adviser to Hammarby football club. We met at a data analytics conference at the Camp Nou. Over beers in one of the stadium cafés afterward, he gave me a Messi tutorial.

Sumpter pointed out something surprising: how often Messi receives the ball unmarked. He's always the main attacking threat on the field, and he's usually walking, so how does he get free when he decides the moment has come to intervene in the action?

Sometimes he simply steps a yard into the right position, giving a teammate an unimpeded diagonal along which to pass to him. As Cruyff always said, there's no point running if the right space is a step away. Sometimes Messi finds space by playing statues, noted Gary Lineker: "It's amazing how many people run away from you if you stop moving."[81] This is what Marcus Rashford of Manchester United was getting at when, at halftime of his first game against Messi, he remarked to a teammate, "He doesn't move, but he's everywhere, because he lets everybody else move."[82] The moment opponents move away from Messi, he demands the ball.

When he does move, he can brake suddenly, more sharply than his markers, in the exact spot where he wants the ball. Often, though, what counts is his second run. When he makes the first run, he isn't yet asking for the ball, but just dragging his opponents out of position, explained Sumpter. Then—like many great forwards—he'll suddenly set off on a second run. Barcelona's players wait to pass to Messi only on the second run; Argentina's players may not have the time on the ball.

Barça aimed to feed him continually, in part just to keep him interested. The club's longtime right-back Dani Alves reminisced, "Pep hates these [vertical] full-back to winger passes because they don't offer progression, but I used to do them with Messi a lot and he'd be annoyed. I told him if Messi doesn't touch the ball every two minutes, he disconnects and we need him connected. He [Pep] agreed."[83]

A good player receives the ball facing the opposition's goal. In fact, for Cruyff that was almost the definition of a good player. But Messi takes correct positioning a step further: he often engineers the situation to receive while his nearest opponent has his back turned to him.

Messi typically receives the ball in the space between the opponent's defense and midfield. He has targeted this zone from the start of his career, though Guardiola's decision in 2009 to play him as a false nine helped orient him toward it. Guardiola rediscovered the innovation of Michels's Ajax: a team without a center-forward.

The false nine has always been particularly confusing to big English center-backs, whose game is winning duels against big center-forwards. The archetypal use of the tactic was the Netherlands' 0–2 victory at Wembley in 1977, when England fielded five specialist center-backs only to find that Cruyff as false nine left them nobody to mark. On the same field in the Manchester United versus Barcelona Champions League final thirty-four years later, United's Rio Ferdinand found himself searching for Messi: "He doesn't even come near you. Me and [Nemanja] Vidić stood on the halfway line at Wembley and just looked at each other and went"—Ferdinand shook his head in bewilderment. "We were standing there thinking, 'I've not even touched anyone.'"[84]

Messi usually changes direction as he receives the ball. He then likes dribbling toward the center-backs, placing them in the dilemma that Cruyff had outlined decades before: if they come toward the dribbler, they leave space in their backs, and if they don't, he can advance.

Messi isn't amazingly fast, but he's as quick with the ball as without it. Often he'll cut inside, suddenly brake so that his marker has to as well, then lose him with an acceleration. Like Cruyff, he also possesses a second acceleration. And like Cruyff, he sees at a glance which foot a defender has planted on the ground, and goes past him on that side. He somehow manages to keep scanning even while on the ball. "He seems to have no blindside," remarked Lineker.[85] Messi is hyperefficient: there's never an excess feint, or a Neymarian trick to humiliate a defender.

Crucially, Messi takes short steps, even relative to his height. That allows him to keep touching the ball, and with each touch, he can do something new. Cruyff remarked, "Ronaldo has two ball contacts per second. But in the same period, Messi touches the ball three times. . . . His changes of tempo and of position are faster."[86] Moreover, Messi's feet touch the ground three times in the stretch of time that some of his markers touch it once. Bigger players spend more time running with both feet off the ground—and someone who is entirely off the ground cannot change direction, explained Seirul·lo.[87] Messi almost always can. That's how he manages to evade defenders like a dog eluding policemen in an old silent movie. In Erskine's documentary, Ferdinand flails his arm through thin air: "When you did get close to him, he's that small and quick he was going underneath." There was nobody "to rough up."[88]

The statistical website FiveThirtyEight calculated in 2015 that Messi's dribbles beat defenders only 55 percent of the time—but that was the best success rate of any regular dribbler in football.[89] Even when he is tackled, and the ball spins loose, he usually regains his balance more quickly than his markers and wins the "second ball."

Sumpter reads Messi's dribbles as a kind of geometry. He has a favorite video of Messi cutting through Athletic Bilbao's defense in 2015. Early in the run, Messi is surrounded on the right touchline by three defenders. He brakes and takes one step inside, leaving the defenders forming a perfect triangle around him. Sumpter explains, "Suddenly . . . each of the players around him are maximally distant from him. Simple mathematical calculation: the greater distance you have from your opposition, the more space, the more time you have." Messi then beats the central opponent, leaving a broken triangle in his wake.

Sumpter goes on, "Most people can't think in more than four dimensions. Messi can think in a few more dimensions than any other player can: twenty-two times two, forty-four, plus the spatial dimensions—forty-eight dimensions." I don't pretend to understand Sumpter's reasoning here, but the point is that Messi is an unmatched interpreter of Cruyffian space.

There is something curiously predictable about Messi's game. We usually know where he is heading. He isn't thinking, "Where is the easiest place for me to receive this ball?" or "How can I get past these defenders?" Instead, he's looking farther ahead: "Where do I want to end up?" His favorite destination is the most valuable space on the field, a space that he visits rather than inhabits: the semicircle on the edge of the opposition's penalty area. When he passes—almost always to his left—he's usually trying to put a teammate in that space. The main beneficiary over the years was Suárez.

"I'm not a typical scorer," Messi has said. "I like to come from deep, get the ball and create. I also like to score goals, but I don't live for that."[90] Sumpter told me that Agüero, and perhaps Harry Kane and Mo Salah, were arguably equally good finishers as Messi, but they didn't repeatedly get into the shooting positions that he did.

I have couched all this in coldly analytical terms, but let's pause for a moment and think of what Messi does for global happiness. To paraphrase Cruyff's biographer, Scheepmaker, he has made our lives richer than they would have been without him. We live in the age of Messi, and it often feels like the best way to spend this time is to watch him. A friend who has struggled with his mental health told me that for years he tried to catch almost every match Messi played for Barcelona: "For me, watching him has something of a therapeutic quality. He's basically an accessible genius, on a weekly basis at a relatively low cost of a yearly subscription."

Messi can even have that effect on opponents during a game. The French striker Djibril Cissé recalled, "I was surprised to find myself watching him, leaving the match and becoming a spectator."[91]

Messi is extraordinary even when playing for his country. If the Messi of Argentina sometimes seems disappointing, that's because we compare him with the Messi of Barça and with the Maradona of the World Cup 1986. In fact, according to the sports statistician Benjamin Morris, the Barcelona Messi and the Argentina Messi have been probably "the two best players in the world."[92] Remember that between 2007 and 2016, Messi reached four finals with Argentina, three in the Copa América and the World Cup final of 2014. He lost them all, but three of them only by the finest of margins. Had Higuaín scored when one-on-one against Neuer early in the first half in the Maracanã in 2014, Messi might now be celebrated at home as a more reliable Maradona, a national savior who turned some unprepossessing teammates into world champions. Argentina lost that game to Mario Götze's goal in extra time, and the Copa América finals of 2015 and 2016 to penalty shoot-outs, both times against Chile. The best explanation for such narrow defeats is probably randomness.

These results don't diminish Messi's greatness. They only diminish his legend. They have also caused him a pain that is hard to gauge. Speaking of Iniesta's winning goal for Spain in the World Cup final of 2010, he once joked, "How lucky Andrés is that he gets to score those goals, at the most crucial moments!"[93] Certainly in Argentina, Messi will never mean as much as Maradona, who lived most of his life there, who beat England four years after the Falklands War, who won a World Cup, who expressed his baroque personality, and who came first. Maradona himself shared the national disdain for Messi. At a publicity event in Paris in 2016, microphones caught his private conversation with Pelé:

PELÉ: Diego?

MARADONA (leaning in, his belly spilling over his tracksuit): Yes?

PELÉ: Do you know Messi personally?

MARADONA: Yes, but . . .

PELÉ: Is he a good person?

MARADONA: Yes, he's a good guy but he has no personality. He doesn't have the personality to be a leader.

PELÉ: Ah, I understand. In our day there were lots of leaders.

MARADONA: Exactly! Many more.[94]

Their claim is not convincing. Messi at Barça became an umbrella for the whole organization. Before him, the club frequently existed in an eternal present where the next match was the next crisis. From 2005 until 2019, he made running Barça relatively easy. When you win the Champions League three times in six years (two more than in the previous half century), anxiety and faction fighting abate. White handkerchiefs disappeared from the Camp Nou. No Barça head coach was sacked during a season from 2003 until January 2020.

Day to day in those years, Messi's presence removed football's usual drama. The ambiance in the Camp Nou was more opera performance than sporting contest. New signings got time to bed in, because nobody needed them to be the messiah. The morning after the first team beats Real Madrid 2–6, every club employee walks into the office relaxed and smiling.

Messi made dubious boardroom decisions look good. Soriano argues that Barça more than doubled its revenues during his time as chief executive from 2003 to 2008 "because we were investing in the product we were offering—the football team—and we were managing the club with the highest degree of professionalism and the best available management tools." Building "a champion team . . . has absolutely nothing whatsoever to do with luck," he insists.[95] Yet I suspect it had something to do with Messi.

Nor until 2020 did the club need to worry much about losing him. "Messi has Barça in his blood, and he will never leave," Barça's president Bartomeu said once.[96] Hardly any other club even summoned the gumption to bid for him. Manchester City did in 2008, but that was an accident, after a Thai senior executive with a heavy accent said (while on a chaise longue having a massage during a transfer panic), "Very messy, messy, it's getting messy," and somebody in club offices misinterpreted this as "We've got to get Messi." An offer of £70 million was made. Barcelona reportedly rang back to ask if it was real.[97]

Messi himself seems to have seriously considered a transfer only once in those years, in 2013–2014, when his troubles with Spain's tax authorities tempted him to leave. In June 2013, Iñigo Juárez, the lawyer tasked with Messi's affairs, emailed Jorge Messi to say that he had met with representatives of Real Madrid who were willing to buy the player for €250 million. Madrid had even offered to enlist Spain's then prime minister, Mariano Rajoy, to help make the tax problem go away. Juárez wrote: "They tell me that they would exert pressure on Rajoy to reach a solution for your son that is as advantageous as possible."[98]

Madrid was making a no-lose offer: even if Messi turned it down, as expected, a bid from the archrivals would help him gouge an even larger chunk out of Barça's wage budget. In May 2014, Barcelona duly gave him another big salary raise,[99] one of nine he received between 2005 and 2020.[100] The clause in his contract allowing him to leave without a transfer fee at the end of each season encouraged the club to keep him happy.

The tax affair left Messi and his father with criminal records, after a Spanish court fined them for tax evasion in 2016 and sentenced them to twenty-one months in prison. Barça compensated Messi for the fine, and the men weren't made to serve the time, as it was their first offense. Yet it was a warning signal that Messi's business affairs were amateurishly run.

The sentence hardly affected his reputation. Few football fans care about Messi's off-field doings. On the field, he is the Ronaldinho who just got better. In fact, he has become unimaginably good. England's cricket selector Ed Smith argued in his book *What Sport Tells Us About Life* (2008) that the most dominant player in any sport in history was the Australian cricketer Don Bradman. From 1928 to 1948, "the Don" scored an average of 99.94 runs per inning in Test cricket. As of 2021, the next-highest Test batting average in history of anyone who had played more than twenty Test matches was Australia's Steve Smith with 61.80. Bradman existed in a universe apart from everyone else.

"There will never be another Bradman," wrote Ed Smith in 2008. He argued that it was impossible to tower that far over everyone else in any modern sport simply because the general standard of opposition had improved. Across sports, weaker opponents had gained in competence. They had learned to defend, and they had more information on their star opponents (from videos, data analyses, scouting trips, etc.). So in our more professional era, the most gifted still ended up on top, but no longer by huge margins, explained Smith.

There's ample evidence for his theory. In baseball, for instance, no hitter has averaged .400 in a season (meaning getting four hits in every ten at-bats) since Ted Williams in 1941. In soccer, better defending by weak teams has reduced the number of goals over time. The gap between the greats and everyone else has shrunk.

And yet we have Messi. It's impossible to make a statistical comparison between a great cricketer and a great footballer, but in John Burn-Murdoch's chart of the best goal scorers since the 1970s, one man does exist in a separate universe from everyone else:

One of these things is not like the others

Goalscoring rates with and without penalties, all senior competitions,
top 194 goalscorers in elite football since the 1970s*

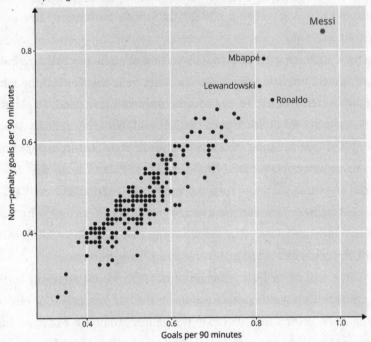

*Players with at least 50 appearances in the English, Spanish, German, Italian, or French top tiers
Source: Analysis of data from worldfootball.net, updated December 3, 2020
Credit: John Burn-Murdoch, *Financial Times*

Messi is another Bradman. There's nobody else like him. Ian Graham, Liverpool FC's director of research, once remarked that a top footballer earns his team five more points a season than an average player in the same position. "And if I'm Barcelona," added Graham, "there is one player over there"—he pointed far off to his right—"adding many, many more than five points."

Mbappé, in second place in Burn-Murdoch's chart, widely regarded as the world's best player of his generation, told me he knew he wasn't as good as Messi and Ronaldo. "It's not only me who knows that," he said, laughing. "Everyone knows it. If you tell yourself that you'll do better than them, it's beyond ego or determination—it's lack of awareness. Those players are incomparable. They have broken all laws of statistics."

No wonder Barça gave Messi the keys to the club. For fifteen years, the choice paid off, keeping him involved and on board. On the downside, though, his presence allowed the organization to get lazy. With him on the field, Barça didn't need to think as hard.

VIII

HIGH STYLE, 2008–2012

I n 2012, Guardiola resigned from Barça, exhausted, after four years as coach of the best football team that many of us have ever seen. A few months later, at a corporate conference in Mexico, he was asked to reveal his team's secret. He replied, "There's only one: the players loved playing football. . . . Some had won everything, but they knew that if they lost that passion another player would take their place."[1]

Most professional players don't love playing football. They experience it as a stressful job. Every match, they are walking on tiptoe: it's not much fun battling relegation, being dropped, threatened by fans, criticized or ignored by the media, wondering how long you can eke out your career, and taking the field simply hoping not to be humiliated by Iniesta or Messi. Mehdi Lacen, who regularly played against Barcelona for smaller Spanish clubs, said his big fear was that a video of Messi putting the ball between his legs would trend on Twitter for a fortnight.[2]

But it is fun to be Iniesta or Messi, or to play with them.

Even while Guardiola's players were having the experience, many of them realized it was the best football they'd ever play. Long after that team had dissolved, it remained in their heads. Henry recalled that often when the referee blew the final whistle, he'd feel surprised and disappointed: "Already? I'm enjoying this."[3] Xavi said he felt "absolute happiness" being the "protagonist," touching the ball 120 times a game.[4] Abidal would tell himself on the field during a match, "How beautiful football is! It's not easy, but it's beautiful."[5] The players' pleasure helped them to keep going, to remain supreme for longer than almost any other modern team. Jürgen Klopp, who during that period was coaching Borussia Dortmund, commented, "They celebrate every goal as if they had never scored before."[6]

Yet Guardiola's reply in Mexico was a deflection. In fact, his team had many secrets, including a number of his own invention. The role of the coach is usually exaggerated in football talk, but Guardiola is one of the rare exceptions, a coach who does make a difference. At Barça he inherited great players, and then helped turn them into a great team. For four seasons, they won everything. Even more than Cruyff's own Dream Team, Guardiola's side was the ultimate expression of Cruyffism. What were the secrets? How did that team become so good?

OVER LUNCH IN THE Camp Nou in March 2008, a Barça director told me she hoped the club would choose thirty-seven-year-old Pep Guardiola as its next head coach. "Really?" I asked, surprised. The man in charge of Barça B hadn't yet coached a minute of senior football. She replied, "We made Victor Valdés goalkeeper when he wasn't the best in the world, and he learned from experience. We should give Catalans a chance." I wrote this off as a nationalist fantasy. Guardiola might become Barcelona's head coach one day, but not as his first job, I thought.

Few big clubs would even have contemplated the appointment. But people at Barça get to know each other well over the decades, and President Laporta, Cruyff, the board member Evarist Murtra, and the then director of football Begiristain had clocked Guardiola as special.

Nonetheless, the obvious candidate to replace Rijkaard in 2008 was the world's winningest coach of the time. Mourinho, who had recently left Chelsea, had the additional benefit of being a Barça old boy. He was eager to coach the most gifted team in football. Some of Barça's decision-makers were eager to merge their club's global brand with his. Mourinho's agent, Jorge Mendes, lobbied Barça officials. At a secret job interview in Lisbon, Mourinho delivered a superb presentation.[7] After Guardiola's own job interview, he asked the director, Marc Ingla, "Why don't you hire Mourinho? It would be easier for you."[8]

Almost anybody in 2008 would have bet on the Portuguese to win more trophies than Guardiola. The problem was that he wouldn't have won the Barça way. Club officials had drawn up a nine-point document on the criteria the new coach had to meet. One section, about the coach's dealings with the media, read:

- He must act cautiously at all times
- Respect opponents, referees, and other institutions in general—fair play[9]

Mourinho was too vulgar to represent the Catalan merchants' club. Nor did his teams play Cruyffian football. Xavier Sala-i-Martin, the Columbia University economist who was then president of Barça's Economic Committee, emailed me later that "this principle guided us when, against ALL RECOMMENDATIONS, we offered the coaching job to Pep Guardiola when everyone recommended Mourinho."[10] After Mourinho found out, he told Laporta that Barcelona had made a terrible mistake.[11]

The crowning of Guardiola was the archetypal Barça moment, a tableau of the club as family: Laporta offered him the job on a visit to a local maternity ward, where Guardiola's daughter had just been born. Like most family scenes, it was less idyllic than it looked: Guardiola had backed one of Laporta's rivals in the 2003 presidential elections. They remained family regardless.

In football terms, Guardiola is Cruyff's son, raised inside the cathedral that Cruyff built. He has had many other influences besides: Guardiola calls himself a "thief of ideas," and will steal them from anyone of any status or none. But his basic ideology has always remained *el cruyffismo*: play one-touch passes in the opponents' half, attack, press, obsess over space, and die with your own ideas. In his first season as coach, at Barça B, he regularly dropped by Cruyff's mansion for beer and advice. After he began coaching the first team, he kept dropping by, now mostly just to show his gratitude.[12]

Guardiola said, during his tenure, "I am the coach of Barça, but of the Barça that Cruyff left behind."[13] Yet he also understood that football progressed week by week. Coaches had professionalized since Cruyff's day, learned more tactics, and become "protagonists," said Eusebio Sacristán, who played with Guardiola on Cruyff's Dream Team. Bits of Cruyff's cathedral had been jerry-built. Guardiola wanted to renovate them.

He always underplayed the coach's role. He once compared himself to a caddy, handing players the right clubs. There was some truth to this. However, César Luis Menotti, former manager of Barcelona and Argentina, snorted, "He says he has good players, but only imbeciles believe that."

So why did Guardiola keep saying it? Menotti replied, "What's he going to say? 'I am the best'? But look where Piqué was before Guardiola, where Pedro was, where Busquets was. Even Iniesta wasn't a starter." Menotti said Guardiola was "one of the few coaches in the world who opens the changing-room door, says, 'Buenas tardes,' and everyone knows how they are supposed to play."[14]

ON JUNE 29, 2008, the evening before Guardiola officially started his new job, a thrilling Spanish passing side featuring four Masia old boys beat Germany 1–0 in Vienna to become European champions. Luis Aragonés, coach of "La Roja" ("the Reds"), had decided to pick all the little ball-playing midfielders that Barcelona's academy and its Spanish imitators kept producing. "I told the players that we had to drop the *furia*, because we were best at just playing good football," Aragonés reminisced in 2013, three months before he died. Finally, Spain had found itself a style, called "Tiki-taka," or "El toque," "the touch."

Catalan fans had historically snubbed the Spanish national team. Spain hardly ever plays matches in Catalonia, for fear of a hostile reception: its last game in the Camp Nou was in 1987. For Euro 2008, Barcelona's town hall refused to set up big screens to show the final against Germany. Yet after the game, cheering locals filled the streets, many of them waving Spanish flags. Polls showed that most people in the city had supported La Roja. The day after the victory, Xavi appeared before a packed square in Barcelona shouting, "¡Viva España!"

That didn't mean he or the fans were rejecting their Catalan identities. Rather, like most Catalans, they felt Catalan and Spanish at once. Here was a new sort of blended Spanish nationalism, one that Franco wouldn't have understood.[15]

Spaniards at the time had a lot to feel nationalistic about. They had been watching TV in delighted bafflement since June 2005, when the nineteen-year-old Rafael Nadal won the French Open tennis title, then reached into the stands with his sweaty hands to grab King Juan Carlos. Nadal, like Xavi, spoke Catalan but identified with the Spanish federal state. Next the Spanish Formula One driver Fernando Alonso and Spain's basketball team became world champions. Between 2006 and 2009, Spanish cyclists won every Tour de France.

Guardiola watched it all in fascination. Like Cruyff, he sought inspiration in other sports. His own right-hand man, Manuel Estiarte, had been "the Maradona of water polo," and Guardiola as a young footballer had occasionally trained with Barça's handball team, building up his body on Seirul·lo's orders.

Guardiola knew that many sports were ahead of football in tactics and training methods. The Camp Nou was a good place to steal their ideas. Once Guardiola had taken office, all Barça's main sports teams were coached by Catalans: the futsal team by Marc Carmona, roller hockey by Ferran Pujalte, basketball by Xavi Pascual, and handball by another Xavi Pascual (splendidly, they really do have the same name). All five teams used the methods of Seirul·lo, "El Druida": training with the ball, communicating through passes, and encouraging players to make their own decisions. The five Catalans began to meet regularly for therapeutic meals, to discuss the problems that were common to all coaches—including issues peculiar to Barça, such as how to play off the director who oversees your sport against the executive who oversees your sport.

Carmona, the futsal coach, told me, "Pep is a very curious person. He wants to know how other people are working. We would talk for hours. I think we all learned a lot, but Pep asked the questions: 'How do you do this? How do you do that?' Pep was quite innovative on corners, for instance, bringing in blocking, which is common in basketball, handball, and futsal." It's true that Guardiola's Barça was one of the first football teams to use organized blocking in dead-ball situations—stopping opponents from reaching the player designated to receive the ball.

Inevitably, Guardiola chose Seirul·lo, his old mentor, as his physical coach. Seirul·lo was "a physical trainer who doesn't believe in physical training," wrote French journalist Thibaud Leplat. The old man rejected football's faith in grueling physical exercise: wind sprints and forest runs as sacrifices to appease the gods and fans. He didn't let players run for more than three minutes at a time, and then only in preseason training. Any physical exercise was made sociable: a player might have to try to sprint away while being held around the waist by a teammate.[16] In training, Seirul·lo told me, "98.93 percent of the time, we are looking for ways to pass the ball."

He believed that since football was high-speed decision-making plus refined foot skills in a tiny space, that was what players needed to practice. He called it "football preparation," as opposed to "physical preparation." Guardiola reportedly clipped this dialogue between El Druida and Argentinian coach Ángel Cappa out of *Marca* newspaper in 2007:

Cappa: I remember one day Diego Maradona and I were watching a Michael Jordan game. I said, "What a great player that Jordan is, don't you think, Diego?" and he replied, "Yes, he's great, I admire him too, but never forget that that guy plays with his hands, hey?"

Seirul·lo: That's the whole difficulty of football: the feet. That brings with it lots of obligations of motor function that also complicate the athlete's interpersonal relationships. Often players say to me, "Paco, why don't we ever train speed?" and I reply that we do that all day, because that's football: speed, acceleration. You never run in a vacuum. You run to adapt to the opponent or the ball. Football consists of playing the ball at the necessary speed and in the direction you want to.[17]

Under Seirul·lo and Guardiola, Barcelona's players trained for football by playing football.

In short, Guardiola started his job with a Cruyffian Mark 2 style handed to him by Spain's Aragonés, with a Cruyffian philosopher by his side and surrounded by ideas from other sports. The other piece of the backdrop was the global financial crisis: on September 15, 2008, two days after Guardiola's first home match on Barça's bench, the American bank Lehman Brothers collapsed. By early 2009, one Spaniard in six was unemployed. Guardiola often urged his players to think of the fan who didn't have enough to eat yet had spent €35 to watch them play.[18]

Piqué told me during the crisis years, "People always think that footballers live in a bubble, that we're disconnected from what happens outside. But people should realize that we have siblings, relatives, friends who are going through this crisis. Obviously, however much I try to put myself in the skin of a person who is suffering, I'll never suffer like he does. But we do know where we are and what is happening." Even more than previous Barcelona teams, Guardiola's felt it had a moral mission. As if to make this explicit, they played for most of his era with UNICEF on their chests.

Rijkaard had left behind a wonderful team that had gone off the rails. Guardiola sold the chief troublemakers Ronaldinho and Deco, and planned to ditch Samuel Eto'o, too, but after Eto'o played a brilliant preseason, Barça's captains persuaded Guardiola to keep him.[19]

Discarding two great players was a brave move by a rookie coach. So was starting young Pedro in place of Thierry Henry. Guardiola was handing the *entorno* all the arguments it needed if results went wrong. But he wanted to die with his own ideas.

IT LOOKED AT FIRST AS if he would die with them. Barça opened the season with a defeat at Numancia, then a home draw against Racing

Santander. Guardiola wasn't too worried. He had the gift of evaluating his team's process, not the results. Xavi Pascual (the handball one) told me, "You can play the right way and lose, and sometimes it's the opposite: you won a game and the process is a disaster." Iniesta reinforced Guardiola's confidence, popping into his basement office to tell him not to change a thing.[20] From their next twenty-one matches, Barça took sixty-one points.

Guardiola subjected his players to an unheard-of discipline. Rijkaard had been an adult who treated his players as adults. When I'd asked the Dutchman why he didn't hold training camps before games to prevent certain players from partying, he said, "You do count on the integrity and the professionalism of the group, of sports people." Guardiola didn't count on anybody's integrity. Barça's left-back Eric Abidal marveled to Leplat, the journalist, "He has everyone's home numbers, sets lots of rules about wearing club polo shirts, not being late to training, being at home at midnight on weekdays, etc. We all signed a document that we took home."

Sometimes Guardiola would tell a player during a team meal, "Stand up and explain why you have to pay a fine." "What fine?" the player would ask, and Guardiola would tell him, in front of everybody, "On such-and-such day, you were in such-and-such a place at such-and-such a time."[21]

At this most fanatical stage of his coaching career, Guardiola tried to micromanage the players' social dynamics. Desperate to stamp out the cliques that had plagued Rijkaard's squad, he banned Abidal and Henry from speaking French to each other.[22]

On-field discipline was just as strict. Each player had to stay in his zone and wait till the ball found him, instead of disorganizing the team by going to find it. In one early game at Sporting Lisbon, Henry, who had played well and scored, was substituted for breaking the rule.[23]

After Cesc Fàbregas rejoined his home club from Arsenal in 2011, he remarked:

> Barça has a very specific system and everyone has to adjust to it. Everything has been studied down to the last millimeter. In my first matches I really had to adjust. I was so used to Arsenal, where I could roam around the whole pitch without worrying about anything. Here it's really very different. Everyone has his own position and you can never lose it from sight. I had to go back to my youth days at Barça to master the basic principles again.[24]

Yet for all Guardiola's rigor, Barça in his era remained a friendly workplace. Several of his players had known each other since the dormitories of the Masia. The club's very style of play—"talking" to each other through passes—enhanced their intimacy. Xavi, in a public message to Iniesta, said he loved "speaking to you in a footballing way, without speaking to you."[25] Sociability is part of the point of Barça's football, Seirul·lo told me. "That's why we pass the ball a lot," he said, "so that all the players are involved." Eamon Dunphy, in *Only a Game?* in 1976, put it even higher:

> If you are just knocking a ball between you, on a training ground, a relationship develops between you. It's a form of expression—you are communicating as much as if you are making love to somebody. If you take two players who work together in midfield, say, they will know each other through football as intimately as two lovers. That would apply to Giles and Bremner, for example. It's a very close relationship you build up when you are resolving problems together, trying to

create situations together. It's an unspoken relationship, but your movements speak, your game speaks. The kind of ball you give each other, the kind of passes you give each other, the kind of situations you set up together, speak for you. You don't necessarily become closer in a social sense, but you develop a close unspoken understanding.[26]

Imagine the emotional charge of doing that together for a decade or more, from adolescence onward, better than anyone else on earth.

Guardiola kept his squad small, to minimize the number of second-raters and discontented reserves, and to preserve harmony. (Cruyff had always been suspicious of harmony.) The only player distinctly short of world-class was the reserve goalkeeper José Manuel Pinto, who survived at Barça from 2008 to 2014 largely because he was close to Messi.

Support staffers such as kitmen and physios were treated as full squad members. They came to the team barbecues that Abidal hosted, where everyone could chat and joke in peace. (In hotels before away games, the waiters were always listening in.)[27]

Piqué lightened the mood. The Catalan merchant had returned home in 2008, aged twenty-one, after four years at Manchester United. With his beard, his loose-limbed lope, and his unhurriedness on the ball, he looked like a chill hipster enjoying a Sunday kick-around in the park. He aimed to play "with a smile," the way his hero Magic Johnson had played basketball.

At ease in his ancestral habitat, Piqué was a noisy presence from the start. He had brought back from United the often infantile humor of an English changing room. He'd take the battery out of Messi's phone, and Messi, a born innocent, wouldn't suspect foul play. Piqué and his partner at center-back, Carles Puyol, had in-match conversations that went like this:

PUYOL: Geri, Geri, Geri!

PIQUÉ: What?

PUYOL: Nothing. I just wanted to make sure you were concentrating.

Guardiola suspected Piqué of gaining weight and taking less care of himself after meeting Shakira, of sometimes coasting in games against small clubs. But Piqué helped his teammates pass the endless hours they spent together. He brought emotional balance to a changing room in which the coach and most of the players were *"obsesivos."*[28]

PEP'S PLAYBOOK

Daily training under Guardiola and Seirul·lo was intense—mentally more than physically. As in Cruyff's Dream Team, the best player in the rondos was the coach, even in his late thirties with a bad back.[29] In training, remarked Henry, "if the ball doesn't stay *by* your foot, it's gone."[30] Seirul·lo's disdain for workouts without the ball meant Barça trained a good ten minutes less each day than other big clubs.[31] In the long term, that helped keep the squad fresh.

Guardiola was the first Barça coach to bar journalists from the training ground;[32] they haven't returned since. Out of the world's sight, he trained his men in a set of rules that would give Cruyffism a new rigor. Cruyff had prioritized attacking: "I prefer to win 5–4 than 1–0."[33] Guardiola wanted to win 5–0. Though he talked about attack, he was equally obsessed with defense. He added buttresses to Cruyff's cathedral.

Watching Guardiola's Barça, you saw what looked like joyous spontaneity. Often it was genuine, but the players were also as drilled as an American gridiron football team. They knew their roles so well that unlike Cruyff's 1970s Ajax, they could play in silence. When Kelvin Wilson faced them with Celtic, he noticed, "They don't tell each other where and when they want the ball. They just know."[34]

Jorge Valdano said, "Cruyff invented the Barça formula, but it took Guardiola to put a method behind the formula."[35]

Here are some of the rules in Guardiola's playbook:[36]

- **The fifteen-pass rule.** In basketball the attacking and defensive phases are distinct: at any given moment, one team is attacking while the other masses in front of its basket to defend. But football has no clear divide between defense and attack. An opponent can appear in your back at any moment—"with bad intentions," jokes Seirul·lo. Attack can change into defense in a second. So the ideal attack simultaneously builds your team's defense. Guardiola devised it: the fifteen-pass buildup. Every time his team had the ball, he insisted they complete at least fifteen passes before trying to score.

  Guardiola called the method *salir en corto*, "coming out with short passes." His players would send the ball up and down and right and left like men filling in a crossword puzzle. While they advanced in compact formation down the field, reaching their pass quota, they were planning three seconds ahead: building their defense ready for the moment when they would lose possession. They always aimed to outnumber their opponents around the ball, so that when they lost it, they could win it back fast.

  Even Cruyff sometimes got bored watching the endless buildup, but he appreciated it. "Do you know how Barcelona win the ball back so quickly?" he asked. "It's because they don't have to run back more than ten meters, because they never pass the ball more than ten meters."

- **Possession is nine-tenths of the game.** For Guardiola, possession was an end in itself. His Barcelona aimed to have the ball about two-thirds of the game. In the 2011–2012 league season, their possession quotient peaked at more than 72 percent.

  The logic was twofold. First, in Cruyff's dictum: "There is only one ball. If we have it, the other team can't score." Guardiola's team, short on good tacklers, had to defend with the ball. Often, after taking the lead, they'd kill the game with endless rondos.

  Second, if Barça kept the ball, their opponents would grow exhausted and lose their structure chasing around after passes, especially as Barcelona rarely gave them a breather by letting the ball go into touch. Effective playing time—the number of minutes the ball was in play—was exceptionally long in their games. Bayer Leverkusen's coach Robin Dutt marveled after one defeat, "By the time you finally have the ball, the whole team already has a pulse-rate of 200."[37] That also made it harder to ward off Barcelona's next wave of pressing. And possession was a psychological weapon: it sapped the other team's optimism, especially if they had just managed to score.

  The saying inside Barça was that there were two kinds of teams: those that organized themselves around the ball, and those that disorganized themselves chasing it.

- **Break the opponents' lines.** Opponents' lines were like trip wire alarms that had to be avoided. Guardiola's players freed themselves to receive the ball by positioning themselves "between the lines." Messi, for instance, typically targeted the spot between the opposition center-backs and the defensive midfielder.

  The best passes beat an opponent's line: think of Piqué sliding the ball past the opposing strikers to Busquets, or Xavi dropping it behind the opposing center-backs for Pedro to run on to.

- **Overload the center.** Where Cruyff had loved wing play, Guardiola prioritized the center of the field, the quickest route to goal. Data analytics confirms the middle is the most valuable zone in football, says David Sumpter, the math professor. Messi knows this instinctively, which is why he almost never passes down his right wing.

  Guardiola said he learned from watching Iniesta "the importance of attacking the center-backs." He added, "No one does it. But watch and you see it. If the central defender has to step out, everything opens up; the whole defense becomes disorganized and spaces appear that weren't there before."[38] Messi, Iniesta, and Xavi—all three of them 1950s inside forwards in spirit—gave Barça control of the middle.

  Barça's wingers were spectators by comparison. Their job was to stick to the touchlines, keeping the field wide. They weren't supposed to get the ball until the attack had reached the opposition penalty area and they were freed to cut inside.

  When Guardiola later coached Bayern Munich and Manchester City, he often pushed his fullbacks into central midfield. Most other coaches, he remarked, "want most of their men on the outside. I'm not saying my way is better. It's just my way."[39] Such was his influence that the focus on the center would soon become the way of many more coaches.

- **The four-second (or five-second) rule.** Cruyff's teams had pressed in a fairly spontaneous, unstructured way (and Romário never bothered). Guardiola's team pressed on schedule. Perhaps no team in football intervened earlier in the opposition's buildup.[40] The moment Barça lost the ball, they spent four seconds hunting as a pack to win it back again. They lost the ball seldom enough for these exhausting efforts to be rare. And the four-second push saved them having to track back fifty yards.

Every player in Guardiola's team was expected to do his pressing duty. Klopp remarked, "I think Lionel Messi is the one who wins the ball back the most when he loses possession. . . . The players press like there's no tomorrow, as if the most enjoyable thing about football is when the other team has the ball. . . . The best example that I've ever seen in football."[41]

Like the fifteen-pass rule, the four-second rule had a simple enough title that Guardiola could remind his players of it in an instant during a halftime talk, or even with a scream from the bench.

The thinking behind the four-second rule was that losing the ball had given Barça an opportunity. The opposing player who had just won possession was vulnerable. In order to make his tackle or interception, he had taken his eye off the panorama of the field and exerted himself. Now he needed two or three seconds to regain vision and energy. Barça aimed to rob him before he could pass to a better-placed teammate.

If Barça could keep winning the ball back fast, the opposition would grow frustrated—and frustration is a difficult emotion to handle in a football match. Seirul·lo believed that a team stopped running in a match not so much because it grew tired, but because it became despondent.[42]

If the opposition still had the ball after four seconds, and was building a dangerous attack, Barça often stopped the game with a foul. Otherwise, they would retreat, set up a ten-man wall, and tell their opponents, in effect, "Try getting through this." The distance between the front man in the wall (typically Messi) and their last defender (Piqué, say) was only twenty-five to thirty yards. Few opponents could pass their way through such a compact maze.

Meanwhile, Barça were giving themselves time to recover from their four seconds of maximum exertion. This rule was built on Seirul·lian physiology.

- **Pressing cues.** Once Barcelona had built their wall, they awaited prearranged cues to start pressing again. One prompt was when an opponent miscontrolled a ball. If the ball bounced off his foot, he had to look down to locate it, losing his view of the field. Barcelona would instantly hound him.

  Another cue was if the opposing player on the ball turned toward his own goal. Now he could no longer pass forward. Barça's players pressed him, forcing him to pass back, and so they gained territory.

- **The "3-1 rule."** Guardiola picked this one up in Italy. If an opposing player got the ball near Barcelona's penalty area, one defender advanced to tackle him, while the other three defenders built a second layer of protection by forming a ring two to three yards behind the tackler.

- **No surprises.** When Barcelona won the ball, they did something unusual: they didn't try to attack immediately. Typically, the player who had lost sight of the field by winning possession simply slotted the ball to the nearest teammate, and the fifteen-pass buildup could restart.[43]

  Most leading teams (especially Mourinho's) treat the moment the ball changes hands—"turnover," as it's called in basketball— as decisive. In that moment your opponents are often out of position. If you can counterattack quickly, you have a good chance of scoring.

  Barça did this only if they won the ball near the opposition's penalty area. In that case, the player who had won possession would head straight for goal. That's where the young Messi's genius for tackling came in. Such were his reflexes that he sometimes won a tackle a split second after losing one. But unless the route to goal was short and open, Barça went into their fifteen-pass routine.

Mourinho carped that renouncing the counterattack was stupid. Counters were the easiest way to score, he argued: if the opposition had lost the ball with several players in your half, their defense lay open. Still, Barça's way seemed to work, too—or at least it did with the quality of players they had.

DAY JOB: WATCHING DVDS

Cruyff never spent much time watching opponents. He left that to his assistant Bruins Slot. At first, the plan was that Bruins Slot would pass on his findings to Cruyff, who would explain them to the team, but since Cruyff always got the details wrong, Bruins Slot ended up briefing the players directly. It hardly mattered. Cruyff wasn't very interested in the opposition. His Barça did their own thing.

Guardiola was different. He said:

> When I was a player, the thing that panicked me most was having to play a match without knowing what . . . the opponent was going to do. So from my first day with Barça B I always tried to tell them before the game, "Gentlemen, this is what's going to happen today. If we do this, we'll win."[44]

In fact, Guardiola was arguably more video analyst than coach. On a typical workday, he might spend ninety minutes training his players and six hours in the head coach's windowless "Cave" buried deep inside the Camp Nou, watching DVDs of opponents.[45] (He had installed a lamp and a carpet to make the room less depressing.) He would watch, he told the Catalan parliament in 2011, until

> finally the brilliant, terrific moment comes that gives sense to my profession. Believe me, if I'm a coach it's for this moment— all the rest is in addition and has to be dealt with. . . . The moment might last one minute twenty seconds, one minute thirty, sometimes just a minute. Sometimes I even have to watch two whole matches of our next opponent before . . . the instant comes when I say: "That's it, I have it. We've won."[46]

In this instant he had spotted the opponent's fatal flaw—most famously, on the evening of May 1, 2009, the space in front of Real Madrid's central defenders that Messi as a false nine could occupy.

Guardiola could explain his insights to his players much better than Cruyff did. Piqué said:

> He made you understand the sport itself. He'd analyze the opposition and then explain that we had to do this because they do that, and then we'd get space in this or that place. And it would turn out that way in the match—which is the most difficult thing—and he'd be very proud because he'd been right. He created the game before playing it.

Under Guardiola, Barça's style became more cerebral than ever. When I quoted Cruyff's dictum "Football is a game you play with your head" to Piqué, he replied, "We maybe took that phrase to its maximum expression." Like Cruyff, Guardiola took his players on a "learning process," teaching them to become cold-headed real-time analysts of the game. He told his overstressed goalkeeper Valdés, "If you go on like this, then one day your career will be over and you won't have enjoyed this wonderful profession for a day. Watch football on TV, try to analyze the game: why is the striker moving left? What pass is the playmaker about to give? The more you understand football, the more you'll love it."[47]

Guardiola regularly devised a special formation to exploit a particular opposition's fatal flaw. Barça would often switch to this formation only ten minutes into the match, making it harder for the other team to react.[48] Sometimes the flaw he had uncovered was a detail—for instance, that the opposing outside-right had no left foot. Barça's left-back, Eric Abidal, would cover the man's right foot, forcing him to turn inside every time and give a short pass backward with his left. With the whole Barça side anticipating that pass, it was easily intercepted. For much of the Guardiola era, Real Madrid's worst flaw was that their forward Cristiano Ronaldo didn't track back, so Barça aimed to finish their attacks on his wing. "This team was nothing but hundreds of little details like that," said Abidal.[49]

Sala-i-Martin compared Guardiola to the Spanish "fast-fashion" retailer Zara, which could put out a new collection once a fortnight, quicker than any of its rivals. The economist said, "Every match he surprises the opponent with small changes to the tactics. Pep is constant innovation!"[50]

CULMINATING IN AN OUTBREAK OF STREET FOOTBALL

"Barça's style is the worst in the world," said Ricardo Moar, when he was sporting director of Deportivo la Coruña.[51] Guardiola denied his own forwards space and the element of surprise. By the time Barça had completed their fifteen passes, the opposition had usually regrouped into a kind of "handball defense": an entire team guarding its goal. Moar had a point. So how did Guardiola's men score?

Sometimes they employed rehearsed set plays: Xavi feeds Messi in the space between the opposing left-back and center-back, while the third man, Abidal, accelerates down the left wing ready for Messi's cross pass. Abidal said later, "It always reminded me of the tactics of a basketball team. You know when they have the ball and start signaling to each other, that they are going to try a certain play? It was a bit like that."[52]

In general, said Guardiola, the secret of scoring in all ball games was to overload one wing, lure the opponent into sending reinforcements there, then switch the ball to the other flank.[53] His rule was, "If you start on the left, you finish on the right." Abidal told Leplat, "You can look at all the goals we scored, it's always the same: we start on one wing and finish on the other."[54]

But once Guardiola's team had switched the ball across the field, in the final twenty-five yards or so they shifted from structure to street football. The ideal attack placed Messi (or Henry, or Eto'o) one-on-one against an opponent near goal. Once this had been done, the forward's individual creativity replaced the playbook. Guardiola wasn't going to tell Messi how to beat a defender. If a forward began to dribble, Barça's other players moved away from him to give him space. At other times, creativity might be the spontaneous interplay of three or four players: Messi to Henry to Eto'o, and goal.

Cruyff had captured the need for an unpredictable soloist in his dictum, "A football team consists of ten people and an outside-left." As defenses became more organized over time, soloists became even more important.

Great soloists were what distinguished Barcelona from the Spanish national team of their era. Spain passed like Barcelona, pressed like

Barcelona, and built walls like Barcelona, but they didn't score like Barcelona, because they didn't have the soloists. They won the World Cup in 2010 by scoring just eight goals and conceding two in seven games.

THE MAGNIFICENT PROCESSION

The emotional peak of Guardiola's first season in charge came ninety-three minutes into Chelsea versus Barcelona on May 6, 2009, when Iniesta's outside-of-the-boot drive put Barça in the Champions League final. Exactly nine months after that goal, Barcelona's almost invariably stable birth rate would spike 16 percent.[55]

The night before the final against Manchester United in Rome, Barça's hotel was packed with the players' children, wives, and hangers-on. Henry marveled later, "I was in my room—midnight! Girlfriend, friends were just talking, having a cup of coffee, chilling. You play for any other team: 'Don't do this, don't do that, no, you have to concentrate.'"[56] Guardiola knew when his players had to be *obsesivos* and when they didn't.

Three of Barça's defenders were missing for the final, handing the coach a stimulating intellectual challenge. He solved it by putting midfielder Yaya Touré in central defense. Guardiola assumed his players were good enough to play anywhere.

Ten minutes into the match, Iniesta's curved pass to Eto'o for the opening goal spoke in the language of Barça, telling the Cameroonian how to beat his marker. Eto'o said afterward, "I actually get past him just by adjusting the shape of my body because the pass does the rest."[57] Barça's second goal—for which Messi rose above the 1.90-meter-tall Rio Ferdinand to head Xavi's cross over United's 1.97-meter-tall keeper Edwin van der Sar—was a statement about height in football. It was also the moment in which he announced himself as the world's best player.

In his first season as coach, Guardiola had won the Treble of Spanish league, Copa del Rey, and Champions League. "That's the end of my career, won everything already," he joked, or half joked.[58]

I attended the match with UEFA officials, and over drinks afterward they recited the stats with glee: eight of Barça's thirteen players in the match had come through the Masia. Here was a model for European football, a return to the days when Cruyff's Ajax won European Cups with a neighborhood team.

The next season, 2009–2010, Barça won the Spanish title with a then record ninety-nine points. Half the team went straight on to South Africa to win the World Cup. When I asked Piqué how he had adjusted emotionally to becoming a world champion at twenty-three, he said:

> It all happened so quickly that I found winning normal. When I began to lose was when I started to understand everything I had won. It was as if you'd go to play a competition like the World Cup, or the league, and you were going to win it. You start winning everything and you think, "You're the best and you must win. You can't waste this opportunity." Because we were going at such a clip that we'd beat any team put in front of us.

Guardiola's team were lucky even in their rivals, Mourinho's Real Madrid. The Portuguese had been hired by Madrid as the antidote to Barça, but in fact he became their perfect foil, a cartoon villain. He baited Guardiola in press conferences, played all-out defense in Clásicos, poked a finger in Vilanova's eye, and slapped an unsuspecting Carles Puyol in the face in the tunnel before one game. These weren't simply mind games: Mourinho hadn't got over the rejection by what he regarded as hoity-toity, virtue-signaling Barcelona.

The pleasure of beating him 5–0 in November 2010 was enhanced for those who could place the result within Barça's history: a callback to the 5–0 victories over Madrid in 1974 and 1994. (Every time Guardiola's team took the field, the ghosts of Cruyff's team sat on their shoulders.) After the 2010 game, Piqué raised five fingers to Barça's supporters, and they raised five back: this was the *manita*, the "little hand," which traditionally marked these moments.[59] Back in the changing room, Barcelona's players gave themselves a one-minute standing ovation.[60]

Yet they needed Madrid. Mourinho's team were good enough to force them to be great every week—not just to beat Madrid, but to beat every other Spanish team, too, because Madrid rarely dropped points. Thanks to the rivalry, a midsize country in economic crisis could accommodate the two best teams on earth.

In mid-March 2011, Abidal was diagnosed with liver cancer. He asked Guardiola to break the news to the squad. Guardiola visited the left-back in the hospital after each of his first two operations, finding him fifteen kilos underweight and looking "yellow like a Teletubby."[61] When Abidal eventually returned home, he struggled just to get up off the sofa. Yet by early May, he was playing again. On May 28, when he was still five kilograms underweight, Guardiola started him in the Champions League final against Manchester United at Wembley.

United inevitably targeted Abidal: in the first few minutes, their winger Antonio Valencia made two runs at him and fouled him three times. Gradually, though, Barcelona achieved near-constant possession. Guardiola would say of the opening twenty-three minutes of the second half, during which his team scored twice, "That was the perfect illustration of how we wanted them to play. We were a young group of coaches trying to convince a unique group of players to do something different, and it worked well for four years."[62]

That match was probably the best display of football I have ever seen. By the end, helpless United players chasing the ball were swearing at their opponents.[63] Barcelona's 3–1 victory was the third Cruyffian European triumph at Wembley, after Ajax's win over Panathinaikos in 1971 and Barça's over Sampdoria in 1992. Afterward Puyol gave Abidal the captain's armband, and the cancer survivor lifted the cup into the sky.

It had been such a perfect night that I was worried Alex Ferguson would spoil it with a rant about the referee. But as he climbed Wembley's thirty-nine steps to receive his loser's medal, he was smiling. "Nobody's given us a hiding like that," he said later. "In my time as manager, it's the best team I've faced."[64] At half past midnight, Barça's kitman walked from the stadium to the bus, a bunch of files in one hand, the Champions League trophy in the other.

When Abidal's cancer returned ten months later, Barça's right-back Dani Alves offered him a part of his own liver for a transplant. The Frenchman's ordeal, with its happy ending, helped bond the squad.

But four years is a long time to maintain intensity. By 2012, having won fourteen trophies, Guardiola had lost almost all his hair, and felt wrung out. The players had tired of his daily perfectionism. With the *directius* fighting each other, he also often had to double up as club spokesman. Laporta gave way as president in 2010 to a former ally-turned-enemy, his teammate in amateur football as a teenager, Sandro Rosell. Guardiola suspected that the new president didn't have his back.[65] Rosell himself was dealing with jealous outsiders, including, by his account, FIFA, UEFA, and the Spanish federation. He told me, "Nobody likes somebody winning always. And I agree: to make the sport big, you have to have others win, too."

When Guardiola resigned, Rosell asked Vilanova to succeed him. Vilanova, like Guardiola four years earlier, had only ever been a head coach in the Spanish fourth division. The appointment upset Guardiola, who seems to have expected his old friend to leave Barça with him. He and Vilanova fell out. In Vilanova's only season in charge, 2012–2013,

Barcelona won the league with a record-equaling one hundred points. Meanwhile, though, Vilanova was diagnosed with cancer. In midseason he flew to New York for several weeks of treatment. Guardiola, who was on sabbatical in Manhattan, visited him only once. Vilanova's family was dismayed. After Vilanova died in 2014, at age forty-five, his widow banned Guardiola from the funeral.[66]

Old friends falling out is an eternal story at Barça: Cruyff and Rexach, Rosell and Laporta, Pep and Tito. More than at other clubs, at Barcelona the professional is personal. Lifelong friendships, individual ambition, and umbilical relationships with Barça end up entangled. "Power divides," sighed Rosell.[67]

What Guardiola and Vilanova left behind, though, is the memory of one of the great football teams—"the best team of the last twenty or thirty years," Mourinho called it.[68]

When Guardiola was asked at the conference in Mexico if he had perfected Cruyff's ideas, he replied, "I don't know, but this goes beyond football: personally, I am better than my parents in many domains, because I benefited from other possibilities, such as travel. And my children will be better than I am. It's normal. Also, the coaches of the future will undoubtedly surpass me."[69] Guardiola surpassed Cruyff, and in the process confirmed Barça as a rare club with an enduring house style: Cruyffism. Guardiola completed Cruyff's cathedral. But then the brilliant artisans took charge of the work, and stopped listening to the architects who succeeded him.

PART FOUR

MEET THE TALENT

IX

DEFINE "TALENT"

During the time I spent at Barça, I became interested in a question that went beyond specific teams and eras: What's it like to be a great footballer, on the field and off it? What kind of people are they? How do they live? What are the aptitudes and attitudes that set them apart from the rest of us? How do they relate to their clubs? How do they integrate—or not—when they move? And what is different about being a great player in Barcelona as opposed to anywhere else? The following four chapters are my attempt to answer these questions, based partly on interviews with club employees and Barça players past and present.

The closest I ever got to understanding what it takes to play top-class football was sitting in front of an ancient computer in Kiev in 1992. I'd met a scientist named Professor Anatoly Zelentsov, who had devised computer tests used by Dynamo Kyiv and the Soviet national team to select players. The test that has stayed with me was the most difficult one: a dot would trace a complicated trajectory through a maze, and then I had to retrace the path, using a joystick. But I could never remember the route, and the maze was so narrow and twisty, and constantly in motion, that I kept bumping into walls. It was, of course, a test of hand-eye coordination and visual memory, and it made me realize what gifts great footballers have. Not after years of practice could I have negotiated that maze.

Most great footballers take their qualities for granted. Cruyff was one of the few who could explain to outsiders what they did. Imagine, he once said, that you're a player receiving a pass in a high-level match:

> An opponent is coming at you . . . the ball is bouncing or there's a curve on it, and you have to pass it into the wind to somebody who has a certain running speed and has to receive it ready to play. A computer can't do in two minutes what that top footballer has to do in hundredths of a second. So those brains have to function superbly. I think that's intelligence. But people often confuse it with knowledge.[1]

Playing top-class football is something like playing chess with your feet at the speed of Formula One. It demands an extraordinary mastery of geometry in motion. Just watch Valverde on Barcelona's training field before a game against Espanyol, showing his defenders which spaces they must occupy depending on which opposing player has the ball, and in which directions they should force Espanyol to pass.[2]

Yet the best footballers can register the frenzied movement around them in an almost leisurely manner. The Portuguese coach Carlos Queiroz told writer John Carlin, "Imagine two cars colliding. For us it happens at normal speed. They [the greats] see it in slow motion, they catch a lot more details in the same time as us. They can compute in their minds more details than you and I can see. Therefore they have more time."[3]

Rapid pattern recognition may be the most important quality in football, said the longtime director of AC Milan's Milan Lab, Belgian doctor Jean-Pierre Meersseman. When I asked which players had it, he named the Brazilian Ronaldo.

A club cannot do much to teach this quality, certainly not to adult players. Barça's data analysts couldn't teach Busquets how to draw an opponent toward him and then at the last moment pass the ball into the space behind the man's back. In fact, it's the reverse: in order to understand how football works, Barça's analysts studied what Busquets and Messi did. When the analysts began using computer modeling to identify high-value spaces on the field, they were surprised to discover how often Barcelona's players were already accessing those spaces with runs or passes.

"I have to say that the great players analyze the game better than I do," Valverde told me, adding:

> Instead of analyzing, I'd say they interpret the play during the game. This is a continuous sport in which the coach has barely any influence, or at least much less than in basketball: we only have three substitutions; the game never stops [for time-outs]. Once the game starts, I'm shouting to the player over there, and he doesn't hear me, and the one beside me doesn't hear me either. Football belongs almost to the players alone.

I queried the word "almost," and Valverde corrected himself: "Not 'almost.' Football belongs to the players. For forty-five minutes at a time, nonstop, the player takes his own decisions." Every moment on the field, players were solving puzzles by themselves: Should I move five yards forward? Who should I pass to? Who will cover the free man?

Valverde always briefed his team on their next opponents, but he attached limited value to his own advice. He admitted, "The beginning of a game is always a surprise, because you don't know what the rival has been preparing. The other day against Athletic Club [Bilbao], for example, we were expecting some very high pressure, and in fact it wasn't that high. So, Christ, in the beginning we were a bit out of place."

Football is a players' game. One of Barça's data analysts told me he didn't think he had ever helped the team win a match. (In that case, why didn't he quit? asked Liverpool's director of research Ian Graham after reading the quote.) When I pressed the analyst, he conceded he may have contributed something: "0.01 percent."

Pattern recognition, decision-making, plus foot skills come close to a definition of talent in football. But a top-class player also needs the right psychological qualities. Which matter most? Inma Puig, who worked for Barça as a psychologist for fifteen years, told me, "Great players experience pressure as a challenge, whereas the ordinary player experiences pressure as a threat. That's the difference."

Every few days, a footballer walks into the Roman Colosseum and has to prove himself afresh. The players who succeed are the ones who relish the unending challenge. The French defender Lilian Thuram told me in 2008, during his stint at Barça:

> What is beautiful in football is this permanently putting yourself into question. Forgetting the match you played before. There is a magical moment in football, when the two teams are lined up side by side, and they walk onto the pitch and greet the crowd, and the referee blows his whistle, because there we have the capacity to write a new match. I think that's why football is fascinating.

But it's terrifying, too. In the changing room before each match, some players are vomiting or making multiple toilet visits. "Floop!" a Barcelona doctor says, miming the diarrhea racing through the intestines. Sometimes a team cannot take the field until a stricken player has finished. Top-class footballers feel fear like anyone else. What distinguishes them is that they use it to motivate themselves. Their gifted peers who couldn't handle fear were weeded out along the way, perhaps on debut for a national juniors team. To quote the American pianist Charles Rosen: "This is what distinguishes the amateur from the professional: they both have stage fright, but the amateur shows it and the professional hides it."[4]

Another element of talent is concentration. Top-class players can focus on their task for ninety minutes as if neither the crowd nor anything else exists. The only sounds that penetrate their consciousness are the calls of their teammates. Meg Rapinoe, who was booed by American crowds for a while after taking the knee during the national anthem, reported, "It turns out that the sound of ten thousand people telling you to go fuck yourself can . . . blend into a solid mass possible to ignore."[5] Thuram said that when a match ended, he always knew which team had won, but he didn't always know the score. He sometimes erased the goals that his team had scored from his mind, because they were irrelevant to his task. He was focused.

There's a common belief that top-class footballers require a manager to inspire them to such heights. The British comedian Peter Cook used to play a football manager who, in a mournful northern English accent, revealed the secret of his trade: "*Moooorrtivation, moooortivation, mooorrtivation!* The three M's." Motivation remains an obsession of many in the football media. The notion is that the player is an inert child, into whom the manager infuses motivation, ideally through a Churchillian pre-match speech.

But the truth is that almost nobody at the top plays for the coach.

Whatever external motivation is needed comes from the group, not the coach. In Barça's changing room just before they take the field, players and coach lock arms in a huddle and shout, "One, two, three, Barça!" And the essential motivation of great footballers is internal. These are driven people. Gerard van der Lem, Van Gaal's assistant coach at Barça, compared their workweek with a pressure cooker: "On Monday the players would go in, and every day the cooker would get a little hotter. When you pulled off the lid on Sunday, 22 murderers jumped out. The intensity of those matches was incredible."[6]

Arsène Wenger, a manager for thirty-five years, told me:

> At the age of twenty-three, the top, top, top players separate from the rest. These are the players who have something more, in the consistency of their motivation, in their desire to push themselves. And money has not too much [of] an influence on them. They have this intrinsic motivation that pushes them to get as far as they can. It's not many of them.

When I asked how much of the manager's role was motivation, Wenger replied:

> It is overrated. . . . If you have every week to motivate the players to be performing on Saturday, forget it. At that level, players want to achieve something, they want to be a star, and you are more there to help them. If they don't like it, they don't want it, leave them at home; you'll waste your time. Of course, sometimes you do it, because they can go through—but globally, the players at that level are motivated.

The Italian manager Carlo Ancelotti concurs: "Our job is not to motivate the players. Our job is not to demotivate them by not providing the challenges and goals that their talents need."[7] If a player senses that his club's management is second-rate, he may decide to succeed somewhere else.

Guardiola, reflecting on his departure from Barcelona in 2012, said, "What happened at Barça is not that I failed to motivate them. No, I failed to seduce them!"[8]

A coach has to seduce players into accepting his ideas. Whereas motivating players is a top-down relationship, seduction implies a relationship of equals. The contemporary manager is more film director than military general. Authoritarian rule has faded out even faster in football than in most high-skill workplaces. The Bosman ruling of 1995 made it easier for discontented players to leave their clubs. The trend since then has been for footballers to amass power. This has happened more at Barça than at other clubs, but it has happened almost everywhere: player power is the standard lament at pre-match meals between directors of rival clubs.

How to seduce footballers? Puig has concluded that they want some of the same things from their employers as any other workers: love and recognition. "Moreover," she laughs, "it's free!" The ultimate gesture of recognition was Rijkaard's bow to his players after Barça won the Spanish title in 2005.

A top-class player has an ego-driven project: he wants to succeed for himself, his vocation, and his career. It's often assumed that ego is damaging to a team, and sometimes it really is. Guardiola said, "Almost the totality of problems that can afflict a team come from egos."[9] In fact, some of them have come from Guardiola's own ego. But the egotistical drive of top-class footballers helps them to succeed. The French striker Kylian Mbappé says he always tells himself, "I am the best," even though he knows that Messi and Cristiano Ronaldo are better. He explains that it's ego that gives him the desire to surpass himself, and stops him imposing limits on himself. "It's important because when things are hard, nobody except you yourself will push you. You have to persuade yourself that you can overturn mountains. . . . There is only you."[10]

Even if a player does temporarily set aside his ego and sacrifice himself for the greater good, by playing out of position or sitting uncomplainingly on the bench, he'll want personal recognition for it from his coach.

The structure of a footballer's career—brief, with frequent job changes and personal ups and downs—encourages egotism. But the most egotistical players tend to be the best. Queiroz said, "These top, top players have a profound awareness of their specialness, of their unique talent, that goes beyond arrogance—that just is."[11] A manager who only wants to manage obedient soldiers will make his own life easier, but he will have to forgo some of the biggest talents.

A realistic manager accepts that his players are in it for themselves, and that they regard teammates as both partners and rivals. Guardiola always assumed the reserves wanted the team to lose, because then they might be picked. He once remarked, "People who say, 'We're all fighting together!,' well, it looks good on a photo but in a changing room nobody believes it."[12]

Teammates need to have good working relationships, but they don't need to be a band of brothers, and they seldom are. Thuram said, "It would be difficult if you demanded that everyone likes you. A Brazilian is not going to think like an Italian. There are cultural differences." Players are free to dislike each other. They just have to trust each other's talent.

For almost all players, football is a job, and their club an employer. Outsiders who grow up as fans and then get a peek behind the curtain—journalists and club officials, say—often suffer lasting disenchantment when they realize this. A Barça director who had been through the experience told me that part of his responsibility after stepping down would be to not talk about the dark side of football, because he didn't want the fans to know about it. "I'm not talking about illegal things," he added. He just meant everyday venality.

When I began writing this book, I thought that most top-class footballers were like highly skilled employees in other fields—that they related to their club in the same transactional way that most surgeons, bankers, or academics relate to their employers. Footballers, I thought, wanted to work for an organization where they could find professional fulfillment, high pay, and recognition. If their current club couldn't give it to them, they would move on unsentimentally. They didn't think like fans. They weren't invested in the club badge, their coach, or their teammates.

Writing this book, I have come to believe that the relationship is even more transactional than that: in fact, most players are like independent contractors. They come together at a particular club to execute a short-term project with other contractors, like actors making a movie together. They hire out their services to the club for about three hours a day, while also working for their sponsors, their national team, and their charities, and perhaps building their personal brands.

The most a manager can do is persuade players that his short-term project will fulfill their selfish ambitions. Mbappé told me he had learned from his father, a local football coach in the Paris suburbs, to think like a coach, but that most players couldn't. He said, "If you're a player, you generally only think about yourself, about your career. Football is the most individual of the collective sports."

A FOOTBALLER WHO WANTS TO survive at the top needs the full package: self-motivation and foot skills, pattern recognition and focus.

The English footballer Phil Neville had the psychological qualities but lacked the foot skills and pattern recognition. Conversely, some gifted players lack the psychology. I recall a talented midfielder of the 1990s lounging beside a swimming pool on the French Riviera, asking rhetorically, in the course of a moan about *obsesivo* colleagues, "What's it all about? It's about being happy with your family." This man failed at Barça, though he did have a good career a level below that.

Some footballers run out of ambition during their careers, perhaps because like many workers in other professions they lose passion for their job with age, or because they have won enough and earned enough to satisfy themselves. Ronaldinho lost his ambition almost the moment he became the best player on earth in the 2005–2006 season. Offered all the pleasures of the city of Barcelona, he chose them instead. His then coach, Rijkaard, told me in 2008 that the Brazilian would return to his best only when he was willing to devote himself mentally and physically to that goal. "It might happen," Rijkaard said, "but it's mostly the internal motivation that has to come forward to achieve that." There is an element of cop-out here: Barcelona lost Ronaldinho. But mostly, Ronaldinho lost himself.

One recent case of a brilliant footballer who lacked the single-mindedness required at the top is Mario Balotelli. His agent, Mino Raiola, who died in 2022, believed that Balotelli was often distracted from achievement by falling in love: "Balotelli has chosen—unconsciously or consciously—not to put football in the center of his life. So there were always marginal phenomena that influenced his performances. Zlatan doesn't have that, Pogba doesn't, Nedvěd didn't."

I suggested to Raiola that many gifted footballers didn't particularly want to reach the top. Why should they? They could make millions playing for slightly lesser clubs, without putting themselves under inhuman pressure.

"Well, that's right," Raiola replied. "That's why in my recent conversations I have an important question for players: 'Why do you play football? What is your drive?'"

What did they answer?

"Well, most haven't thought about it yet. I send them home saying, 'Go think about it.'"

A footballer who has the full array of skills and mental qualities doesn't need to be a physical superhuman. Extraordinary physical qualities—like pace or strength or size—have always been less important in football than in other sports. In cycling, or in certain positions in American football or rugby, a driven athlete with the perfect body who eats and trains right every day (and perhaps takes performance-enhancing drugs) can compensate somewhat for a lack of talent. That doesn't work in top-class football. In fact, until quite recently, a player who possessed the rest of the package from pattern recognition to foot skills could succeed while putting in less physical effort and living less professionally than everyone else. Exhibit A was the chain-smoking Cruyff. The prime example on his Dream Team, Romário, hardly ever gave 100 percent in training or minor matches. The Brazilian's priorities were sex, nightclubs, and parties in Rio de Janeiro. Cruyff always defended him against the complaints of harder-working players, and Romário understood the flip side of the deal: in big matches, he had to perform.

You find similar types in the equally skill-based sport of basketball. Allen Iverson refused to lift weights during his career because "that shit was too heavy."[13] There wasn't much his coaches could do about it. He was still Allen Iverson, the team's best player.

In football, at the level of FC Barcelona, the talent is irreplaceable. There may be nobody else on earth who can perform a particular player's role as well as he can. Even if there is, the replacement could cost €100 million in the transfer fee alone, and he might fail to adjust to Barça. The adage "No player is bigger than the club" may be true in the middle reaches of the game, where a club can replace an obstreperous striker with someone else of similar quality. It doesn't apply at the highest level.

A top-class football club is the most meritocratic of workplaces. Nobody today gets to play for Barcelona because of nepotism or where he went to school. His teammates won't care about his skin color or possibly his sexuality, or even much about his social skills, as long as he meets their stringent performance standards.

Thuram, who after his career became an antiracism campaigner, said, "Sincerely, I've never met a racist person in football. Maybe they were, but I didn't see it. You know why? Because people who are racist tend not to know the Other. In football, we share things. And in football it's harder to have discrimination, because we are judged on very specific performances."

The best footballers feel they are the winners of a weekly meritocracy. They are often disobedient (because they can afford to be) and opinionated (because they "interpret" football better than the coach can). When they look at the rest of us, they see misshapen fatties spending decades in mediocre low-adrenaline jobs. No wonder they sometimes struggle to hide their disdain.

Cruyff said, "At the top you're dealing with very special people: people with the highest qualities, people with a lot of pride, and people who are super-intelligent. These are the people you have to try to persuade.... Top players who are easy hardly exist. Top players push back.[14]

X

THE TALENT RULES

On Monday December 20, 1999, the Brazilian forward Rivaldo woke up in the Princesa Sofia, the hotel up the hill from the Camp Nou that serves as Barça's unofficial business center and guesthouse. His family had already flown to Brazil for their Christmas holidays, and he hadn't wanted to be alone in the big house.[1]

He was due at the club at nine a.m. After Barcelona's coach Louis van Gaal finished analyzing the previous night's 2–1 victory over Atlético Madrid, Rivaldo requested permission to speak. Listen, he said in his Portuguese-tinted Spanish, I have respect for the coach and for everybody here, but I won't play outside-left anymore. "OK," said Van Gaal calmly. "Does anybody else have something to say?"

A light training session followed, after which Rivaldo gave a press conference. Twenty journalists, still unaware of his speech to the squad, interrogated him about the vote for European Footballer of the Year.

The magazine *France Football* has awarded the prize since 1956. Whoever wins it becomes a legend.

No comment, said Rivaldo. The result of the vote isn't known yet. "Everybody knows it's you," pleaded the journalists.

Then he drove to the airport to collect the handball player Iñaki, a son-in-law of King Juan Carlos. That afternoon they did an event for charity. Rivaldo and his agent, Manuel Auset ("I'm not his agent, I'm his friend"), asked me not to write about it. Rivaldo didn't do these things for his image.

Three hours late, dressed in black, the exhausted Brazilian arrives on the nineteenth floor of the Princesa Sofia. Iñaki had been delayed and the charity event had run late. Rivaldo groans when he sees my long list of questions, but sits down and tries to answer. At one point he says, "I have played on the wing for a while and now I want to play in the center again. For years I have been doing things for the team and I do nothing for myself. I want to enjoy more, to play in my own position."

When we finish, he poses for photographs for his boot sponsor. Meanwhile, his Nokia phone keeps ringing, so he hands the thing to Manuel. Everyone is calling to congratulate him, because many media are reporting that he has won the Ballon d'Or. "I'm not here," says Rivaldo, posing with a flat ball. "Is he now officially Player of the Year?" I ask Manuel. "Well, I don't know," says Manuel. "We haven't heard anything."

"Call *France Football*," Rivaldo suggests. Good idea. Manuel taps in the number and the phone rings for a long time. Finally somebody in Paris answers.

"Vincent!" says Manuel. Rivaldo goes and stands next to him and listens in. Vincent confirms that Rivaldo has been voted European Footballer of the Year for 1999. "Vale, vale, vale," ("OK, OK, OK") says Rivaldo. We congratulate him.

"Thank you," he says. He takes the phone from Manuel and walks onto the roof terrace. Alone, he looks across the city toward the dark Tibidabo mountain. Directly in front of him is a branch of El Corte Inglés, the department store. The clock on its outside wall gives the time as 19:23 hours. From now on Rivaldo is officially a legend.

Did he already know he'd won? "Yes," says Manuel with a grin. "He had to pose for a photograph with the Golden Ball."

Has he celebrated yet?

"Celebrated? He hasn't even had his lunch today! He's just been busy."

Rivaldo returns the phone to Manuel and resumes posing. Manuel shows me the thing. The screen constantly reports three callers waiting. Whenever one of them hangs up, a new one appears immediately.

Then Rivaldo sits for an hour in a small, hot, windowless room under a barrage of lights, giving TV interviews. People stream in and out to get a photograph with him, an autograph, a kiss. Everyone who notices his exhaustion makes a little joke or consoling remark. At about nine p.m. he finally reaches the hotel lobby, where he feints his way past a pack of journalists. He has almost speed-walked to his Mercedes people carrier when the hotel concierge imprisons him in a hug. The journalists catch up. Rivaldo struggles into his Mercedes, but they stand in front of it. After a standoff lasting several minutes, they finally let him drive to his empty house. In the bath he'll have a chance to think about the day.

The day after, Van Gaal kicked him off the squad for refusing to play on the wing. But Barça drew their first game without Rivaldo, and public opinion sided with the player. Guardiola, the captain, went to Van Gaal to ask him to let Rivaldo play number ten. The Dutchman reluctantly agreed. Years later, he grumbled to the journalist Jonathan Wilson, "Then he played at ten and we didn't win anything anymore because it was chaos."[2]

Van Gaal left at the end of that season after multiple conflicts with his Brazilian players, and no prizes. He had learned what happens in modern football when the talent clashes with the club: the talent wins.

Many fans find this incomprehensible. They still expect a manager to command his players like the no-nonsense headmaster of a 1950s reform school for bad boys. In fact, a macho coach who tries to break the players' will, or who attempts heavy-handed "motivation," will prompt talent flight. Modern clubs have abandoned the fantasy of dominating their mobile, multinational, multimillionaire, near-irreplaceable players, most of them armed with egos, agents, and journalistic sycophants. In a talent-driven business, rule by talent is inevitable. Barça's former president Sandro Rosell told me:

> This is an activity that depends on eleven persons. And it's not a machine. These eleven persons have to perform perfectly for you to be or not to be a good president. You cannot change eleven persons, but you can change the coach.
>
> This is a very strange situation where the big boss, the president, his salary is zero. The sporting director has a lower salary than his employee, the coach. And the salary of the coach is lower—not always now—than [that of] his employees, the football players. This is the only place in the world where the higher position you have, the lower salary you have. It's mad! You work for Volkswagen, the guy who makes the car earns a hundred times more than the chief executive? Explain to me—how can this happen?

Money is the best measure of player power in football. Big clubs spend about 50 to 70 percent of their revenues on footballers' salaries, and another 20 to 40 percent on transfer fees, calculates Ian Graham of

Liverpool. In other words, the talent is able to command up to 90 percent of clubs' revenues.

Barcelona uses a system of performance-related pay, introduced by Cruyff during his reign as manager.[3] Raúl Sanllehí, Barça's director of football, explained to Harvard in 2015:

> About 60 percent of the salary is fixed. If a player is available to start in the first team and not injured, we add 10 percent. If the team reaches a certain level of success in the Champions League, we add another 10 percent. We reserve the last 20 percent for titles won: the King's Cup, the Spanish league and, especially, the Champions League.[4]

But each time Barça won a prize, the players' agents demanded more money, said Rosell. "So the club is always the victim of its success." After all, the players have the negotiating power. Rosell's predecessor Laporta had made the same discovery. On the plane home from Barça's victory in the Champions League final in Paris in 2006, Messi, who in those days never spoke, grabbed the cabin microphone, possibly emboldened by the first alcoholic haze of his life, and shouted, "President! Is there a bonus or not? *Presi*, come and fix the bonus! And no more watches, *presi*. You think we're joking, but I'm serious. We want houses, *presi*!"[5]

As footballers' pay has soared, they have surrounded themselves with support staff who form a barrier against the club. Nowadays, a leading player runs a small business that might include his agent, social media manager, personal physiotherapist, stylist, and so on. To cite an extreme example, in 2021 Real Madrid's striker Vinícius Júnior had twelve full-time employees, including a personal chef, cameraman, photographer, and family-office staff, as well as twenty-seven part-time ones. Inevitably, his support system reduced his dependency on his club.[6]

Jorge Valdano had lamented as early as 2010, when he was Real Madrid's sporting director:

> Twenty-five years ago, the contact between the club and the player was very direct. It was all much simpler. A footballer was the club's employee, with rights but above all obligations. Now there are many layers between club and player. Sometimes your interlocutor is still the player himself. But sometimes the interlocutor is the player's father, the player's agent, the player's communications director, the player's girlfriend.[7]

Arsène Wenger, too, complained about "lawyers, agents, advisers who are really family members, all those middlemen who would gradually get between a player and his coach."[8] At Barcelona, Seirul·lo grumbled to me, "Before, Johan [Cruyff] said something and it was law. Now the people around the player are protagonists." A modern club has so little power over its players that it will be tempted to find illicit ways to fight back. Laporta's board in the 2003–2010 era hired private detectives to spy on Barça's squad,[9] just as Bartomeu's was accused of hiring a communications company to attack players on social media. Yet as long as the talent performs on the field, it will win most power struggles.

ADAPT OR DIE

One of the most stressful moments in a footballer's career is changing clubs. When a new signing and his entourage land in Barcelona for the final contract talks, they might be sneaked out of the airport through a side entrance. While the agent negotiates with Barça, the player may spend anxious hours hiding from journalists in a suite in the Princesa

Sofia. The standard contract bans the player from paragliding and water-skiing without the club's express permission (which presumably isn't often granted). Once he signs, he is expected to hug middle-aged board members. It's only the first of many trials he will face.

Gary Lineker, who joined Barcelona from Everton in 1986, recalled decades later:

> From the moment I got off the airplane, there were hundreds of photographers and press people. You don't get that in England. . . . Then of course, they had the thing they call the "presentación," when they'll have a training session on the pitch with the new signings. But they'll do it at the Camp Nou! I was there with Mark Hughes [the Welsh striker]. We'd just signed and we were told, "We're going to train on the pitch today, it's when they introduce you to the crowd," and we thought, "Well, who's going to turn up? Maybe thirty people, maybe forty." There was about sixty-odd thousand people there, just to cheer [on] the new players and watch a bit of training, so you start to think: well, this is a little bit different.

Then comes a more private initiation rite at Barça's training ground. New signings sprint through a kind of guard of honor formed by their teammates, who administer (ideally gentle) taps on the head. The newcomers' next test is on the training ground: coping in football's most demanding rondo. "What's happening to me?" thought Lieke Martens after joining Barça's women's team. "A rondo goes very quickly here." Players who cannot handle probing fireballs to their wrong foot can lose their reputation in seconds.

On the men's team in the Messi era, the new-kid-at-school effect was enhanced by the fact of landing among a core of players who had known each other for years, in some cases since childhood. The four club captains in the 2020–2021 season—Messi, Busquets, Piqué, and Sergi Roberto—were all homegrown.

At any club, a newcomer is a threat to the established senior players: he could oust one of them from the team. Their selfish incentive is to form a clique that excludes him. On the other hand, players who spend their career at a club tend to come to feel responsible for its long-term functioning. This tempers the standard footballer's egotism. Fernando Torres, the Spanish forward who played for and supported his boyhood club, Atlético Madrid, explained, "You miss [a chance of scoring]—it hurts, because you know it's your fault. The team you're supporting didn't win because *you* didn't do well. Every year, because you are a better player than when you start, the responsibility is bigger." In a few rare cases, love creeps into the player–club relationship. Andrés Iniesta wept at the press conference where he announced his departure from Barça, and Carles Puyol had to fight hard not to.

Barça's old guard seems to be relatively welcoming to new signings. The silly pranks of the Catalans Piqué and Sergi Roberto (hiding a teammate's phone is the height of football humor) help to initiate newcomers. Neymar says that when he arrived in Barcelona, "I was quite shy. But they were great with me, joking around from the beginning, saying they were getting ready to beat Brazil at the World Cup. Everyone's playing around, but it's something healthy."

Yet even with friendly workmates, immigration is tough. Whether an expat player lands in Barcelona or Manchester, he has to deal with a new home, a new changing room, new schools for his children, possibly a new language, and the loss of his old life. He might encounter little sympathy in a workplace of men, especially at a club like Barça, where the dominant players have never extended their horizons by leaving their hometown. No wonder Barça pays a premium for players who already know Spain and its football. "Dani Alves cost more to FC Barcelona than defenders in other leagues because of the added value of the five years he had played for Seville," notes Soriano.[10] Seydou Keita, Adriano, Ivan Rakitić, and Clément Lenglet also acclimatized to Spanish football in Sevilla before joining Barcelona.

Like all big clubs, Barça has bought many foreigners who failed the integration test. Lineker witnessed a case study. He recalled, "I got off to a good start, which helped; two goals in my first twenty minutes. Mark Hughes didn't, and they got on his back quickly."

Was Hughes one of the players of whom it's said that they "die" of nerves in the Camp Nou? "I think there's a degree of that," agreed Lineker.

> Mark's a very robust footballer. He's backing into people, and every time he did that in Spain, they gave a free kick against him, where that wouldn't have happened in England. I think he got a bit frustrated, and the crowd got a bit frustrated with him giving fouls away.
>
> He was about twenty-one at the time and he hadn't had the experience I'd had. I think it was probably a bit early for him. You could see him really struggling, and I felt that. I went to Spanish school with my first wife two or three times a week. Mark started the Spanish school and then gave up after a couple of weeks, and I think he became a bit lonely. We did our best, but it was difficult. I think he was just a bit too immature. But the expectancy levels there: the foreign players that they'd had, Cruyff himself, Maradona. They were used to having top-class players. That's added pressure.

When the Argentinian playmaker Juan Román Riquelme signed for Barça in 2002, he was a top-class player who could already speak Spanish. Nonetheless, Van Gaal, the coach, immediately informed Riquelme that he had neither requested nor wanted him. That wasn't even the player's biggest problem. A staffer who gave him a lift home a year after his arrival noticed that his apartment was almost bare of personal items, except for a container of Argentinian maté tea. When the club's new chief executive, Soriano, heard that, he decided to research Riquelme's background. He discovered that the player had lived in the neighborhood of his birth west of Buenos Aires until he was eighteen, when he signed for Boca Juniors and moved about twenty miles toward the city center. Soriano recounts:

> Those who knew him well and know the details of his career say he never managed to adapt. He missed his small neighborhood, his friends, the steaks on the patio. . . . So he had a very lovely house built in El Viejo Vivero in Don Torcuato, just a few hundred meters from the spot where he had been born. . . . In other words, in 2002 Barcelona signed a man who had not been able to get used to a different neighborhood in Buenos Aires—and brought him to Barcelona! . . . It was logical and predictable that this would not work . . . He lives in Buenos Aires now, probably in Don Torcuato.[11]

Some newcomers succeed at Barcelona because they treat immigration as a challenge. Thuram said, "Succeeding abroad means having to adapt to something. And from the moment you have adapted to another situation, another club, another life, it makes you much stronger."

Others succeed by not thinking too hard about the jump they have made. One morning soon after joining Barça in 1998, Boudewijn Zenden opened the curtains of his hotel room and gazed out over the city and the Camp Nou. "Strange, isn't it?" he remarked to his roommate Phillip Cocu, his fellow Dutchman who had come from PSV Eindhoven with him. "Here we are living in Barcelona and playing for Barça." Cocu replied that it was indeed strange, but that was just the way it was. Then he got on with his day. Cocu went on to set the record (later broken by Messi) for most appearances by a foreigner for Barça.

The newcomer's next trial is Barça's unique brand of football. Thuram said that when he joined Barcelona at age thirty-four and discovered the club's Cruyffian principles, he felt for the first time that he was fully a footballer. He even wondered what sport he had been playing until then.[12] For many newcomers, the discovery comes as a mixture of delight and shock. They spend much of their training time at Barça trying to break old habits acquired at their previous clubs, such as retreating after losing the ball. "I had to learn this language of football," said the Ukrainian Dmytro Chygrynskiy.[13] But at the top of the game, there's almost no time to learn. Joan Oliver, during his time as Barça's chief executive, formulated what he called the "one-second rule": "If a player needs just one more second to discover who is the player waiting for the ball, that's the difference between winning and losing."

Barça tries to allow for an adaptation period. "If you look at the performance of the player in the first year of the contract, probably it's very, very poor," said Oliver in 2009, soon after signing Chygrynskiy. "Typically the player is trying to understand, 'OK, what's my role in the team and how is it trying to play?' For instance, the newcomer probably doesn't yet know Messi's body language on the field—the signs that reveal he wants the ball *now*. But by the time the player has worked it out, the coach, his teammates, and the *entorno* may have given up on him." Chygrynskiy was gone within a year.

Newcomers also have to cope with a change in status. Typically, a player who joins Barça has been the Lionel Messi of his previous club, his national team, and quite likely every team he has played on since age six. Suddenly, he is Messi's subordinate, making decoy runs to create space for the great man, then doing Messi's defensive work. As Cruyff said, "Nine out of ten players you buy are big players in a small club. But will they be big players at a big club?"[14]

TALENT IN FOOTBALL VERSUS "TALENT" IN BUSINESS

Many managers of ordinary companies model themselves on successful sports coaches. Some retired coaches and athletes make fortunes on the corporate speakers' circuit, passing on insights like, "We looked each other in the eyes and said, 'There's no *I* in team,' and that's why we won the World Cup." If you're running an unglamorous marketing department somewhere, it's an inspiring message.

But the truth is that sport isn't a very useful model for business. On the contrary: many sports clubs are so badly run that they ought to model themselves on ordinary companies. (The only sphere of excellence inside many clubs is the playing squad.)

More fundamentally, though, a football club is a different kind of animal than a bank, a law firm, or a multinational oil business. The biggest difference is the importance of talent.

Corporate leaders love making speeches about "the talent of our people," but in fact, most businesses are based on the concept of replaceability. If your chief procurement officer leaves, you hire another one. The second one will be a little different than the first, but then these people don't need to be highly talented. They just have to be good enough every day (in many jobs, 90 percent of success really is just showing up), and ideally they won't be nightmares to work with. (The Stanford professor Robert I. Sutton popularized the "No Asshole Rule.")

The typical workplace relies on efficient processes, not extraordinary talent. A supermarket chain, for instance, has to get the right food to the right outlets quickly and cheaply. In most jobs, creativity and extraordinary talent only cause trouble. A hospital wants its surgeons to perform knee operations using standard methods validated by large-scale studies. Creative surgeons who prefer to follow their personal inspiration can endanger their patients.

The financial sector does cherish a belief in talent and even "superstars," but a man called Robert Pickering skewered it in a celebrated letter to the *Financial Times*, in 2014:

> I ran an investment bank for a number of years and was regularly held up at gunpoint and told that we had to jack up so-and-so's pay to prevent him or her from leaving (usually for Goldman Sachs and invariably for "twice what they get here"). Sometimes I paid up and sometimes I didn't, but the outcome in the long term was usually the same; people came and went, the business went through peaks and troughs but life carried on. In the febrile days of 2000, my predecessor was told that the very survival of our 200-year-old firm was dependent on the continued employment of a 20-something individual who had been in the industry for about 18 months. We offered him a partnership but he left anyway. A few years later, I reminded my senior management team of this incident and none of us, myself included, could remember his name.[15]

Now compare this to football clubs. They, too, are constantly having to jack up the wages of some "20-something individual." Like Pickering's bank, the club will survive even if said individual leaves. But unlike the bank, the club's performance will suffer if it loses its best talent. Just think of what might have happened to Barcelona had it let Messi, Xavi, Iniesta, and Busquets walk out the door in their prime. In football, the best talent is irreplaceable.

Unlike ordinary companies, top-class sports teams really do strive for excellence every week. Wenger, who went from running Arsenal to giving management talks at corporate conferences, admitted that lessons from sport weren't easily transferable: "Players have to be as close as possible to 100 percent of their potential to be efficient—which is not the case in daily life." A football team needs to come close to human perfection to beat Real Madrid. If an "asshole" can help you do it, you need his talent. That gives him power.

XI

HOW THE TALENT LIVES

Gerard Piqué's dad is driving him to his football game, Barça–Real Madrid, in October 2018. In the car they chat about mushrooms on the mountain. On arrival, Piqué goes to a room in the bowels of the Camp Nou where the players are gathering for the pre-match buffet. There's a fruit bowl, bananas, salads, but also less-healthy ham. Players tease arriving teammates about their fashion sense.

Luis Suárez and his Castelldefels neighbor Messi, car-sharing as usual, pull up in the stadium's parking lot with Suárez's son and daughter and Messi's son in the backseat. Suárez's wife has just given birth to a third child. Messi, his arm in a sling, isn't playing today. Wearing a hoodie for anonymity, he sits in the stands with Suárez's children. When Suárez scores a penalty, Messi beams at the children like a proud uncle. Then Suárez scores again and runs to the stands to embrace his kids.

When he completes his hat trick, Messi throws his free arm around Suárez's son. Barça win 5–1 and there are five-finger *manitas* all over the stadium, including from the fans' rep on the field, Piqué. (He made the sign twice, he boasts later, in case "they" missed the first.)

After the game Messi and Suárez each take a son into the changing room. Players sit gazing at their phones, watching the messages pour in. Then Piqué goes to a dinner for Barça's sponsor Rakuten (the "Japanese Amazon"), where he gives a welcome speech in English. Afterward he reminisces with Rakuten's chief executive, Hiroshi Mikitani, about the time he asked permission from the coach, Valverde, for the players to attend a post-match party in New York. "Do you remember?" asks Piqué. "I went to him and I said, 'Listen, Mr. Valverde, we go to a party.'" He mimics Valverde: "Why? Why? Why?" Piqué continues, chuckling, "I had five meetings to convince him that it's necessary for the team to go party. He didn't understand: 'I see no reasons to leave you go to party.' I said, 'Doesn't matter, we will go anyway!'"[1]

These scenes are from a documentary, *Matchday*, made by Rakuten itself. Piqué brokered the access to the players' intimate spaces, overriding the club's hesitation, just as he had brokered Rakuten's sponsorship of Barça in the first place. Censored though *Matchday* undoubtedly is, it offers rare glimpses of the players' lives.

Almost every sports fan wonders, "What's it really like to be them?" How do modern footballers live, at home and at work? And how are they deformed by stress, fame, and money?

CHANGING-ROOM LIFE

Barça's changing room is generally described as a convivial place. When Louis van Gaal arrived from Ajax as coach in 1997, he noticed, "Here the radio is on in the changing room, they drink coffee. It's much noisier before a match."[2] Neymar told me in 2014, "I was really surprised: the Barcelona changing room is cheerful, everyone chats and fools around, similar to Brazilians. In the changing room there is music—pregame, postgame—similar to Brazil." Boudewijn Zenden found Barça's changing room "a warmer place" than its Dutch equivalents. "Players visit each other at home, meet with the families, go out for dinner together. They hug."

One condition of that warmth is that players and managers in Spain rarely tell each other hard truths. Van Gaal, a purveyor of Dutch-style full-frontal criticism, encountered pushback at Barça. Zenden said, "If we were 1–0 down at halftime, and Van Gaal said, 'Listen boys, the wingers have to move inside a little,' [Luis] Figo was already raising his hand to say, 'What's this? We're not 1–0 down because of us. They just have to defend better.' He immediately felt attacked."

At Barça—and in Spanish life more generally—there are high expectations of courtesy. Public tellings-off are not tolerated. This indirectness can be a problem. It helps explain (along with the family nature of Barça) why nobody ever took Busquets or Piqué aside to tell them they had got old and it was time to go.

"It's part of top-level sport that you say things, and discuss things," said Zenden. But in Spain, "if you have an open clash with a player, it won't automatically come good again." Any criticism needs to be delivered in private and carefully phrased. A shrewd coach will first invest time building a relationship of trust with a player before trying to broach sensitive issues.

There is one other important aspect of changing-room life that's almost never mentioned: nudity. Imagine that in a regular office, or a restaurant, all employees of one gender stripped and showered together daily. In football, nudity surely affects the social dynamic, but since it's a taboo topic within the game, I haven't been able to discover just how this works.

STRESS, MEAN TWEETS, AND THE SILENCE OF THE CAMP NOU

Pressure to perform is essential in top-level sports, because otherwise athletes grow nonchalant. But this pressure eats away even at the most successful players. In the documentary *Nummer 14*, made in 1972, Cruyff explains the young footballer's sudden realization that journalists and teammates treat him worse after a bad game. "You notice a different attitude. Then you go home and turn on the TV and watch yourself being panned. Monday in the paper, more of the same. It's a feeling of loneliness, that everyone is against you." The next time you walk onto the field, he continues, you look at the stands and wonder, "Are these people here for me? What should I do, how should I behave, how should I play? Should you run beautifully, or should you really play football?"

He reflects, "You belong to everyone, but as soon as it ends, I'm alone and then I drive home and—I don't know." He looks pleadingly at his interviewer. "Then you feel so lonely."

He says it's like being the Queen of the Netherlands: people see her and think, "Loads of money, big house, I'd like to swap with her." Yet she could never be herself or say what she thought. Cruyff scratches his head, pushes aside his mop of hair. "It's terribly difficult to say how you really feel." This was his level of anxiety in a season that he won a second straight European Cup with Ajax and was about to be named European Footballer of the Year for the second time running.[3]

There are few professions in which a twenty-year-old gets regular hammerings in global media. A mean article or tweet can ruin a footballer's day, even give him a psychological complex. Players are particularly sensitive to the marks that websites and newspapers award for their match performances. Lineker said that all footballers look at those marks "even if they say they don't."

Sometimes a stressed player will confide to a teammate, perhaps one of Barça's captains, "I need help." Others withdraw from the squad into their entourage. Unhappiest of all is the player who ends up sitting in silence in the changing room, locked in his own world. It's hard for a club doctor to tell a coach that a player is unfit to play due to chronic stress, because there are no clear biological markers.

Barça tries to help. After the struggling Philippe Coutinho played badly yet again and was substituted during a victory over Espanyol in 2019, the club president Josep Maria Bartomeu and vice president Jordi Mestre visited him in the changing room with consoling words. "The majority supports you," Bartomeu told him. "A small section boos you, and me, and him [pointing to Mestre]. You are in a good team and you are an excellent player. Don't think about it." And the besuited president hugged the shirtless, tattooed, miserable superstar, who would soon be sent away on loan.[4]

Criticism can be especially harsh at the Camp Nou, where the *socis* have impossible standards, focus almost all their attention on the home team (the opposition is usually mere decor), and aren't particularly supportive. Cruyff spoke of "the problem of the stadium . . . [which] creates enormous pressure, especially on the Spanish players in our side."[5] Lineker saw it when he arrived in 1985:

> It wasn't an incredible atmosphere. It was like you needed to perform for them to applaud, like the theater, like the opera. And there was a kind of silence for most of the game. It wasn't like working-class British people that went to football and had a few drinks and wanted to shout, sing and applaud. These were the kind of middle classes that went. They were all season-ticket holders, members.
>
> The atmosphere was different, more reserved. You had to entertain them before they got on their feet, with the one exception

of the Clásico, the Real Madrid game, which was something else—the atmosphere from the very start was electric. But pretty much all the other games, unless you scored a couple in the early stages, you'd get a few whistles, and the old *pañuelos blancos*, the white handkerchiefs, so it could be hard.

You had to get the crowd going, they didn't get you going. All that really matters is what you do on the pitch. If you're scoring the goals, they love you, if you're not, they really don't like you at all.

There are no hardworking or funny-looking cult heroes at Barça. There are only successes and failures.

The atmosphere at the Camp Nou didn't change much between Lineker's departure in 1989 and the start of the pandemic in 2020. The crowd would sing along to the decorous Barça hymn before and after the game, but otherwise remained pretty quiet. The *socis* treated victory as their right. When Zenden left Barcelona for Chelsea, he started his English career with a home draw against Newcastle. Afterward, Chelsea fans came up to him in the parking lot to say, "No worries, son, well done," and "Next week we're going to win." He was amazed: "If you drew the first league match with Barcelona, you would know about it afterward."[6]

Still, perhaps footballers in Europe have it easy. Rivaldo set me straight in 1999 when I naively suggested that the pressure from fans in Barcelona was the biggest in global football. "I don't think so," he said. "I experienced the greatest pressure in Brazil, at Corinthians and Palmeiras. They threaten your family, they damage your car and it's a little complicated. If you were to have the results at Palmeiras that we've been having at Barcelona recently, you wouldn't be able to walk down the street."

What makes Barça fans almost uniquely demanding is that winning isn't enough. They also demand beautiful attacking Cruyffian football. Thuram, who had come from Juventus, said, "In Italy, whether you play well or badly isn't what's important. What counts is that you win. Here, even if you win 2–0 but there isn't spectacle, the spectators won't be satisfied." Valdano told me that Madrid's fans had a different attitude: "At Real there is an enormous passion for triumph. There's an admiration here for the player who gives everything. And there's also a desire for spectacle. But that's the order of things here. In Barcelona that order is reversed. First it's the play, then the result."[7]

There is no expectation at Barça of supporters getting behind the team even when it's playing badly. The Camp Nou sets the standards; the players' job is to meet them. Guardiola, who understood *socis* because he was one himself, told the crowd in the stadium on the day his new squad was presented in 2008, "It's a marvelous challenge for us to try to convince you."[8]

The peculiar nature of the Camp Nou—giant yet unenthusiastic— makes a player's life at Barcelona still more demanding than at other giant clubs. When Ronald Koeman left Barça for Feyenoord Rotterdam in 1995, Cruyff mused, "In one way, of course, you can understand it because at this level, in this climate, it takes so much out of you."[9] A retired Barcelona player once told Rosell, "Sandro, when I was put on the bench, I was happy, because on the days when I was playing, my leg was shaking." Even Messi has said, "It's not easy to step onto the field in the Camp Nou."

The German goalkeeper Robert Enke's only full season at Barça was ruined by a disastrous defeat to a third-division team in the Copa del Rey. He then sank into depression. After moving to Fenerbahce, in summer 2003, he wrote on a sheet of hotel notepaper:

My year in Barcelona has changed me a lot. All the self-confidence that I built up in three years in Lisbon has been taken away from me. . . . I was always glad when I didn't have to play, even in training games. . . . In reality I was always relaxed and happy when I was watching from the sidelines. I'm also really scared of the opinion of the public, the press, and people's eyes. I'm paralyzed by fear.[10]

Six years after that, as recounted in Ronald Reng's biography *A Life Too Short*, Enke threw himself in front of a train. Every suicide has multiple causes, but Reng believes that the stress of football contributed to this one.

Even the almost incomparably successful and popular Iniesta said after leaving the club for Japan, "Playing for Barça is not just playing a football match. It's a brutal pressure, constant tension, training perfectly every day, being the best in every match." It was hard, he concluded, "to enjoy it 100 percent."[11]

THE ENTOURAGE AND THE GOLDFISH BOWL

Away from the game, top-class players need to learn how to live the superstar life. Not all of them manage.

The big divide is between players who live in families and those who live in entourages. Young foreigners often set up in a mansion in Barcelona with their agent, physio, girlfriend of the moment, an older relative or two, the odd unidentifiable camp follower, and friends from the old neighborhood who have become their financial dependents. (A footballer from a poor country, like the Cameroonian Samuel Eto'o, might be supporting dozens of people back home.) Especially if the player doesn't speak much Spanish, there's a risk of him retreating from the club into the comforting circle of his support group. After training he'll return to the mansion to complain about his teammates and coach.

Maradona, who played for Barça from 1982 to 1984, lived with a "clan" of friends, relatives, personal doctor, and trainer in a house in the chic neighborhood Pedralbes. A local journalist who once visited him at home when he was recovering from hepatitis recalled in 2020, after Maradona's death, "Diego was in a bed in the garden. Around him were more than ten people eating and drinking at six in the afternoon as if it were a party. It was the first time I saw white powder snorted, from the corner of the ping pong table."[12]

Barça's then manager, Menotti, who also liked his nightlife, sometimes in his compatriot's company, moved the team's training sessions to three p.m. to suit their habits.[13] Ronaldinho and Neymar later brought tamer versions of the Maradona entourage to Barcelona; Neymar's included his hairdresser.

Not all entourages are dedicated to the player's success. The friends from the old neighborhood sometimes have interests that are contrary to the footballer's. They rattle around the mansion all day with nothing to do. At night they want to go out, ideally in the footballer's company so that they can get free drinks at the best table in the nightclub, and attract women. The footballer goes with them, and doesn't immediately notice a drop in match performance, but the nights out take a cumulative toll.

Then there are visits from friends and family, which tend to be more frequent in Barcelona than in, say, Dortmund or Newcastle. During Neymar's time at the club, "his friends were flown to Spain every two months for an all-expenses paid holiday in Barcelona—a relatively common benefit among top players," writes the football lawyer Daniel Geey.[14] Some visitors understand that the player needs an afternoon siesta and can't go out with them every evening; others don't.

Barça finds married players easiest to manage. Marriage bumps the footballer into a new life stage: from yellow Ferrari to black Range Rover, and from central Barcelona to a quieter beach town. But inequality is baked into most footballers' marriages. A former banker in Barcelona recalls an agent setting up three bank accounts for a new Barça signing: a joint account for player and wife, an account for their fixed outgoings such as rent, and a third account that the wife wasn't told about. Whether the player lives with a family or an entourage, it's he who dominates the household. Everything is structured around his desires, moods, up and downs. Nobody else is allowed to distract him with theirs.

Once Barça players become fathers, they are encouraged to treat the first-team squad as extended family. Piqué, Suárez, and Messi set up a kids' team for their sons to play on,[15] and with discipline slackening in the post-Guardiola years, every day at Barça seemed to be bring-your-children-to-work day. Frenkie de Jong marveled, "If guys aren't in the squad, they'll kick a ball with their kids in the room where you can warm up. At Ajax I'd never seen kids in the changing room." Even Barça's plane to the Spanish cup final in 2019 was full of relatives, with Piqué's young sons loitering purposefully behind Messi's seat.[16]

Barça's players often limit their social circles to family, childhood friends, a few teammates, and perhaps some longtime staffers at the Masia, because they learn to distrust anyone they meet after becoming a star. Piqué said, "It's difficult now to cultivate real friendships. People like me attract, seduce. That's why I protect myself. I don't open up easily, to the point of appearing distant."[17]

He has mastered the modern celebrity's box of tricks to keep the world at bay. For instance, he and his wife, the singer Shakira, post photographs of their sons online so as to reduce the value of the pictures and thereby deter paparazzi. At least there is less off-pitch scrutiny in Barcelona than in Madrid, headquarters of Spain's showbiz media.

The worst thing to happen to footballers in the twenty-first century is probably the smartphone camera. They live in fear that somebody will take an indiscreet picture or video, or post their restaurant conversations on social media, so people who are permitted to hang out with them often have to hand in their phones. In a nightclub, a footballer might watch the dance floor from a private area, and have club security walk him to the toilets.

All this fear and suspicion is rational. Footballers really are surrounded by people who are trying to use them, for money or simply to boost their own status. My interview with Neymar in 2014 was commissioned by his sponsor Red Bull, as part of a promotional shoot for another of his sponsors. Fifteen people—photographers and their assistants, public-relations types, makeup girls, and I—stood around a Barcelona loft studio ogling his fat-free body as he changed shorts between photographs. Everybody there wanted something from him. A couple of young Brazilian men, presumably friends from childhood who had become entourage members, sat waiting patiently on the side of the room. I sold my unrevealing forty-minute interview to Red Bull for good money, and here I am years later selling the experience all over again.

No wonder footballers often respond in kind by using other people, either as sex objects or as unpaid valets to handle everyday chores. In the case of one young Barça player of the past, that meant commissioning a club fixer to supply him with Viagra. If a footballer needs a new phone, somebody else gets it for him instantly. Nor will he ever go online to book his own plane tickets. Watch the video of the litter that Barça's squad left strewn across their changing room after a game at Slavia Prague in 2019: there's always someone to pick up after players. They learn to walk past people as if they aren't there.

One former agent told me that footballers outsourced everything to gofers except football, sex, and sometimes shopping. He thought that most of them lacked empathy because they had grown up in a competitive, suspicious, all-male business, in which anyone who couldn't meet standards was cut and disappeared.

Many footballers learn to see the outside world as smelly strangers rubbernecking at the gate of the training ground, grabbing their hair and bodies, or shouting abuse at them. A footballer eating with his wife and children in a restaurant might have to pose for fifteen selfies, unable to talk to his family or even eat his food. Most Barcelona players report that they can go out to dinner in town (Piqué said that even he and Shakira could, and Neymar said it was certainly easier than in Brazil), but footballers develop an extraordinary tolerance for being bothered in public. Zenden summed up his experience: "If you're eating out in England, they wait till you finish and then they say, 'We waited half an hour, please can we have an autograph?' In Spain they come to you while you're eating and say, 'I have to go now, so I'm coming to ask for your autograph,' and in Italy they literally join you at the table."

A few players don't mind the goldfish bowl: during Ivan Rakitić's years with Barça, he went to the supermarket, waited for his kids at the school gate, and posed for selfies at the beach. But most players prefer to stay home or stick to celebrity hangouts where they can be among their peers.

Inma Puig, the psychologist, found that the big risk for footballers at Barça was becoming "dehumanized" through fame. She explained, "People see the player as a superman. If you lose contact with reality, nothing will work."

This isn't only the players' fault. It's the fans who do the most to dehumanize them. One day when my sons were about ten, they were invited to a friend's birthday party at the Parc des Princes, Paris Saint-Germain's stadium. (Like many clubs, PSG does this kind of thing as a nice little earner.) The children were walking out of the stadium afterward when PSG's striker Edinson Cavani happened to drive past with his partner. The birthday boy's dad later sent me the video. On it, the group of small boys swarm the windows of Cavani's sports car, shouting, "Look! It's Cavani!" while the two dads chaperoning them yell, "Boys, step back!"

Absent from the children's response is any awareness that Cavani is a human being.

Yet Cavani's response was striking, too. He presumably experienced this kind of invasion of his personal space every day, but he sat there smiling, patiently waiting for it to end. Cavani knew the boys would always remember this moment, and I suspect he wanted to be generous. Many footballers are awed when they realize how much they mean to fans. Cruyff often spoke of the time after Barça won the league in 1974, when an old woman came up to him on the Costa Brava and said not "Congratulations," as he'd expected, but "Thank you." That was how deep the feeling went, he marveled.

A footballer can even make a dying child happy with a bedside chat. Sandro Rosell, Barça's ex-president, said that after he visited children's cancer hospitals with Messi and Carles Puyol one Christmas, a doctor told him, "You cannot imagine what it does. The vital statistics of the children"—Rosell raised his arm skyward.

RICH PEOPLE'S PROBLEMS

Money—*pelas* in Spanish slang—can destroy a footballer's equilibrium, especially when he first becomes rich. In 2003, while Barça's young center-forward Javier Saviola was having a bad spell, an anguished club director told me, "Saviola! If you know that in Argentina at River this guy was earning sixty thousand dollars, and here he's earning six million, then you know the problem."

Cruyff understood. He once said in an interview, "The money you have left at the end of the ride is what you earned after age 26. Everything you earn before then, you spend. . . . If you earn a fortune tomorrow, what's the first thing you do? Buy a Porsche."

"Or something else of value," interjected the journalist.

"No, a Porsche!" said Cruyff. "That's just the way it is. Even if you only enjoy it for a year. And why? Nobody knows, but it happens. There's no sense to it."[18]

When the Cameroonian midfielder Alex Song joined Arsenal in 2005, he later recalled,

> I signed my first professional contract and I was so excited, I came to training and saw [Thierry] Henry arrive in his car, which was a gem, and I thought I needed the same car no matter the cost. Since I was a footballer, I could just go to the dealership, sign some papers and they would give you the car, that's how I ended up with the same car as Henry. After two months I understood that my money was going to run out and I asked for a Toyota instead.

For years, Song spent everything he earned. Then, in 2012, he was approached to join Barcelona. "Their sporting director spoke to me," said Song. "He told me that I wasn't going to play much football there. I told him that I didn't care, I knew that now I was really going to be a millionaire." Song's spell at Barcelona was mediocre, but he achieved his goal.[19]

If the footballer doesn't spend it, someone else will. Players are surrounded by vultures who want their money. Cruyff succumbed to the disastrous business adviser Michel Basilevitch. Often the chief vulture is the player's agent, yet the agent can simultaneously protect him from other vultures. Mino Raiola said, "You now have players who can earn fifty million to two hundred million euros [over their careers]. How do you invest that—or not? Players are always getting offers from people." He put on an overexcited young voice: "'Mino, a friend of mine has a real estate company, and they're going to do this, and I'll get fourteen percent, guaranteed!'"

Raiola added:

> But you also have to watch out for banks. Banks want to sell you products, too. . . . I always say to players, "We do not invest." We just want the player to finish his career with the money he earned, and more—but not less.
>
> What I suggest is, "Buy your own house quickly, buy bricks, and otherwise keep your money in the bank, even if it's at low interest. You don't have to live off the interest. Don't put it into businesses you know nothing about." All my players, in the beginning, want a restaurant, a hotel, or café. I come from the restaurant business and I say, "Don't come to me with that, zero. Because I know what that is."

Raiola (who grew up working in his father's pizzerias) was pinpointing a key difference between today's footballers, who don't need to find more ways to make money, and those of the recent past, who did. As late as 2008, in the changing room of the European champions Milan, players such as Cafu, Clarence Seedorf, and Mathieu Flamini would put on suits after training and drive into town for business meetings. They had started out in an era when even top-class footballers expected to need a second career.

Nowadays players earn so much that anyone who lasts a couple of seasons at Barcelona and hangs on to his money can maintain his extended family forever. In 2019, the average basic first-team player's pay at Barça was $12.2 million a year, the highest for any sports club on earth, according to the Global Sports Salaries Survey by Sporting Intelligence. (Real Madrid and Juventus were second and third in the rankings, with NBA teams making up the rest of the top ten.)[20] Barça pays above-market wages in part because the club is run by *directius* who have spent their careers in more conventional businesses. When they find themselves face-to-face with football agents, they are like gazelles among lions. And like many senior officials of football clubs, they tend to be terrified of their own players.

Even after the pandemic pushed down pay, top-class footballers were still earning more than at almost any other time in history. Huge salaries encourage monomania and infantilization. From adolescence onward, the player's entourage, family, or club shields him from life so that he can focus on football. Financial advisers—often chosen chiefly for their charm and proximity rather than any expertise—are hired to handle the money. That's how Messi, for instance, could have no inkling of his own illegal tax dealings. "He doesn't know what a bank account is," one former Barça official told me.

It's in the interest of both the club and the agent that a player be kept dumb. He typically isn't even at the table while they conduct the negotiations that determine his career. They might agree a secret deal between themselves—perhaps the club pays the agent a bonus if the player stays—that he doesn't know about. Or the player might suddenly be dispatched to a new club, grinning as he holds up the team shirt for the cameras while wishing he wasn't there. Players often come to understand this power dynamic only late in their careers, or after retiring, or in many cases, never.

Footballers are encouraged to shut up and play. Unlike musicians or online influencers, they have little financial incentive to build controversial personal brands. They are raised on media training that teaches them to say nothing: "We're happy with the win, but Saturday is another big game." Thuram, who was a rare player with outspoken political views, explained his colleagues' caution: "The moment you give your opinion in public, you no longer have unanimous approval."[21] Neymar's entourage spent years crafting his brand, but it was all about teaching him to smile rather than say anything interesting. When I interviewed him, I felt that he was a nice young man who had lost the ability to speak frankly even if he wanted to.

A rare modern footballer with an alternative career is Piqué. The center-back is a compulsive entrepreneur who while winning the World Cup with Spain in 2010 used his long hours of downtime in the team hotel to set up a video game company.[22] He has since created a string of businesses. He can present a business plan live to investors, remembering the numbers for every income stream, pivoting on the spot when necessary. The name of the company he founded in 2017, Kosmos Global Holding, sounds like a parody of plutocratic globalization. Piqué is also happy to say controversial things, often antagonizing other Spaniards with his support for a referendum on Catalan independence.

He is exquisitely aware of his wealth, as witness a somewhat shocking scene in the Rakuten documentary. Dressed in a 1950s intellectual's black polo-neck and a Berlin clubber's leather trousers, Piqué appears on a local radio show in front of a studio audience. Grinning, he recites the song that fans of Barça's local rival Espanyol sing about his family:

> Piqué, scoundrel,
> Shakira is a man,
> Your son is fathered by Wakaso [a Ghanaian then playing
>   for Espanyol]
> And you are gay.

Piqué finishes the song with a thumbs-up and a hoot of laughter. The show's host asks whether his salary is comparable to the budget of a small town. Piqué replies, "My net wealth is higher than Espanyol's budget."

"¡Joder!" ("Fucking hell!") swears the host, laughing.

A producer interjects that Espanyol's annual budget is €57 million.

Piqué corrects him: "It's much more." The audience members—many of whom probably live on less than €1,000 a month—laugh.[23]

One of the things going on in this scene is a spilling over of professional footballers' culture into civilian life. Inside a football team, pay is the main measure of status. Cruyff said, "The degree of appreciation is expressed in money. So it's not about the sum that you earn, but the hierarchical position that you occupy."[24] Piqué was signaling, in the grossest possible way, that his status was stratospheres above that of the people who abuse him.

Since money in football equals status, players keep trying to gouge more of it from their club, no matter how much they already have. Even local boys who grew up as *culers* are unsentimental in salary negotiations, said Rosell. He paid tribute to the exceptions: "Carles Puyol: when he retired he didn't ask for the salary for the remaining years on his contract. Second time in my life. First time was [Marc] Overmars. And Van Gaal."

Yet footballers often struggle to spend much of their money. That's especially true at Barça, with its club culture of modesty, where players are encouraged to come to work in their Audi-sponsored cars. When I snooped around the first-team parking lot at the Gamper complex one morning, the only exceptions I noticed were a couple of Range Rovers, a Jeep, and a red Ferrari—the sole vehicle that would have caused comment on, say, a street on the Upper East Side.

Proud as footballers are of their wealth, many of them simultaneously feel guilty about it, especially ones like Maradona and Romário, who grew up in slums and considered themselves political radicals. This sense of guilt can prompt self-destructive behavior. Many footballers try to assuage their unease by spreading their wealth around, sometimes almost randomly. Ferran Soriano, the former Barcelona chief executive, writes, "Over the years I have seen players spend hundreds of thousands on cars they can't use, but I have also seen them give €500 to a beggar or leave a €50 tip on a €65 restaurant bill."[25] There is a yearning here to reconnect with the society that they have left behind.

A NEW KIND OF TALENT

On Valentine's Day in 2020, the coronavirus was already racing through Spain, but nobody knew it yet. That morning, I went to watch Barcelona's women's team train at the Gamper.

I found a seat in the low concrete stand beside the only other spectator, a man who introduced himself as the personal physio of the women's keeper. On an artificial mini-field smaller than a penalty area, twenty-two players were performing a spectacularly difficult Cruyffian exercise. The blue team attacked, and the red one defended. The blues had to complete three passes before they could shoot into any one of the six mini-goals lining the field. There were also points awarded for completed passes. Anyone who could play in that small a space could play football.

Talk about the male gaze: surrounding the women were ten male coaches, their arms folded as they scrutinized play. The men's presence ratcheted up the intensity: everything that each player did, good or bad, would be seen by somebody and analyzed at the coaches' meeting afterward. After each round, the red and blue teams swapped bibs, while a coach shouted out the points totals. Gamification helped keep daily training interesting.

The physio pointed out to me how seriously the women worked. At a male training session, he said, some players would be messing around. Indeed, on the adjoining training field, Barça's youth keepers were enjoying a moment of hilarity after one of them had got sprayed by a sprinkler.

Barça's women's team was founded in 1988, but it only turned pro in 2015, when female football in Europe began to boom. In 2017, the club's

Dutch winger Lieke Martens won the Euro with the Netherlands and was voted Best FIFA Women's Player of the year. She and her parents flew to Monaco for the awards ceremony on a private plane with Messi. He told her he'd followed her exploits at the Euro and was proud of her trophy. In Monaco, Cristiano Ronaldo, winner of the men's award, joked with her like a colleague.

In March 2019, in a league game at Atlético Madrid, Martens played in front of a crowd of 60,739, the largest attendance ever in women's club football. Two months later, she appeared in Barça's first-ever women's Champions League final, a 4–1 defeat to Lyon. Yet her daily reality remained less glamorous. She made do with a few visits from family a year, and didn't have a mansion to accommodate them in. She told me, "Male footballers bring their whole family, can bring anyone they want, create their own house. It doesn't yet work like that in women's football. I still sometimes suffer from homesickness."

One Sunday, I went to see FC Barcelona Femení play Logroñés, in the little Estadi Johan Cruyff next to the Gamper. The 1,842 spectators sang along joyously to the Barça hymn. After decades watching men's football, it was an odd sensation to sit right beside the field, listening to female voices calling to each other. The similarity was the style: the Femení played Barcelona's fast-passing Cruyffian football, and quickly went 4–0 up.

When Barça missed a penalty, a middle-aged Scandinavian couple at the front of the stands—the man wearing a football shirt with "Johansen 1" on the back—jumped up and applauded. A sympathetic collective chuckle went up as the crowd realized that these were the parents of the Logroñés keeper. She hadn't even stopped the penalty (it had rolled wide), but at 4–0 down you celebrate when you can. After the game the keeper ran over to her parents for long hugs. This wasn't the Camp Nou.

Barça's women earn less in a year than their male teammates in a week. That differential will shrink. There was delight in Barcelona when Real Madrid finally launched its female team, adding spice to the Spanish women's league. In October 2020, on field 11 of Madrid's training complex, Barça won the inaugural women's Clásico 0–4. Though the stands were empty because of the pandemic, the game was shown live on Spanish public TV. In May 2021, the Femení won their first women's Champions League, thrashing Chelsea 4–0 in the final. In March 2022, the female Clásico drew a crowd of 91,553 to the Camp Nou—the world record for a women's game, despite rain and an early evening kickoff.

There is potential here—perhaps more so outside Spain than inside. Officials in Barça's office in New York have been surprised to discover the impact of the Femení in the American market. Stanley Black & Decker, the maker of drills and lawnmowers, keen to shed its male image, put its name on the women's team's shirts. Generally, the Femení give Barça a handy sheen of gender equality. In years to come, as the status of female talent rises, the women may acquire some of the airs of the men.

XII

———

EAT, PLAY, SLEEP: THE TALENT AND THE PRIVATE CHEFS

L uis Suárez's kitchen in Castelldefels has a barbecue built into it. The Uruguayan striker gets the indoor grill going and salts the raw steaks while his neighbor from across the street, Leo Messi, drinks South American maté tea. On the kitchen table are nearly empty glasses of red wine, and what appears to be a cheese plate. Bottles of champagne and a large Moët-branded cooler fill the counter.

There is brief disappointment when fullback Jordi Alba arrives without the promised bottle of wine. He explains that he'd hidden it from the baby, then forgotten it. "He didn't want to bring it," teases Messi. But soon a bottle of red appears from somewhere. For dessert, Messi spears strawberries from the communal bowl on the table, eating them off his knife.[1] Nothing in this scene amounts to Maradonaesque excess. Still, it would give the nutritionist of an Olympic rowing team a heart attack.

Leading football clubs have learned a lot in the past decade about how players should eat, sleep, and generally manage their health, even if huge knowledge gaps remain. One problem persists, though: how to persuade the talent to take the advice, especially in a city as full of temptation as Barcelona. Frenkie de Jong said that after he signed for the club, Ronald Koeman, then his coach with Holland, warned him not to "go to restaurants too much or eat too much because life is really good in Barcelona and sometimes you can feel like you're on vacation the whole year."[2] Then there's the issue of sleeping habits in Spain, a country that averages fifty-three minutes less shut-eye per night than the rest of Europe.[3] Getting footballers to eat and sleep right turns out to be as hard as getting your children to do it.

BARÇA'S FOOTBALLERS CERTAINLY live more healthily than their predecessors did. The club's first foreign star, the Hungarian refugee Ladislao Kubala, famous for his nights on the town, favored the pre-training regimen of "a cold shower, a sleep on the treatment table, coffee filled with aspirin and back out on to the pitch," records Sid Lowe. Asked once by a customs officer if he had anything to declare, Kubala patted his belly and said, "Yes, two liters of whisky."[4]

Some of these habits were passed down. In 1973, Barça lost 3–1 at Sevilla in the Copa Generalísimo (the Spanish cup, then named after General Franco). Barcelona's manager, Rinus Michels, rejected his players' request to go out that night, so a few of them got together and ordered two bottles of cava from room service. Michels, who had stationed himself in the lobby, intercepted the waiter carrying the drinks tray and asked which room he was going to. The Dutchman remarked that he himself happened to be heading that way, and offered to take the tray. When the knock came at the door, the players opened it, expecting to see a waiter. Instead, De Generaal, screaming in Dutch, hurled their bottles to the floor, splintering glass everywhere.

After the Peruvian Hugo Sotil signed for Barça a few weeks later, the first question at the press conference was, "Do you like champagne?"[5]

Michels's outburst didn't change habits at Barça. Catalans had been drinking wine since Roman times and weren't going to stop for some overexcited Dutchman. Lineker recalled:

> When you sat with the Barcelona team for your pre-match meal, there would always be bottles of red wine on the table. Most players would have a single glass of it with their food, perfectly naturally, without comment. There was quite simply no English club where that would have happened. Wine on the lunch table? With an English football team in the eighties, it would have been inviting carnage.[6]

Good wine was one of the perks of playing for Barça. For decades, the team were accompanied on away trips in Europe by a crate of Marqués de Arienzo, a powerful red rioja.[7] Many foreign players became connoisseurs during their time at the club. Cruyff, in the late 1970s, dabbled unprofitably in wine exports.[8] Michael Laudrup, a generation later, founded a more successful business in his native Denmark. One industry blog calls Laudrup Vin & Gastronomi "the most important importing company for wine and gourmet products from Spain to the Scandinavian country."[9]

The food at Barça has always been good, too. In 2006, the year they won the Champions League, one player would regularly bring luxury foie gras into the changing room. The club's medics failed to dent his belief that it was healthy.

At the time, it was just about acceptable for a footballer to live the good life. Since then, though, the game's fitness standards have soared.

High-intensity running—defined as moving at over fifteen kilometers an hour—increased 30 percent in the English Premier League between 2006 and 2013, according to the Gatorade Sport Science Institute. The number of sprints rose sharply in the Champions League, too. "We have to have a much better physical condition to play our game," Paco Seirul·lo told me.

Modern coaches push players almost every day for eleven months of the year, leaving little time for recovery. Most players can perform optimally in the autumn, but struggle to maintain that level between February and May—the period that Barça defines as "high competition," with lots of matches, travel, and sleep loss.

Gil Rodas, a specialist in sports medicine at the University of Barcelona who has worked with Barça for many years, said the game's rising "intensity and density" had prompted an increase in muscle and tendon injuries, which he called "the cancer" of football. The packed schedule didn't help: one study found "a 6.2-fold higher injury rate in players who played two matches per week compared with those who played only one."[10] As players' pay rose, so did the cost of injury: on a salary of €8 million, spread across forty club games, each match appearance was worth €200,000.

In short, footballers needed to get fitter. How best to achieve that? An unspoken truth in the game is that doping will do more for you than broccoli. I'm sure there are some illegal drugs in football. On the other hand, clubs, doctors, and players have strong incentives not to risk getting caught. I am not aware of any proof that Barcelona has used doping, even if there have been many allegations.[11]

In any case, Barça's style doesn't rely on running more or faster than the opposition—to the contrary. In the good years, Barcelona players got ample opportunity to rest on the ball.

Still, all clubs had to up their physical game. Nutrition had the advantage over drugs of being legal. It was also a growing obsession among the millennials who increasingly staffed the football industry. Gradually, clubs everywhere began to supervise players' dining habits. In 2010, the health fanatic Guardiola appointed Antonia Lizárraga to the new role of Barça's nutritionist. She became only the second person in that job in the Spanish league. Football's conventional wisdom in those days, she told me years later, was, "The most important thing is not nutrition, but that the ball goes in."

Guardiola insisted that Barça's players eat lunch together after training.[12] Football's traditional match-day meal had been chicken or pasta without sauce, or in the more hidebound institutions, steak. Lizárraga introduced quinoa and fish. She began planning nutrition for all Barça's teams from the Masia upward. She helped many first-team players find personal chefs, and communicated constantly with the chefs about individualized daily menus. (Chefs tend to be stronger on cooking than nutrition.)

During the 2010s, the game's feeding support structures burgeoned into a mini-industry, with Barça at the forefront. One day in November 2019, sports nutritionists from thirty-five countries, "performance chefs," and players' personal chefs gathered in an auditorium beside the Camp Nou for FC Barcelona's Sports Nutrition Conference—another step in the club's attempts to build football's knowledge base. The largest national delegation was British. Outside the auditorium, athletic-looking young chefs served the delicious "functional protein muffins" and non-alcoholic Bloody Marys that Barça now tries to feed its players. I found myself leaving panel debates about healthy eating early so as to stuff myself at the food stalls.

Still, I learned a lot about what footballers should (in theory) eat. I discovered that the main principle of sporting nutrition was "periodization": eating the right thing at the right time. A booklet called *Sports Nutrition for Football*, published by the Barcelona Innovation Hub, the club's research wing, proved particularly helpful. Here are some of Barça's recommendations:

- Cheeringly, caffeine appears to improve everything in football from cognition through sprinting to passing accuracy. Barça's booklet recommends tea or coffee at pre-training breakfast, and caffeinated sports drinks (or gum) on match days, ideally to be taken during the warm-up.[13]

- Carbs are an essential part of the pre-match meal, usually eaten about three hours before kickoff. Most clubs also provide them at halftime, often in the form of a gel or a drink. A player with a high workload needs to pack in the carbs, but if he doesn't have a high workload (perhaps because he's injured), lots of carbs will make him fat.

- Nutritionists have long obsessed about pre-match meals. More recently they have begun to think about post-match nutrition, too.[14] Straight after exercise is when the body is most receptive to nutrients. Post-match is also a time when the club has some control over what its players consume. That is why Juventus installed a dining table in its home changing room. Away teams often eat on their drive home in a team bus equipped with a top-class chef serving from a ditto kitchen.

  Within an hour of a match ending, players should ingest protein to help their damaged muscle fibers recover. (The player's cycle is "damage/recovery, damage/recovery," said Lizárraga.) The anti-inflammatory protein recovery shake—which some clubs personalize for each player—has become a ritual in the industry after training and matches.

- High-fiber vegetables such as broccoli, cabbage, cauliflower, and brussels sprouts should be eaten twice a week, but—given that they are gassy and take time to digest—not immediately before taking the field.[15]

- Inflammation of body tissues tends to increase throughout the season. In the toughest months, from February onward, players should ramp up anti-inflammatory foods such as dry fruits and bone broth, rather than mainlining football's traditional painkilling drugs. Ideally, food becomes medicine, said Lizárraga.

YOU CAN LEAD A FOOTBALLER TO A PROTEIN RECOVERY SHAKE BUT YOU CAN'T MAKE HIM DRINK

It's one thing for a club to draw up a nutritional plan, and quite another to get players to stick to it. Imagine being a Barça footballer. You have been the star of every team you ever played for. By definition, everything in your career has worked out: you've made it to Barça. Now you're bursting with health. You're the most popular man in every nightclub you walk into. (Barcelona is not New York; footballers are practically the only A-list celebrities in town.) You can afford to eat or drink whatever you want. And some nutritionist who earns in a year what you make in a weekend wants to restrict your diet? Come on, this isn't prison.

The cliché is that being a footballer is a short career. In fact, at the top nowadays, it's a fairly long career. It effectively starts in a youth academy in adolescence and lasts about twenty years, eleven months out of twelve. That's too long for most people to live like monks—or like Olympic athletes, who typically have to exercise self-denial for just a handful of years, and who know exactly which day they need to peak.

American team sports have off-seasons lasting several months, with time for burgers and nightlife. Footballers cannot toggle between famine and feast, and so they rarely give themselves over entirely to either.

Many footballers, especially younger ones, simply don't know what to eat, or are cooked for by someone who doesn't understand sporting nutrition. The ones who do take an interest often care more about looking good in the nightclub than being top-fit on the field. Others just don't see the point of good nutrition. Some players tell medical staff that they can't finish a whole bottle of water at halftime, although marathon runners might drink eleven bottles during a race. Some say they don't feel hungry after a match, then go for a late dinner with their entourage. Some players at giant clubs spend weeks at a time with national teams that don't even have a nutritionist.

In Barcelona, there's an additional hazard: Spanish dinnertimes of ten p.m. or later. Late-night meals tend to increase inflammation, blood sugar levels, and weight gain, and to impair sleep.

Barça and its nutritionists are sometimes left looking on in horror. After the twenty-year-old Frenchman Ousmane Dembélé arrived in Barcelona in 2017, he fired four private chefs in quick succession. The fourth, Mickael Naya, said afterward, "Ousmane is a nice boy but he doesn't have his life under control. He's always living with his uncle and best friend, who don't dare tell him anything. It's a bumpy life. I've never seen alcohol, but he doesn't respect his times for rest at all, there is no high-level structure around him."[16] Spanish newspapers reported on the Frenchman's love of fast food.

After Dembélé got injured again during Barça's first match of the 2019–2020 season, the club called him in for an X-ray the next day. He didn't show up, preferring to fly home to visit his mother. On his return, Barça's doctors diagnosed him with a thigh injury that kept him out for five weeks.[17] With medicine as with nutrition, Dembélé was doing his own thing.

This is common in football. A player might avoid the club doctors because he is trying to hide an injury (especially if he's in the last year of his contract). He might have superstitious beliefs about the right treatment. He might be listening to his personal physiotherapist or unlicensed quack, who steers him toward the latest unproven treatment (such as ice baths), usually without telling the club.

Barça has to try to coax its talent into the treatment room. The club is always trying to market its services to its own players. To dissuade injured footballers from going private, Barça bought what it believes to be the best MRI machine on earth, a device that can produce images of a single millimeter of muscle, showing exactly where a tear is.

But footballers, like most people, like to keep control over their own bodies. Even at hyperprofessional Bayern Munich, Guardiola had to nag his squad to sit down to the catered post-match gourmet meal in the club restaurant. Few footballers have the nutritional discipline of individual athletes, who make their own decisions and cannot easily blame sporting failure on anyone else: the athlete Carl Lewis and tennis player Martina Navratilova were vegan pioneers decades ago.

Even some individual athletes indulge. I had wondered before my breakfast with Federer on his plane whether he would eat human food. But when the flight attendant brought us mini-croissants, muesli, fruit skewers, and three different detox juices, he scarfed everything except the fruit. When I assumed breakfast was over, the flight attendant reappeared to suggest an omelet.

"I'll try an omelet," said Federer. "Why not? We're brunching!"

I remarked on his appetite, and he said, "I don't want to become too serious. It also reminds me, maybe, I'm more than just a tennis player. I'll have a coffee before every match, and if there is a chocolate on the side, I'll have a chocolate. Or a cookie." The most gifted don't have to sacrifice like mortals.

In football clubs, nutritionists have limited influence. They are usually at the bottom of the staff hierarchy, competing with doctors, physical coaches, and psychologists for the players' ears. Nutritionists can recommend certain foods, but they can't break into players' mansions and force-feed them. They rarely get to sit with the players at mealtimes. (At some clubs, even a younger player cannot join the senior players' table.) The team's pre-match meal—the centerpiece of the nutritionist's week—is usually presented as a buffet. How to persuade players to make the right choices?

In a hierarchical environment like a changing room, influencers matter. The main influencer on almost any subject in football is the coach. If he disdains nutrition, he may never let the club nutritionist address the team, even presuming he knows who the nutritionist is. He certainly won't help her calibrate each player's feeding schedule by telling her who will be playing in the next game and who will not.

A canny nutritionist might draw up a personalized diet plan for the coach, convert him, and then let him evangelize among the players. Simply having the coach attend player weigh-ins can make a big difference.[18] Guardiola was that kind of coach. However, his successors relaxed some of his nutritional rules. In 2019, Barça's players still sat down for their main meal of the day together after training (which could be in the morning or the afternoon), but anyone who preferred to go home was given a takeaway, in hopes that he'd eat it.

"Only at twenty does your body function perfectly," mused Alfredo Di Stéfano, star of the 1950s, and younger footballers often feel, with some justification, indestructible. Many of them start their careers short on discipline, commitment, and listening skills. Yet most athletes grow up over time, "get over themselves," and become more coachable, said Gregg Popovich, coach of the San Antonio Spurs basketball team.[19] Often the prompt is reaching a certain age, starting a family, failing at a club, or entering an exciting new career phase—making a big transfer, say. That can be the most fruitful moment for a nutritionist to have the Talk with a player about food.

Other than the coach, a club's main influences are the senior players. Older footballers who have been through injury and have started worrying about extending their careers tend to develop an interest in beet juice. Messi has followed that trajectory. Long an aficionado of the Argentinian breaded steak, ham, Parmesan, and mozzarella dish milanesa a la napolitana, he realized by his late twenties that he was facing early decline. He sometimes vomited during games. He looked exhausted throughout the World Cup of 2014.

Like many footballers, he sought expert advice outside his club: from the dietician Silvia Tremoleda[20] (who later followed Guardiola to Manchester City) and on visits to the Venetian clinic of the Italian nutritionist Giuliano Poser. Messi is reported to have gone mostly vegetarian during the season, a new trend in football. Some players have even become vegans.

Messi managed to lose multiple kilos. (His rival Cristiano Ronaldo adapted his own already spartan diet in 2016, dropping from eighty-two to seventy-nine kilos so as to regain some speed.) Looking back, at age thirty, Messi said, "I ate badly for many years—chocolates, soft drinks, everything. That was what made me vomit during games. Now I take better care of myself with fish, meat, salads."[21]

His conversion benefited Lizárraga's work at Barça.[22] He became a lifestyle influencer in the changing room, publicly warning Dembélé, "He needs to make that change to be more professional . . . I hope he doesn't keep having the bad luck he's had with injuries."[23]

Helpfully, many footballers have been influenced by society's growing obsession with nutrition. By managing their own intake and following eating routines, they can control their stress, instead of simply feeling like victims of injuries and luck, observed Lizárraga. But especially in a gourmet city like Barcelona, it's not enough to give footballers healthy food. To keep them from straying, it needs to be tasty, too, ideally delivered as a cake or shake.

What finally appears on the table tends to be a compromise between club and players. After a draw at Malaga in September 2014, Barça's individual post-match meal requests leaked to the media. For the main course, the club had offered players a menu of options, each one rich in the sugars and carbs that help rebuild damaged muscles. Here are some of the players' choices:

Ter Stegen: Sushi and a Nutella sandwich

Piqué: Nutella sandwich and fruit

Rakitić: Sushi (two helpings) and fruit

Busquets: Ham pizza and fruit ("ONLY PINEAPPLE AND STRAWBERRY")

Xavi: Chopped chicken breast and ham pizza

Iniesta: Ham-and-cheese pizza and a sandwich of bologna and chorizo

Suárez: Ham-and-cheese pizza and Caesar salad

Messi: Cheese pizza

Neymar: Ham-and-cheese pizza and fruit

Mascherano: Pasta salad and two pieces of fruit

Sergi Roberto: Sushi and "triple sandwich" with Nutella[24]

Even given that the post-match meal is the most sugar-rich of the footballer's cycle, these choices look suboptimal. A ham-and-cheese pizza comes packed with saturated fat and salt. Still, at least it's a protein-and-carb delivery system that footballers will actually ingest. And compared to what some players eat at home, it's practically health food.

THE MYSTERY OF THE FOOTBALLER'S BODY

For all the effort invested in getting footballers to eat right, there is still little scientific evidence that it makes a difference. We just don't know whether good nutrition wins football matches or does much to prevent injury. It's quite possible, for instance, that Dembélé's muscular injuries stemmed from bad luck and his sprinter's body type rather than from bad eating. The French physical trainer Sébastien Lopez argued that Barça's low-paced training sessions in the 2017–2020 era, tailored to older players, limited the winger's sprint training.[25] In other words: Dembélé's procession of personal chefs might have been irrelevant. We don't know.

This points to a larger, uncomfortable truth: we have little scientific evidence of any kind about the tiny demographic of top-class footballers. That's because their bodies and needs are so atypical that they have barely been studied by medical researchers.

If a footballer pulls his hamstring and has to miss matches, it's a crisis that could cost his team a title. However, if the average office worker pulls her hamstring, or has suboptimal muscle tissue for a fortnight, she'll barely notice. No wonder medical research hasn't taken these issues seriously. Nor can Barça conduct much in-house research, because the club's sample size of elite adult male footballers is only about twenty-five. The dozen or so top-class clubs that make up Barcelona's peer group are unwilling to share their medical data. That's why big decisions in football (Does this player need surgery?) have historically been made on intuition.

And clubs lack knowledge because footballers' bodies follow different rules from those of the rest of us. Barça's athletes carry several "paradoxical biomarkers"—ones that are unhealthy for ordinary mortals but beneficial to top-class sportspeople. For instance, during the season Barcelona's footballers have high levels of both good and bad cholesterol. They have high levels of the amino acid homocysteine, which in ordinary people seems to raise the risk of heart attack and stroke.

Players are also unusually likely to have Gilbert's syndrome, a mild genetic disorder that prompts the body to produce higher than normal amounts of bilirubin, a yellow substance in the blood. Gilbert's syndrome can cause mild jaundice, but it has an important upside for athletes: the excess bilirubin reduces inflammation.

Footballers constitute a human subspecies that requires its own kind of medical care. We just have very little idea yet what that might be.

SLEEPLESS IN THE CAMP NOU

Football is still so far from being optimized that Barça is exploring all sorts of new frontiers in the field of "player wellness." While I was writing this book, the Barça Innovation Hub had entered into partnerships with scientists in dozens of studies of muscle and tendon injuries. The club was attaching chips to players in training, in hopes of learning how to predict stress or injuries.

Another holy grail of football is to get players to play with as much power in the second half as they do in the first. One recent theory is that players fade partly because their body temperature drops too much while they are sitting down at halftime. That could be avoided with measures as simple as giving them jackets, turning up the heat in the changing room, and making them perform a "re-warm-up" before the second half.[26]

Now Barça is trying to individualize care. It wants to progress from measuring each player's "external load" (how many games and of what intensity he has played recently) to measuring his internal load: how he is reacting psychologically, biomechanically, and physiologically to the external load. After all, a player might experience more stress reading social media about football than he does playing.

Of all the new frontiers in football, the most promising is probably sleep. Scientists keep discovering more about its importance to human functioning. "Sleep loss leads to a decline in physical performance, eye-hand coordination, attention span—almost everything one can measure," reports ESPN in an exposé of sleeplessness in the NBA.[27] The issue is especially relevant to elite athletes, who are among the rare people whose jobs require them to be at their best. So it's remarkable how little sleep some of them get.

Messi, in his first months on Barça's first team, shared a small apartment with his brother Rodrigo, Rodrigo's wife, and their baby. He said at the time, "The club tells me I need to have a good sleep every night so it's a bit difficult with the baby crying, but I pretend that I don't lose any sleep."[28] Piqué admitted in 2019 that between football and entrepreneurship, "I hardly sleep four or five hours. I lack time for everything."[29] Busquets once remarked that in the years before he met his partner, he was awake eighteen hours a day, "thinking about football."[30] Then there was Dembélé in his early Barça seasons, spending his nights on PlayStation[31] and (according to his ex–private chef) not "respecting his rest periods."[32]

Sleeplessness isn't always the players' fault. It's an inevitable consequence of playing sixty or so matches a season, around the world. The excitement of a game prompts the body to release cortisol, a hormone that promotes wakefulness, and it suppresses melatonin, the hormone that regulates sleep.[33] "I can't sleep after games," confessed the long-time English center-forward Peter Crouch.[34] Especially after he had played for Liverpool at Anfield, he writes, "My head was so clear, my body tingling, buzzing so much that it would be several hours and many beers until I could even think about going to bed."[35]

Post-match insomnia is a particular plague for players at Barça, who regularly kick off games at ten p.m., finishing at around bedtime. Lizárraga, the club's nutritionist, recommends milk or turkey to promote sleep, but there are nights when even a glass of *leche merengada* ("200 ml lactose-free milk, 1 cinnamon stick, ¼ lemon peel, 1 tsp agave or maple syrup, 20 g casein powder, cinnamon powder")[36] won't do the trick.

Then there's travel. In the 2019 preseason, Barça's squad flew to Japan for friendly matches on July 23 and 27. They then returned home for a friendly against Arsenal on August 4. Three days later, they faced Napoli in the Hard Rock Stadium in Miami, thirteen time zones away from Japan. Next, they flew three hours to Michigan for a rematch against Napoli, before returning to Spain on their fourth transcontinental flight in three weeks. "Physiologically speaking, I don't know whether that was so good, but commercially I understand it, and so there isn't a player who complains about it," commented Frenkie de Jong.[37]

In international weeks, a footballer might play an away game with Barça on Sunday night, return home at two a.m., finally fall asleep at four thirty a.m., and then be on a flight at seven a.m. to join his national team. "I did experience that as hard," De Jong admitted soon after moving to Barcelona. Football traditionally has little patience with such complaints. "That makes a big man out of you," said the Netherlands' manager Ronald Koeman, who a few months later would take over at FC Barcelona.[38] But the footballers' trade union Fifpro reported in 2019, "Sixty-three percent of national team players say that long-distance travel impacts their performance."[39]

Barça's South Americans regularly cross an ocean and back to play a match. In 2016, Neymar gave his club teammates Messi and Mascherano a lift in his private plane to a Brazil–Argentina qualifying match for the World Cup 2018, even though they were playing against him.[40]

When clubs play away games, they often arrive in the host city the day before the match, sleep a single night in a hotel, then fly home straight after the game. That leaves them prey to so-called first-night effect (FNE): the first night you sleep in an unfamiliar place, half your brain (typically the left side) remains unusually awake, according to researchers at Brown University. The connection between the two halves of the brain is also unusually active. This is probably an evolutionary adaptation: the brain is ascertaining whether the unfamiliar territory is safe. The upshot is that if you sleep just one night somewhere, you'll probably sleep badly—and for footballers, that night often precedes a big game.

One way to combat first-night effect is always to stay in the same hotel chain, so that the room becomes familiar. A better solution would be to stay two nights. "FNE alertness is drastically reduced or even disappears during the second night sleeping in the same unfamiliar environment, almost as though the brain simply shuts off its alarm after ensuring that the area is safe," reports the Barcelona Innovation Hub.[41] Staying a third night after the game would be better still, because it would save players from returning home in the early morning and notching up yet another broken night.

The only problem with this advice is that players don't like it. They generally want to spend as little time as possible on the road, returning home straight after the match.[42]

It's a tricky call for Barça to make: either exert more control and risk alienating star players, or keep them happy and accept that they won't be optimally fit. In recent years, Barça has generally chosen to keep them happy. Hoping to oblige the talent, the club tries to minimize travel. For away games in Spain, if kickoff is at six p.m. or later, the team flies out on the morning of the match, and returns home that night. De Jong said he liked it that way:

> Imagine that you go to another club—then you leave on the Saturday morning, [sleep in a] hotel, play on Sunday, and on Sunday you stay the night there. Then you're only home that

Monday evening. And some [teams] also go into a hotel before home games. Here in Barcelona it's much more relaxed. We only have to arrive two and a half hours before the game if we're playing at home, and for away games we often leave on the day itself. So you're home more.

When I asked why he thought Barça followed this policy, De Jong said he imagined the players had indicated that they liked being at home. He added, "I don't see the problem. I don't think it makes much difference." He said Barça was happy to talk to a player about sleep if he wanted, but he added: "It's not that they tell me, 'That's when we're playing, so that's when you need to go to sleep.' They leave that very much up to the players. The guys here have played ten or so seasons at the highest level, they know how to deal with that. I think they wouldn't like it if people said, 'You have to do such-and-such.'" De Jong had had a different experience at Ajax, a young team: "They'd say, 'You have to be in your hotel room at eleven.' They'd think, 'Maybe they'll be home with their mates or having a pizza or something.'"

Clubs still know very little about how their players sleep. Some ask players to report on their quality of sleep each day, but a man who has been up all night has an incentive to lie. People at Barça told me of plans to get more reliable data by making players wear night garments with sensors. At last, football clubs are catching up on sleep.

AN AGING SOCIETY

Football's advances in sleep, nutrition, and medical knowledge have improved fitness, even if the talent doesn't always listen. Players, clubs, medics, and referees—each on their own, and sometimes in concert—have raised the game's standards of care. One piece of evidence: "[E]lite athletes are getting older," writes sports scientist Carlos Lago Peñas in a report for the Barcelona Innovation Hub.[43] The average age of players in the Champions League rose from 24.9 years in 1992–1993 to 26.5 in 2018–2019. An increase of 1.6 years is bigger than it might seem, given that the average ages of almost all leading teams fall into a narrow band of 23 to 29.

When Megan Rapinoe was crowned as winner of female Ballon d'Or for best player on earth in December 2019, she was 34. Messi was the same age when he lifted the male version of the prize again two years later. Cristiano Ronaldo was then also still near the zenith of the game, aged 36. Despite growing physical demands, elite careers are lengthening.

This trend is echoed in other sports. In tennis, the average age of the top 100 male players rose in a decade from 26.2 to an all-time high of 27.9 years. By April 2021, Novak Djokovic (age 33) was the highest-ranked male player, Rafael Nadal (34) was in third place, and Roger Federer (39) sixth. Serena Williams (39) remained a power in the women's game. The quarterback Tom Brady had just won the Super Bowl with the Tampa Bay Buccaneers at age 43. Studies of baseball players and triathletes also suggested "a marked increase in the age of peak performance of elite athletes during the last two decades," according to a paper that Lago Peñas wrote with colleagues at the University of Vigo.

Decision-making and football intelligence—pattern recognition, in effect—seemed to improve with age, he explained. "The percentage of successful passes is 3–5 percent higher in players over 30 compared to players between 16 and 29 years old." That could compensate for a decline in speed. Lago Peñas cited a study of players in Germany's Bundesliga: after age thirty, their number of sprints (defined as runs faster than 6.3 meters per second, maintained for at least a second) was 21 percent lower than for younger players.[44]

A healthy veteran player is the perfect combination of an old head on reasonably young legs. But an old head on old legs is a problem. Ominously, no top-class team in the years to 2020 took aging further than FC Barcelona. Aging happens naturally at Barça because players who are starters here rarely choose to leave—a fact that rival clubs have come to accept. Barça's players have surprisingly few options elsewhere, noted Rosell: "They can only go to three, four clubs in the world, because nobody can pay their salaries."

Barça's players also know they will struggle to find a better team, a nicer city, or more enjoyable daily training (compare the brutal endurance battles at Juventus or Atlético Madrid). De Jong said, "In Barcelona the weather is fantastic, the training sessions are super fun. Every day I appreciate that I'm allowed to be on the field with these players." Barça is the footballer's final destination, not a staging post.

And players come to realize as they approach retirement that it won't offer them a more fulfilling experience than football. Piqué told me when he was twenty-eight: "Now I'm hoping my career as a footballer will be as long as possible, whereas a few years ago I thought I'd quit at thirty. That change happens to all players: the footballer's syndrome."

Active footballers may not be any happier than the rest of us, but they do have more intensity. The basic illusion of top-class sport is that it is more important than life and death. Winning in front of a hundred thousand fans provides a buzz unmatched in ordinary life. So, perversely, does losing. You sit in the changing room with all your teammates, your body hurting, too tired to lift a bottle of water to your lips, slumped in misery, and it is a shared intensity of emotion that you will never experience again after football. Retirement in one's thirties is a widespread fantasy among Dilberts in office cubicles, but most top-class athletes have too much internal motivation to spend their remaining decades on the sun lounger.

They struggle to understand how the rest of us put up with our low-adrenaline lives. The highlight of a civilian career might be a promotion, a piece of work that wins a nod from the boss, or simply an office junket to the seaside. No wonder successful footballers play for as long as they can, and then often seek a new buzz in risk-taking afterward: think of Cruyff's business investments, or Maradona's lifestyle.

Consequently, Barça's best players usually stick around and grow older together. An ideal at the club is for a player to leave "through the front door," before everyone has grown fed up with him, but few manage to get out on time. Barça's president is typically keen to renew the contracts of the fans' idols, sometimes even giving them pay rises in their thirties. That might mean wasting tens of millions of dollars when the idol becomes an unshiftable thirty-five-year-old crock, but often that's the next president's problem. For the short term, the renewal buys the current regime some happy front-page photographs. Age changes the team's dynamic. Older players tend to pick their moments to peak. You'll rarely see an aging elite team give its all in a home game against weak opposition. Fernando Torres, who spent much of his career at hardworking Atlético Madrid, observed that the most talented teams were often able to coast: "Sometimes you are not having a good game, the opposition is doing better, and in one second"—he snapped his fingers—"a player wins you the game. Madrid and Barcelona have this situation many times."

Barça's team aged almost unnoticed for years, until suddenly the problem became obvious. The club had failed either to grow or to recruit young players to replace its old ones.

PART FIVE

THE CATHEDRAL
CRUMBLES

XIII

MISADVENTURES IN THE TRANSFER MARKET

n any talent business, the most important management decision is recruitment—"the war for talent," the McKinsey consultancy called it. By the time Barça won its fifth Champions League in 2015, it had the money to sign almost anybody in football. The Masia's production machine had saved it fortunes on the transfer market, and the Catalans were generating the highest revenues of any sports club on earth. They could have gradually bought a new great team. They didn't. Even by the standards of football's inefficient transfer market, Barcelona botched the job of identifying new talent and persuading it to sign. The club has ended up a case study of the pitfalls of talent recruitment in football. What went wrong?

Finding a player who will thrive at Barça is a messy process. Some clubs, such as Lyon or Liverpool, have a small committee of experts that decides whom to buy. Barça is less organized. Rival currents inside the club might each push for different signings, often without bothering to check with the coach of the moment. Presidential candidates campaign on promises of the stars they will buy if elected. Certain sponsors and agents (including Guardiola's brother, Pere) can influence transfers. The sporting director of the moment will have his own views, as will senior players, especially Messi.

Here's how Barça's recruitment procedure works at its best: After the club identifies a weakness in the first-team squad, the senior executives on the football side discuss who might fill it. If there are budding players in that position in the Masia, the sporting director will make sure they are considered. The club tries not to let the coach drive transfers. After all, he probably won't be around for long, and he doesn't have the time to research the transfer market. When Guardiola pushed Barça into buying the Ukrainian defender Dmytro Chygrynskiy in 2009, against the misgivings of other officials who had met the player, the transfer failed. And the last thing the club wants is a squad full of the previous coach's pet purchases whom his successor decides to clear out. One official told me: "Never sign a player because the coach wants him, but never sign a player that the coach doesn't want."

Once Barça decides it needs to buy someone—a right-back, say—the sporting director and the director of football will handle the matter. They will ideally pursue four potential targets simultaneously. That allows them to compare prices and put pressure on the selling clubs. The president ideally comes in only at the end of negotiations, to decide which final details to yield on—shall we pay the extra €5 million that the selling club or agent wants?—and then shake the player's hand for the cameras.

The man nominally in charge of Barcelona's disastrous transfer policy between 2014 and 2020 was Josep Maria Bartomeu. Nothing in his experience had equipped him for the role. An amiable chap, he runs a family company that makes the jet bridges that you walk through from plane to terminal. In 2003, he joined Barcelona's board as the *directiu* overseeing basketball, handball, and field hockey. He resigned two years later after clashing with President Laporta, then returned in 2010 as the little-noticed vice president of Sandro Rosell, a pal of his from student days at Barcelona's upmarket ESADE business school. In January 2014, Rosell stepped down because of legal troubles over the purchase of Neymar, and his loyal follower Bartomeu became the accidental president. Elections were due eighteen months later, and he was considered a mere caretaker. However, in June 2015, Barça sealed the treble of league, Spanish cup, and Champions League. A month later, Bartomeu cantered home in the presidential elections.

In early 2015, he had told me: "Economically, our club is, I think, in the best position in its history." He certainly deserves some credit for the jump in revenues during his reign. The problem was that he didn't know how to spend the money that was flooding in. He knew little about either football or the football business. His sporting director, Andoni Zubizarreta, did—"Zubi" had signed Neymar, Suárez, Rakitić, and Marc-André ter Stegen—but Bartomeu soon sacked him. In all, the president had five sporting directors in six years. He and some of his senior board members—who were themselves new to football—began getting involved in the early stages of transfers. Sometimes they even approached a player without telling Barça's executives. If the executives then approached the same guy, the result was confusion and embarrassment. Contrast this naive lot with Real Madrid's experienced duo of Florentino Pérez and his silent counselor, the philosophy graduate José Ángel Sánchez.

Another constraint on Barça's purchases: at the very highest level of European football, poaching players from rivals is considered ungentlemanly. Paris Saint-Germain's chief executive Jean-Claude Blanc told me:

The honor code among big clubs is to have good relations with the other big clubs. If a player interests us, we talk between clubs, and don't send agents or other intermediaries to act as go-betweens. If a big club wants to buy one of our players, they call this office or [president] Nasser [Al-Khelaifi] and ask, "Would you consider selling this player?" If the answer is no, then 90 percent of the time the conversation is over.

The same rules apply to coaches: Barça hired Tata Martino in 2013 partly because he was a rare unattached candidate.

You'd think that a club planning to spend tens of millions on a player would base its decision on statistics or other objective measures. Liverpool does: it was the club's data department that identified Mo Salah as a great striker. Jürgen Klopp, the manager, initially didn't want him. (After Salah came good at Anfield, Klopp apologized to the analysts.) Barça, by contrast, makes little use of data in the transfer market—a reluctance that has earned the club some friendly ribbing from Liverpool's head of research, Ian Graham.

Data mostly reveal what a player does on the ball, explained Javier Fernández, when he was Barça's head of sports analytics. But it's hard to obtain "tracking data" that show what the guy does in the other eighty-eight minutes of the game.

Valverde, when he was coaching Barça, told me, "Sure, we look at the data of a player we're interested in. For example, if we're going to buy [Clément] Lenglet [the center-back signed from Sevilla in 2018], we look at his speed, his number of ball recoveries, the attacks he has interrupted." But, above all, Valverde went on, the club asked people who knew the player about his psychology. "Because if a guy comes here with amazing data but he's a satellite . . ."

The player's psychology is the great unknown in almost any transfer.

A team is a fragile thing, like a glass bottle hanging from a thread, said Guardiola. Buying an emotionally weak or undisciplined player can break it. Hence the saying: 99 percent of recruitment in football is about who you don't hire.

When Barça is considering a player, Barça also will often dispatch a senior executive to meet him and his agent before approaching his club. This is against FIFA's rules, but it's common practice in football. After all, it's the most direct way to take the measure of a potential employee. Barça has an international network of alumni it can draw on for intelligence. In 2002, while the club was plotting the ill-fated purchase of the keeper Robert Enke from Benfica, it consulted Porto's young manager, José Mourinho. He gave a glowing report, even though that ruined his own hopes of buying Enke.[1] Presumably he was keen to stay in Barça's good books.

But as Enke's psychological unraveling in Barcelona shows, no new signing is a fully known quantity. "When you buy a player, you can't exactly carry out a brain operation to see how he's put together mentally," lamented Cruyff in 1990.[2]

Once Barça approaches a player, he's almost invariably willing to listen. "The door is always open," Rosell told me. "Sometimes you cannot reach an agreement, but everybody sits at the table." When Enke's wife said she didn't want to go to Barcelona, her husband's agent corrected her: "If Barça calls, you run to get there."[3] The Dutch striker Memphis Depay asks, "How often are you going to say no to Barcelona? It's Barcelona."[4]

Yet Barcelona in the Messi era has often faced a peculiar hurdle: Many potential signings felt they weren't good enough for the club. They thought Barça had made a mistake in approaching them. These players were suffering from impostor syndrome, but, of course, they might have been right.

Rosell said, "Sometimes an agent comes and says, 'No, no, no, we are not ready.' This is very honest. I liked it when it happened to me, two or three times when I was president."

Bartomeu concurred, telling me:

> Not all the players I wanted to sign have come to Barcelona. I have examples that I cannot say—very important players now playing in other clubs. We told them to come, they were excited, but at the last moment they said, "I can't sign because I will be on the bench." We don't want them.
>
> Sometimes, they are not strong enough to say, "Where do you want me to play? Xavi is playing, why do you want me? You want me to play in the Leo Messi position, I can't." At the time [goalkeeper] Víctor Valdés was there, nobody wanted to come to Barcelona. Why? To sit on the bench? So that's the big difficulty.

Paul Pogba made these sorts of calculations when deciding to join Manchester United in 2016. His agent, Mino Raiola, explained, "Pogba could have gone to all the top clubs. But Real Madrid had just won the Champions League. He'd have been a trophy player there. Barcelona: their three trophies are Messi, Neymar, and Suárez." Raiola believed that a player should join a club that needed him, and for Pogba that club was United. In this case as in many others, the agent may have had the biggest say in the player's decision. "What you see is the final result of years of sculpting," said Raiola. "I spent two years working on Manchester United's deal with Paul."

Barcelona's best transfer this century was probably the purchase of twenty-one-year-old Neymar from Santos in 2013, just before the Bartomeu era. Most of Europe's big clubs were chasing the Brazilian. When Barça's then director of football, Raúl Sanllehí, left for Sâo Paulo to try and persuade the player's family, he told his wife he'd be gone for three days. He ended up staying away nearly two months, competing in what felt like a "beauty contest" with Real Madrid, Bayern Munich, and the others. Using his fluent Portuguese, Sanllehí became pally with the key decision-maker, Neymar's father, who even invited him to stay in the family home. This proved handy: after dinner Neymar Senior would tell Sanllehí about his talks with other clubs. But Sanllehí held the ace: Neymar couldn't hide his desire to join Barça. The club ended up paying less for him than some rivals had offered.

The transfer arrangements were so murky that they eventually forced Rosell to resign as club president, but the cost to Barcelona has been put at around $100 million, much of it in payments to the player and his family.

It was a bargain. Neymar understood from the start that he had to subordinate himself to the king, telling the Camp Nou at his presentation that he aimed "to help the team, and also Messi, so that he can remain the best player in the world."[5]

A year later, the Uruguayan striker Luis Suárez arrived—another easy transfer, because joining Barcelona had always been his career plan. His wife's family already lived in the city. His agent was a local man: Pere Guardiola, Pep's brother. Almost every summer, Pere phoned senior Barça people from the president downward to ask if they were interested in Suárez, until in 2014 Sanllehí rang him to say: actually, yes we are. Bartomeu said the player turned down better offers from other clubs to join Barça.[6] Suárez bonded with Messi over shared South American *maté* tea from day one. From then until 2017, Barcelona was able to field the magnificent Messi-Suárez-Neymar "MSN" attack. The team increasingly skipped midfield to supply the brilliant trio early. The style was too random for Cruyff's taste—"a team that prefers individuals rather than a team that plays good football,"[7] he sniffed—but on the upside, it worked. Bartomeu told me in 2015, channeling Barça's Franco-derived paranoia, "Sometimes I feel surprised that football let us have Messi and Neymar and Suárez in one attack. I was thinking someone would say, 'Stop! No! You can't!'"

Neymar peaked by Messi's side. The Brazilian says that when he was struggling early on at Barcelona and needed help, "the best person in the world came to me, held my hand, and spoke to me: 'Come here. Just try to be yourself, you must become happy again, you must be the same boy you were at Santos. Don't be shy, don't be scared of me or anyone else in the team. I'm here to help you.'" Neymar claims to have been so moved that he burst into tears in the changing room, thinking, "If Leo says these things, it must be the truth." He recalled, still sounding like an afternoon soap opera: "Suddenly I became calm. At last. It was the start of a warm friendship."[8]

Neymar at Barcelona was a hyperefficient, nippy goal-scoring winger who ran onto Messi's passes, and accepted being exiled from the center of the field. Expected goals (xG) is a measure of how many goals a team is likely to score based on its quality of chances. Barça's xG peaked at about three per game in 2015–2016. Of that total, Neymar accounted for 1.2 xG per game, only slightly behind Messi's staggering 1.4, reports my *Financial Times* colleague John Burn-Murdoch. But Neymar wanted to be Messi: the fulcrum of every attack, winner of the Ballon d'Or. In 2017, to Messi's dismay, the Brazilian left to become main man at Paris Saint-Germain for a transfer fee of €220 million, a world record.

It was a landmark moment for Barça: for the first time in years, a star with a regular first-team place had decided to leave the club. It also proved possibly the most consequential football transfer of the 2010s. From September 2017 through the end of 2020, Neymar at PSG averaged 1.16 goals and/or assists per Champions League game, more than anybody else in football in that period. In addition, he created the most chances and completed the most dribbles.[9] He developed an unfortunate habit of missing the knockout rounds of the competition through injury, though the one season he did play, in 2020, he led his team to the final against Bayern.

But deprived of Barça, he lost some of his discipline. At times he degenerated into a number ten who liked to receive the ball standing still, then taunt opponents by doing tricks while they kicked him. It was his natural game, and perhaps he preferred it to brilliant servitude at Barça. Stuck in the French league, the most gifted player of his generation effectively retired from weekly top-class football.

When a club sells a player for €220 million, it doesn't actually have €220 million to spend. There are taxes, agents' fees, and payments by installment. Still, every other football club in 2017 knew that President Bartomeu now had a wad of money in his back pocket, and a need for a human trophy to wave in front of his Neymar-deprived *socis*. The smart thing for Bartomeu to do would have been wait for a year to let the memory of his windfall fade, and the selling clubs' demands with it, but he wanted to please the *socis* at once.

Barça rushed around hunting for a star. The Spanish agent Junior Minguella offered the board the eighteen-year-old French forward Kylian Mbappé, already a sensation at Monaco. Mbappé's family had decided that Barcelona was the right team for him. Monaco preferred to sell him to Barça rather than French rivals PSG. Barcelona would have had to pay a transfer fee of about €100 million plus bonuses. But Minguella waited in vain for a reply from Barça until finally a WhatsApp message arrived from a board member, Javier Bordas: "Thanks for passing him on to me. But as you see, neither the coaches nor Presi [the president] wanted him." According to Minguella, one Barça *directiu* had asked, "What has Mbappé done yet to warrant that price?"[10] Bordas would say years later that Barça had also turned down the young Erling Braut Haaland, because the technical staff thought the Norwegian wasn't "a player in the Barça model."[11]

Instead Barça decided to replace Neymar with a different young Frenchman, Borussia Dortmund's promising twenty-year-old winger Ousmane Dembélé. Bordas would recall, "The explanation at the time was that Mbappé plays for himself and Dembélé plays for the team."[12]

There were misgivings inside the club about Dembélé. Nobody at Barça had managed to speak to him before the time came to make an offer. Club officials had been unimpressed when he refused to train with Dortmund in an attempt to force the transfer. But they needed a star, fast. Three weeks after selling Neymar, Bartomeu and another Barcelona official flew to negotiate Dembélé's transfer with their Dortmund counterparts in Monte Carlo, a favorite hub of the football business. The Barça duo arrived with a firm plan, reported the *New York Times*:[13] They had resolved to pay a transfer fee of at most €80 million. Any more than that and they would walk away. According to Dembélé's agent, Dortmund had indicated earlier in the summer that the fee would be in that sort of region—but that was before the Neymar transfer. Before knocking on the door of the assigned hotel room in Monte Carlo, the two Barça men hugged each other. But when they walked into the room, recounted the newspaper, they got a surprise: "The Germans told their guests that they had a plane to catch. They had no time to exchange small talk, and they were not here to negotiate." If Barça wanted the promising youngster, it would have to pay about $193 million, or double the budgeted sum.

Bartomeu succumbed. After all, he was president of the world's richest club, and still something of a football virgin. He committed to pay $127 million up front for Dembélé, "with a further $50 million in easily-achieved performance bonuses," wrote the *New York Times*. That was more than what Mbappé would have cost.

Not six months later, Barça paid Liverpool €160 million for Coutinho. Neymar's transfer fee had been blown, and more. A transfer fee of over €100 million should come with a guarantee against failure, but neither

Dembélé nor Coutinho would ever quite fulfill their promise in the Camp Nou. Deprived of Neymar, Barça lost their dominance.

The move that taught me most about the human considerations that go into any Barcelona transfer was Frenkie de Jong's from Ajax in 2019. The player had grown up with a very Dutch love of Barça. During one of his childhood holidays on the nearby Costa Brava, the family had taken the tour of the Camp Nou, and his grandfather had bought him an early yellow-green Messi shirt with the number 30 on the back. Interviewed by a local newspaper as a ten-year-old, De Jong had said, "My dream is to play for Barcelona one day."[14]

Around New Year's Day 2015, a pretty teenaged Dutch couple flew to Barcelona for a weekend break, armed with tickets for the Camp Nou. Before the match they took a selfie in the stands. Looking at the photograph now, it feels premonitory. "It was the first time I ever saw Barça live," recalled De Jong, who in 2015 was an eighteen-year-old reserve with the little Dutch club Willem II. "I didn't necessarily have the feeling: in four years' time I'll be playing here myself. Of course you hope that, but so do ten thousand players, I think."

Yet when Barça tried to sign him from Ajax in 2019, he was torn. He considered Busquets the world's best defensive midfielder, and was worried he wouldn't get onto the team. He had other good offers, and joining Manchester City or Paris Saint-Germain felt more realistic. He sometimes lay awake at night fretting over what might well be the biggest decision of his professional life. As Wenger says, "What counts the most in a player's career is the club he chooses and the moment he chooses it."[15]

De Jong's worries encapsulated many of the issues that shape Barcelona's transfer negotiations. Like Pogba three years earlier, the Dutchman was wondering: Did Barça need him? Or would he be just another squad member bought primarily for the bench? He was reassured when Bartomeu and a small party of club executives made the effort to come and see him in Amsterdam.[16]

Bartomeu recalled the first thing De Jong told him: "I want to enjoy my life with my girlfriend, playing." As Bartomeu recounted the conversation to me, that was his opening. He told the player and his father:

> Whoever is the coach of Barça, the style will be always the same. Now we have Ernesto Valverde as coach. The following coach will be another name, but you won't see too many differences. Other clubs, depending on the coach they choose, change the style or the idea of the football. If you look for a coach, go with Pep Guardiola, but when he will leave City, I don't know who is going to be the following coach at City. If you look for money, go to PSG. You will be a billionaire. But if you want to enjoy your life for the next twelve, fourteen years, come to Barcelona.

And Bartomeu promised, "If one day you say, 'I don't like it,' we will talk. We are not a prison." Barcelona had let Pedro, Alexis Sánchez, and Marc Bartra go when they asked to leave.

De Jong finally decided he had to take the risk of joining Barça, rather than spend the rest of his life wondering whether he could have made it there.

The Catalans don't appear to have made him the highest offer. For a player choosing between different giant clubs, each of which will make him an instant multimillionaire, money often isn't the main consideration. De Jong reportedly didn't even ask his agent what salary each club was offering.[17]

Barcelona paid Ajax a transfer fee of €75 million. According to the football agent Hasan Cetinkaya, who was advising the Dutch club, this was nearly double what Ajax had initially hoped to get for a twenty-two-year-old who at that point had been playing top-level football (meaning for the Dutch national team and in the Champions League) for only three months. Cetinkaya said:

> There was tremendous pressure on Barcelona's sporting management to get the deal done, and they really wanted to protect themselves. Those in Barcelona's sporting leadership were so relieved that the then sporting director Pep Segura began to cry as soon as the papers were written.[18]

Since about 2010, Barça had gotten used to overpaying. Whereas most clubs target a type—say, a young defensive midfielder with a good forward pass who costs under €30 million—Barcelona until 2020 shopped at the top of the market, and could afford to target an ideal. In this case, the club didn't want a "De Jong type." It wanted De Jong himself. As so often in the boom years when bidding for a player, Barça had no alternative in mind, and the selling club understood this. "You know you will pay more than another club," Rosell said with a shrug. Barça presidents tended to be relaxed about overpaying. After all, the money they were spending was never their own, or indeed anybody's in particular. Club owners like John Henry at Liverpool had a personal incentive to be tight-fisted.

When De Jong arrived in Barcelona, he found that the player who did the most to make him feel at home was the very man he had been signed to succeed, Busquets: "The first day, even before training began, he sent me a message asking if I needed anything. He also reserved a restaurant table for my girlfriend and me."

De Jong had experienced more cutthroat rivalry at his previous Dutch clubs, Willem II and Ajax. At little Willem II, a player who couldn't get onto the first team risked dropping out of the Dutch premier division entirely. "That's more stress," reflected De Jong. "Financially you have much less security. And many guys there still have to prove themselves. But here [at Barça] you have lots of players who are already top players. They have confidence in themselves. They know: 'I'm very good and I'll do everything to play here, but if I don't it will come next year, or the year after, or I can go to another top club.' They have more inner peace."

In early summer 2019, a few months after De Jong's signing, Neymar messaged Messi to say he wanted to leave PSG. (The "MSN" attack lived on in a WhatsApp group.) Messi saw the chance to repair Barcelona's mistake of 2017. He replied, "We need you to win the Champions League." He then summoned Bartomeu and let him know. Having learned to talk, Messi made the same case in the media, using his platform to put pressure on the club. He was turning into a low-volume version of Cruyff.

But Barça took one look at the injury-prone, fun-loving, twenty-seven-year-old Neymar and decided it wasn't going to pay PSG's asking fee of approximately €200 million. By this time, Barcelona was running out of money, partly because of its five-year run of bad purchases, and partly because the Messis were bleeding the club dry. The pay raises that Messi's father, Jorge, extracted each season, which also encouraged teammates to demand more money, finally made it impossible to buy the player Messi most wanted.

Barça spent the summer of 2019 more or less pretending publicly to sign Neymar, so that it could eventually go back to Messi and say, "Sorry, we did our best but we couldn't get him," Eric Abidal, sporting director at the time, recalled later, possibly with some attempts at buck-passing:

> Ten days before the end of the transfer window [in 2019], I went to Paris to talk with Leonardo (PSG's sporting director) and I was with my CEO, and we were talking about Neymar. I

think if the CEO goes to Paris Saint-Germain, it's because we can sign him. . . . The president decided to sign [Antoine] Griezmann. One of the arguments against Neymar was that he had a court case against the club, so it's not easy. They said he would have to stop the court process if he wanted to come back.[19]

A year after Griezmann had publicly rejected Barcelona in a tacky reality-TV documentary produced by Piqué's company, the club paid Atlético Madrid €120 million for him. When Barça belatedly realized it didn't have that sum lying around, it had to borrow most of it in a hurry.[20] The transfer fee was a record for a footballer older than twenty-five; the Frenchman was twenty-eight at the time.[21] It also enriched Barcelona's rivals Atlético over and above the peculiar arrangement of Barça paying the Madrilenes €5 million a year for "first refusal" on all their players.[22]

The first thing Griezmann did on arrival in Barcelona was sit down with Messi. The Frenchman later admitted, "He told me that when I turned down the first chance to go [to Barça], he was screwed because he had asked for it publicly." He added, "But he told me he was with me and I notice it every day."[23]

Barça's ostentatious pursuit of Neymar doesn't seem to have fooled Messi. Asked by *Sport* newspaper if the club had done everything possible to get the Brazilian, he replied, "I don't know. . . . In the end, not everything is very clear." Asked if he ran the club, he issued his usual irritable denial: "Obviously I don't direct things, I'm just another player."[24]

A club staffer who has worked with Messi since before his first-team debut disagrees. "He's calling the shots," this man told me. "He knows he can take out anyone. He's not looking for fights—he's a nice guy. But he knows he has the power." When Messi lost a battle, the staffer said, he would remain silent but would metaphorically "write it down in his notebook." The failure to buy Neymar was Messi's biggest defeat inside Barça, and it went into his mental notebook. He couldn't forgive the board.

Messi wasn't like Cruyff. He didn't particularly want power. He sometimes felt blamed for every problem at Barça. He would have preferred that the directors and coaches handled everything—but only as long as they surrounded him with exactly the players he wanted.

A youngster like De Jong was willing to spend most of his first season at Barça playing uncomplainingly out of position. A drop in status was harder for a veteran superstar like Griezmann, especially when for the first time in his career he found himself on the bench. The night the Frenchman was substituted after a dreadful performance against Napoli in August 2020, he looked about to cry. Later he began to grumble about playing out of position. Griezmann's problem was that he was a left-footer who liked to cut in from the right, a mini-Messi on a team that already had Messi. The only way the Frenchman might have succeeded at Barça was to copy Neymar's strategy of becoming a golden valet. Jorge Valdano says: "It seems to me that the players who arrived and subordinated themselves to Messi showed proof of intelligence."[25]

It's precisely the attacking midfielders and forwards who have provided the lowest return on investment in Barça's recent history. Coutinho, Griezmann, Dembélé, Arda Turan, and Malcom all either flopped or at least struggled for long periods in the Camp Nou, at a combined cost in transfer fees of about €425 million. In total, Barcelona spent over €1 billion on transfers between 2014 and 2019, more than any other football club,[26] running up the club debt, yet ending up with a decaying team of old men almost devoid of transfer value. "Every year we were a little bit worse," admitted Piqué.[27]

By January 2020, when Barça needed a striker to replace Suárez, who was out for five months after knee surgery, the club was reduced to discount shopping. Two days before the transfer window closed,

Abidal contacted the agents of Cédric Bakambu, a twenty-eight-year-old French-Congolese forward playing for Beijing Guoan. Was Bakambu interested in joining Barcelona?

When Bakambu got the call that every journeyman footballer dreams of, he had just landed in Seoul, via Dubai, to prepare for an Asian Champions League game. He got straight on a plane to Hong Kong, from where he could catch a connecting flight to Catalonia. Exhausted though he was, he sat wide awake with excitement during the four hours to Hong Kong. As the plane came in to land and the signal on his mobile phone resumed, a message from Abidal arrived: Barça had changed its mind. Bakambu could turn around and go back to Seoul.[28] Instead, the club signed a different twenty-eight-year-old journeyman striker, the Dane Martin Braithwaite, who had recently flopped at Middlesbrough in the English Championship. Braithwaite had never been mistaken for Neymar.

Yet the most peculiar signing of the Bartomeu era was surely Matheus Fernandes. He was an unknown twenty-one-year-old reserve midfielder at the Brazilian club Palmeiras when on the last day of that same January transfer window in 2020, he joined Barcelona. The transfer fee was €7 million, plus another €3 million in potential add-ons.

Fernandes was almost a secret signing. Barça never gave him an official presentation, and immediately dispatched him on loan to little Valladolid. After his first training session there, a teammate asked him what he'd thought of their rondo. "High rhythm, high rhythm!" Fernandes exclaimed admiringly. "Well, get used to it," said the teammate, "because this is nothing compared with Barcelona."[29]

Fernandes played just three matches for Valladolid. When the season ended, the club no longer wanted him. Nor, it seemed, did Barcelona, but he was understandably eager to stay on the club's books and keep drawing his salary. Returning to the Camp Nou, he was given the "COVID" shirt number 19, which nobody else wanted. By spring 2021, "the Brazilian Phantom" had played just seventeen minutes on the first team, during a 0–4 romp at Dynamo Kyiv. No one could work out why Barça had bought him. Was it a favor to an agent, or just another misjudgment? Palmeiras's sporting director, Alexandre Mattos, explained later that he had somehow managed to lure Abidal, his counterpart at Barcelona, to come and see the club's reserve team train. "I told him: 'Watch No. 35,'" Mattos recounted. "At that moment, they called me crazy: 'You want to sell a player from the Palmeiras reserves, who doesn't play much, to Barcelona?'"[30] Two years previously, Mattos had succeeded in selling Barcelona the Colombian central defender Yerry Mina, who didn't set the Camp Nou alight either. One wonders what Messi made of Braithwaite and Fernandes.

By summer 2020, Barça's transfer deficit had become a source of personal anxiety to Bartomeu and his board members. Under the rules that governed Spanish member-owned clubs like Barça, the directors had to repay a portion of any losses out of their own pockets. The board needed to book some profits urgently before the end of the financial year on July 1, 2020. And so a bizarre swap transfer was concocted. The counterparty was Juventus, which also needed to improve its books to comply with UEFA's "financial fair play rules." It was agreed that Juve would "sell" the Bosnian midfielder Miralem Pjanic to Barça for a basic fee of €60 million (plus potential add-ons), while Barça would "sell" the Brazilian midfielder Arthur Melo to Juve for a basic €72 million.

These sums would never actually be paid. They were invented only for accounting purposes. Under bookkeeping rules, each club could book its handsome supposed selling price as immediate income. The notional payments would be spread out over the years of the players' contracts. In the long run, only €12 million in actual money would change hands, the difference between the two players' fictional prices, paid by Juve to Barça. What mattered was that the swap would help both giants clean up their books quickly.[31] It was a good deal for Bartomeu's board, but less so for Barça: the aging squad would now acquire another thirty-year-old in Pjanic, while losing twenty-three-year-old Arthur. Pjanic was soon warming Barcelona's bench.

Bartomeu does deserve credit for the signing of seventeen-year-old Pedri from Las Palmas that summer, for a fee of just €5 million. The boy from a family of Barça fans took taxis to the Camp Nou for his first few games because he couldn't yet drive, but he almost instantly became a regular in the team. Months later he made his debut for Spain. Soon he was considered probably the world's best teenage footballer. Still, that success doesn't stack up against all Bartomeu's failures.

Barça had the money to replace Guardiola's great team. It wasted it. The club's sorry record on the transfer market eventually became self-perpetuating. The most sought-after transfer targets scanned the club's long list of past failures and decided to take their careers somewhere else. Barça lost the war for talent.

XIV

EVERYONE BECOMES THE MASIA

T alent is the only essential commodity in football. Clubs either have to buy it or produce it in-house. But around the time that Barça lost the knack for buying great players, it stopped producing them, too. The team of homegrown boys that won everything between 2008 and 2012 have so far proved an off-the-charts exception. The seven Masia players in history who played the most games for Barça's first team—Xavi, Messi, Iniesta, Puyol, Valdés, Busquets, and Piqué—all came from that single generation. The Masia didn't produce an unquestioned star in the decade after Busquets emerged (though as I write in spring 2022, Gavi, Nico, and Ansu Fati have shown the potential to attain that status). Who killed the Masia? What went wrong?

Most days I make the short car journey from the Camp Nou to the Gamper training complex with Oriol, one of Barça's press officers and my appointed babysitter. Oriol has worked for the club for over fifteen years. Between interviews, we spend hours debating fatherhood and barbecuing strategies (he isn't a big football fan) or sitting in the Tapas 24 franchise beside the stadium eating *jamón*.

This morning in October 2019, we're heading for the Masia. It's been exactly ten years since I first visited the academy, in October 2009, when it was still based in the old brick farmhouse beside the Camp Nou. Two years later, the Masia moved into a glass-and-steel building in the Gamper complex, known as the Centro de Formación Oriol Tort.

Walking through the front door now, you think: student residence of an expensive private college in California. Seventy-odd boarders, age thirteen and up, including some girls, sleep in bunk beds in the building. Some of them play Barça's other professional sports—basketball, handball, or even roller hockey. The boarders, remember, are a minority: nearly 90 percent of the club's youth athletes live with their families within a car ride of the academy.

In reception there's a photograph of three Masia graduates: Messi holding the Golden Ball for European Footballer of the Year for 2010, flanked by the runners-up, Iniesta and Xavi. Together they incarnate the three lineages from which Barça has always recruited: the foreigner Messi, the Spaniard Iniesta, and the Catalan Xavi. The seven hundred athletes on Barça's various youth sports teams today come from all over the world, but as of 2017, 592 of them were from Spain, including 328 from Catalonia alone.

Academies at other clubs are still mostly changing rooms, but at the Masia, the Californian-college ambiance lingers inside: large windows flooded with sunlight, employees tapping on laptops, teenagers watching TV in the main hall, a teachers' lounge, a little library, and mathematical formulas on a whiteboard in one of the classrooms.

The Masia's nurturing has been professionalized since my visit a decade before. In the corridors there's a to-ing and fro-ing of teachers, psychologists, nutritionists, and "mentors," who act as substitute mums and dads. Specialists come in to teach kids about the downsides of cocaine, the creation of personal brands, and how to detach from people on social media who say you are rubbish. Barça even employs pedagogical taxi drivers. Some kids spend two hours a day in a taxi, commuting to training at the club's expense. The chauffeurs have been trained to detect behavioral changes and to deliver quasi-informal talks about nutrition.

The Masia's psychologists never speak publicly, and I'm not allowed to quote them, but inside Barça they are regarded as crucial employees. The club understands it has done something cruel to the children in its care: it has plucked them from their families and placed them under daily pressure to perform.

Most of the kids in the Masia aren't going to have professional careers. True, Barcelona still produces more big-league players than just about any other club in Europe barring Real Madrid and Olympique Lyon, but that's not saying much. A senior Barça official told me, "The academies of football clubs are regarded as centers of high performance. In reality they are centers for failure."

Barça can destroy a family's dream in a moment by cutting a child from the Masia, but success can also create problems within a family, such as idolatry or jealousy. After Geoff Hurst scored a hat trick for England in the World Cup final of 1966, he noticed that his parents began treating him like a celebrity.

Barcelona's club psychologists have to rescue the children. When the best player of an amateur club arrives in the Masia, Barça gives him (and his parents and agent) time to adjust. Often the child thinks he's not good enough for Barcelona. The psychologists tell him: You don't need to perform at once. You're here to improve, with time and patience.

Each child is taught to see himself clearly, both his strengths and his weaknesses. The children are also trained in empathy, so that they can support each other. One coach told me that when a boy was cut, his rival sometimes cried from guilt at having been the better player, and asked the loser for forgiveness.

The child has to learn to deal with pressure to perform. Life rituals help, such as fixed times for meals and sleep. The Masia sometimes uses loudspeakers to blast out the sounds of a full stadium, so that the kids can get used to them.

The psychologists talk to the children about performance rather than results, including performance outside sport. How is the kid performing at school? In family life? The children mustn't see themselves only as athletes—an identity that can vanish in a day if they get cut—but also as sons, daughters, siblings, pupils, and friends.

And the children are taught mindfulness: focusing on the now. Don't beat yourself up about something that went wrong before, and don't worry about the future—it's pointless. Only today matters. The club has concluded over the years that possibly the main psychological characteristic of people who make it in sport is that they are good at putting failures and disappointments behind them.

The Masia holds workshops for athletes' families, because a family can determine a player's success or failure. Successful players believe in themselves, and they get much of that belief from their family, said Inma Puig, the psychologist who treated Iniesta in 2009–2010. She added that child athletes tended to do better if their parents respected the coach. If the parents regard him as a fool whose comments are best ignored, they will generally end up disappointed.

It all sounds wonderful, like a blueprint for producing great footballers. Few other football academies have forty years of experience, much of it embodied in coaches who have been around most of that time. The Masia's reputation remains stellar: Fati said he chose Barça over Real Madrid partly so that he could live in the academy.

But throughout the 2010s, the supply line to the first team stagnated. Messi remarked, "Recently Barcelona is a bit less committed to the academy. Some big talents have left. It's strange that something like that happens at the best club in the world."[1] Masia coaches could end up feeling they were wasting their careers. They might spend a decade nurturing a talented kid. If he was sold before getting so much as a chance to fail on the first team, it could all seem pointless.

Many good players in the Masia today don't even dream of the Camp Nou. Arnau Tenas, a goalkeeper born in 2001 who first appeared on Barça's first-team squad at age eighteen, told me, "Life doesn't end with Barcelona. If they don't give you confidence, you have to find a club where they do give you confidence and minutes." Masia players for years even struggled to break into Barça B, which increasingly consisted of adult players signed from elsewhere. Andreu Cases Mundet, the Masia keeper who ended up with a soccer scholarship at Santa Clara University, said that between 2015 and 2018, while he was trying to break into senior football, Barça B signed thirty-four players from outside. None of them became a regular first-teamer.

If a Masia talent moves to another club and succeeds, Barça regards it as a "second victory." But that hasn't happened much since 2010. Among the rare examples are Thiago Alcântara at Bayern and Liverpool, Héctor Bellerín at Arsenal, and Ajax's goalkeeper André Onana.

THE MAN WHO HAD BEEN tasked with reviving the Masia was Patrick Kluivert. As he walked me to his little office, I recognized the brilliant former center-forward just from the back view: long legs, high small butt, narrow hips, boxer's torso. The Dutchman, who played for Barça around the turn of the century, was named head of the academy in 2019. "I was already living in Barcelona, so that was fantastic," he said.

As a boy, Kluivert had come through the Cruyffian sister academy at Ajax. "I must say that it's pretty much the same," he'd noticed. Like the Masia kids, he had been made to play different positions as a child in Amsterdam, especially center-back. "Just for my education. Because as a striker you're really the only player who plays with his back to the opponents' goal. But of course it's good to see how it is when you have the game in front of you: a lot easier, I can tell you."

Kluivert, Clarence Seedorf, and Edgar Davids were the junior stars of a mostly homegrown Ajax team that won the Champions League in 1995. In the final against Milan, Kluivert, age eighteen, scored the only goal. If the next Kluivert, Seedorf, and Davids came out of the Masia today, could they make Barcelona's first team?

"Very, very difficult," Kluivert replied. "Of course, it also depends on whether you have people who believe in you. Ajax is a club that gives players a chance sooner. Barcelona is a club—of course they won't *not* give top players a chance, but you really have to show it."

He added:

> Our players are constantly being called by English clubs. "We want your son, we'll give you something as well, as the father." The agent gets money, too. If a boy comes from a family that doesn't have much money, and in one go gets an offer like, "You can earn so much abroad, much more than what Barcelona is offering you," players can succumb to that. Is it good for the boy's progress? Imagine that it doesn't work, then they do have guaranteed money. Everyone knows that the TV money in England for a top club is much higher than here in Spain, so they have a bigger budget.

It wasn't a hugely convincing argument. In the 2018–2019 season, the last before the pandemic, Barcelona claimed annual revenues of

€990 million, the most in global sports. Kluivert wasn't the only Barça official with an unfounded small-club complex.

When I asked what he had changed in his first months at the Masia, he talked about the vending machines stationed around the Gamper complex. "You see all this cola and Fanta in those things. I'm busy putting healthy things into the machines."

He added, "What I changed is that we quickly go to talk with the players about contracts. Here you have to give a lot of players a pat on the shoulder, but also say: 'You have to do this and that better.' That used to not be done so much. And apart from that: just make sure everything runs well."

Kluivert is a likable guy, but our chat helped me appreciate the other Barça staffers I had interviewed. Whether they worked in nutrition, social media, or data analytics, they were itching to explain in detail the thing they had been thinking about all those years. Kluivert—appointed chiefly for his reputation as a footballer—didn't give that impression. After our conversation, I checked out the vending machine next to the first-team parking lot. He was quite right: the thing was full of soft drinks and crisps. However, another official pointed out to me that the stuff was intended for nonplaying staffers, not for Masia kids.

If the vending machines don't explain the Masia's decline, what does? When I put this question to several current and former Masia employees, they all said Barcelona couldn't hope to reproduce the Messi generation. No academy on earth was ever going to do that again. Still, admitted Seirul·lo, Barça hadn't spent enough time trying to understand what made that generation so good. "We didn't generate enough information," he said.

During my first visit to the Masia in 2009, at the peak of its fame, its coordinator Albert Capellas had drawn a circle in the dirt of the driveway, to show Barça's full circle: Guardiola had gone from the Masia to the first team as a player, and as coach was bringing Masia boys to the first team again.

But by the time I returned in 2019, the circle wasn't round anymore. Barça's short-lived head coaches no longer came through the Masia themselves, had no time to find out what was cooking there, and preferred to field ready-made players signed for €100 million.

Who could blame them? Every match they won gave them another week in the job. And expectations at Barça had soared over the years. When Messi made his first-team debut in 2004, the club had won one Champions League in its history. The Messi-Xavi-Iniesta generation had added four more in under a decade. They set a new standard: after that, Barcelona's first team was expected to be world-class. The problem is that very few footballers (and hardly any goalkeepers or defenders) are anywhere near world-class when they graduate from an academy at eighteen. They might get there by age twenty-four, but Barça cannot easily send them on loan for six years and see if they are ready then. Thiago Alcântara wasn't willing to spend two years on the bench waiting for Xavi to leave, so at twenty-two he joined Bayern. The coach there was Guardiola: in Munich, the circle was round. Meanwhile, Barcelona turned into a buying club like Real Madrid.

In 2019, I reconnected with Capellas. He was the person who taught me the most about why the Masia had declined—not only through what he said, but also through the circumstances of our chats. We'd have coffee or lunch in Barcelona during his visits home from Denmark, where he was coaching the national under-21s team. Before that, he had coached in the Netherlands, Israel, and China. In other words, Capellas was part of a brain drain from Barcelona that was spreading the Masia's methods to the world.

Several of his old colleagues in the Masia had fled the infighting within Barça's bureaucracy and gone off to earn bigger salaries at foreign clubs where they might actually get a boy onto the first team. A global market had opened up for them that hadn't existed in the days when the Masia really was the best academy on earth. Along with some carpetbagging Dutch and even German coaches, they were preaching the Cruyffian creed from Paris to India.

The brain drain from Barça operated at senior level, too. The managers of Manchester City, Spurs, and Arsenal in the 2020–2021 season had all started in Barcelona. City had become almost a colony club of Barça's, run by people who were not simply former Barça directors and coaches but Barça *socis*, too. They had brought their knowledge to England and were updating it daily.

In short, the Masia, and Barcelona more generally, fell victim to its own success. European football is just about the most innovative sector in business—much more innovative even than tech. In tech, if you were lucky, you only had to innovate once: in the early years of the World Wide Web, you invented a novel platform like Amazon or Facebook, drew millions of users to it, and raked in a fortune. If competitors emerged, you bought them up. Users tended to stick with your platform, because everyone else was on it, too. That's how Jeff Bezos and Mark Zuckerberg could each make tens of billions of dollars out of a single (albeit evolving) invention.

But there are no monopolies or patents in football. Clubs steal ideas from each other every week. In Guardiola's phrase, "Football is evolution."[2] Other academies copied the Masia. This started in Spain, where junior national teams finally stopped discriminating against small footballers.[3] Between 2008 and 2012, the country won two European titles and the World Cup with a team built around Masia ballplayers. Even Real Madrid adopted Cruyffian innovations. One day on a TV screen in the Barcelona underground, I saw footage of a Merengues training session, led by Zinedine Zidane: they were doing the rondo.

After Barça's homegrown team won the Champions League in 2009, Masia imitation became the global orthodoxy. My visit to the farmhouse had been part of a mass pilgrimage by football people from around the world come to steal ideas. Clubs everywhere invested in their academies, hired psychologists, gave young and small players a chance, and redefined football as a passing game that you play with your head. The once-radical tenets of Cruyffism became football's conventional wisdom.

Meanwhile, the Masia itself stopped learning. Never once did a Masia staffer tell me about having made a study visit to a foreign club. Seirul·lo admitted, "We were so good, so we didn't look around enough." Nor did the Masia hire top-class foreign coaches.

Other countries caught up. Countless short footballers of the 2020s will owe their careers to Xavi. (There were few lessons to be learned from Messi, because he was a one-off.) In France, the next Griezmann will get into an academy. My twin sons in Paris have spent their childhood playing eight-a-side on small pitches, in the Cruyffian spirit. When I was a kid, slogging across muddy adult-size fields from age seven, the best players were the ones who could win tackles and kick farthest. Even England has started producing skillful little ballplayers and keepers who can pass. Germany has become practically an intellectual outpost of the Masia. Bayern Munich, for decades a club without a house style, finally acquired a Barcelona-inspired one under the head coaches Louis van Gaal and Guardiola. A subsequent Bayern head coach, Hans-Dieter Flick, who in 2021 became manager of Germany, had made a study visit to the Masia earlier in his career, trying to understand how the place worked. When Germans begin to think, the rest of football struggles to compete. Today Bayern is arguably a more Cruyffian club than Barcelona.

Only in the 95 percent of the world outside western Europe does youth football remain pre-Cruyffian. U.S. kids soccer, in particular, still prioritizes winning over learning. In about 2013, at half-time in an under-12s game in New York, the Hispanic-looking dad of one of the Downtown United players wandered over to give the opposing team's striker some unsolicited advice about his game. The boy's father charged across, shouting something like, "Who do you think you are to coach my son?"

The Hispanic-looking man, on sabbatical in New York after four draining years coaching Barcelona, replied: "I am Pep Guardiola."

XV

MORE THAN A CLUB?

It was a perfect summer day in late October 2019, and the former Barça president Sandro Rosell was drinking beer on the deck of his beach club in the town of Gavà Mar, gazing out over a waveless Mediterranean.

I know I keep coming back to the weather. But as I write this in a dark Paris during winter lockdown, I struggle to imagine that Gavà Mar exists. Rosell appreciated the sea view even more, because he had only recently been released from jail. He had been accused of laundering millions in illegal commissions linked to the sale of TV rights for the Brazilian football team, during his time working for Nike. He was locked up awaiting trial for 643 days, the longest period of "preventive detention" for anyone accused of economic crimes in the history of

Spain. At times, when temperatures in his unheated cell fell below zero, he slept in all his clothes, including his anorak.[1]

The Madrilenian judge overseeing his case, Carmen Lamela, refused thirteen requests for bail. Since she had also jailed nine Catalan separatist politicians, popular opinion in Catalonia did not regard her as a friend of the region. Rosell's claim, "If I hadn't been president of Barcelona, I wouldn't have gone to jail," was widely believed there. It may even have been true. Four days into his trial, the court released him. The first thing he did was go to a hotel bar and down a beer in one gulp: "That was so good, *madre mía*. Going from jail to liberty in three seconds."[2] A few weeks later, he was acquitted.[3]

This afternoon in Gavà Mar, Rosell doesn't want to talk about jail. He savors his beer, the Mediterranean, and the impending arrival of his parents for the traditional Catalan weekend family lunch. His benevolence extends to proposing a title for my book. "You should call it *More Than a Club*," he says.

"I don't know if Barça still is more than a club," I reply.

"It is," he corrects me, and, touching my hand to reinforce his points, he tells a story. When he became president in 2010, the club was overspending as usual. Rosell told his general manager, "I want you to go through the expenses and let me know which we can cut immediately."

Very quickly, they agreed to scrap the baseball team. It was an easy call: hardly any of the baseball players were *socis*, Barça rented the baseball field from a competitor, and the sport had no roots in Catalan culture. The team's annual budget was somewhere between €500,000 and €1 million—a handy little savings.

Yet the moment Barça announced the decision, the city went nuts. Local media accused him of trampling on the club's traditions. One day, a group of *socis* collared him as he was leaving the basketball arena. Rosell reenacts the conversation for me:

SOCIS: You canceled baseball!

ROSELL: I will ask you three questions. If one of you answers them correctly, we will restart baseball. One: How many players in a baseball team?

[*Socis* look blank.]

ROSELL: Two: give the name of one of our baseball players.

[*Socis* look blank.]

ROSELL: Where do we play baseball?

[*Socis* look blank.]

So baseball stayed canceled. But Rosell thought he had made his point: the *socis* saw Barça as "more than a club." For them, it was an institution with a spiritual-national purpose.

He didn't persuade me, though. Researching this book, I have come to believe that Barcelona is now just a club. It's no longer a more meaningful institution than rivals like Real Madrid and Manchester United, or even Paris Saint-Germain and Manchester City.

This represents a fall from grace, because for decades the Catalan-nationalist, member-owned democracy certainly was more than a club. Joan Laporta had summed up the meaning of "more than a club" as "Cruyff, Catalonia, Masia, UNICEF."[4] When Rosell took office in 2010, Barça was still more than a club: a team of homegrown kids, coached by Cruyff's disciple Guardiola, which played glorious Cruyffian football in front of an almost entirely local crowd. Their chief rival at the time was the cartoon villain Mourinho, coach of Inter Milan and then Real Madrid, who, in his own language, "parked the bus" and aimed (again, in his phrasing) to break opponents' wheels or put sugar in their tanks. Against him, Barcelona could only look like the good guys.

And Barça in 2010 still helped unite the Catalan nation. A Catalan separatist, a pro-Spanish federalist, a communist, and a factory owner could all share a group hug over a Messi goal.

Off the field, too, Barça in 2010 was still more than a club. At the time it was a rare football club with a charitable foundation (launched in 1994), which did good work for refugees and children around the world. It was the only big club never to have sullied its shirts with a sponsor's name. Its brilliant team wore UNICEF on their chests, and even paid the UN's children's charity €1.5 million a year for the privilege.

But by 2021, almost all the elements of "more than a club" had faded or disappeared. Let's take them one by one. We've seen that the Masia stopped producing great players. Other clubs were playing more authentic versions of Cruyffian football than Barcelona did.

And modern Barça has been careless with its legends. Cruyff left the building the moment his enemy Rosell took charge, resigning as honorary president and ceasing to attend matches. Guardiola left Barcelona in 2012, and Messi in 2021.

Meanwhile the shirt was sold. Since the 1990s, commercial executives at Barça had been inspired by the front-runner in the football business, Manchester United.[5] Ferran Soriano, Barça's chief executive from 2003 to 2008, later confessed that "inspired" was a euphemism: "All we did was copy everything Manchester United was doing right and which could be of use to us."[6] "Manchester," as Barça people call the club, didn't have UNICEF on their chests. Nor did Real Madrid. They had shirt sponsors that paid them fortunes. As these clubs began tapping revenues worldwide, Barça faced a stark choice: either match them, or eventually lose their best players to their rivals. In 2005, Barça came close to doing a deal with the Chinese government to put "Beijing 08" on their shirts. Next it considered the betting company Bwin (which ended up on Real Madrid's shirt instead).[7] Finally, in December 2010, in the biggest shirt deal in football's history, Barça accepted €165 million from the Qatar Foundation for a five-year contract. "So far there is nobody who pays more," Rosell shrugged. UNICEF moved to the back of the shirt.

The knee-jerk response is to pan Barça for rank commercialism. Of course, getting into bed with an absolute monarchy like Qatar didn't sit brilliantly with the club's historic image as the democratic resistance to dictatorship. Thousands of fans signed a petition to revoke the contract. Rosell himself told me that with his *soci* hat on, he opposed getting a shirt sponsor. Cruyff, from the comfort of his mansion in Bonanova, called the deal "vulgar": "No other club had kept its shirt clean for more than 100 years. You don't sell something like that for money . . . We have sold our uniqueness for 6 percent of the budget." He said Barça had gone from *més que un club* to "a typical club."[8]

But I suspect that had Cruyff still been coaching Barça, he would have backed the deal, too. (This is the man who made a beeline for Franco's Spain in 1973 and then asked, "What is fascist?") And the harsh truth is that rank commercialism funds beautiful football. Qatar paid Messi's wages. Even so, the deal dented Barça's claims to moral superiority.

I'm not pinning the demise of "more than a club" on Rosell. Most people and clubs at the top of modern football found themselves taking tainted money. Guardiola, for instance, boarded the Qatari train as a paid ambassador for the country's bid to host the 2022 World Cup. He said people in Qatar had "all the freedoms of the world, within the frame that the government gives them." The same claim could be made of any country on earth, noted the German author Dietrich Schulze-Marmeling.[9]

In 2013, FC Barcelona replaced the Qatar Foundation with the club's first corporate sponsor, Qatar Airways. Gradually, executives who had worked in prestigious companies outside football moved into offices in the Camp Nou and the surrounding streets, tasked with raising the club's revenues. A tension arose that has only worsened since: Barça was trying to turn itself into a global entertainment business while remaining a Catalan-nationalist social club.

It wasn't that Barça had suddenly become "big business." The club wasn't trying to make profits. The point of bringing in more money was to spend every cent of it on good footballers. Still, many *socis* and staffers—and even some *directius* and executives—worried that money-grabbing was turning Barça into what Cruyff called "a typical club." This anxiety went back a long way. After Cruyff's Barça won the league in 1974, the local comedy band La Trinca had warned:

> *While the tit keeps dripping*
> *They'll treat us like puppets*
> *and they'll even invent*
> *armpit deodorants*
> *with the Barça colors.*

In 2022, "FC Barcelona—Original Blue Deodorant Spray—For Men (200ml)" is for sale online.

One of the new executives in Barça's digital department told me that *socis* often grumbled, "Guys, play football. This is not Disney." The executive would retort that Barça was still leaving a lot of money on the table that could improve the football team: "We're one of the most recognized brands in the world, but we generate just one billion dollars in revenue a year. We have the recognition of brands that have two hundred times as much revenue. So there's a big opportunity." Barça believed it was better known in some countries than Apple or Amazon. Most *socis* didn't care about any of that, though. They wanted their club to fund its charitable foundation and its baseball team and also beat Real Madrid, but without concocting grubby moneymaking schemes.

Barça's foundation still did good work, yet by the 2020s it was no longer unique: other big European clubs now also had foundations, and most English clubs ran some kind of "football in the community" scheme. In January 2019, thirty-two English clubs joined a program to deliver coaching and refereeing courses in local prisons.[10] They were all more than clubs, too.

Inside Barça, arguments between the football and business sides of the club got edgier. The head coach might not like the exhausting multicountry preseason tour of Asia; the brand people insisted on it. The same conflict plagues all big clubs now, writes Arsène Wenger: "The technical side—the team, the players, the academy—is becoming smaller within companies where the commercial, marketing and press departments take up ever more space."[11]

FROM *SOCIS* TO FOLLOWERS

Barça's path to higher revenues ran beyond Catalonia, even beyond little old Europe. About 45 percent of the world's population lives in four countries—China, India, Indonesia, and the United States—which have begun to switch on to football. That was where Barça needed to be. It had to go global while trying to remain Catalan.

In December 2008, in an anonymous office block on the northwestern edge of Miami, I knocked on a door with a plaque that read "332 Marcelo Claure." Inside sat Claure, a six-foot-five-inch (1.95 m) Bolivian-American former amateur goalkeeper who hardly fit into the poky little room. From here he ran the wireless services company Brightstar, which at the time was the biggest Hispanic-owned business in the United States. He was also partnering with Barça to start a new team, Miami Barcelona. The day we spoke, Claure had just returned from a Clásico at the Camp Nou, where he had attended the pre-match directors' banquet as a guest of Barça's board: "This is the first time in history that they invited a stranger. So I came back very happy."

Miami, or so Claure had gathered, was Barça's "number one priority outside their day-to-day business." He said the directors liked to think of Barcelona as the most important sports institution in the world, and they were "going to put the same pressure on this team."

He marveled that Barça received "over five thousand videos a week" sent in by hopeful players and agents dreaming of a contract in the Camp Nou. Well, many of these players might want to play for Barcelona's sister team in the United States' most Hispanic city.

"Is your team really going to happen?" I asked. "One hundred and twenty-five percent that this is going to happen," said Claure. He even planned to turn the launch into a reality TV show.

His team didn't happen. Three months after our conversation, Miami Barcelona was canned, a victim of the financial crisis and Barça's reluctance to stretch its brand.[12] But the great world remained out there. In 2013, Barça opened an office in Hong Kong, and then, in 2016, another in a skyscraper on New York's Park Avenue. Armed with data showing that only 36 percent of Americans followed soccer, the club saw the United States as a growth market.

Doing business in America was tough. In Spain, what counted most was who you knew. If you were friends with a chief executive, or, especially in Catalonia, if your families had known each other forever, he (or occasionally she) would generally do business with you. But American executives wanted to see metrics if they were going to persuade their boards and their shareholders to sponsor a soccer club playing four thousand miles away.

The metric that Barcelona liked to show Americans was social media followers. By the end of 2019, the club had 214 million followers, or more than 1,400 for every *soci*. In all of sports, only Real Madrid (with

224 million) had more. Barça had over five times as many followers as the number one American sports team, the Los Angeles Lakers, and more (as of 2016) than all NFL teams combined.[13] Many of these 214 million people, though not all, were more than followers: they were fans of Barcelona.

Companies like McDonald's and Amazon were always trying to convert their customers into fans. Barça had the opposite problem: it had to convert fans into customers. A supporter in Mumbai, India, might walk around in a pirated Messi shirt and watch all the team's games in a local bar, without ever paying a rupee to the club. If he was one of Barcelona's 100-million-plus Facebook followers, then Facebook rather than Barça had his personal details. Barça might not even know the guy's name. It had to pay Facebook for access to him. If Barça wanted to monetize him directly, it needed to build a relationship with him. That started with persuading him to register on the club app, by offering some incentive or other—for instance, the chance to buy the official new team shirt two weeks early. Then Barcelona would have his name, address, and credit card details. The club would become a mini-Facebook: a data acquisition company.

Barça also aimed to become a mini-Amazon, selling stuff to its fans. It could help its sponsors market their fridges and cars to the guy in Mumbai, though the trick would be to do this while making him feel that his beloved club was still "more than a club," not just another grasping corporation. Club executives told me about their plans to create a "Netflix of Barça," on which fans could pay to watch club-related videos, maybe with some behind-the-scenes stuff on match days, if the players were willing to cooperate. (Modern footballers care more about reaching their own social media followers, or those of their sponsors.)

If Barça could turn its fans into customers, then in the future it would depend less on sponsors, TV rights, and ticket sales. That was where the whole football industry was heading, one executive told me:

instead of selling to sponsors and TV companies who sold to fans, cut out the middleman and sell directly to fans. The executive said Barça had to think more "like a digital start-up." Picking up a napkin from his plate, he said football clubs used to think, "Let's put our logo on this napkin, and sell it." That was too primitive.

Barça's new foreign fans came in countless varieties. A minority of them were passionate about Barça. Imagine a taxi driver who lives in a slum in Bangkok or Lagos, sends his children to poor schools, and will never escape his circumstances: for him, supporting Barça might be his one personal connection to something world-class. In TV images from conflict zones or refugee camps, there were always kids in pirated "Messi 10" shirts. Some people on social media cited their football fandom as their only identity: "@Barcabaajabal: Lives Somalia/Mogadishu Support Barcelona/Chelsea."

But few new fans were as committed as the traditional fan base in Catalonia. In recent years, the club has come to mean less and less to more and more people. It would be misleading to say that Barça is now loved around the world. Rather, Barça now evokes lukewarm sympathy around the world. Its games have become part of the global decor, showing half watched in innumerable hotel lounges.

For most new fans, the club is more a source of entertainment than of identity. And if Barça fails to entertain, well, there are endless other sources of fun nowadays. One club executive told me, "We are competing against [the video game] *League of Legends*, Real Madrid, and Netflix. If we don't understand that, we may in twenty years be in serious trouble." On social media, the club was shifting its content from information toward entertainment.

The new fans also included many Messi supporters who might decide to leave Barça in his wake. There were some people who supported Barça *and* Real Madrid simultaneously. European sympathizers outside

Spain generally already supported a club in their own country, and treated Barcelona as their second team. (There aren't many heart-and-soul British fans of Barça.) Fans from Asia or the United States might know almost nothing about football.

As for Catalonia, many new fans had never heard of it. They did usually know that Barcelona was a city, but they had an unfortunate tendency to call the place "Barça," which is only the nickname of the club. (The city's local nickname is "Barna.") For new fans, Barça didn't so much represent its hometown as overshadow it. Perhaps the thing that drew them to the club was precisely its international glamour.

The challenge, as Soriano had foreseen, was to explain "more than a club" to a Chinese child.[14] That could get tacky fast: selling Barça's history as a Disneyfied heritage story. In the club megastore opposite the museum one day, I watched an advertisement for the new turquoise away shirt, featuring a bored-looking Piqué intoning in English, "The sentence 'more than a club' represents this club very well."

In the years before the pandemic, more and more of the new global fans had been showing up at the Camp Nou. One of the first things passengers saw after landing at El Prat airport was a poster telling them where they could get match tickets for Barça. The club had created a "smart-booking" system for *socis* to sell their seats for matches they didn't attend. An algorithm predicted how many places *socis* would give up for a certain game, depending on the opponent, kickoff time, the weather, and so on. Barça then sold that number of seats online before *socis* even released them. For some matches, foreign visitors took thirty thousand seats. That way the *socis* made a bit of money (some probably sell enough matches to turn a profit on their season tickets), the club took a cut, and visiting Indians or Brazilians got to watch a game.

One night in October 2019, when Barça hosted mid-table Valladolid, I tried the system myself. I bought tickets for me and my children, at

€59 plus €2.50 administration fee each—a hefty markup over the *soci* price. It was a typical Barcelona home match: about a third of the seats empty, the hardcore supporters' group Boixos Nois behind one goal the only people singing, a couple thousand locals waving Catalan Estelada separatist flags, and many thousands of tourists. "Is that Messi?" asked an English boy behind us as the teams came out. The people sitting around us spent much of the match taking selfies and checking their phones. The queue for popcorn at halftime buzzed with several European languages. Perhaps the next Frenkie de Jong was there with his parents. When Griezmann was ritually substituted, my kids and other French people cheered him up with "*Allez*, Grizi!" When Suárez scored, some of his compatriots chanted, "Uruguay!"

My children won't forget that night. We saw Messi at his greatest, scoring twice and giving two assists. What suspense there was surrounded Barça's pursuit of the elusive sixth goal. After the final whistle went at 5–1, tourists held up their phones to record the playing of the Barça hymn. As we came out of the stadium, waiting rickshaws were offering rides into town.

The flip side of all this is that locals who aren't *socis* are being pushed out. They won't pay €61.50 for a ticket, especially not for games that now often kick off at ten p.m., which even in Spain is late for kids on a school night. It's also an untraditional time: Catalans expect to watch football at nine p.m. on a Saturday, or five p.m. on a Sunday. But Barça's games are no longer scheduled for Catalans. The club is outgrowing them. One business executive at the Camp Nou told me that Barça had always put players and *socis* at the heart of the club. Now, he said, it needed to put global fans there.

It was precisely to cater to the new fans that Barcelona in 2014 launched the most expensive project in its history: the Espai Barça, or "Barça Space," a planned wholesale renovation of the Camp Nou and its surroundings.

The Espai Barça was originally supposed to open in 2021, but it has been repeatedly delayed, most recently by the pandemic. The estimated cost has risen to about $1.85 billion, more than double the original figure.[15] If all goes well, then by the end of 2025 the club hopes finally to unveil the Espai: a vast, gateless "campus," with a renovated Camp Nou at its heart, expanded from 98,000 to 105,000 seats. It will be surrounded by a new indoor arena, club offices, restaurants, and a modernized megastore and museum.

The Espai will be "the best sporting complex in the world in the center of a great city," promises Barça. The existing megastore is to be upgraded from a species of supermarket into something more like an Apple Store, offering experiences as well as products. There will be facilities for virtual reality: one day you should be able to stand (virtually) on the field and watch Pedri or Ansu Fati run at you, hear his breathing and the shouts of the defenders.

Above all, the plan is to keep foreign fans on-site longer. These people, often attending the only Barça game of their lives, yearn to maximize the experience. Already, the Camp Nou complex is busier day to day than most stadiums. There is a walk-in-off-the-street quality to the place: without any security checks, you can stroll along the row of souvenir stands and outdoor cafés, past the ice rink where your kid can skate for €10, to the museum (the third-most visited in Spain) and the megastore. On the stadium tour you trudge down the staircase from the changing room, passing the chapel on your right, climb up the seven steps to the edge of the field, gaze up at the stands to savor your own insignificance like a medieval pilgrim in a cathedral, then recline in the dugout on what look like first-class plane seats. The upper tiers of the stands are decorated with giant yellow logos: the main sponsor's name, the Nike swoosh, and *"Més que un club."*

Pre-pandemic, the Camp Nou complex already attracted about four million people a year. But Barça wants to offer visitors more. For now, there aren't enough places at the ground to hang out. After games, you see supporters spending their money in tapas joints outside the stadium.

The plan is that in years to come, fans will be able to spend all of match day (or even the day before) at the Espai Barça, like "tailgating" fans in American gridiron football. There'll be outdoor cafés everywhere, just like in the city. Sensors will track where fans go and where they don't, allowing Barça to keep tailoring the complex to their tastes. In other words, the Espai will be a shopping mall as much as a stadium. It will also carry a sponsor's name—quite likely, the "Spotify Espai Barça." But I'm sure "*més que un club*" will always be emblazoned on the stands.

PRE-PANDEMIC, JUST AS BARÇA was becoming a tourist club, so Barcelona had become a tourist city. The place had succumbed to Airbnb-ification, with visitors driving out residents. (I plead guilty.) The pandemic provided a natural experiment of what the city would look like without tourists and conference-goers: quieter, but also a lot poorer. There is no easy path back to a city for locals.

When a city goes global, its local institutions do, too. Three and a half miles from the Camp Nou, at the other end of the city center, stands a twin Catalan-nationalist project, started, like Barça, by the late-nineteenth-century *burgesia*. Like the Camp Nou, Antoni Gaudí's still-unfinished Sagrada Família is meant to awe you with its majesty: when finished, it will be the tallest cathedral on earth. Like Cruyffian football, it was created by a mad genius who abhorred straight lines. Gaudí fought with the local merchants who funded his work,[16] just as Cruyff did with their descendants who sat in Barça's boardroom. Both men aimed to give pleasure to their congregations. "Fa goig!"—"Give joy!"— were the last words the aged Gaudí spoke to his cathedral's workmen on June 7, 1926, just before he stepped out to be run over by a tram.[17]

"Salid y disfrutad," "Go out and enjoy it," Cruyff told his players at Wembley in 1992.

The Sagrada Família is almost certainly the only nineteenth-century building project that's still being built, writes Gaudí's biographer, Gijs van Hensbergen.[18] Barça is a nineteenth-century project that is never supposed to finish at all.

The cathedral will be completed one day, possibly around 2030. Not everyone will cheer. As the art critic Robert Hughes argued decades ago, "The building seems to die as it advances." He accused the sculptors and architects who succeeded Gaudí of creating "rampant kitsch."[19] Many architects in Barcelona today agree. I'm no Robert Hughes, but having taken in the gorgeous realism of Gaudí's Nativity facade—the infant Christ as a real kid—I suspect the cathedral's creator would be dismayed to see what his disciples have added. Yet it's hard to blame them. Though Gaudí's vision survives him, nobody is entirely sure what it is. Like Cruyff, Gaudí worked ad hoc, making things up as he went along, finding solutions in the moment.[20] Cruyff never wrote anything down, and Gaudí didn't trust two-dimensional drawings to capture a cathedral. The drawings and models that he did leave behind were burned and smashed by anarchists in an attack on the Sagrada Família in 1936.[21]

And the cathedral no longer serves a Catalan congregation, as Gaudí had intended. Once the pandemic ends, it will go back to welcoming more than ten thousand visitors a day from around the world,[22] many of them armed with selfie sticks and sporting "Messi 10" shirts. There's a Barça gift shop opposite the cathedral. Like the football club, the Sagrada Família was conceived for a city of locals that no longer exists.

THE UNARMED ARMY OF CATALONIA
FIGHTS WITH ITSELF

The biggest component of "More than a club" has always been *catalanisme*, Catalan nationalism. That isn't a very divisive ideology in Catalonia. It's a slogan that almost all Barça *socis* can unite behind, the local version of motherhood and apple pie. But what is divisive is Catalan independence: the idea that Catalonia should break away from Spain and form its own state. For years, polls have shown that about half the region's inhabitants want it and the other half don't.[23] In the 2010s, *catalanisme* spiraled into an independence movement that split friends and families, and risked splitting Barça itself.

The dream of creating a Catalan state used to be a marginal, almost crackpot pursuit. No Catalan political party last century seriously pursued independence. Only from about 2010, amid the global financial crisis, did the movement for independence—*el procés*—start going mainstream. One of the claims of *independentistes* was that modern, hardworking, "European" Catalonia would get richer if it could just separate itself from poor, backward Spain.[24] This was a dubious argument. Catalonia had actually managed to emerge from the era of *franquista* repression about as well-off as Madrid. Only in the decades after the 1992 Olympics, when it had much more autonomy than before, did its economy gradually fall behind the booming capital city's.

Still, the financial crisis boosted momentum toward independence. When Barça met the Basque team Athletic Bilbao at the King's Cup final of 2012, fans of both clubs booed the Spanish national anthem and the watching Crown Prince Felipe.

Barça had always done its best to avoid taking sides on independence. The romantic image of a "rebel club" perennially yearning for freedom from Spain is false. Most Barça *directius* and *socis* are probably *indepes* (to use the local slang), but others are happy in Spain. For years, the club tried to keep both groups on board. It distanced itself from politicians who used the club's name to push their own platforms. Rosell for a time was in the same jail in Madrid as the *indepe* politicians, and he'd ask them why they were always interfering with Barça's elections, when Barça—a potentially much more influential entity— stayed out of theirs.

The club in the 2010s took only one political position: it backed Catalonia's right to hold a referendum on independence. Importantly, so did the world's most famous Catalan. "We have no other option but to vote," Pep Guardiola told a rally of forty thousand people in June 2017. When he urged "all democrats—in Europe and around the world" to support the referendum, many people in far-flung continents found out that Catalonia existed.

The Catalan government finally called the referendum for October 1, 2017. "Do you want Catalonia to become an independent state in the form of a republic?" was the question on the ballot.

Spain's prime minister, Mariano Rajoy (the man Real Madrid had once tried to enlist to help lure Messi away from Barcelona), dismissed the vote as an "act of disobedience." On referendum day, Spanish police officers flooded the rebel region, closing polling stations and beating up people on live TV. That afternoon Barça was due to play Las Palmas in the Camp Nou. Hours before kickoff, President Bartomeu went to tell the squad that he was calling off the game in protest against police violence. The board had made the decision even though the Spanish FA had said it would punish Barça by deducting six points. An emotional Gerard Piqué backed Bartomeu: the violence at the polling stations was "a disgrace," he said.

But then employee number one spoke. Messi, who was as uninterested in *catalanisme* as the club's other figurehead, Cruyff, didn't want to lose the points. Let's play in front of spectators, he said. Bartomeu proposed a compromise: play, but in an empty stadium. The captain Iniesta and the other players agreed.[25] The team warmed up in red-and-yellow shirts, the colors of Catalonia's flag, and beat Las Palmas 3–0. According to a report years later by the Spanish newspaper *El Mundo*, *indepe* leaders had secretly asked Barça to finance their movement through fictional contracts. Bartomeu refused to turn the club into a sort of piggybank of independence.[26] But his awkward balancing act on independence only succeeded in antagonizing both sides. To *indepes* he was a coward, and to federalists, a crazed Catalan nationalist.

Broadly speaking, only *indepe* Catalans voted in the referendum that day, while federalists boycotted the vote, so the "yes" side got 92 percent, but of a turnout of just 43 percent. The referendum looked to outsiders like "a disorganized public relations stunt," commented the Danish political scientist Marlene Wind.[27]

Spain's constitutional court then declared the vote illegal. The Catalan president, Carles Puigdemont, who had called for the referendum, fled to Brussels, somewhat to the chagrin of the nine *independentiste* politicians who went to jail. They were later sentenced to between nine and thirteen years in prison each for misuse of public funds, and for the oddly archaic crime of sedition. Spanish jails, Spanish police batons, an exiled Catalan leader: many Catalans heard echoes of the Franco era. Some protesters in Barcelona enjoyed pretending they were taking on El Caudillo's forces, this time without risk of execution. Among the broken windows and the street barricades, graffiti on the city's walls attacked "Fascist Spain."

The prospect of years of political instability scared local companies. True, the separatist movement was something of a pantomime. Catalonia wasn't really being suppressed again by a Fascist dictatorship. In most practical matters, Catalans already ruled themselves: modern Spain is one of the most decentralized democracies on earth, and Catalonia a particularly autonomous region.[28] And hardly anyone expected that independence would actually happen. Even if Catalonia somehow found a way to leave Spain, Madrid could use its veto to block the new state from joining the European Union, and then the region would be out in the cold. Still, a noisy long-term independence movement would be bad for Catalan business. In the weeks after the referendum, at least twenty-five hundred local companies moved their legal headquarters (though almost never the physical ones) elsewhere in Spain.[29] Even Catalonia's giant CaixaBank moved. Rosell, who came from a prominent business family, famously said he'd vote for independence, but that he'd leave town the day independence happened.

The turmoil in Catalonia made Madrid look like a safe haven. In 2018, the capital city attracted 91 percent of foreign direct investment into Spain; Catalonia got 6 percent. By then, average income per capita in Madrid was 15 percent higher than in Catalonia.[30]

People in the rest of Spain were growing fed up with the perennially dissatisfied region that apparently considered itself too good for them. The traditional nickname for Catalans in Spain is *polacos*, Poles, to denote their foreignness. In national elections in 2019, the far-right Spanish nationalist party, Vox, came from nowhere to get 15 percent of the vote, on a platform of *franquista* dog-whistling, anti-immigration, and Catalan-bashing. It was the first far-right group since Franco's death to win seats in Spain's parliament. When a Catalan boys' football team played in the championship of the Spanish regions, there were anti-Catalan chants at their games.

During my visits to Barcelona in 2019 and 2020, independence remained the local hot topic. In the mornings I'd sometimes walk past broken windows in the city center, where policemen had battled separatist demonstrators the night before. Local TV news often led with Barça's latest statement on the conflict: violence wasn't the solution; jailing Catalan politicians wasn't the solution either; Catalans should have the right to vote on independence.

The violent Spanish crackdown made many Catalans even angrier with Madrid. But Catalans also grew angrier with each other. The rough divide is that most people who grew up speaking Spanish at home want to stay in the union, whereas most who grew up speaking Catalan at home want independence. In other words, migrant families from other Spanish regions and from abroad are federalist, while the homegrown *burgesia* is largely *indepe*. Support for a referendum on independence was "dramatically higher among the upper classes, particularly those with the highest incomes,"[31] noted the French economist Thomas Piketty.

In *burgesia* circles, anyone who comes out for federation with Spain now risks getting dismissed as not a "real" Catalan, perhaps even as a *franquista* apologist. Some dissidents find themselves informally boycotted in their professional lives. It's notable that inside Barça, Spanish-speaking staffers or players such as Busquets and Iniesta never made even the mildest statement against independence. It wouldn't have gone down well.

Most people in Catalonia still say they feel both Catalan *and* Spanish,[32] and speak both languages interchangeably. But a growing group of mostly well-off or rural people now say they feel exclusively Catalan. This group tends to consume only Catalan TV, radio, and newspapers, and so has come to inhabit a separate reality from the rest of Spain.[33] In some of their workplaces and social settings, speaking Spanish has become taboo.

In short, the issue of independence has split Catalonia down the middle. During the peak years of the independence movement, from 2017, you could often read the divide off the front of an apartment building: on the balconies, you might see five Estelada flags with the independence star, five regular Catalan flags without the star, and perhaps a Colombian flag, or just the Barça colors, but very rarely a Spanish flag.

Anyone who has lived through Brexit in Britain or Donald Trump in the United States knows what a divided society feels like. Mutual hostility over politics becomes so bitter that sporting rivalries feel benign by comparison: even Red Sox and Yankees fans, or Madrid and Barcelona fans, have a shared love of sports and mostly understand that it's only a game. In Catalonia today, people stomp out of Sunday family lunch or break up with old friends because of quarrels about independence. Catalonia has become an even more distrustful place than the rest of Spain, which is itself low-trust by European standards. In the World Values Survey for 2010 to 2014, only 14 percent of people in Catalonia strongly agreed that "most people can be trusted"—less than half the level of Madrid.[34]

Just as Queen Elizabeth didn't take sides on Brexit, Barça continued trying to stay neutral on independence. But the political divide penetrated the Camp Nou. One federalist told me he had stopped going to games because it upset him too much to hear part of the crowd chant for independence 17.14 minutes into every game. (The timing is a nod to the year 1714, when Barcelona fell under the control of Spain's Bourbon monarchy.) Ominously, Barça, Catalonia's biggest institution, was struggling to unite Catalans. And then in fall 2020, two out-and-out *indepes*, Joan Laporta and Victor Font, began to compete for the club presidency.

XVI

MESSI'S CLUB

After Messi renewed his contract with Barça in 2017, the club's head of legal services, Román Gómez Ponti, sent CEO Óscar Grau an email that consisted of one word: *"ALELUYA,"* with the final *A* repeated sixty-nine times. Grau replied, "The extension of Leo Messi was important for the survival of FC Barcelona."[1]

The three separate contracts written by the club guaranteed Messi an annual salary of over €100 million, according to a document obtained by Football Leaks and passed to Germany's *Spiegel* magazine. One internal club document recommended, "The player needs to be aware of how disproportionately high his salary is relative to the rest of the team."[2] Indeed: Messi was earning about as much as a typical top-class team of the time. Pretty soon, Barça were paying him even more. Aided by the release clause in Messi's contract, which allowed him to walk out the door free at the end of each season, his father, Jorge, negotiated large annual pay hikes.

Over the four years from 2017 through 2021, the player earned more than €555 million ($674 million) in total, according to highlights from his thirty-page contract published in *El Mundo*.[3] That was nearly 30 percent of the club's total staff costs.[4] Barça and Messi announced they would sue the newspaper, and Messi made plans to sue the five senior Barça officials who were in a position to leak the contract, but nobody denied the figure.[5] Bayern Munich's chairman, Karl-Heinz Rummenigge, said he "had to laugh" when he saw the contract. "I can only compliment him on managing to negotiate such an astronomical salary."[6]

A senior Barça official told me Messi's salary had tripled between 2014 and 2020. He added, "Messi is not the problem. The problem is the contagion of the rest of the team." Whenever Messi got a raise, his teammates asked for one as well. Even on the plane back from victory in the Champions League final in Berlin in 2015, players had shouted at Bartomeu, "*Presi*, bonus!" Though their contracts already guaranteed them bonuses for lifting the trophy, Bartomeu agreed to pay them millions more.[7]

Over time, Barça morphed from *més que un club* into Messi's club. *Messidependencia* is an old concept in Barcelona, but originally it described an incidental phenomenon: Messi winning a tight match. Gradually, *Messidependencia* became the system. Barça parasited off Messi, until he began eating the club. In 2020 and 2021, sporting disaster, economic disaster, and Messi's departure all struck at once.

DURING MESSI'S FIRST DECADE on the team, Xavi and Iniesta had enough status not to give him the ball too early in an attack. They would build on the other flank, waiting for the moment when they could switch across and put him one-on-one against a defender. But as the duo faded from the team, and Neymar left, Barça's strategy simplified into *Messidependencia*. From 2017 until 2019, Messi's shots and assists accounted for between 45 and 49 percent of Barcelona's annual expected goals, calculates Burn-Murdoch. Almost the only other big modern club more reliant on a single player was Real Madrid (with its *Ronaldodependencia*) in 2014–2015. One level below that, Lucas Pérez was practically a one-man team for Deportivo la Coruña in 2015–2016.

Barça have become exceptionally reliant on Messi
Share of a team's goalscoring chances scored or created by one player, in one season

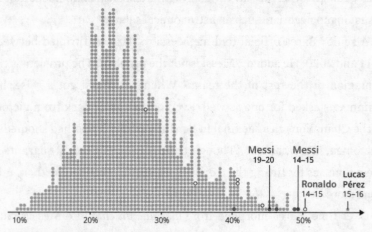

Source: Analysis of data from Understat for seasons 2014–15 to 2019–20
Credit: John Burn-Murdoch, *Financial Times*

Barça's system became "get to the final third, then give the ball to Messi, wherever he is." It was turning into a team almost like Argentina, without a shared passing language, playing simple, practically playground football. In Messi's final years, Barcelona's first team was abandoning Barcelona football. That made it harder still for Masia boys to make the leap to the Camp Nou. Even if they got the chance, they landed in an alien system.

Instead of Messi moving as part of a fluid Cruyffian collective, now his teammates simply reacted to his moves. Most were awed by him. Frenkie de Jong told me:

Messi's really much better than the other players. I think people underestimate that. They see it every week, and eventually they start to find it normal. You're playing here with the very best players in the world, in principle, but he's quite far above that. You have to make sure you're always trying to keep an eye on him, so that when you get the ball you know if he's free or not.

Meanwhile, although nobody at Barça wanted to talk about it, the king was growing old. Messi (and for the most part, Luis Suárez) stopped defending—an almost unheard-of privilege in top-class football. When Barça lost the ball, opponents aimed to play the ball out through Messi's zone, while he just stood there and watched them go. Then he would often trudge back alone, yards offside behind the opposition's defenders, watching play unfold at the far end of the field. Teammates like Rakitić, Arturo Vidal, Sergi Roberto, and Griezmann acted as his legs, pulling forty-yard sprints to cover the holes he left. That dragged Barça's midfield out of shape.

As the team aged with Messi, Barça's training sessions slowed down. This was a shock for Griezmann, who had come from Atlético Madrid. There, he recalled, "Every training session was at the intensity level of a match."[8] To the quiet dismay of Barça's younger players, football's most demanding rondo descended into a warm-up routine. In matches, Barcelona's defenders and midfielders rarely overlapped anymore.

This went against the grain of modern football. The sport continued to evolve weekly, and the onetime innovators Barça were being overtaken. The economist Joseph Schumpeter labeled the same process in business "creative destruction": new entrepreneurs come along with new ideas, and the pioneering systems of yesteryear are junked.

"Every day football gets more spectacular, the players physically, technically, and tactically stronger," remarked Gerard Piqué. "I always say that the best defenders in history are those of today." Even Franz

Beckenbauer, he added, was "worse on the ball, slower and understood the game less well" than Piqué's generation. As for defenders who just kicked people, they had died out.[9]

Piqué was right that football kept improving—but most of all outside Barcelona. While Barça neglected pressing, other teams updated it. *Gegenpressing,* the Germans called the latest version: chasing up the opposition the moment you lose possession, so as to win the ball near their goal, before their defense could organize. It was Ajax's "hunting" of the 1970s on fast-forward—a game so rapid it should be called "storming."

Storming teams adopted some of Barça's innovations, such as Guardiola's five-second pressing rule, but discarded others, like the obsession with possession. Whereas Guardiola's Barça had hated losing the ball, for teams like Klopp's Liverpool, losing the ball and then winning it back was the strategy.

In 2014, Germany's 1–7 thrashing of Brazil with rapid forward pressing had seemed like a hilarious one-off. It turned out to be the portent of a new phenomenon: blowout wins by teams playing at a pace that would have seemed impossible as recently as 2010. By 2020, storming had become the orthodoxy, practiced even by traditionally cautious teams like Juventus and Chelsea.[10] Wing-backs pelted forward nonstop. Midfielders pulled sprints when their team won the ball, and also when they lost it.

Wenger told me in 2020:

> In the last ten, fifteen years we have gone for real athletes, and from the day on where everybody could measure the physical performance, all the players who could not perform physically well were kicked out of the game. Today football goes at two hundred miles an hour, so you have to show first that you can go on the train. Once you're on the train you can express your talent, but if you cannot get on the train, you don't play.

A football field is about seven thousand square meters in size. Teams like Bayern and Liverpool, said Wenger, squeezed their defending into 8 percent of that space: they massed players around the ball in a zone of about six hundred square meters in the opposition's half. Storming had become so overwhelming that a brilliant lightweight like Mesut Özil was squeezed out of the Premier League at Arsenal.

"It has killed some artists," said Wenger. "I think it has uniformized a little bit too much the way to play football. . . . Everybody presses on the first ball from the keeper. . . . It has emphasized the chain defending to close balls down. And it has killed a little bit the creativity."

Yet storming produced lots of goals. After a team went ahead, rather than sitting on their lead they just kept on storming. The Champions League had never averaged three goals per game in any season between 2003 and 2004 (when the competition's new format was adopted) and 2015–2016. Between 2016 and 2020, the average exceeded three in three seasons out of four.[11]

One oddity of storming is that the method tends to work best against skillful attacking teams like Barcelona. It's hard to storm defensive teams, because they keep ten men back. It's also hard to storm long-ball teams, because they will go long, bypassing the storm. But teams like Barça, which pass out from defense, can be caught in storms.

Used to having the ball in the other team's half, Barcelona got confused when they lost it in their own. Suddenly the effective playing area stretched across the whole field, rather than the fifty yards that they preferred to play in. A *pivote* like Busquets, master of the square yard, sometimes ended up "swimming" in a vast midfield. To use Cruyff's analogy, an intelligent slow footballer can defend a table, but not an entire restaurant.

In February 2017, a storming PSG beat Barcelona 4–0 in the Champions League. Barça won the second leg 6–1 with their famous *remontada* ("comeback"), but then lost 3–0 at Juve in the quarterfinal and were eliminated. In 2018, they lost 3–0 at Roma at the same stage and were eliminated again.

The good news was that Cruyffian attacking pressing football still worked. The bad news was that other clubs had modernized it. Barcelona were "forced to compete with their own influence," remarked the writer on tactics, Michael Cox.[12] Yet the club didn't hire a coach to turn its aging players into a high-intensity storming unit, or to replace them with younger ones. Barça's thinking was that with a core of veteran world-class players topped by Messi, plus the remnants of the Cruyffian house style, a strong coach would only get in the way.[13]

Every Barça coach after Guardiola understood his own shrunken role. When I visited Valverde in 2019 at the first team's training ground, the Camp Tito Vilanova, his white office walls were almost bare except for the team's schedule. There was barely a personal touch in the room. Valverde knew he was just a caretaker. He couldn't tell Messi, Busquets, and Piqué how to play, though he could give them useful information about, say, an opposing keeper's weaker side.

In the changing-room scenes of the *Matchday* documentary, Valverde resembles a friendly schoolteacher who doesn't scare the class. Before kickoff, he always gives a brief tactical talk, after which senior players say a few words. Messi usually makes much the same short speech, in his characteristic monotone, emphasizing the need to think coolly. Before a game against Atlético Madrid, for instance, he tells his teammates, "*Tranquilo*, like always, without losing our heads. Not too quickly."[14]

On May 1, 2019, at halftime in the home leg of the Champions League semifinal against Liverpool, with Barça leading 1–0, Messi says, "Try to calm the match. I know it's hard, but try. If we play one against one, they are stronger. We're not used to it; they're quick. Then we're going up and down; it's a lottery. If we have control, it's another story."[15]

In a seven-minute spell in the second half that night, Messi sealed a

3–0 win by scoring his 599th and 600th goals for Barça (the latter an unforgettable long-range free kick). Afterward, a smiling Klopp bounded into Liverpool's forlorn changing room shouting, "Boys, boys, boys! We are not the best team in the world. Now you know that. Maybe they are! Who cares? Who cares! We can still beat the best team in the world. Let's go again."[16]

That night, it sounded like bravado. Barça really did look like the best team in the world. Three days after clinching their second straight Spanish title, they had one foot in the Champions League final, where they would be favored to beat Ajax or Spurs. There was life in the old dog yet.

Six days later, in the second leg at Anfield, Barça returned to their changing room at halftime 1–0 down. Jordi Alba, whose error had given Liverpool the goal, was in tears. The whole team was anxious. Once a group of players has been together for years, every new match becomes an echo of past matches. The thrashings at PSG, Juventus, and Roma had given Barça a complex.

It was at this point at Anfield that Messi decided to stand up and remind his teammates of their deepest fear. "We have to start strong," he said, his monotone louder than usual. "Remember Roma was our fault. Nobody else's. We mustn't let the same thing happen. It was our fault, nobody else's."

As the Irish journalist Ken Early remarked, Messi seemed to believe that "'Let's talk about the thing that we desperately don't want to happen, and get that very firmly in our heads before we go out and play,' is a sound basic format for a captain's gee-them-up speech."[17] In the second half, Barça crumbled, succumbing 4–0 to Liverpool's storm. Piqué reflected later, "Everything made us think of Roma, the experience we had, and everything reproduced itself in the end."[18]

In Barcelona's changing room after the elimination, nobody spoke. A few players stared at their phones, but most sat with heads in hands, showing penance to their teammates, probably wondering whether their team's time was over.[19] Later, four *socis* who had traveled to the game shouted insults at Messi. The player's father demanded that Bartomeu punish them, but the president thought the request small-minded, and did nothing—no doubt worsening his relationship with the family.

The thrashing at Anfield was a callback to Barça's 4–0 thrashing by a fitter, faster Milan in the Champions League final in Athens a quarter century earlier. There was a constant at work across time: when things went wrong with Barça, they went very wrong, because there were so few defensive safeguards.

Ronald Koeman, a veteran of Athens who by 2019 was managing the Netherlands, must have noticed the similarities. By his own admission, he had "spent his whole career trying to become coach of Barcelona one day,"[20] and having learned from Cruyff the importance of cultivating friendly journalists, he was forever nurturing his contacts in Catalan media. Even before Anfield, he had reminded a local TV channel that Suárez, Messi, Piqué, and Busquets were all over thirty. Once they left, he noted, "You have no central defender, no midfielder, no striker and no Messi. Good luck with that."[21]

After Anfield, Messi gave his first press conference with Barcelona in four years. "The worst thing," he said, "and for that we can never forgive ourselves, is that we didn't fight."[22] When the team needed a rocket up the arse, in the English phrase, he saw it as his job to deliver it.

The 4–0 at Anfield turned out to be premonitory. If 1992 had been Barça's *annus mirabilis*, 2020 was its *annus horribilis*. Everyone had seen the cracks in the cathedral's ceiling. But nobody expected the building to collapse. That year, an almost carnivalesque string of mishaps occurred.

It started on January 13, when Bartomeu sacked Valverde after a 2–3 defeat to Atlético Madrid. Though the role of Barça's head coach had been denuded of most of its responsibilities, one remained: the coach serves as designated scapegoat. He is sacrificed so that the president can live on.

The sacking looked harsh. Admittedly Barça hadn't been playing well, and Valverde had closed the team's door to gifted players from the Masia. Still, he had won two Spanish titles in two seasons, and he left with the team top of the league again. The sacking upset Messi: though he doesn't care much who the coach is, he thought Valverde was a nice guy.

The Argentinian was outraged when Barça's sporting director, Eric Abidal, told a newspaper, "Lots of players were not satisfied [with Valverde] and nor did they work much." Messi posted Abidal's interview on Instagram, with a red circle around those words, and wrote that the players had no responsibility for the sacking.[23]

The candidates to replace Valverde included Xavi, Koeman, and Mauricio Pochettino (who had once said that as an Espanyol fan, he could never manage Barça, and had joked that he'd rather work on a farm in Argentina than "in some places," which was "a problem for some people's egos," recalled Eric Abidal, Barça's sporting director at the time[24]). None of these men wanted to take over in midseason. And so the obscure, jobless sixty-one-year-old *cruyffista* Quique Setién, who had spent the previous day walking among the cows of his home village in northern Spain, received a surprise call.

At his presentation, Setién tactfully avoided mentioning that he'd grown up supporting Real Madrid.[25] "Not in my wildest dreams could I have imagined being coach of Barcelona," he marveled. "Honestly, I just could not imagine them going for me."[26] Nor could most people. But in fact, Setién's unremarkable CV reassured Barcelona. At least a C-list coach wouldn't delude himself that he was the boss of Messi.

Setién understood that Messi was his hierarchical superior. At half-time of one of his first matches, away at Betis, he asked him what he thought. "What do you think I think?" snapped Messi. He was irritated that the inexperienced Junior Firpo (a protégé of Setién's in their days at Betis) had started at left-back instead of Messi's friend, the veteran Jordi Alba. "This isn't a youth team!" Messi shouted. "Play your best players." Soon after halftime, Jordi Alba replaced Firpo.

IN EARLY FEBRUARY 2020, an official from the European football association UEFA visited Barcelona. At a restaurant next to the Camp Nou, he met a Barça official for a catch-up. During the conversation, the Barça man accused UEFA of kowtowing to two clubs effectively owned by Gulf states, Paris Saint-Germain and Manchester City. Barça felt that if these clubs were allowed to spend their owners' oil and gas money on players, the Catalans couldn't compete. UEFA's "financial fair play" (FFP) rules supposedly restrained such spending, but Barça felt the association was applying the rules selectively. Eventually, the Barça official asked: "Is there anyone in your FFP department we could pay?" The UEFA official understood that his counterpart was trying to find somebody to bribe. Reading this as a sign of "the almost feral culture around football governance," he thought: "And these are supposed to be the good guys! 'Més que un club' and all that."

The Barça official was voicing a growing anxiety within the club: that it no longer had the money to win the big prizes, because it was owned by its members rather than by a billionaire sugar daddy. Some senior people within Barça felt they had no alternative but to join the secret scheming for a lucrative European Super League. But this self-pity rather ignored the fact that another member-owned club not a million miles away, Real Madrid, was still racking up Champions League trophies, as were other clubs without sugar daddies such as Bayern Munich and Liverpool. The truth was that Barça's problems stemmed more from bad management than an outdated ownership model.

Amid all this anxiety, the scandal around the small Uruguay-based communications company I3 Ventures blew up. It seemed that Bartomeu had hired I3 to tackle a problem that presidents of other football clubs simply don't have: an active opposition inside the club. I3 appears to have created fake online media accounts and bots to defend Bartomeu and undermine his perceived opponents, who included the pantheon of modern Barça's heroes, Piqué, Messi, Guardiola, and Xavi, as well as potential candidates for the presidency. Barça had paid I3 €900,000—a sum far above market rates, and divided into tranches just small enough for Bartomeu not to have needed authorization from the board. The scandal inevitably became known as "Barçagate."

Bartomeu denied that I3 had attacked anyone, saying the firm had only been hired to "monitor" social media. In a meeting with Barça's captains, he handed them a dossier of supportive posts published by the accounts in question. The captains were unconvinced. Barçagate helped prompt the resignation of six more directors, taking total resignations from the board to eleven under Bartomeu's reign.[27]

On the field, Barça were faltering. By March 2020, their expected goals had dropped below two per game. Griezmann's 0.42 xG was just over a third of Neymar's at his peak. Koeman, observing from the Netherlands, remarked, "The best teams right now play at a massively high tempo for 90 minutes. It's hard for Barcelona to keep up."[28] Messi appeared to agree: "The way we are right now I don't think it's enough to win the Champions League."[29]

At that point, the coronavirus came along to shut down football and devastate Spain. By May, the country had forty-three thousand deaths above usual levels—at the time, the highest rate of death in the pandemic for any country for which good-quality data existed.[30] Spaniards suffered an extraordinarily strict lockdown. For six weeks that spring, children weren't allowed to leave the house.

Across Europe, the closure of stadiums ravaged football's finances.

In the 2017–2018 season, Barça had become the first club in any sport to hit $1 billion in annual revenues (or €914 million). In 2018–2019, it claimed revenues of $1.1 billion (€990 million).[31] With hindsight, that looked like a peak that no football club would revisit anytime soon. In May 2020, Barça's vice president, Jordi Cardoner, himself recovering from a bout with the virus, told me the pandemic had already wiped about €130 million off the club's revenues.

When Spain's lockdown began, Barça asked its players to accept a wage cut so as to preserve the full salaries of the five hundred or so nonplaying permanent employees. Messi messaged a senior club official to express his outrage at the very suggestion. Another senior player, when told that the average club employee earned €30,000 (about $33,000), said he thought that was quite a generous monthly wage. In fact it was their annual wage. Eventually Barça's four captains agreed in teleconferences with directors that the team would take a 72 percent reduction. Admittedly that would apply only from the start of the lockdown in March until the season's end, meaning that players would lose less than 10 percent of their annual pay. Still, it was enough to allow the regular employees to keep their full salaries. That did matter to the captains, who had all grown up at the club.

Yet anyone who read the pay cut as a victory for the board over the squad was mistaken. After the deal was agreed, Messi went on Instagram to take a swipe at Barça's leadership. Overlooking his initial opposition to the cut, he wrote:

> We want to clarify that our desire has always been for our salaries to be reduced, because we understand that this is an exceptional situation and we have ALWAYS been the first to help the club with what they have asked of us . . . it surprises us that there would be people inside the club who want to put

us under a magnifying glass or try to pressure us into something that we were always clear we wanted to do.[32]

Messi at that point had 145 million Instagram followers, about sixty million more than Barça. In any conflict, he owned the bigger megaphone.

In late May 2020, a smartphone video went around the world. It showed a white policeman in Minneapolis holding his knee against the neck of George Floyd, a black man, until he died. Protesters took to the streets across the United States and Europe. Even footballers—historically an apolitical lot—spoke out like never before. Teams from Liverpool on down photographed themselves "taking a knee," the symbol of the Black Lives Matter protest movement. When matches resumed following the first COVID-19 lockdown, teams in the Premier League wore the slogan "Black Lives Matter" on the backs of their shirts. For months, players and match officials kneeled before kickoff. There were protests in the Bundesliga, too. In France, Kylian Mbappé spoke out repeatedly against police violence. FIFA, which normally punishes players for any "political" action, sniffed the wind and didn't interfere.

The activism by this unprecedentedly educated and powerful generation of footballers went beyond Black Lives Matter. Players in England, led by Liverpool's captain Jordan Henderson, made large donations to Britain's National Health Service. Manchester United's twenty-two-year-old forward Marcus Rashford, a local man who knew what it was like to grow up without enough to eat, led a successful campaign to push the British government into providing free school meals for poor children during the summer holidays.

Yet there was almost no activism at Barcelona. It was as if all the squabbles over Catalan independence and players-versus-board had crowded out bigger issues. "More than a club" seemed like a defunct marketing slogan. Megan Rapinoe, the activist American soccer player, marvels in her autobiography that Messi—like Cristiano Ronaldo and Zlatan Ibrahimović—hasn't spoken out against racism and sexism.[33]

Spanish football resumed in June 2020. If only it hadn't. Barça lost the league to Real Madrid, and then, in the Champions League quarterfinal in a mercifully empty stadium in Lisbon on August 9, went down 8–2 to Bayern Munich. Six of their starting outfield players that night were age thirty-one or over.

The result was both extraordinary and typical: Barça's fifth "storming" defeat by three goals or more since 2017. Wenger diagnosed, "The weakness of Barcelona was mainly physical, and that's why they were in trouble for three years now." The epitome of this in Lisbon was Messi watching almost like an armchair viewer as Bayern's left-back Alphonso Davies launched attack after attack unimpeded.

It was a scoreline too definitive to argue with. A decade earlier, when Barcelona lost to Mourinho's Inter Milan, they could claim moral superiority: they had played football, and he had parked the bus. But to borrow the football writer David Winner's line on the Netherlands–Spain World Cup final, Barça's defeat to Bayern was a case of "Jungian mirroring": they had lost to the more authentic version of their better selves. Now it was Bayern that played Cruyffian football. The Germans' playmaker, Thiago Alcântara, was a Masia *pivote* who had left Barcelona in 2013 because he couldn't see a way of breaking into the Xavi-Iniesta-Busquets midfield.

An era—an unusually long era, by football standards—had ended in one night in Lisbon. Now Barça needed to recruit a new team. The problem was that they had run out of money.

Setién, whose fifteen minutes of coaching fame had at least secured him a nice pension, was dispatched back to his village. Interviewed by Spain's former manager Vicente del Bosque in *El País* newspaper months later, he unburdened himself about Messi. "There's another facet that's not that of a player, and that is more difficult to manage," said Setién. "He is very reserved but he makes you see the things he wants. He doesn't speak much. But he watches." During Setién's seven months at Barça, he had always been aware that Messi could get him sacked at any moment. He had felt helpless around the player, unable to be himself: "Who am I to change him if they have accepted him for years here and have never asked him to adapt?"[34] Setién diagnosed in Messi a permanent anxiety fueled by the pressure to win matches.

Barça replaced Setién even before officially sacking him. After the 8–2 loss, Ronald Koeman had rung one of his journalistic allies in Barcelona, the TV presenter Lluís Canut, and started chatting about his situation with the Dutch national team. Canut, who was dining in a pizzeria, got the message: Koeman wanted the Barça job. The journalist informed the right people at the club.[35] When Koeman got the call from Bartomeu, he thought, "If I don't do it now, I probably never will."[36] He was fifty-seven, recovering from a heart attack a few months before, and sensed that time was running out to realize his last career goal. "Who says we'll live another thirty years in all health?" As luck would have it, he and his wife had just finished renovating their recently purchased Barcelona holiday apartment, with its roof terrace that looked out over the Camp Nou. His family had retained a love of Catalonia from his playing days there from 1989 to 1995. In fact (ironically given the identity of Koeman's future successor) his blond Dutch grandson was named Xavi.[37] The Dutchman's agent, Rob Jansen, wasn't worried about the risk of his client failing and getting sacked. He shrugged: "What happens then? You go home."[38] Wearing a black mask like an albino Zorro, Koeman signed the contract for his dream job.

He came without a great coaching track record, but with the kind of symbolic capital that mattered at Barça. A former Barcelona player like his predecessors Guardiola, Vilanova, Luis Enrique, and Valverde, Koeman had also been the hero of Wembley in 1992. For decades, Barça fans had come up to him on the street to thank him for that goal, and to tell him where they had been when it went in. And he was one of the last coaches in football personally anointed by Cruyff, his former next-door neighbor in Barcelona. Bartomeu and the CEO Grau (his imposing belly hanging over his shorts) took Koeman for a welcome lunch at the La Venta restaurant on the foot of the Tibidabo mountain, a traditional hangout for Barça people. The Dutchman explained his plan to take control and bring in younger players. Messi would have to decide for himself whether he was on board with the project or not. The men clinked cava glasses. "To many years," they toasted. It was that eternally recurring football moment: the optimism of new beginnings.[39]

As the son, brother, and father of professional footballers, Koeman had spent his life in a competitive environment. Messi didn't scare him. The coach arranged a meeting at his captain's house. Messi returned from Cerdanya, on the Franco-Spanish border, where he was holidaying with his family and those of Suárez and Jordi Alba,[40] to lay out his grievances with Barça. Koeman was struck by Messi's commitment, and his enormous interest in football.[41] But the coach explained that he only controlled the first team, and reportedly told the player, "Your privileges in the squad are over, you have to do everything for the team. I'm going to be inflexible."[42]

As so often before in Barcelona's history, Dutch directness had encountered Latin etiquette. Messi was offended—nobody spoke to him like that—and more so when Koeman then told Suárez he wasn't needed in a phone call that lasted (according to the Uruguayan) forty seconds. "It's not the way to say goodbye to a legend," Suárez complained later.[43] Worse, nobody from the board rang the "El Pistolero" to thank him for his 198 goals for Barcelona. Messi could accept Barça's decision to discard his best friend, but he couldn't forgive the disrespect.

It hardly mattered anyway. Messi had decided to leave the club regardless, as he had told Bartomeu several times that year. The president had always asked him to wait, assuring him that if he still felt that way when the season ended, he would be free to go. Messi later explained his reasoning to the website Goal.com:

> I thought the club needed more younger players, new players, and I thought my time at Barcelona was over. I felt sorry because I'd always said I wanted to finish my career here. It was a very difficult year. I suffered a lot in training, in the matches and in the changing room. . . . The moment came when I decided to look for new ambitions.

The one thing he had always wanted, he said, was "a winning project."

> And the truth is that there hasn't been a project or anything else for a long time. They juggle and cover the holes as things come up. . . . I want to compete at the highest level, win titles, battle in the Champions League. You can win or lose, because it's very difficult, but at least you have to be competitive and not melt down like we did in Rome, Liverpool or Lisbon.[44]

"Leo's big problem is that he competes with himself," according to Barça's former keeper and sporting director Andoni Zubizarreta. Messi had been carrying around the responsibility to win matches for fifteen years, explained Zubi:

> We have all had that responsibility. When you're in the tunnel about to go out to play, you know who the good ones are in your team, the ones who'll win it for you, especially in finals. . . . A day comes when you look in the mirror and you say, "Ooof, this isn't going to be so easy."[45]

A male athlete of a previous generation might have made the decision to change clubs without worrying what his wife and kids thought. After all, Daddy's job came first. But today's sportsmen are from a generation of involved fathers. When seven-year-old Thiago asked his father whether he was leaving Barça, Messi couldn't bring himself to tell him he might have to make new friends at a new school. Thiago cried anyway, and said, "We're not going." At the family meeting where Messi broke the news, his wife and three sons all burst into tears. "It was a drama," he admitted later.[46]

Nonetheless, on August 20 he sent Barcelona a *burofax*—a sort of registered letter carried by the Spanish postal service—officially stating his decision to go. The Messis knew that his contract specified he could leave on a free transfer only if he announced his departure by June 10. However, a cavalier lawyer assured the family that the deadline wouldn't apply in the special circumstances of 2020. What the clause really meant, the lawyer said, was that Messi had to announce his departure soon after the end of the season. It was a mere quirk of fate that in 2020, uniquely, the season ended in August. Messi was sticking to the spirit of the agreement, said the lawyer, who was no doubt eager to come up with an interpretation that would please the great man. The family seems to have accepted the assurance unthinkingly. Messi himself was sure he was free to go. Hadn't Bartomeu always told him to decide after the season?[47]

Like Cruyff before him, Jorge Messi had succumbed to the fantasy that he was a brilliant businessman who could negotiate huge contracts alone. Yet in the biggest decision of his son's career, with hundreds of millions of euros at stake, the family displayed the amateurism of a mom-and-pop shop.

The Messis' counterparty, Barça, wasn't thinking like a business either. Had it been a more corporate club, a Catalan Manchester United, it might have met the family halfway: pointed out that the deadline for a free transfer had passed but let Messi leave, probably to Manchester City, for a fee of perhaps €150 million. By also shedding his salary, Barça would free up a total of about €300 million to rebuild the team. Losing the best-paid player would have put downward pressure on everyone else's salaries. It would have been the pragmatic decision. After all, Messi, then thirty-three, was free to walk out the door ten months later for nothing, while pocketing a hefty loyalty bonus.

But Barcelona isn't a business. It's a neighborhood club run by local merchants who plan to live in town until they die, and who care above all about their reputations there. Bartomeu, already despised for his disastrous transfers and conflicts with players, said, "I won't be the president who loses Messi." His predecessors Rosell and Laporta had each had occasion to use almost exactly the same phrase. With masked demonstrators outside the Camp Nou demanding his resignation, Bartomeu said the player could leave only if a club paid his release clause of €700 million. No club was going to do that.

That was when Messi gave in. Some Barça fans were already angry with him for asking to leave, and he didn't want to make things worse by taking the club to court, as Cruyff had done after being sacked in 1996. In any case, like Cruyff's family, Messi's wanted to stay in Barcelona. And at least everyone at the club now saw the need for new, younger players. Perhaps Barça could rebuild.

IN SEPTEMBER 2020, I took a train from Paris to Catalonia. Except for an (unrelated) interview about nuclear espionage in an Antwerp pizzeria that summer, I hadn't left France in six months. I disembarked in a stricken Barcelona. Tourism had collapsed, destroying the livelihoods of everyone from the city's Michelin chefs to the pickpockets who haunt the port. Spain's economy had shrunk by 18.5 percent in the second quarter of the year, the largest fall since records began. In Catalonia alone, nearly six thousand people had died of COVID-19.

But selfishly, I felt I was making a last stop in paradise before a long COVID winter in Paris. Barcelona was sunny, gorgeous, empty of tourists, and enjoying the respite between two onslaughts of the virus. I stocked up on sensory pleasures. Every evening I swam in the rooftop pool of my hotel, where I was paying a pandemic price of €60 a night for a lovely room. I had a long, slow lunch with friends in a seafood restaurant on the water that was normally booked out a week in advance.

The club's post-Lisbon meltdown felt like a subplot of the city's. On a terrace in Pedralbes, a club staffer offered me a Barça-branded mask and said, "We have everything! Well, we don't have a team or a board of directors, but we have masks."

I found the Camp Nou semi-abandoned and tatty, nothing like the swish new grounds elsewhere in Europe. It was like walking around Rome after the barbarians had arrived. The stadium bars were closed. The electrical capacity was so low that the catering staff couldn't use the ovens.[48] Renovations had stagnated. The Miniestadi opposite the ground, where Guardiola had played in his Masia days, had been torn down to make way for a new basketball arena that showed no sign of materializing anytime soon. Meanwhile, Real Madrid was already well advanced on its $900 million overhaul of the Bernabéu stadium.

Barça's headquarters behind Gate 11 were deserted, with almost everyone working from home. I'd come to meet a director for a postapocalyptic briefing, and after bumping elbows, we went to sit in the president's empty office. Bartomeu wasn't there; perhaps he was hiding.

On the walls of the little office hung a portrait of the mustachioed Hans Gamper, the club's founder, and a shocking fluorescent orange shirt from Wembley in 1992. But the pièce de résistance was an artwork donated by a *soci*: a framed collection of Barça membership cards for every year from about 1900 to 2000.

The director said the pandemic had slashed revenues by a total of €300 million across two seasons. Barça had offered refunds to its 85,000 season-ticket holders (435 of whom had said, "Keep the money"). The club's debt was ballooning out of control.

The director played down the dreadful figures. The banks were still willing to lend, he assured me. One banker had said that the only one of his customers that he was confident would still exist in a hundred years' time was Barça. The director recalled that in 2010, the club had borrowed €155 million from seventeen different banks to pay the players' salaries. This time, he said, the whole world was in crisis, and other clubs were harder hit than Barcelona.

But no other big football club had as urgent a need to buy a new team. No club had been more dependent on tourism: the Barça museum, the megastore, and the tens of thousands of foreign fans paying premium prices for match tickets had all melted away in the pandemic. And no other club in all of sports had a higher annual wage bill than Barça's €500 million, more than a quarter of which went to Messi. On top of that sum, noted the director, Barça had to write off another €200 million a year on transfer fees. If a club signs a player for a fee of €100 million and gives him a four-year contract, it writes off €25 million a season in its accounts. That's not a problem if he's a youngster who can be resold later, but Barça's collection of oldies had little resale value.

Adding together the salaries and write-offs, Barça's total outlay on players was about €700 million a year. Worryingly, that was almost as much as the €750 million in revenue that it was expecting for the 2020–2021 season. (Before the pandemic, the club's target for 2021 had been to surpass €1 billion.)

In short, salaries at Barça had got out of hand. Now an era of austerity loomed. La Liga, hoping to prevent bankruptcies during the pandemic, had tightened its spending controls on Spanish clubs. The league had slashed Barcelona's total permitted spending on transfer fees and players' salaries to €383 million—down sharply from €656 million the season before.[49] Any cuts that Barça didn't make at once it would have to make the season after. The director obviously didn't say it, but Barcelona's twin brother, Real Madrid, had managed to keep a much tighter cap on wages. In the 2019–2020 season, it spent only €411 million on salaries and transfer write-offs—about €275 million less than Barça.[50] Madrid was a sustainable business, and Barcelona wasn't.

Now Barça was frantically trying to lighten the wage bill by discarding expensive players such as Rakitić, Suárez, Vidal, and Rafinha without transfer fees. The club was about to pay Suárez millions to leave. It would still end up hundreds of millions over La Liga's limit, and without money to sign new players. The director sighed. "I feel bad because there are millions of people, and we can't give them what they want."

Barcelona had to lower its sights for a while, another senior club official told me; "not try to win every year La Liga or the Champions." In thirty years of visiting Barcelona, I had never seen the club laid so low. It was now possible to imagine that football's biggest spenders of the 2014 to 2019 period would eventually have to sell rising stars like Pedri and Ansu Fati to richer clubs.

During the 2020 transfer window, Barça was reported to be chasing sixty different players.[51] Its initial main target was Inter Milan's striker Lautaro Martínez. Once the club realized it couldn't afford him, it switched to the discount option, Memphis Depay of Olympique Lyon. It agreed to a fee of €26 million with the French club, only to discover that it couldn't even afford that. Its biggest signing of the window ended up being the promising twenty-year-old Portuguese winger Francisco Trincão, bought from little SC Braga for €31 million. Once the season began, he mostly sat on the bench.

In October, Barça's shirt sponsor Rakuten renewed its contract for only one more season, until 2022, and for just €30 million plus bonuses, which was €25 million a year less than the previous deal. Cinto Ajram, in charge of sponsorships under Bartomeu, later said the price had fallen because of uncertainty over Messi's future. Ajram mused:

> I would even ask myself right now if the agreement is worth €30 million. Rakuten began the relationship with Barcelona when there was the trident of Messi, Suárez and Neymar. . . . When you sell the Barcelona brand around the world, you use Messi's face. In these conditions, no one would dare to renew for three or four years because they don't know what the value of the club will be without this player.[52]

The board was left to haggle with the squad over further pay cuts. The club's tactic became to pick out individual players and offer them longer contracts, with most of the pay back-loaded onto later years. Bartomeu's board—whose primary interest was survival week by week—was spending its successors' money. Piqué signed a captains' letter to the board rejecting the "embarrassing" plans for pay cuts,[53] but almost simultaneously signed a new contract that would keep him on the pay-roll until 2024, when he would be thirty-seven. (Soon after signing, he suffered an injury that put him out for months.) Meanwhile, over in Madrid, the Spanish tax authorities published a list of the people and companies who owed them the most money. Their single biggest individual debtor at the end of 2019: Neymar, who owed €34.6 million from his time at Barça.[54]

At the Gamper training ground, Koeman's efforts to change club culture earned him the nickname "Sergeant Koeman." Players had to report an hour before practice started. Training sessions were extended from one hour to ninety minutes, and became quite strenuous, by Barça's standards.

Koeman struggled to enjoy his dream job. He said that coaching Barcelona was "the most stressful job" he'd had in his life. He admitted to a documentary maker, "To really win something big, you need a better team." His wife, Bartina, lit candles in the Buddha statue in their apartment before big games,[55] but she often couldn't bear to watch Barça's first few matches, and instead went out with Frenkie de Jong's girlfriend, who couldn't watch either.[56]

The constraints of COVID-19 weighed on Koeman's attempts to build a new team. The players were allowed to assemble for home games only an hour before kickoff, already wearing their match kit, and could spend just five minutes in the changing room together. Koeman hated the silence of the Camp Nou during matches, with no crowd to drive on his exhausted players.[57] He hardly saw the players after games, because they had to go straight home without showering. During the week, he had scant opportunities to talk to them. "All clubs have to deal with this," he conceded, "but the difference is that we are trying to change things so that we can then build something up. That's when you really need that personal contact." He observed that with the sanitary rules, constant testing for COVID-19, and empty stadiums, players at many big clubs seemed to be struggling for motivation.[58]

In games, Koeman played Messi more centrally, as a number ten, with two *pivotes* behind him to compensate for his defensive absences. Yet initially Messi seemed ghostlike, mooching around the field in the empty stadiums with his head down, still coming to terms with his aborted departure. "At first Lionel Messi didn't want to [play]," recalled Koeman's assistant Alfred Schreuder.[59] In the first ten matches of the 2020–2021 season, Barça lost to Getafe, Real Madrid, Atlético Madrid, and tiny Cádiz. It was the club's worst league start since 1987, the year before Cruyff arrived. Koeman's wife complained about the players: "Sometimes it's really a mess—they take it much too easy, and my husband is such a hard worker."[60] Meanwhile, Barça's reject Luis Suárez was firing in the goals for league leaders Atlético.

Bartomeu was forced out when, despite the pandemic, a motion of no confidence against him rapidly collected signatures from 20,731 *socis*. That ouster couldn't have happened at Manchester United, where the despised Glazer family had stuck around relatively unbothered for fifteen years. It turned out that at least one bit of "more than a club" survived at Barcelona: democracy. Bartomeu resigned with his board on October 27, saying their families had been threatened, presumably by angry fans. As he left, he announced that Barça would be joining the planned European Super League.

Bartomeu had gone from king to leper of Barcelona, and in the months to come he found that he was pleased to have to wear an anti-COVID mask in public, because it stopped people recognizing him. But he couldn't free himself from the mess he had left behind. In March 2021, he would spend a night in jail as police investigated the I3 affair. Later the prosecutor's office in Barcelona began investigating him for possible "economic crimes."

In late November 2020, the club mortgaged another slice of its future. The squad agreed to forgo about €122 million in basic pay over the season, and another €50 million in possible bonuses. However, Barça promised to repay the players over the next three seasons. Short term, the deal got it halfway out of a big hole. Longer term, the promises shrank the future budget to refresh the squad. An austere Barça wasn't going to attract stars.

The club's debt at this point was €1.17 billion, most of which had accumulated since the pandemic. Laporta, the front-runner in the presidential election, called Barça "the club of three billion: one billion in income, one billion in expenses and one billion in debt."[61] This was two-thirds true: in mere months, income had melted down to well below a billion.

The only other European club that owed more than €1 billion was Tottenham Hotspur, and the vast majority of that was long-term debt stemming from the building of its new stadium, explained the respected blogger on football finance, the Swiss Ramble. He wrote, "FC Barcelona have more of a debt problem than other clubs, as they have by far the highest short-term debt of £641 million"—or £262 million more than the runners-up in that category, Atlético Madrid.[62] There was no immediate crisis: creditors weren't about to risk getting tough with such a popular club. But given football's various financial rules, Barça didn't have much scope to keep running up the debt.

The players were given just four days off for Christmas. Messi and his wife and sons took a private jet to his hometown, Rosario, in Argentina. Once there, a convenient ankle injury obliged him to extend his vacation by two days, and he missed the game against Eibar. But he returned rejuvenated. For his first game back, the team traveled to Huesca by bus instead of plane. The three-hour ride saved €30,000.[63] Barça won 0–1, with Messi getting the assist. He then seemed to rediscover his pleasure in football, and began combining happily with his young teammates Pedri, De Jong, Sergiño Dest, and a newly professional Dembélé. Opposing teams relearned their old fears. Koeman's former assistant Alfred Schreuder remarked, "Without crowds you can literally hear what opponents say to each other. When Leo gets the ball you hear, 'Make a foul! Kick him down!' But that doesn't work, and then they just smack him down with an open hand."

The Dutch coaches were struck by Messi's rediscovered alertness in training. When Piqué rejoined the squad after injury, Schreuder began explaining a new training exercise to him that the other players already knew, only to be interrupted by Messi: "Alfred, no need, I've already filled him in." Schreuder had laughed to himself and thought, "That's how clever you are." He reflected: "That's Messi: he sees everything, understands everything, keeps track of everything relevant to the team, and thinks ahead."[64]

Koeman said,

> If we did a shooting exercise in training, there were players who would sometimes lob an easy ball, mess around. But with Messi it was always: boom, boom, boom, boom. Nothing fancy, always functional. . . . With him, the old players never lost an exercise against the young ones. It happened once and Messi was seriously angry about that for a week. . . . Other than Cruyff, I've never met anyone with his football intelligence. Alfred sometimes explained the exercises in English, which Messi doesn't speak well. But he'd understand it within a couple of seconds.[65]

Barcelona recovered in the league that winter, rising to second place by spring 2021. However, the team continued its four-year run of getting thrashed in the Champions League, losing 0–3 to Juventus and 1–4 to Paris Saint-Germain, both times in the Camp Nou. Mbappé, who could have joined Barça at age eighteen, scored a hat trick for Paris. ("The best match of my career," he told me, "because it was complete.") The emotional summary of that night was Piqué—fully audible in the empty stadium—screaming at his deflated teammates, "Can't we have a long possession just once?" and then exchanging graphic insults of their respective mothers with Griezmann.

This was the club that Joan Laporta inherited on March 7, when he returned as president eleven years after leaving office. The biggest democratic election in sports had been held in the thick of the pandemic. Of the 110,000 club members eligible to vote for a new president, about half did, many by mail. Laporta (member number 13,352) won 54 percent of the vote in a three-way runoff. Messi, who showed up in a mask to cast his vote at the Camp Nou, is assumed to have backed him.

Laporta had campaigned on bullish talk about Barça's future. He said he would renew Messi's contract over an *asado*, an Argentinian barbecue. His optimism was genuine, because he had a secret plan: he believed that almost immediately after becoming president, he could access €300 million, the fee from the American bank J.P. Morgan for joining the Super League. That, he thought, would make the club's short-term problems go away, and even allow Barça to bid for stars like Mbappé. But Laporta didn't explain his scheme because he wanted to cast himself as the only candidate who could save the club.

His ascension instantly cheered up many Barça fans. The handsome lawyer is a grinning politician who draws energy from interactions with voters—sometimes too much energy. There was trouble on election day after he told a young woman with whom he'd posed for a photo: "Call me when you're eighteen." The only female member of his campaign slate was sent out to explain that he'd meant he'd be signing the girl to a sports contract. But his problems had only just begun. No wonder some members of rival campaigns exhaled in silent relief when they lost.

First, Laporta and his board members had to come up with a collective bank guarantee, or *aval*, worth €124.6 million, or 15 percent of that season's budget.[66] If Barça lost that amount during their tenure, which seemed very possible, the money would automatically be deducted from their personal accounts. The quickest, most obvious way to slash costs—letting Messi leave—was taboo to mention. In fact, Laporta had campaigned on the promise that he was the ideal person to persuade Messi to stay.

Laporta eventually found a Midas figure to put up the largest single chunk of the *aval*: the entrepreneur José Elías, an electrician's son from the poor suburbs outside Barcelona who had ended up running the renewable energy company Audax. The *aval* was notarized at three a.m. on the last day before the deadline.[67] Elías wasn't eligible to join Barça's board because he had only been a *soci* for one year.[68] But any businessperson taking on that much personal risk to save a new president was going to demand power in return. This was where Barcelona's future seemed to lie: the club would start offering rich outsiders a say. Bartomeu's board had already looked into doing this. Now the situation had become so desperate that the *socis* might even let Laporta sell a minority stake in Barça to a sheikh, an oligarch, or an investment fund. For the first time ever, a slice of football's biggest democracy could be up for sale.

There was one other, little-noticed but potentially revolutionary aspect to Laporta's presidency: for the first time ever, Barça was being run not simply by a Catalan nationalist but by a committed *indepe*, a man who believed Catalonia should break away from Spain. From 2010 to 2012, Laporta had sat in the Catalan parliament with his own separatist party. He skirted the issue during the club elections, campaigning as a uniter of all *socis*, but he received strong support from *indepes*. As president, he would face temptation to turn the most beloved Catalan institution into a vehicle for the secessionist cause—perhaps even to help fund it. It would be like a hardline Republican taking over the New York Yankees and using the club to promote Donald Trump. If that happened, federalist *socis* would walk away from Barça, and the club would divide Catalans rather than unite them.

Even more fundamentally, there was no obvious way for Laporta to keep Barcelona at the top. Over the last three decades, the club had always had a competitive advantage of some kind: first Cruyff's pioneering ideas, then the golden Masia generation, and finally the unmatched revenues it threw off.

By 2021, Cruyff's ideas had gone mainstream, the Masia had stopped producing stars, the Messi generation was having its last hurrah, and the money had run out. In April, Laporta tried to take Barça into the Super League, but the project collapsed within forty-eight hours when nine of the twelve founding clubs pulled out. This was a humiliation for the two chief conspirators behind the league, Florentino Pérez at Real Madrid and Andrea Agnelli of Juventus, but it was a disaster for their junior accomplice Laporta, whose club needed the money the most. Florentino understood this. In fact, he wanted to help his Catalan rivals: if a penniless Barça descended into long-term mediocrity, then the *Clásico* and the entire Spanish league would lose value, and Madrid would suffer, too.

Even after the Super League collapsed, Barcelona stuck with the project. It was a mark of poor management that the club that so recently had notched up the highest revenues in sporting history was on a desperate quest for higher revenues. True, Laporta's board was busy identifying untapped income sources—such as selling the naming rights of the Espai Barça—but then so were rival clubs.

Barça at this point still had one last unique selling point. In the first months of 2021, *Messidependencia* reached a new extreme. More than ever before, Barça looked like a one-man team. From the start of January through to the end of the season, the thirty-three-year-old accounted for 55 percent of the team's league goals and assists, despite missing three matches in the period. That's an astonishing proportion, almost unmatched in football history (even if Harry Kane at Spurs was matching it that very season). All told, from 2016 through 2021, Messi accounted for about half of Barça's goals and assists.[69] A measure of his teammates' reverence for him is that after their victory over Athletic Bilbao in the Spanish cup final, they took turns posing for individual selfies with him and the trophy.

A team that depended so heavily on one old and irreplaceable man had ceased to be a team. True, talented youngsters had come into the side, but it seemed improbable that Pedri, Dest, and Mingueza would turn out to be the next Xavi, Dani Alves, and Piqué. And Barcelona no longer had the money to buy in the world's best. The cost of keeping Messi for that extra, ultimately disappointing, season was somewhere around €300 million: his salary plus the transfer fee the club had forfeited by not selling him the previous September.

Barça finished the 2020–2021 season in third place with seventy-nine points—its lowest points total since 2008. Atlético Madrid won the Spanish title, largely thanks to Barcelona's free gift of Luis Suárez. After scoring the winning goal in the last match, the Uruguayan sat on the field crying with happiness as he phoned his family. "The way they showed contempt for me at Barcelona at the start of the season," he had said before the game, "and then Atlético opened all its doors for me—I'm so grateful for that." He scored twenty-one league goals and was the striker that Barcelona lacked all season—the umpteenth bad transfer of the Bartomeu era.

When the season ended, Laporta told Koeman that he wouldn't sack him just yet, but wanted to spend a fortnight looking out for a better coach. In private, the usually stoic Dutchman was reduced to tears by the uncertainty.[70] In the end Laporta let him hang on for a while, perhaps because Barça didn't have the €12 million required to pay off Koeman's contract. In fact, it still hadn't paid off his sacked predecessors Setién and Valverde.

It was hard to see why the club's intellectual lead would ever return. Maybe the Barcelona model was coming to an end. The club's business executives were already planning for a future of failure on the pitch. One told me that Barça should expect to be less successful in the next twenty-five years than it had been in the previous twenty-five. The worst-case scenario was becoming AC Milan: from European champions to national also-rans.

If that happened, Chinese kids would stop watching Barcelona's matches and buying their shirts. In that case, Barça would probably drop out of the top three of European clubs with the highest revenues. The foreign fan base—which by this time consisted largely of youngsters in love with Messi—might start to age. Once again, Barcelona's role model was Manchester United: its commercial executives had milked the club's historical brand to maintain high revenues despite on-field mediocrity since Alex Ferguson's departure. United still had more Chinese fans than Barcelona did. "Manchester" had managed to brand itself as something more than just a winning team. Perhaps a post-Messi Barça, too, could make itself almost independent of success?

When Messi left, Barça would have to reinvent itself—but how? A senior club official told me, "After Messi you see the desert, you see darkness."

XVII

THE END?

In summer 2021, Messi had decided to stay at Barcelona. He had been shaken after his attempt to leave the previous year reduced his wife and sons to tears. He knew that Barça's team was no longer world-beating, but it wasn't terrible either, and anyway, he was above all a dad. So he agreed to sign a new contract for half his previous pay and play out his last peak years in the Camp Nou.

When Barça's 2020–2021 season ended, he went off to Brazil and finally won Argentina the Copa América—the country's first prize in twenty-eight years. This really was his trophy: he topped the tournament's rankings for most goals scored, most assists, most chances created, most successful dribbles, and most moves that led to a goal.[1] While he was away his contract with Barça expired, but that seemed to be just an administrative formality.

At the start of August, the Messi family was on a yacht in their favorite holiday spot, Ibiza. On the island, he met Neymar and some other

Paris Saint-Germain players, who jokingly urged him, "Come to Paris."[2] It didn't mean anything: the Messis were headed back to Castelldefels for the long haul. Messi thought that the only thing missing on his new contract was his signature.[3]

But in the late afternoon of August 4, his dad rang: the deal with Barça was off.[4] Jorge Messi had just seen President Laporta, who had finally dropped the upbeat campaign talk and admitted that the club couldn't afford to offer Leo any sort of new contract. Barça's total wage bill then still amounted to about 110 percent of revenues, well above the Spanish league's limit of 70 percent.[5] Barcelona was desperately trying to unload overpaid players—Coutinho, Griezmann, Dembélé, Umtiti, Pjanic—but at that point no other club was keen to take on their salaries, let alone pay their transfer fees. That meant Messi had to go. He was stunned. He had little notion of the club's structural financial crisis, let alone his own role in it; after all, his dad handled the money.

Even had Messi agreed to continue at Barça for La Liga's minimum wage of €155,000 ($177,000), it wouldn't have been enough: the club's ratio of player costs to revenues would still have been about 90 percent,[6] so La Liga would have refused to register his new contract.

When Koeman heard Messi was leaving, he thought, "This isn't true."[7] Millions of people felt the same way. Some speculated that Barça was playing a complicated game of bluff with La Liga.

The following Sunday, at the press conference confirming his departure, Messi sobbed on stage for two minutes before he managed to speak. He explained, frankly, that he was crying chiefly for the loss of his family's happy existence in Barcelona rather than for love of the club. "My family and I were convinced we would stay, because this is our home. I've done everything I can to stay, but it's just not possible." Even the world's best player had discovered his lack of control over his own life. The audience—which included many of his teammates past and present—gave him a minutes-long standing ovation.

On August 10 he jetted off to Paris to join the club that was replacing Barça's as the payer of football's highest salaries. On the plane, along with his family, was Pepe Costa, his body man of the last seventeen years, who was leaving Barça to join his master in France.

Jorge Messi had been in touch with Paris Saint-Germain's chairman, Nasser Al-Khelaifi, for years.[8] But Paris wasn't what Leo Messi wanted. His family, freshly installed in their suite at the Qatari-owned Royal Monceau hotel, had not chosen this adventure. What's more, PSG, already equipped with a non-defending genius in Neymar, didn't particularly need him. In his first few months in Paris, Messi often looked to have lost interest in club football, and mused about returning to Barça one day as sporting director.[9] I suspect he will eventually settle in Catalonia for good, like Gamper, Kubala, and Cruyff before him.

His locker at the Joan Gamper sports complex was taken by Barcelona's new loan signing from Sevilla, Luuk de Jong,[10] a big Dutch target-man who had been sitting on the bench in Andalusia. The Dutchman's main attraction to Barça was that he cost almost nothing: the Catalans would have to pay only his Sevilla-level wages.

La Liga had ordered Barça to slash their player costs from about €670 million in the 2019–2020 season[11] to €97 million in 2021–2022—lower than Real Sociedad's. In practice, Barça's actual wage bill in early 2022 was still somewhere over €400 million,[12] but presuming it continued to shrink, it was hard to see how the club could keep competing for prizes. In club football, salaries predict league position with an almost iron logic. Already, by the time Barça lost 3–0 at Benfica in September 2021, it was the team's fifth Champions League defeat by a three-goal margin or worse in thirteen months.

Meanwhile, Messi had been replaced as the power within the club by Goldman Sachs. The bank had lent Barça $700 million to help restructure the club's debt, by then estimated at $1.7 billion, and had also agreed a thirty-five-year plan to finance the $1.85 billion Espai Barça.

Having made the biggest loan to a football club in history, Goldman was now calling the shots.[13]

Messi and the money had gone simultaneously. Cruyff would have found this a thrilling moment: time to start thinking. But what to do? The cliché was that Barça should return to its old "formula": stick boys from the Masia in the first team. Certainly, a group of talented youngsters led by Gavi, Nico, and Ansu Fati was finally emerging from the academy. However, beating all comers with a homegrown team was a low-probability bet. That formula had worked for Barcelona precisely once in the club's history, for about a decade from 2005 through 2015, in an era when the Cruyff-built youth academy was years ahead of its time. Since then, football had evolved: other clubs had copied the Masia, and they now produced exceptional passing players, too. What's more, there's a reason why hardly any leading club in Europe consistently gets a large chunk of its first team from its academy. It's simply unreasonable to expect that half a dozen novices coming out of one academy at eighteen or twenty will be among the best two hundred or so footballers on earth. The Messi-Xavi-Iniesta generation was an unrepeatable one-off.

Still, Barcelona initially seemed fixated on re-creating its glory days of the early 2000s. Laporta—who had been president in that era, too—brought back the right-back of the time, Dani Alves, by then a gnarled thirty-eight-year-old, and hired another early-century icon, Xavi, as coach after Koeman was finally dispatched.

But in football you can never go backward. Instead, Barça needs to go out to find the future: identify the most innovative clubs, and the most innovative people inside those clubs, and either poach them or copy what they were doing. In other words, the Catalans have to do precisely what other clubs had done to them.

Xavi, an instinctive futurist, seems to understand this. But without enough money, even innovation probably won't be enough. I doubt that

Barça can stay at the top. I suspect the era of Messi has given way to the era of Luuk de Jong. The club may return to being the defeatist bastion of regional pride that it was before Cruyff landed at El Prat in 1973.

I seem to have ended up burying Barcelona. Yet I started writing this book because I wanted to praise the club, and I still do. The phrase "beautiful game," popularized by Pelé, has always been associated with a South American ideal of football, with the brilliant individualist. I don't think that's enough, though. My ideal of the beautiful game unites the brilliant individualist with the brilliant collective system. That's FC Barcelona: Messi plus *el cruyffismo*. The Argentinian can dribble past half a team, but for fifteen unforgettable years he was also a cog in a side that could whizz the ball from player to player, find space between lines, press opponents, and perfect all the other elements of the style that had been invented in Amsterdam-East in the 1960s.

The ideal football was always going to be played somewhere in the sport's economic heartland, Western Europe. It happened to be in Barcelona because of the emotional needs of a city without a nation-state. In the decades after Catalonia was crushed in the Spanish Civil War, *socis* and local elites channeled their pride and money into their football club. They found the cash to sign Cruyff, the best player of his day. Later, as coach, he built an original tradition in which Messi could become the best version of himself.

None of this is trivial. What Barça created, in the world's most beloved sport, is one of the most cheering of human achievements. It has touched people from Catalonia to Patagonia.

Maybe this story is now winding down. I'm just grateful I was there to see it, and to eat the *pa amb tomàquet*.

THANKS/*GRÀCIES*

I've been fascinated by FC Barcelona ever since I discovered Johan Cruyff over forty years ago, but the final prompt to write this book happened (like so much in modern soccer) in Qatar. At a *Financial Times* conference there in 2018, I got talking to Javier Sobrino, FC Barcelona's chief strategy and innovation officer (though he's actually from Madrid). A charming and courteous guy, Javier invited me to visit Barcelona to write about his Barcelona Innovation Hub. When I got there, Barça's then president Josep Maria Bartomeu, Jordi Cardoner, Marta Plana, and Albert Mundet were all exceptionally helpful.

My article appeared in the *Financial Times* in February 2019. A few days later, I got an email from Rebecca Nicholson at Short Books in the UK wondering if there was a book in it. I'd been wondering the same thing myself. Rebecca and my editor at Penguin Press in the United States, William Heyward, understood this project from the start and fired my enthusiasm for it. Thanks to both of you and to Natalie Coleman for making it happen.

My colleagues at the *Financial Times* were essential to the book. Jeff

Wagner, Chris Doneley, and their colleagues organized the conference in Qatar that kicked it all off. Esther Bintliff, Piero Bohoslawec, Alice Fishburn, Sophie Hanscombe, Jane Lamacraft, Anthony Lavelle, Neil O'Sullivan, Cherish Rufus, Alec Russell, and Josh Spero and Matt Vella commissioned, edited, and published several articles of mine on Barcelona. They have been a pleasure to work with all these years. Daniel Dombey, the *FT*'s Spain correspondent, helped correct at least a few of my misapprehensions about the country, even while we waited in the clinic to get his broken toe fixed. In return, my children helped look after his. Thanks to Elcin Poyrazlar for putting up with us all.

My fellow journalists and friends Ramón Besa, John Carlin, Jimmy Burns, and Jordi Puntí were fantastically generous with their knowledge of and contacts in Barcelona. I couldn't have written this book without them. John was such a star that he felt bad when Pep said he'd speak to me and then didn't. John, you know you went above and beyond in asking him.

Barcelona's lovely and hyperefficient international communications team of Oriol Bonsoms, Sandra Hors, and Chemi Teres, always polite and smiling, set up dozens of interviews for me. Anyone who has ever worked in football journalism will know that this is not standard industry practice.

This book is the result of hundreds of conversations and interviews over the past thirty years, in Barcelona and elsewhere. I want to thank every interviewee quoted in the book, and also Yael Averbuch, Oriol Barrachina, Roger Bennett, Antoni Bosch Domènech, Carl Bromley, Pierre-Henri Cachera, James Campbell, Maria Carreras, John Davies, Rachel Donadio, Robert Edelman, Pep Ferré, Richard Fitzpatrick, Gloria Garcia Castellvi, Michael Goldenberg, Isaac Guerrero, Mateu Hernández, Sam de Jongh, Enric Jove, Simon Lister, Jill Litt, Matías Manna, Anna Marques Corbella, Jaume Masferrer, Branko Milanovic, Benjamin Miller, Albert Montagut, Felipe Monteiro, Marc Murtra, Dominic Peters, Alex Phillips, Roger Pielke Jr., Will Pryce, Jerome Pugmire, Amy Raphael, Arthur Renard, Xavier Roig, Helena Rosa-Trias, Xavier Sala-i-Martin, Esther Silberstein, Ed Smith, Henk Spaan, Russell Stopford, Francesc Trillas, Darren Tulett, Carles Tusquets, and Xavi Vilajoana.

I haven't thanked all my interviewees at FC Barcelona here, or named them all in the text, because I don't want to risk causing any of them embarrassment by anything that I've written. But you know who you are, and I am intensely grateful.

Albert Capellas is quoted many times in the book, but I want to single him out for a shout-out, because he did more than anyone to shape my thinking about FC Barcelona. May his academy produce many more great players.

This book is about a beautiful place, and I wrote much of it in two other beautiful places. Thanks to Mark Mazower, Marie d'Origny, James Allen, and Eve Grinstead for lending me an office at Reid Hall, the academic center in Paris managed by Columbia University. Amid the insanity of 2020, it was a morale boost to write much of this book in a sunny courtyard off the Rive Gauche.

Many thanks also to Antoine Flochel, proprietor of the Can Cab *masia* in the Catalan mountains, and to Colombe Schneck and Thomas Chatterton Williams, who arranged a spot for me in Can Cab's writers' retreat. It was the perfect place to get my head around this book, with a special mention for the pool. Thanks, too, to Can Cab's lovely staff and to my fellow writers, French and American. It was a moving sight, fetching the umpteenth cup of tea of the day from the kitchen, to pass each person in a different room or terrace, each bowed silently over their own lonely project. I hope all your books have worked out.

My agent, Gordon Wise, at Curtis Brown was always there to answer my boring and pointless emails. With his colleagues Niall Harman and Sarah Harvey, he ruthlessly foisted this book on unsuspecting foreign publishers.

My father, Adam Kuper, was an essential editor and ideas man, as he has been for all my books. Thank you.

My wife, Pamela Druckerman, and our children, Leila, Leo, and Joey, got on board my selfish project more fully than I had ever imagined. They made the ultimate sacrifice and came along on some of my trips to Barcelona, where the kids took Spanish-language courses and became Ansu Fati and Frenkie de Jong fans. We also ate a lot. The most immediate outcome of this book is that as I revise these lines for the paperback edition, we are spending the school year 2021–2022 in Madrid. Why not Barcelona? Well, for reasons touched on in this book, it's easier to learn Spanish in Madrid. But I'm taking the fast train to Barcelona as often as I can.

Pamela, a much better writer than I am, read so many pages of this book in so many different drafts that she could now produce a decent biography of Johan Cruyff herself. But I owe her so much more than that, forever.

EATING WITH BARÇA: A RECIPE APPENDIX

All Recipes Courtesy of the
Barça Innovation Hub

▌▌ Protein Brownies

Ingredients for 10 brownies

150 g dark chocolate, 200 g butter, coconut oil, or extra-virgin olive oil, 200 g brown sugar,* 80 g flour, 4 eggs, 10 g baking powder, 12 chopped walnuts, 50 g dried cranberries, pure cocoa powder, 100 g whey protein, 80% (chocolate flavor).

> *To make this a low-carb recipe, replace half of the sugar with a few drops of Stevia.

METHOD

In a bowl, stir the flour and baking powder. Set aside. Melt the chocolate in a double boiler. Set aside. Work the room-temperature butter until soft and smooth.

In another bowl, beat the sugar into the eggs. Add the olive oil, coconut oil, or softened butter to the eggs and sugar. Add the melted chocolate. Slowly add the flour mixture. Add the whey protein, chopped nuts, and cranberries. Pour the batter into a baking dish, spreading evenly. Bake at 180°C (350°F) for approximately 20 minutes.

KEY INFO
One brownie has approximately 15 g of protein
4/1 recovery recipe
Afternoon snack for players

▌▌ Sleepy Time—*Leche Merengada*

Ingredients for 6 servings

200 ml lactose-free milk, 1 cinnamon stick, 1/4 lemon peel, 1 tsp agave or maple syrup, 20 g casein powder, cinnamon powder

METHOD
Bring the milk, lemon peel, and cinnamon stick to a boil in a pot. Remove from the heat, cover, and let the mixture infuse for 20 minutes. Remove the lemon peel and cinnamon stick. Mix in the casein and syrup. Let cool and serve with cinnamon powder sprinkled on top.

KEY INFO
One glass (approximately 200 ml) has 20 g of casein

▌▌ Coffee Delight

Ingredients for 5 servings

5 instant freeze-dried coffee sachets, 25 g icing sugar, 25 g butter, 25 g coconut oil, 25 g coconut flour, melting chocolate.

METHOD

Melt the butter and coconut oil together. Mix in the instant coffee. Add the sugar and coconut flour. Mix well. Pour into 5 small, round molds and freeze.

Melt the chocolate. Dip the frozen pieces into the chocolate and cool quickly.

KEY INFO

Each piece has approximately 80 mg of caffeine
Quick and easy to eat

SELECTED BIBLIOGRAPHY

Books

Ballús, Pol, and Lu Martín, *Pep's City: The Making of a Superteam* (Backpage and Polaris, Edinburgh, 2019).

Barend, Frits, and Henk van Dorp, *Ajax, Barcelona, Cruyff: The ABC of an Obstinate Maestro* (Bloomsbury, London, 1998).

Burns, Jimmy, *Barça: A People's Passion* (Bloomsbury, London, 1999).

——, *Cristiano and Leo* (Macmillan, London, 2018).

Cox, Michael, *Zonal Marking* (HarperCollins, London, 2019).

Cruijff, Johan, *Boem* (Gooise Uitgeverij, Bussum, 1975).

Cruyff, Johan, *My Turn: A Life of Total Football* (Nation Books, New York, 2016).

Davidse, Henk, *Je moet schieten, anders kun je niet scoren, en andere citaten van Johan Cruijff* (BZZTôH, The Hague, 1998).

De Galan, Menno, *De trots van de wereld: Michels, Cruijff en het Gouden Ajax van 1964–1974* (Bert Bakker, Amsterdam, 2006).

Fieldsend, Dan, *The European Game: The Secrets of European Football Success* (Arena Sport, Edinburgh, 2017).

Ghemmour Chérif, *Johan Cruyff, génie pop et despote* (Hugo Sport, Paris, 2015).

Hornby, Nick, *Fever Pitch* (Indigo, London, 1996).

Hughes, Robert, *Barcelona* (Vintage Books, New York, 1993).

Ibrahimović, Zlatan, *I Am Zlatan Ibrahimović* (Penguin, London, 2013).

Illan, Montse, and Xavier Torrado, *High-Performance Nutritional Cuisine: Practical Recipes for Football* (Barça Innovation Hub, Barcelona, 2019).

Iniesta, Andrés, *The Artist: Being Iniesta* (Headline, London, 2016).

Kok, Auke, *Johan Cruijff: De biografie* (Hollands Diep, Amsterdam, 2019).

Kuper, Simon, *Ajax, the Dutch, the War: Football in Europe During the Second World War* (Orion, London, 2003).

——, *Football Against the Enemy* (Orion, London, 1996).

Leplat, Thibaud, *Guardiola, éloge du style* (Hugo Sport, Paris, 2015).

Lineker, Gary, and Danny Baker, *Life, Laughs and Football* (Arrow Books, London, 2020).

Lowe, Sid, *Fear and Loathing in La Liga* (Yellow Jersey Press, London, 2013).

Minder, Raphael, *The Struggle for Catalonia: Rebel Politics in Spain* (Hurst & Co., London, 2017).

Montalbán, Manuel Vázquez, *Barcelonas* (Verso, London, 1992).

Perarnau, Martí, *Pep Confidential: The Inside Story of Pep Guardiola's First Season at Bayern Munich* (Arena Sport, Edinburgh, 2014).

Preston, Paul, *The Spanish Civil War: Reaction, Revolution and Revenge* (William Collins, London, 2016).

Puntí, Jordi, *Messi: Lessons in Style* (Short Books, London, 2018).

Reng, Ronald, *Barça: Die Entdeckung des schönen Fussballs* (Piper, Munich/Berlin, 2016).

——, *A Life Too Short: The Tragedy of Robert Enke* (Yellow Jersey Press, London, 2011).

Rollo, Ian, and Asker Jeukendrup, *Sports Nutrition for Football: An Evidence-Based Guide for Nutrition Practice at FC Barcelona* (Barça Innovation Hub, Barcelona, 2018).

Scheepmaker, Nico, *Cruijff, Hendrik Johannes, fenomeen 1947–1984* (Van Holkema & Warendorf/Unieboek, Weesp, 1984).

Schulze-Marmeling, Dietrich, *Der König und sein Spiel: Johan Cruyff und der Weltfussball* (Die Werkstatt, Göttingen, 2012).

Soriano, Ferran, *Goal: The Ball Doesn't Go In by Chance* (Palgrave Macmillan, London, 2012).

Tóibín, Colm, *Homage to Barcelona* (Simon and Schuster, London, 1990).

Van den Boogaard, Arthur, *Het laatste seizoen: Het andere gezicht van Johan Cruijff* (Thomas Rap, Amsterdam, 2019).

Van Hensbergen, Gijs, *The Sagrada Família: Gaudí's Heaven on Earth* (Bloomsbury, London, 2018).

Van Os, Pieter, *Johan Cruijff: De Amerikaanse jaren* (Uitgeverij 521, Amsterdam, 2007).

Wilson, Jonathan, *The Barcelona Legacy* (Blink, London, 2018).

Winkels, Edwin, *Johan Cruijff in Barcelona: De mythe van de verlosser* (Brandt, Amsterdam, 2016).

——, *Van Johan tot Frenkie: Het Barcelona-gevoel van 30 Nederlandse voetballers en trainers* (Brandt, Amsterdam, 2020).

Winner, David, *Brilliant Orange: The Neurotic Genius of Dutch Football* (Bloomsbury, London, 2000).

Zwart, Pieter, *De val van Oranje—en hoe we weer kunnen herrijzen* (Das Mag, Amsterdam, 2018).

Films

Castellet, Oriol Bosch, *Andrés Iniesta: The Unexpected Hero* (2020).

De Vos, Maarten, *Nummer 14: Johan Cruijff* (1973).

Erkelens, Piet, and Pim Marks, *Schijnbewegingen* (NOS, 1988).

Erskine, James, *This Is Football*, season 1, episode 6: "Wonder" (Starbucks Production, 2019).

Gieling, Ramon, *En un momento dado* (Pieter van Huystee Film, Humanistische Omroep, 2004).

Goslinga, Jop, *Força Koeman* (Videoland, 2021), seasons 1 and 2.

Llompart, Jordi, *Barça Dreams: A True Story of FC Barcelona* (2015).

Marcos, Jordi, *L'últim partit. 40 anys de Johan Cruyff a Catalunya* (2014).

McMath, Duncan, *Take the Ball, Pass the Ball* (Zoom Sport International, 2018).

RMC Sport, "Leo, le film" (2021).

Rodríguez, Pol, and Oriol Querol, *Matchday: Inside FC Barcelona* (2019).

Tifo Football, *Tifo Guide to La Masia: The History* (September 17, 2019).

Webster, Justin, and Daniel Hernández, *FC Barcelona Confidential* (JWP-Alea, 2004).

Magazines

Hard Gras: God is dood, Cruijff niet: De mooiste gedichten en verhalen over Johan Cruijff (Ambo/Anthos, Amsterdam, 2016).

Hard Gras, issue 15, June 1998, Edwin Winkels, "De eenzame kampioen" (L. J. Veen, Amsterdam, 1998).

Hard Gras, issue 29, December 2001, "In Barcelona" (L. J. Veen, Amsterdam, 2001).

So Foot, issue 128, summer 2015, "Johan Cruyff."

Other

Carreras, Maria Victoria, "A Second Renaissance: Football Club Barcelona, Camp Nou, and the Re-emergence of Catalan Nationalism, 1950–1975" (unpublished MA thesis, California State University, Long Beach, August 2013).

Elberse, Anita, "Futbol Club Barcelona" (case study 9-516-031, Harvard Business School, September 1, 2015).

NOTES

Introduction: Getting to Know Barça

1. Wilson, *The Barcelona Legacy*, 153.

I: Who's Who in the House of Barça

1. Lowe, *Fear and Loathing in La Liga*, 7.
2. Hughes, *Barcelona*, 495.
3. Lowe, *Fear and Loathing in La Liga*, 24, 27–28.
4. Preston, *The Spanish Civil War*, 295.
5. Conxita Mir, "The Francoist Repression in the Catalan Countries," *Catalan Historical Review* 1 (2008): 133–47.
6. Preston, *The Spanish Civil War*, 306.
7. Lowe, *Fear and Loathing in La Liga*, 59.
8. Minder, *The Struggle for Catalonia*, 66–68.
9. Schulze-Marmeling, *Der König und sein Spiel*, 138.
10. Lowe, *Fear and Loathing in La Liga*, 63.
11. Minder, *The Struggle for Catalonia*, 268.
12. Hughes, *Barcelona*, 18.
13. Jimmy Burns, *La Roja: A Journey Through Spanish Football* (London: Simon and Schuster, 2012), 99–100.
14. Lowe, *Fear and Loathing in La Liga*, 47–52.
15. Lowe, *Fear and Loathing in La Liga*, 2.
16. Mike Ozanian, "FC Barcelona First Team Ever to Surpass $1 Billion in Revenue," *Forbes*, October 2, 2018.
17. Lowe, *Fear and Loathing in La Liga*, 232–33.

18. "Barça: comment Piqué et Shakira ont favorisé l'arrivée du nouveau sponsor," *RMC Sport*, November 16, 2016.

19. Winkels, "De eenzame kampioen," 76.

20. Soriano, *Goal*, 89.

21. "Barcelona gana población y alcanza la cifra más alta desde 1991," *La Vanguardia*, July 14, 2019.

22. Minder, *The Struggle for Catalonia*, 270.

23. Elberse, "Futbol Club Barcelona."

24. "Price of Football: Full results 2017," BBC, November 15, 2017.

25. Shilarze Saharoy, "Barça to Offer Compensation to Camp Nou Season Ticket Holders," *Times of India*, June 23, 2020.

26. Duncan McMath, *Take the Ball, Pass the Ball* (Zoom Sport International, 2018).

27. "90 Minutes with Pep Guardiola—Part 4—Leadership, Cruyff and Managing Dressing Rooms," Caño Football, August 18, 2019.

II: The Man Who Talked on the Ball

1. Ghemmour, *Johan Cruyff, génie pop et despote*, 11.

2. Hornby, *Fever Pitch*, 36.

3. Hans Werner Kilz, Kurt Röttgen, and Ludger Schulze, "Ballack sächselt wenigstens noch: Interview mit Angela Merkel," *Süddeutsche Zeitung*, May 17, 2010.

4. Cruijff, *Boem*, 42.

5. Cruijff, *Boem*, 45–46.

6. NOS Studio Sport, "Johan Cruijff: Een eerbetoon," April 26, 2020.

7. Jean Issartel and David Espinar, "Cruyff: 'J'avais l'élégance de la rue,'" *L'Équipe*, March 24, 2016.

8. Simon Kuper, "Old Scores: The Message in Johan Cruyff's Memoir," *Financial Times*, October 6, 2016.

9. Cruijff, *Boem*, 51–55.

10. De Vos, *Nummer 14*.

11. Cruijff, *Boem*, 81.

12. Kok, *Johan Cruijff*, 59.

13. Kuper, "Old Scores."

14. Davidse, *Je moet schieten*, 71.

15. Cruijff, *Boem*, 85.

16. Kok, *Johan Cruijff*, 43.

17. Cruijff, *Boem*, 86–87.

18. NOS Studio Sport, "Johan Cruijff: Een eerbetoon."

19. Schulze-Marmeling, *Der König und sein Spiel*, 77.

20. The best account of the early years of the great Ajax is in Menno de Galan, *De trots van de wereld*.

21. *So Foot*, "Johan Cruyff," 39.

22. Jurryt van der Vooren, "De wereldberoemde uitspraak 'Voetbal is oorlog' is precies vijftig jaar oud," Sportgeschiedenis.nl, November 17, 2019.
23. Schulze-Marmeling, *Der König und sein Spiel*, 126–27.
24. Kok, *Johan Cruijff*, 93.
25. Van den Boogaard, *Het laatste seizoen*, 61 and 97.
26. *Voetbal International*, "Johan Cruijff 50," April 23, 1997.
27. Jonathan Wilson, *Inverting the Pyramid: The History of Football Tactics* (London: Orion, 2008), 62.
28. Ghemmour, *Johan Cruyff*, 163.
29. Cox, *Zonal Marking*, 4.
30. Scheepmaker, *Cruijff, Hendrik Johannes, fenomeen 1947–1984*, 89–90.
31. Wilson, *The Barcelona Legacy*, 14.
32. Schulze-Marmeling, *Der König und sein Spiel*, 103.
33. Ghemmour, *Johan Cruyff*, 162.
34. Cruijff, *Boem*, 184.
35. NOS Studio Sport, "Johan Cruijff: Een eerbetoon."
36. Van den Boogaard, *Het laatste seizoen*, 369.
37. Voetbal International, "Johan Cruijff 50."
38. Van den Boogaard, *Het laatste seizoen*, 112.
39. Cox, *Zonal Marking*, 5–6.
40. Erkelens and Marks, *Schijnbewegingen*.
41. Schulze-Marmeling, *Der König und sein Spiel*, 133.
42. NOS Studio Sport, "Johan Cruijff: Een eerbetoon."
43. Ghemmour, *Johan Cruyff*, 70.
44. Cruijff, *Boem*, 136.
45. Davidse, *Je moet schieten*, 56.
46. De Vos, *Nummer 14*.
47. Kok, *Johan Cruijff*, 99.
48. Ballús and Martín, *Pep's City*, 30.
49. NOS Studio Sport, "Johan Cruijff: Een eerbetoon."
50. Cruijff, *Boem*, 204.
51. Leo Verheul, "Rinus Michels ziet om," *Hard Gras*, issue 29.
52. *So Foot*, "Johan Cruyff," 60.
53. De Vos, *Nummer 14*.
54. De Vos, *Nummer 14*.
55. Cruijff, *Boem*, 201–2.
56. Ghemmour, *Johan Cruyff*, 134.
57. Kok, *Johan Cruijff*, 337.

III: FC Barcelona—From an Original Idea by Johan Cruyff

1. Kok, *Johan Cruijff*, 343.
2. Winkels, *Johan Cruijff in Barcelona*, 251–53.

3. Davidse, *Je moet schieten*, 11.
4. Scheepmaker, *Cruijff, Hendrik Johannes, fenomeen 1947–1984*, 225.
5. Verheul, "Rinus Michels ziet om," 21.
6. Burns, *Barça*, 206.
7. Lowe, *Fear and Loathing in La Liga*, 223.
8. Kok, *Johan Cruijff*, 450.
9. Cruijff, *Boem*, 249–50.
10. *So Foot*, "Johan Cruyff," 140.
11. Verheul, "Rinus Michels ziet om," 15–16.
12. *So Foot*, "Johan Cruyff," 82.
13. Winkels, *Johan Cruijff in Barcelona*, 135.
14. Marcos, *L'últim partit*.
15. Kok, *Cruijff*, 355.
16. Burns, *Barça*, 206.
17. Andrés Rodríguez-Pose and Daniel Hardy, "Reversal of Economic Fortunes: Institutions and the Changing Ascendancy of Barcelona and Madrid as Economic Hubs," *Growth and Change* 52, no. 1 (2020): 48–70.
18. Burns, *Barça*, 230–31.
19. Winkels, *Van Johan tot Frenkie*, 26.
20. Cruijff, *Boem*, 35.
21. Cruijff, *Boem*, 27–28.
22. Cruijff, *Boem*, 8–10.
23. Verheul, "Rinus Michels ziet om," 22.
24. Josep Maria Casanovas, "Cruijff, een leven voor Barça," in *Hard Gras: God is dood, Cruijff niet*, 110.
25. *So Foot*, "Johan Cruyff," 27.
26. Winkels, *Johan Cruijff in Barcelona*, 104–5.
27. Davidse, *Je moet schieten*, 7.
28. Kok, *Johan Cruijff*, 369.
29. Marcos, *L'últim partit*.
30. *So Foot*, "Johan Cruyff," 140.
31. Cruijff, *Boem*, 272–3.
32. Marcos, *L'últim partit*.
33. *So Foot*, "Johan Cruyff," 82.
34. Schulze-Marmeling, *Der König und sein Spiel*, 104.
35. *So Foot*, "Johan Cruyff," 80–82.
36. Cruijff, *Boem*, 270.
37. Cruijff, *Boem*, 271–72.
38. Verheul, "Rinus Michels ziet om," 22–23.
39. Kok, *Johan Cruijff*, 368–69.
40. *So Foot*, "Johan Cruyff," 39.
41. *So Foot*, "Johan Cruyff," 145.
42. Gieling, *En un momento dado*.

43. Schulze-Marmeling, *Der König und sein Spiel*, 146.
44. *So Foot*, "Johan Cruyff," 140.
45. Ghemmour, *Johan Cruyff*, 145.
46. Verheul, "Rinus Michels ziet om," 23.
47. *So Foot*, "Johan Cruyff," 120.
48. Kok, *Johan Cruijff*, 386.
49. Kuper, "Old Scores."
50. Kok, *Johan Cruijff*, 411.
51. Winner, *Brilliant Orange*, 92.
52. Details in Kok, *Johan Cruijff*.
53. *So Foot*, "Johan Cruyff," 39.
54. Schulze-Marmeling, *Der König und sein Spiel*, 169.
55. *So Foot*, "Johan Cruyff," 43.
56. Jimmy Burns, "Cruyff was sinterklaas," in *Hard Gras: God is dood, Cruyff niet*, 139.
57. Gieling, *En un momento dado*.
58. Barend and van Dorp, *Ajax, Barcelona, Cruyff*, 241.
59. Winkels, *Van Johan tot Frenkie*, 262.
60. Kok, *Johan Cruijff*, 562.
61. Burns, *Barça*, 217.
62. Lowe, *Fear and Loathing in La Liga*, 241.
63. Minder, *The Struggle for Catalonia*, 290.
64. Kok, *Johan Cruijff*, 430.
65. Winkels, *Johan Cruijff in Barcelona*, 148.
66. NOS Studio Sport, "Johan Cruijff: Een eerbetoon."
67. Sander Schomaker, "Totaal mislukte ontvoering Cruijff had toch gevolgen," *Metro*, October 6, 2016.
68. Van Os, *Johan Cruijff*, 257.
69. *So Foot*, "Johan Cruyff," 88.
70. Van Os, *Johan Cruijff*, 233–35.
71. Ghemmour, *Johan Cruyff*, 222.
72. Winkels, *Johan Cruijff in Barcelona*, 58–59.
73. NOS Studio Sport, "Johan Cruijff: Een eerbetoon."
74. Van Os, *Johan Cruijff*, 62.
75. Van Os, *Johan Cruijff*, 82.
76. Van Os, *Johan Cruijff*, 12–13.
77. NOS Studio Sport, "Johan Cruijff: Een eerbetoon."
78. Van Os, *Johan Cruijff*, 105.
79. Schulze-Marmeling, *Der König und sein Spiel*, 106–7.
80. Matty Verkamman, "Voor Cruijff is voetbal altijd een spel gebleven," *Trouw*, April 19, 1997.
81. Van den Boogaard, *Het laatste seizoen*, 345.
82. *Voetbal International*, "Johan Cruijff 50."

83. Davidse, *Je moet schieten*, 70.
84. Van den Boogaard, *Het laatste seizoen*, 106–7.
85. Kok, *Johan Cruijff*, 511.
86. Van den Boogaard, *Het laatste seizoen*, 102.
87. *So Foot*, "Johan Cruyff," 106.
88. Davidse, *Je moet schieten*, 62.
89. Van den Boogaard, *Het laatste seizoen*, 360.
90. Scheepmaker, *Cruijff, Hendrik Johannes, fenomeen 1947–1984*, 200.

IV: The Choreographer

1. Marcos, *L'últim partit.*
2. *Voetbal International*, "Podcast over eeuwige voetbalvader: 'Guardiola door Cruyff verliefd op voetbal,'" April 15, 2020.
3. Davidse, *Je moet schieten*, 70.
4. Davidse, *Je moet schieten*, 66.
5. Ghemmour, *Johan Cruyff*, 260.
6. Erkelens and Marks, *Schijnbewegingen.*
7. Zwart, *De val van Oranje*, 220.
8. Kok, *Johan Cruijff*, 542.
9. Davidse, *Je moet schieten*, 86.
10. Ghemmour, *Johan Cruyff*, 259.
11. Kok, *Johan Cruijff*, 547.
12. Barend and van Dorp, *Ajax, Barcelona, Cruyff*, 224.
13. Schulze-Marmeling, *Der König und sein Spiel*, 249.
14. Erkelens and Marks, *Schijnbewegingen.*
15. Erkelens and Marks, *Schijnbewegingen.*
16. See, for instance, Barend and Van Dorp, *Ajax, Barcelona, Cruyff*, 88 and 92.
17. Burns, *Barça*, 229–30.
18. Burns, *Barça*, 297.
19. *Voetbal International*, "Johan Cruijff 50."
20. Kok, *Johan Cruijff*, 558.
21. "Tonny Bruins Slot," Edwin Winkels, https://edwinwinkels.com/tonny-bruins-slot/.
22. *So Foot*, Johan Cruyff, 128.
23. Davidse, *Je moet schieten*, 17.
24. Barend and Van Dorp, *Ajax, Barcelona, Cruyff*, 104.
25. *Voetbal International*, "Johan Cruijff 50."
26. Wilson, *The Barcelona Legacy*, 96.
27. Kok, *Johan Cruijff*, 559 and 562.
28. José Luis Hurtado, "The Similarities Between the Hesperia Mutiny of 1988 and Messi's Rebellion of 2020," *Marca*, April 2, 2020.
29. Gieling, *En un momento dado.*

30. Winkels, "De eenzame kampioen," 90.

31. Winkels, *Johan Cruijff in Barcelona*, 189.

32. Winkels, *Van Johan tot Frenkie*, 107.

33. Marcos, *L'últim partit*.

34. Barend and Van Dorp, *Ajax, Barcelona, Cruyff*, 150.

35. Ghemmour, *Johan Cruyff*, 286–87.

36. *So Foot*, Johan Cruyff, 43.

37. "Las frases más geniales de Johan Cruyff," *Mundo Deportivo*, March 29, 2016.

38. Verkamman, "Voor Cruijff is voetbal altijd een spel gebleven."

39. Marcos, *L'últim partit*.

40. Llompart, *Barça Dreams*.

41. Martijn Krabbendam and Sjef de Bont, "Ronald Koeman en de onverwoest-bare Barça-band: nog één droom te gaan," May 20, 2020, in *Voetbal International*, 25:51.

42. Ronald Reng, *Barça: Die Entdecking des schönen Fussballs* (Munich/Berlin: Piper, 2016), 20.

43. Davidse, *Je moet schieten*, 66 and 85.

44. "Las frases más geniales de Johan Cruyff."

45. Davidse, *Je moet schieten*, 18.

46. Marcos, *L'últim partit*.

47. "Guardiola: 'Vraag me nog vaak af wat Johan zou doen,'" *Voetbal International*, March 25, 2016.

48. Pierre Escofet, "Francisco 'Paco' Seirul-Lo, le maître inconnu du Barça," *Le Temps*, February 20, 2017.

49. Joshua Robinson and Jonathan Clegg, *The Club: How the Premier League Became the Richest, Most Disruptive Business in Sport* (London: John Murray, 2019), 275.

50. Marcos, *L'últim partit*.

51. Marcos, *L'últim partit*.

52. Lineker and Baker, *Life, Laughs and Football*, 152.

53. Barend and van Dorp, *Ajax, Barcelona, Cruyff*, 104.

54. Lowe, *Fear and Loathing in La Liga*, 283.

55. Simon Zwartkruis, "Het Spanje van Jordi Cruijff: 'Mijn vader heeft echt iets achtergelaten,'" *Voetbal International*, November 2019.

56. *Voetbal International*, "Podcast over eeuwige voetbalvader."

57. Marcos, *L'últim partit*.

58. *So Foot*, "Johan Cruyff," 76.

59. Issartel and Espinar, "Cruyff: 'J'avais l'élégance de la rue.'"

60. Enrique Ortego, "El gran problema de Messi es que compite consigo mismo," *El País*, September 20, 2020.

61. Erik Jonk, "Força Koeman van Videoland mooie kijk achter de schermen van 'bizar Barcelona,'" Metronieuws.nl, February 17, 2021.

62. Cox, *Zonal Marking*, 13.

63. Winkels, *Van Johan tot Frenkie*, 254.
64. *So Foot*, "Johan Cruyff," 45.
65. Winkels, *Johan Cruijff in Barcelona*, 47 and 161.
66. McMath, *Take the Ball, Pass the Ball*.
67. Carles Ruipérez, "Cruyff bautizó hace 27 años en Praga el ruido eterno que acompaña al Barça," *La Vanguardia*, October 23, 2019.
68. Ghemmour, *Johan Cruyff*, 289.
69. Kok, *Johan Cruijff*, 592.
70. Gieling, *En un momento dado*.
71. Eusebio Sacristán, interview with author, November 15, 2019.
72. Winkels, *Van Johan tot Frenkie*, 105.
73. Lowe, *Fear and Loathing in La Liga*, 289.
74. Winkels, "De eenzame kampioen," 139.
75. Ghemmour, *Johan Cruyff*, 299.
76. Ballús and Martín, *Pep's City*, 227–28.
77. George Orwell, "As I Please," *Tribune*, December 6, 1946.
78. Lowe, *Fear and Loathing in La Liga*, 299.
79. Leo Verheul, "Vijf stellingen," *Hard Gras* issue 29, December 2001.
80. Ortego, "El gran problema de Messi es que compite consigo mismo."
81. Janan Ganesh, "What the Dream Hoarders Get Wrong About Parenting," *Financial Times*, November 27, 2020.
82. Cox, *Zonal Marking*, 12.
83. Barend and Van Dorp, *Ajax, Barcelona, Cruyff*, 196.
84. Ghemmour, *Johan Cruyff*, 316.
85. Barend and Van Dorp, *Ajax, Barcelona, Cruyff*, 239.
86. *So Foot*, "Johan Cruyff," 74.
87. Schulze-Marmeling, *Der König und sein Spiel*, 246.
88. See https://twitter.com/90sfootball/status/1252663390188830726?lang=en.
89. Kok, *Johan Cruijff*, 600.
90. Henk Hoijtink, "Johan Cruijff spreekt tot hart, geest en fantasie," *Trouw*, April 24, 2007.
91. Winkels, *Johan Cruijff in Barcelona*, 205.
92. "Sierd de Vos over eten en slapen in Barcelona, over Cruijff, Guardiola en el Loco Bielsa," YouTube video, 8:49, posted by "elsierd," March 31, 2012, https://www.youtube.com/watch?v=qA34XIjBtGg.
93. Burns, *Barça*, 286–87.

V: Cruyff: My Part in His Downfall

1. *Voetbal International*, "Johan Cruijff 50."
2. Marcos, *L'últim partit*.
3. Schulze-Marmeling, *Der König und sein Spiel*, 56.
4. *So Foot*, "Johan Cruyff," 35.

5. Schulze-Marmeling, *Der König und sein Spiel*, 278.

6. Soriano, *Goal*, 127.

7. Schulze-Marmeling, *Der König und sein Spiel*, 78.

8. Ghemmour, *Johan Cruyff*, 366.

9. *So Foot*, "Johan Cruyff," 122.

10. *So Foot*, "Johan Cruyff, 120–22; Winkels, *Johan Cruijff in Barcelona*, 87.

11. "Property Developer and Former FC Barcelona President, Josep Lluís Núñez, Goes to Jail for Tax Fraud," *Catalan News*, November 17, 2014.

12. Cruijff, *Boem*, 21.

13. Michel van Egmond, *Wandelen met Cruijff, en andere bijzondere voetbalverhalen* (Rotterdam: De Buitenspelers, 2011), 268–70.

14. *So Foot*, "Johan Cruyff," 51.

15. Winkels, *Johan Cruijff in Barcelona*, 239.

16. Winkels, *Van Johan tot Frenkie*, 59.

17. Simon Zwartkruis, "Koopclub Barcelona verlangt terug naar talentenvisie Cruyff," *Voetbal International*, August 15, 2019.

18. Llompart, *Barça Dreams*.

19. *So Foot*, "Johan Cruyff," 82.

20. Perarnau, *Pep Confidential*, 58.

21. McMath, *Take the Ball, Pass the Ball*.

22. Schulze-Marmeling, *Der König und sein Spiel*, 87.

23. Zwart, *De val van Oranje*, 165.

24. Duncan Alexander, "The Exploration of Space Through Goal Kicks," Stats Perform.

25. McMath, *Take the Ball, Pass the Ball*.

26. Lowe, *Fear and Loathing in La Liga*, 382.

27. "Guardiola: 'Vraag me nog vaak af wat Johan zou doen.'"

28. Lineker and Baker, *Life, Laughs and Football*, 231.

VI: Shorties at Boarding School: More Than a Youth Academy

1. Cruijff, *Boem*, 104.

2. De Vos, *Nummer 14*.

3. Kok, *Johan Cruijff*, 607.

4. McMath, *Take the Ball, Pass the Ball*.

5. Callum Rice-Coates, "Oriol Tort: How One Man Helped Turn Barcelona's La Masia into a Bastion of Talent," *These Football Times*, April 9, 2018.

6. Schulze-Marmeling, *Der König und sein Spiel*, 229.

7. Rice-Coates, "Oriol Tort."

8. Email exchange with Maria Carreras, June 23, 2020.

9. "La Masia: The History of Barcelona's Academy," YouTube video, 10:18, posted by "Tifo Football," September 17, 2019, https://www.youtube.com/watch?v=tResxp9hOHo.

10. Llompart, *Barça Dreams*; and Lowe, *Fear and Loathing in La Liga*, 370.

11. Leplat, *Guardiola, éloge du style*, 59.

12. McMath, *Take the Ball, Pass the Ball*.

13. Wilson, *The Barcelona Legacy*, 25.

14. Duncan Hamilton, *Immortal: The Approved Biography of George Best* (London: Century, 2013), 24.

15. Van Os, *Johan Cruijff*, 63.

16. Van den Boogaard, *Het laatste seizoen*, 162.

17. Barend and Van Dorp, *Ajax, Barcelona, Cruyff*, 223.

18. *So Foot*, "Johan Cruyff," 22.

19. Kok, *Johan Cruijff*, 625.

20. NOS Studio Sport, "Johan Cruijff: Een eerbetoon."

21. Andrew Murray, "Xavi: Master the Pass," *FourFourTwo*, April 11, 2014.

22. Sid Lowe, "I'm a Romantic, Says Xavi, Heartbeat of Barcelona and Spain," *Guardian*, February 11, 2011.

23. Schulze-Marmeling, *Der König und sein Spiel*, 233.

24. John Carlin, "Nou sensation," *Guardian*, February 2, 2008.

25. Xavier Ortuño, "Revealed: The Secrets of the Barcelona Method Have Been Unveiled," *Sport*, October 7, 2014.

26. Murray, "Xavi."

27. NOS Studio Sport, "Johan Cruijff: Een eerbetoon."

28. Schulze-Marmeling, *Der König und sein Spiel*, 269.

29. "Een serieuze poging tot Cruijffkunde," *Neerlandistiek*, June 7, 2020.

30. Mark Williams and Tim Wigmore, *The Best: How Elite Athletes Are Made* (London: Nicholas Brealey, 2020), 89.

31. *So Foot*, "Johan Cruyff," 43.

32. Kok, *Johan Cruijff*, 597.

33. Llompart, *Barça Dreams*.

34. Reng, *A Life Too Short*, 163.

35. Soriano, *Goal*, 134–36.

36. Rodriguez and Querol, *Matchday*, episode 3.

37. Reng, *Barça*, 27.

38. Alexandre Gonzalez, "Iniesta, le gentil fantôme," *So Foot*, February 2009.

39. Andrés Iniesta, *The Artist: Being Iniesta* (London: Headline, 2016), 99.

40. *Voetbal International*, "Podcast over eeuwige voetbalvader."

41. Wilson, *The Barcelona Legacy*, 53.

42. Raffaele Poli, Loïc Ravenel, and Roger Besson, *Historical Analysis of Compositional Strategies for Squads (2010s)*, CIES Football Observatory Monthly Report no. 50 (December 2019).

43. Cox, *Zonal Marking*, 245–48.

44. Kuper, *Football Against the Enemy*, 150.

45. Elberse, "Futbol Club Barcelona."

46. Elberse, "Futbol Club Barcelona."

47. Reng, *Barça*, 123.
48. Gonzalez, "Iniesta, le gentil fantôme."
49. Ibrahimović, *I am Zlatan Ibrahimović*, 1–2, 10.
50. Schulze-Marmeling, *Der König und sein Spiel*, 262.
51. Castellet, *Andrés Iniesta*.
52. Wilson, *The Barcelona Legacy*, 149.
53. See Mark Hyland, *Until It Hurts: America's Obsession with Youth Sports and How It Harms Our Kids* (Boston: Beacon Press, 2009).
54. Simon Kuper, "Pushy Parents and Fantasies That Last for Life," *Financial Times*, March 13, 2009.
55. "Michiel de Hoog interviewt Michael Lewis," June 17, 2020, in *De Correspondent*, produced by Jacco Prantl, podcast.
56. "Michiel de Hoog interviewt Michael Lewis."

VII: How Does He Do It? Understanding Lionel Messi

1. James Erskine, *This Is Football*, "Wonder."
2. John Carlin, "Peter Pan en el olimpo del fútbol," *El País*, May 24, 2009.
3. Puntí, *Messi*, 37–39.
4. RMC Sport, "Leo, le film" (2021).
5. Rodriguez and Querol, *Matchday*, episode 6.
6. Dermot Corrigan and Adam Crafton, "Jorge Messi: The Agent Father Behind Leo's Fortunes," *The Athletic*, September 1, 2020.
7. Andy Mitten, "Introducing the Messiah," *FourFourTwo*, January 2006.
8. Jimmy Burns, *Cristiano and Leo* (London: Macmillan, 2018), 99.
9. Cox, *Zonal Marking*, 276.
10. Ronald Reng, *Barça*, 100, 104; and Luis Martín, "La proyección Messi," *El País*, February 4, 2006.
11. Soriano, *Goal*, 53, 87.
12. Soriano, *Goal*, 96.
13. *Voetbal International*, "Toen Rijkaard de voetbalwereld kennis liet maken met het fenomeen Messi," October 16, 2019; the other ten Cate quotes are from his appearance at the Dublin Web Summit in November 2014.
14. Reng, *Barça*, 104–5; and Carlin, "Peter Pan en el olimpo del fútbol."
15. Webster and Hernández, *FC Barcelona Confidential*.
16. Ballús and Martín, *Pep's City*, 6–7.
17. Reng, *Barça*, 103.
18. Mitten, "Introducing the Messiah."
19. Reng, *Barça*, 106–7.
20. Mitten, "Introducing the Messiah."
21. Burns, *Cristiano and Leo*, 134.
22. Mitten, "Introducing the Messiah."
23. Reng, *Barça*, 89.

24. Reng, *Barça*, 95.
25. "Barça: L'anecdote étonnante sur le départ de Ronaldo en 1997," *RMC Sport*, November 7, 2018.
26. Soriano, *Goal*, 77.
27. James Yorke, "Messi Data Biography Analysis: Young Messi 2004–05 to 2007–08," StatsBomb, July 12, 2019.
28. James Yorke, "Messi Data Biography Analysis: Young Messi."
29. Alana Fisher, "Lionel Messi Joins Facebook, Reaches 6.7 Million Fans, Gains 40,000 Interactions in a Few Hours," *Brand New Directions*, April 7, 2011.
30. De Vos, *Nummer 14*.
31. Erskine, "Wonder."
32. "Leo Messi: 'I've Learned to Read the Games Better,'" FC Barcelona, October 28, 2019.
33. McMath, *Take the Ball, Pass the Ball*.
34. McMath, *Take the Ball, Pass the Ball*.
35. Cox, *Zonal Marking*, 271.
36. Carlin, "Peter Pan en el olimpo del fútbol."
37. RMC Sport, "Leo, le film."
38. I. Trujillo, "Así es Pepe Costa, el escudero de Messi, que llega al PSG donde su hijo se forra como 'toiss' de Neymar," *La Razón*, August 11, 2021.
39. Reng, *Barça*, 110.
40. Burns, *Cristiano and Leo*, 178.
41. Soriano, *Goal*, 126.
42. Burns, *Cristiano and Leo*, 169.
43. Burns, *Cristiano and Leo*, 178.
44. Cox, *Zonal Marking*, 283.
45. Dermot Corrigan, "How Much Power Does Messi Really Hold at Barcelona?," *The Athletic*, July 8, 2020.
46. Leplat, *Guardiola*, 197.
47. Leplat, *Guardiola*, 198.
48. "Afellay: 'Ik kreeg de maaltijden niet door mijn keel, Messi moest vaak overgeven,'" Voetbalprimeur, June 16, 2021.
49. Joan Oliver, interview with author, Barcelona, November 24, 2009.
50. Oliver, interview.
51. Ghemmour, *Johan Cruyff*, 372.
52. McMath, *Take the Ball, Pass the Ball*.
53. "Lionel Messi: Entretien exclusif avec le meilleur joueur du monde," *So Foot*, February 2009.
54. "Jerzy Dudek no se corta un pelo: 'Leo Messi es falso y provocador, y Cristiano Ronaldo, arrogante,'" LaSexta, April 23, 2020.
55. "Messi's Stern Telling-Off from Champions League Referee: 'Show Some Respect!,'" *AS*, November 12, 2020; UEFA, "Man in the Middle," trailer, retrieved at https://www.youtube.com/watch?v=nFxgrnWY21Q on March 30, 2021.

56. Roberto Palomar, "The Psychologist That Messi Never Visited," *Marca*, January 3, 2021.

57. Puntí, *Messi*, 111.

58. R.Bx, "Neymar, Messi, les JO: les confidences de Kylian Mbappé" *Le Parisien*, December 23, 2019.

59. RMC Sport, "Leo, le film."

60. Winkels, *Johan Cruijff in Barcelona*, 250.

61. RMC Sport, "Leo, le film."

62. RMC Sport, "Leo, le film."

63. Marcos, *L'últim partit*.

64. Lineker and Baker, *Life, Laughs and Football*, 178.

65. Mitten, "Introducing the Messiah."

66. Marcos, *L'últim partit*.

67. Wilson, *The Barcelona Legacy*, 245.

68. "Mourinho Changes His Tune and Says Messi Deserves the Ballon d'Or," *Sport*, April 20, 2019.

69. Carlos Silva Rojas, "El día en que Messi vio todo negro y casi golpea a compañero de la selección en Argentina," *RedGol*, April 5, 2020.

70. Van Os, *Johan Cruijff*, 271.

71. Tim Reedijk, "Steenrijke voetballers gewilde targets voor criminelen," *Algemeen Dagblad*, March 18, 2021.

72. Cristina Cubero and Fernando Polo, "Entrevista a Messi: 'Amo Barcelona, ésta es mi casa,'" *Mundo Deportivo*, February 20, 2020.

73. Carlin, "Peter Pan en el olimpo del fútbol."

74. Puntí, *Messi*, 95.

75. Erkelens and Marks, *Schijnbewegingen*.

76. Data provided by John Burn-Murdoch, *Financial Times*.

77. Data provided by John Burn-Murdoch.

78. Erskine, "Wonder."

79. Perarnau, *Pep Confidential*, 336.

80. Erskine, "Wonder."

81. Lineker and Baker, *Life, Laughs and Football*.

82. Murad Ahmed, "Marcus Rashford: 'The System Is Broken—And It Needs to Change,'" *Financial Times*, September 18, 2020.

83. The Pep (@Guardiola Tweets), "Dani Alves 'Pep hates these full-back to winger passes because they don't offer progression. But I used to do them with Messi a lot and he would be annoyed,'" July 9, 2019, https://twitter.com/guardiolatweets/status/1148654468269051904?lang=en.

84. Erskine, "Wonder."

85. Lineker and Baker, *Life, Laughs and Football*, 281.

86. Schulze-Marmeling, *Der König und sein Spiel*, 268.

87. Erskine, "Wonder."

88. Erskine, "Wonder."

89. Benjamin Morris, "Lionel Messi's Majestic Season," FiveThirtyEight, June 5, 2015.

90. "Leo Messi: 'I've learned to read the games better,'" FCBarcelona.com, October 28, 2019, https://www.fcbarcelona.com/en/news/1470325/leo-messi-ive-learned-to-read-the-games-better.

91. Mickaël Caron, "Football: ce documentaire qui ausculte Messi et Ronaldo comme jamais, *Journal du Dimanche*, May 30, 2019.

92. Benjamin Morris, "Lionel Messi Is Impossible," FiveThirtyEight, July 1, 2014.

93. Castellet, *Andrés Iniesta*.

94. Soriano, *Goal*, 4, 46–47.

95. RMC Sport, "Leo, le film."

96. "The Day That Manchester City Accidentally Bid 80 Million Euros for Messi," *Marca*, December 26, 2019.

97. RMC Sport, "Leo, le film."

98. "FC Barcelona Star Lionel Messi: Tax Troubles, an Audit and a 100-Million-Euro Contract," *Der Spiegel*, January 15, 2018.

99. "FC Barcelona Star Lionel Messi."

100. Corrigan, "How Much Power Does Messi Really Hold at Barcelona?"

VIII: High Style, 2008–2012

1. Josep Guardiola, "J'ai fini par me fatiguer de moi-même," *So Foot*, October 2012.

2. Michel Bezbakh, "Sur RMC Sport, les 'monstres' Messi et Ronaldo racontés par ceux qu'ils ont traumatisés," *Telerama*, March 23, 2020.

3. McMath, *Take the Ball, Pass the Ball*.

4. Marcos, *L'últim partit*.

5. Leplat, *Guardiola*, 237, 242–43.

6. Elmar Neveling, *Jurgen Klopp: The Biography* (London: Ebury Press, 2020), 142.

7. Llompart, *Barça Dreams*.

8. Lowe, *Fear and Loathing in La Liga*, 369.

9. Soriano, *Goal*, 127–32.

10. Xavier Sala-i-Martin, email message to author, July 10, 2019.

11. Wilson, *The Barcelona Legacy*, 119.

12. Donald McRae, "Pep Guardiola: 'I would not be here without Johan Cruyff. He was unique,'" *Guardian*, October 7, 2016.

13. Marcos, *L'últim partit*.

14. "Menotti y una entrevista a fondo: Guardiola, Messi, Pelé, Agüero, Simeone, la Selección del 78," *El Gráfico*, December 2, 2014.

15. Simon Kuper, "Spain's New Nationalism," *Financial Times*, September 5, 2008.

16. Reng, *Barça*, 34–36.

17. Leplat, *Guardiola*, 153–55.

18. Leplat, *Guardiola*, 243–44.

19. McMath, *Take the Ball, Pass the Ball*.

20. Iniesta, *The Artist*, 124–25.

21. Leplat, *Guardiola*, 230, 233.

22. Leplat, *Guardiola*, 142–43.

23. Pieter Zwart, "Via Michels en Cruyff naar Van Gaal en Guardiola: Het geheim van Juego de Posición," *Voetbal International*, November 29, 2019.

24. Simon Kuper, "Pep's Four Golden Rules," *The Blizzard*, June 1, 2013.

25. Castellet, *Andrés Iniesta*.

26. Eamon Dunphy, *Only a Game?* (London: Penguin, 1987), 30.

27. Leplat, *Guardiola*, 236.

28. Simon Kuper, "What's Going On at Barça?," *Financial Times*, February 6, 2015.

29. Leplat, *Guardiola*, 241–42.

30. McMath, *Take the Ball, Pass the Ball*.

31. See also Paul Bradley, "FC Barcelona: how our new research helped unlock the 'Barça way,'" *The Conversation*, September 19, 2018.

32. Reng, *Barça*, 222.

33. "Las frases más geniales de Johan Cruyff."

34. Oliver Kay, "How to mark Lionel Messi, by the defenders who kept him quiet," *The Times*, April 30, 2019.

35. *So Foot*, "Johan Cruyff," 82.

36. With many thanks to Albert Capellas for a tutorial over espressos in Papendal, the Netherlands, in February 2012.

37. Schulze-Marmeling, *Der König und sein Spiel*, 273.

38. Iniesta, *The Artist*, 130.

39. Perarnau, *Pep Confidential*, 208.

40. Michiel de Hoog, "De uitvinder van tiki-taka haat tiki-taka, onthult dit geweldige boek over Pep Guardiola," *De Correspondent*, January 29, 2015.

41. Neveling, *Jurgen Klopp*, 141.

42. Leplat, *Guardiola*, 156.

43. Kuper, "Pep's Four Golden Rules."

44. Leplat, *Guardiola*, 166–67.

45. Perarnau, *Pep Confidential*, 161.

46. "Discurso subtitulado (español/english) de Pep Guardiola en la Medalla de Honor del Parlament," YouTube video, 12:09, posted by "andreu24x," September 8, 2011, https://www.youtube.com/watch?v=oVuZwBGlpRc.

47. Reng, *Barça*, 128–29.

48. Cox, *Zonal Marking*, 308.

49. Leplat, *Guardiola*, 235.

50. Reng, *Barça*, 210.

51. Reng, *Barça*, 172.

52. McMath, *Take the Ball, Pass the Ball*.

53. Perarnau, *Pep Confidential*, 139.

54. Leplat, *Guardiola*, 150, 241.

55. Jesus Montesinos et al., "Barcelona Baby Boom: Does Sporting Success Affect Birth Rate?," *BMJ* 347 (2013): f7387.

56. McMath, *Take the Ball, Pass the Ball*.

57. Iniesta, *The Artist*, 152–53.

58. Reng, *Barça*, 198.

59. Cox, *Zonal Marking*, 301.

60. Lowe, *Fear and Loathing in La Liga*, 385.

61. Leplat, *Guardiola*, 236–37, 248.

62. McMath, *Take the Ball, Pass the Ball*.

63. Leplat, *Guardiola*, 237–38.

64. "Barcelona Gave Us a Hiding, Says Man Utd Boss Ferguson," BBC, May 28, 2011.

65. Perarnau, *Pep Confidential*, 15, 243.

66. Silvia Taulés, "La mujer de Tito Vilanova 'vetó' a Guardiola en su funeral," *El Mundo*, June 5, 2014.

67. Webster and Hernandez, *FC Barcelona Confidential*.

68. Lowe, *Fear and Loathing in La Liga*, 403.

69. Guardiola, "J'ai fini par me fatiguer de moi-même."

IX: Define "Talent"

1. *Voetbal International*, "Johan Cruijff 50."

2. Rodriguez and Querol, *Matchday*, episode 4.

3. John Carlin, *White Angels: Beckham, Real Madrid and the New Football* (London: Bloomsbury, 2004), 194.

4. Simon Callow, "A Taste for the Difficult," *New York Review of Books*, February 11, 2021.

5. Megan Rapinoe with Emma Brockes, *One Life* (New York: Penguin Press, 2020), 14.

6. Maarten Wijffels, "Barça-assistent Schreuder: 'Ze slaan Messi neer, gewoon met de vlakke hand,'" *Algemeen Dagblad*, March 6, 2021.

7. Mike Forde and Simon Kuper, "Game of Talents: Management Lessons from Top Football Voaches," *Financial Times*, May 15, 2015.

8. Pernarnau, *Pep Confidential*, 302.

9. Leplat, *Guardiola*, 197.

10. "Mbappé assume son ego: 'Je me dis toujours que je suis le meilleur,'" RMC Sport, April 2, 2021.

11. Carlin, *White Angels*, 194.

12. Leplat, *Guardiola*, 191.

13. Rivea Ruff, "Allen Iverson Says He Didn't Lift Weights in NBA Because They Were 'Too Heavy,'" Bleacher Report, December 16, 2016.

14. *Voetbal International*, "Johan Cruijff 50."

X: The Talent Rules

1. I have previously written about this interview in Simon Kuper, *Soccer Men* (New York: Nation Books, 2014), 15–18.
2. Wilson, *The Barcelona Legacy*, 56.
3. Kok, *Johan Cruijff*, 562.
4. Elberse, "Futbol Club Barcelona."
5. Reng, *Barça*, 107.
6. Pablo Polo, "El universo Vinícius," *Marca*, October 6, 2021.
7. Simon Kuper, "The Sage of Real Madrid," *Financial Times*, January 21, 2011.
8. Arsène Wenger, *My Life in Red and White: My Autobiography* (London: Weidenfeld & Nicolson, 2020), 78.
9. Reng, *Barça*, 218.
10. Soriano, *Goal*, 120–22, 158.
11. Soriano, *Goal*, 121–22.
12. Escofet, "Francisco 'Paco' Seirul-Lo, le maître inconnu du Barça."
13. McMath, *Take the Ball, Pass the Ball*.
14. Barend and Van Dorp, *Ajax, Barcelona, Cruyff*, 229.
15. Robert Pickering, "Death Spiral Is a Myth to Perpetuate High Pay," *Financial Times*, April 28, 2014.

XI: How the Talent Lives

1. Rodriguez and Querol, *Matchday*, episode 1.
2. Winkels, "De eenzame kampioen," 63.
3. De Vos, *Nummer 14*.
4. Rodriguez and Querol, *Matchday*, episode 4.
5. Barend and Van Dorp, *Ajax, Barcelona, Cruyff*, 133.
6. Arthur Renard, "You Ask the Questions: Boudewijn Zenden," *FourFourTwo*, April 6, 2020.
7. Kuper, "The Sage of Real Madrid."
8. Leplat, *Guardiola*, 139.
9. Barend and Van Dorp, *Ajax Barcelona, Cruyff*, 186.
10. Reng, *A Life Too Short*, 187.
11. Castellet, *Andrés Iniesta*.
12. "The Maradona I Knew the Year He Discovered Cocaine," *Sport*, November 26, 2020.
13. Burns, *Barça*, 251, 254.
14. Daniel Geey, *Done Deal: An Insider's Guide to Football Contracts, Multi-Million Pound Transfers and Premier League Big Business* (London: Bloomsbury, 2019), 39.
15. Jesús Ruiz Mantilla, "Gerard Piqué: 'Sé cuándo la voy a liar y lo hago porque me apetece," *El País*, November 11, 2019.

16. Rodriguez and Querol, *Matchday*, episode 7.
17. Mantilla, "Gerard Piqué."
18. *Voetbal International*, "Johan Cruijff 50."
19. "Alex Song: I Made 15,000 Pounds per Week and Saved Nothing," *Marca*, May 18, 2020.
20. Ben Morse, "Barcelona Remains Best Paid Sports Team, Ronaldo's Juventus Up to Third," CNN, December 23, 2019.
21. Lilian Thuram, interview with author, March 13, 2008.
22. Mantilla, "Gerard Piqué."
23. Rodriguez and Querol, *Matchday*, Episode 4.
24. *Voetbal International*, "Johan Cruyff 50."
25. Soriano, *Goal*, 139.

XII: Eat, Play, Sleep: The Talent and the Private Chefs

1. Rodriguez and Querol, *Matchday*, episode 1.
2. "Frenkie de Jong on Ronald Koeman and Life at Barcelona," UEFA, October 26, 2020.
3. Congreso de los Diputados, "Boletín Oficial de las Cortes Generales," September 26, 2013, 63.
4. Lowe, *Fear and Loathing in La Liga*, 104–5.
5. Winkels, *Johan Cruijff in Barcelona*, 123–26.
6. Lineker and Baker, *Life, Laughs and Football*, 217.
7. Edwin Winkels, "Vis, vlees en voetbal," *Hard Gras*, December 2001.
8. Kok, *Johan Cruijff*, 452.
9. Marerlma, "Football and Wine: A Passionate Combination," *Drinks & Co.*, February 26, 2016.
10. Rollo and Jeukendrup, *Sports Nutrition for Football*, 88.
11. The most frequently cited charge against them concerns Eufemiano Fuentes, the Spanish doctor arrested in "Operación Puerto," cycling's drug scandal of 2006. Fuentes had also worked with Barça and Real Madrid. Since Spain didn't have anti-doping laws at the time of the cycling scandal, the gynecologist was charged only with "endangering public health" and sentenced to a year in prison. He was later cleared of all charges. In 2021, in an interview in which he discussed his work at the 1992 Olympics and named three smaller football clubs he had worked for, he said that he had "a couple of contacts with" Barcelona and would have liked to "work with the club" but hadn't. See Stéphane Mandard, "Le Real Madrid et le Barça liés au docteur Fuentes," *Le Monde*, December 7, 2006, and "Eufemiano Fuentes desvela los contactos que tuvo con el Fútbol Club Barcelona," *La Sexta*, March 28, 2021.
12. McMath, *Take the Ball, Pass the Ball*.
13. Rollo and Jeukendrup, *Sports Nutrition for Football*, 74–75.

14. Isabel Arquero, "La nutricionista del Barça: brócoli sí, pizza no tanto," *El País*, March 12, 2019.

15. "Foods That Are Very Healthy but Are Not Recommended During Exercise," Barcelona Innovation Hub, August 5, 2019.

16. François David, "Dans l'intimité d'Ousmane Dembélé: 'Il n'y a pas de structure de haut niveau autour de lui,'" *Le Parisien*, August 20, 2019.

17. David, "Dans l'intimité d'Ousmane Dembélé."

18. Rollo and Jeukendrup, *Sports Nutrition for Football*, 27.

19. Forde and Kuper, "Game of Talents."

20. Fernando Polo and Roger Torelló, "Messi trabaja con una dietista que es una crack del triathlon," *Mundo Deportivo*, November 9, 2013.

21. "Me inyectaba las hormonas solo y lo tomaba como algo rutinario," TyC Sports, March 18, 2018.

22. Arquero, "La nutricionista del Barça."

23. "Leo Messi: 'Barça is my home, I don't want to leave but I want to play in a winning team,'" *Sport*, September 12, 2019.

24. "¿Qué come cada jugador del Barça tras los partidos?," *Sport*, September 25, 2014.

25. Hugo Guillemet, "Dembélé, les raisons de sa fragilité," *L'Equipe*, March 3, 2020.

26. Carlos Lago Peñas, "Half-Time Strategies to Improve Player Performance in the Second Half of the Game," Barcelona Innovation Hub, October 19, 2019.

27. Baxter Holmes, "NBA Exec: 'It's the Dirty Little Secret That Everybody Knows About,'" ESPN, October 14, 2019.

28. Mitten, "Introducing the Messiah."

29. Mantilla, "Gerard Piqué."

30. Luis Martín, "Sergio Busquets: 'Yo estoy para dar soluciones,'" *El País*, June 18, 2015.

31. François David and Yves Leroy, "Ousmane Dembélé, dernier avertissement?," *Le Parisien*, November 12, 2018.

32. David, "Dans l'intimité d'Ousmane Dembélé."

33. Holmes, "NBA Exec."

34. Peter Crouch with Tom Fordyce, *How to Be a Footballer* (London: Ebury Press, 2019), 180.

35. Peter Crouch with Tom Fordyce, *I, Robot: How to Be a Footballer 2* (London: Ebury Press, 2019), 146.

36. Illan and Torrado, *High-Performance Nutritional Cuisine*.

37. Martijn Krabbendam, "Frenkie de Jong over Messi, zijn eerste Barça-rondo en de snelle aanpassing," *Voetbal International*, November 25, 2019.

38. "Frenkie de Jong begrijpt dat hij kerel moet worden: 'Zoiets vertelde Koeman al,'" *NOS Voetbal*, October 13, 2019.

39. Fifpro, *At the Limit: Player Workload in Elite Professional Men's Football* (2019).

40. "Neymar Gives Messi and Mascherano Lift on Private Jet," AFP, November 8, 2016.
41. "Our Brain Hinders Sleep the First Night Away from Home, but We Can Stop This from Happening," Barcelona Innovation Hub, July 26, 2019.
42. Carlos Lago Peñas, "Happiness Versus Wellness in Elite Sport," Barcelona Innovation Hub, February 11, 2020.
43. Carlos Lago Peñas, "Are Football Players Getting Older?," Barcelona Innovation Hub, October 1, 2019.
44. Carlos Lago Peñas, "The Influence of Age on Footballers' Performance," Barcelona Innovation Hub, October 15, 2019.

XIII: Misadventures in the Transfer Market

1. Reng, *A Life Too Short*, 119.
2. Edwin Winkels, "Johan Cruyff en de kritiek," *Voetbal International*, March 10, 1990.
3. Reng, *A Life Too Short*, 120.
4. Trailer of the Força Koeman documentary, Videoland.com.
5. RMC Sport, "Leo, le film."
6. "No 'Bite' Clause in Luis Suárez Contract," PA Sport, August 5, 2014.
7. Wilson, *The Barcelona Legacy*, 240.
8. Bjorn Goorden, "Hoezo Grote Twee? Neymar is Messi en Ronaldo zelfs al voorbij," *Voetbal International*, December 28, 2020.
9. Goorden, "Hoezo Grote Twee?"
10. Aymeric Le Gall, "Barça-PSG: 'Oui, le Barça a bien refusé Mbappé pour prendre Dembélé,' raconte un agent espagnol proche des Blaugranas," *20 minutes*, February 17, 2021.
11. Fernando Polo, "Bordas lo cuenta todo sobre Morata, Courtois, Haaland y Monchi," *Mundo Deportivo*, November 15, 2020.
12. Fernando Polo, "Bordas: 'Mbappé pudo venir por 100 milliones,'" *Mundo Deportivo*, November 15, 2020.
13. Tariq Panja and Rory Smith, "Barcelona and the Crippling Cost of Success," *New York Times*, February 12, 2021.
14. Danielle Pinedo, "Frenkie de Jong: 'Ik ga liever anoniem door het leven," *NRC Handelsblad*, November 1, 2020.
15. Wenger, *My Life in Red and White*, 160.
16. "De Jong doet onthulling over transfer: 'Daarom twijfelde ik over Barcelona,'" Voetbalprimeur, February 3, 2021.
17. Edwin Winkels, "Familie van Frenkie de Jong geniet mee in Barcelona: 'Is dit de winter hier?,'" *Algemeen Dagblad*, December 25, 2019.
18. Sam France, "De Jong Agent Reveals How He Doubled Ajax's Asking Price for Barcelona Star," *Goal*, September 28, 2019.

19. Matt Law, "Eric Abidal Exclusive: Quitting Barcelona, Courting Pochettino, Talks with Messi—and the Future," *Daily Telegraph*, March 22, 2021.
20. Juan Jiménez, "La noche antes de fichar a Griezmann no lo podían pagar," *AS*, October 6, 2021.
21. Omar Chaudhuri (@OmarChaudhuri), "European window yet to close, but three transfer-records-by-age broken this summer, including Harry Maguire becoming the most expensive 26-year-old in history (overtaking Van Dijk). Hazard was briefly the 28-year-old record holder," Twitter, August 9, 2019, https://twitter.com/OmarChaudhuri/status/1159785348387549184.
22. Panja and Smith, "Barcelona and the Crippling Cost of Success."
23. "Griezmann: I Spoke with Messi When I Arrived He Told Me He Was Screwed When I First Turned Barcelona Down," *Marca*, November 24, 2020.
24. Ernest Folch, "Entrevista exclusiva a Leo Messi: 'El Barcelona es mi casa, no quiero irme pero quiero un proyecto ganador,'" *Sport*, September 12, 2020.
25. RMC Sport, "Leo, le film."
26. "Big spender Barcelona troeft Premier League-elite af: één miljard in vijf jaar," *Voetbal International*, July 12, 2019.
27. Juan Jiménez, "Piqué: El club está como está," *AS*, November 4, 2020.
28. "Bakambu a failli signer à Barcelone," *L'Équipe*, January 30, 2020.
29. Jordi Quixano, "Matheus Fernandes, el futbolista invisible," *El País*, November 17, 2020.
30. Robin Bairner, "'They Called Me Crazy'—Palmeiras Director Talks Selling Matheus Fernandes to Barca," *Goal*, April 19, 2020.
31. Sid Lowe, "Barcelona Swapping Arthur for Pjanic Was a Business Move but for All the Wrong Reasons," ESPN.com, June 29, 2020.

XIV: Everyone Becomes the Masia

1. Zwartkruis, "Koopclub Barcelona verlangt terug naar talentenvisie Cruijff."
2. Perarnau, *Pep Confidential*, 400.
3. Wilson, *The Barcelona Legacy*, 253.

XV: More Than a Club?

1. Ángel Pérez, "El infierno de Sandro Rosell," *Mundo Deportivo*, February 8, 2018.
2. Luz Sánchez-Mellado, "Sandro Rosell: "La cárcel huele a rancio," *El País*, July 18, 2020.
3. Sergi Font, "La pesadilla de 643 días de Sandro Rosell en la cárcel," ABC, April 25, 2019.
4. Lowe, *Fear and Loathing in La Liga*, 232–33.
5. Burns, *Barça*, 355; and Soriano, *Goal*, 17–18.

6. Soriano, *Goal*, 178.
7. Soriano, *Goal*, 67–69.
8. Schulze-Marmeling, *Der König und sein Spiel*, 279–80.
9. Schulze-Marmeling, *Der König und sein Spiel*, 281.
10. "Twinning Project: 32 Football Clubs Join Prison Scheme to Help Tackle Reoffending," BBC, January 23, 2019.
11. Wenger, *My Life in Red and White*, 212.
12. "Miami Barcelona MLS Campaign Is Dead," *Goal*, March 3, 2009.
13. Diego Martín, "Real Madrid Lead the World in Social Media Followers," *AS*, December 29, 2019; and Kurt Badenhausen, "FC Barcelona Ranks as the Top Sports Team on Social Media," *Forbes*, July 14, 2016.
14. Soriano, *Goal*, 64.
15. Bobby McMahon, "Barcelona Estimates That Espai Barça Project Will Now Cost Almost $1.5 Billion," *Forbes*, October 8, 2020.
16. Toíbín, *Homage to Barcelona*, 77.
17. Van Hensbergen, *The Sagrada Família*, 106–7.
18. Van Hensbergen, *The Sagrada Família*, 5.
19. Hughes, *Barcelona*, 538–39.
20. Van Hensbergen, *The Sagrada Família*, 110.
21. Van Hensbergen, *The Sagrada Família*, 42, 106, 129–30; and Hughes, *Barcelona*, 538.
22. Minder, *The Struggle for Catalonia*, 186.
23. Minder, *The Struggle for Catalonia*, 12, 124.
24. Minder, *The Struggle for Catalonia*, 3, 6, 11, 233.
25. Albert Masnou, "Exclusive: How Bartomeu Took the Decision to Play Behind Closed Doors," *Sport*, October 2, 2017.
26. "Las relaciones peligrosas entre el Barça y el 'procés,'" *El Mundo*, January 18, 2022.
27. Marlene Wind, *The Tribalization of Europe: A Defense of Our Liberal Values* (Cambridge, UK: Polity Press, 2020).
28. Rodríguez-Pose and Hardy, "Reversal of Economic Fortunes."
29. Michael Stothard, "Barcelona Brand Suffers After Independence Turmoil," *Financial Times*, November 30, 2017.
30. Rodríguez-Pose and Hardy, "Reversal of Economic Fortunes."
31. Thomas Piketty, *Capital and Ideology* (Cambridge, MA: Harvard University Press, 2020), 919.
32. Simon Kuper, "Us and Them: Catalonia and the Problem with Separatism," *Financial Times*, November 9, 2017.
33. José M. Oller, Albert Satorra, and Adolf Tobeña, "Unveiling Pathways for the Fissure Among Secessionists and Unionists in Catalonia: Identities, Family Language, and Media Influence," *Palgrave Communications* 5, no. 1 (2019): 148.
34. Rodríguez-Pose and Hardy, "Reversal of Economic Fortunes."

XVI: Messi's Club

1. "FC Barcelona Star Lionel Messi: Tax Troubles, an Audit and a 100-Million-Euro Contract," *Der Spiegel*, January 15, 2018.
2. "FC Barcelona Star Lionel Messi."
3. Andrew Davis and David Hellier, "Lionel Messi's Contract with Barcelona Worth $674 Million: Mundo," *Bloomberg*, January 31, 2021.
4. Christoph Nesshöver, "Wirtschaftswunder," *Manager Magazin*, February 2022.
5. "Messi slaat hard terug en klaagt vijf Barça bobo's aan na lekken supercontract," *Voetbalprimeur*, February 3, 2021.
6. "Vorstandsboss Karl-Heinz Rummenigge vom FC Bayern: Lionel Messi? 'Musste lachen,'" *Goal*, February 16, 2021.
7. Nesshöver, "Wirtschaftswunder."
8. "Griezmann: I Spoke with Messi."
9. Jordi Quixano, "Gerard Piqué: "Anfield fue una pesadilla que perdurará en el tiempo," *El País*, May 25, 2019.
10. Michael Cox, "It's Time for Barcelona to Stop Obsessing over 'the Guardiola Way,'" *The Athletic*, September 24, 2020.
11. UEFA Champions League, *Technical Report 2019/20* (Nyon, Switzerland: UEFA, 2020).
12. Michael Cox, "The Bielsa Paradox: How Can Someone So Influential Also Be So Unique?," *The Athletic*, November 24, 2020.
13. Simon Kuper, "At Barcelona It's Lionel Messi, Piqué and the Players Who Hold the Power, Not the Manager," ESPN, January 22, 2020.
14. Rodriguez and Querol, *Matchday*, episode 5.
15. Rodriguez and Querol, *Matchday*, episode 6.
16. Neveling, *Jurgen Klopp*, 308–9.
17. Ken Early, "Did Lionel Messi's Team Talk Help Liverpool Beat Barcelona?," *Irish Times*, December 2, 2019.
18. Rodriguez and Querol, *Matchday*, episode 7.
19. Rodriguez and Querol, *Matchday*, episode 6.
20. Martijn Krabbendam, "Ronald Koeman: het jaar van corona, een hartinfarct, en de hoofdrol in een Barça-storm," *Voetbal International*, December 17, 2020.
21. "Monsterklus Koeman: Frenkie's rol, Messi's onvrede en vernieuwen zonder geld," Voetbalprimeur, August 19, 2020.
22. Rodriguez and Querol, *Matchday*, episode 7.
23. Sid Lowe, "Barcelona in Meltdown After Lionel Messi Hits Back at Eric Abidal," *Guardian*, February 4, 2020.
24. Law, "Eric Abidal Exclusive."
25. Sámano and Enrique Ortego, "Quique Setién: "En el Barça no fui yo, no pude o no supe," *El País*, October 31, 2020.
26. Sam Marsden, "Setien on Barcelona Job: Beyond My 'Wildest Dreams' to Go from Cows to Camp Nou," ESPN, January 14, 2020.

27. Tom Sanderson, "FC Barcelona Contract Social Media Firm to Attack Messi, Pique and Others, Claims Scandalous Report," *Forbes*, February 17, 2020; Sid Lowe, "Messi: Barcelona Not in Shape to Win Champions League but I Want to Stay," *Guardian*, February 20, 2020; Santi Giménez, "Barcelona: Piqué Makes It Clear That Bartomeu Not Believed," *AS*, February 19, 2020; Javier Miguel, "Audit Company Points Finger at Barcelona over I3 Ventures Affair," *AS*, April 11, 2020; Sid Lowe, "Carry on Barcelona: The Comic Tale of Tragedy and Drama That Keeps on Giving," *Guardian*, April 11, 2020; Cillian Shields, "Barça President Accused of Corruption in Catalan Police Investigation," *Catalan News*, September 4, 2020.

28. "Monsterklus Koeman."

29. Cristina Cubero and Fernando Polo, "Messi: 'Hoy no nos alcanza para pelear por la Champions,'" *Mundo Deportivo*, February 20, 2020.

30. John Burn-Murdoch and Chris Giles, "UK Suffers Second-Highest Death Rate from Coronavirus," *Financial Times*, May 28, 2020.

31. Sam Carp, "Barcelona Profits Down Despite Hitting Record €990m Revenue," SportsPro, July 25, 2019.

32. "Messi carga contra Abidal por implicar a los jugadores en el cese de Valverde: 'Se nos está ensuciando a todos,'" *La Vanguardia*, February 4, 2020.

33. Rapinoe, *One Life*, 211.

34. Sámano and Ortego, "Quique Setién."

35. Jop Goslinga, *Força Koeman* (Videoland, 2021), season 1, episode 1.

36. Krabbendam, "Ronald Koeman."

37. Goslinga, *Força Koeman*, season 1, episode 2.

38. Trailer of the Força Koeman documentary, Videoland.com.

39. Goslinga, *Força Koeman*, season 1, episode 1.

40. Javier Miguel, "Cumbre inminente entre Koeman y Messi," *AS*, August 20, 2020.

41. Martijn Krabbendam, "Het beste uit 2021: een openhartig gesprek met Koeman over het gemis van Messi," *Voetbal International*, December 27, 2021.

42. "Koeman Tells Messi: 'Your Privileges Are Over' as Captain Demands Barcelona Exit," *AS*, August 26, 2020.

43. Krabbendam, "Het beste uit 2021."

44. Rubén Uría, "EXCLU—Lionel Messi reste au Barça et brise le silence!," *Goal*, September 4, 2020.

45. Enrique Ortego, "El gran problema de Messi es que compite consigo mismo."

46. Uría, "EXCLU—Lionel Messi reste au Barça et brise le silence!"

47. Uría, "EXCLU—Lionel Messi reste au Barça et brise le silence!"

48. Cristina Navarro, "Elena Fort: 'Hay operarios vigilando que no salten los plomos durante los partidos,'" *Marca*, October 17, 2021.

49. Murad Ahmed, "Fire Sale at Spain's Top Football Clubs Forced by Lower Spending Limit," *Financial Times*, November 17, 2020.

50. Tom Knipping, "Zwarte cijfers Real Madrid pijnlijk voor Barça," *Voetbal International*, January 5, 2021.

51. Sid Lowe, "La Liga Kept Messi at Barcelona, but the Talent Drain to the Premier League Is a Concern," ESPN, October 16, 2020.

52. Sergi Escudero, "Cinto Ajram: 'La incertidumbre de Messi ha afectado al acuerdo con Rakuten,'" EFE, November 13, 2020.

53. Javier Miguel, "Barcelona Captains Issue Scathing Letter to Board," *AS*, October 22, 2020.

54. "Neymar entra en la lista de morosos de Hacienda con una deuda de 34 millones," *El Español*, September 30, 2020.

55. Goslinga, *Força Koeman*, season 2, episode 2.

56. Yanick Vos, "Ronald Koeman: 'Ik zie wel parallellen met Frenkie en Mikky,'" Voetbalzone, February 18, 2021.

57. Vos, "Ronald Koeman: 'Ik zie wel parallellen met Frenkie en Mikky,"

58. Krabbendam, "Ronald Koeman."

59. Martijn Krabbendam, "Club Brugge krijgt de beste versie van Alfred Schreuder," *Voetbal International*, January 12, 2022.

60. Goslinga, *Força Koeman*, season 2, episode 3.

61. Panja and Smith, "Barcelona and the Crippling Cost of Success."

62. See the Twitter thread at https://twitter.com/SwissRamble/status/1358675740 145950720?s=20, February 7, 2021.

63. "El Barça, en bus a Huesca para ahorrar," *Mundo Deportivo*, January 5, 2021.

64. Wijffels, "Barça-assistent Schreuder."

65. Martijn Krabbendam, "Het beste uit 2021," *Voetbal International*, December 27, 2021.

66. Jordi Blanco, "El Barcelona da inicio a su carrera electoral con la entrega de papeletas a precandidatos," ESPN Deportes, December 23, 2020.

67. Roger Pascual and Albert Guasch, "Laporta consigue al fin el aval," *El Periódico*, March 16, 2021.

68. "José Elías, el nuevo socio de Laporta: ingeniero, emprendedor y una de la grandes fortunas de España," *Marca*, March 17, 2021.

69. Nesshöver, "Wirtschaftswunder."

70. Goslinga, *Força Koeman*, season 2, episode 3.

XVII: The End?

1. John Carlin, "Inside the Mind of Lionel Messi—and What Next for Barcelona?," *The Times* (London), September 10, 2021.

2. Robin Bairner, "Messi to PSG: Transfer 10 Years in the Making and Completed in a Matter of Days," *Goal*, August 14, 2021.

3. Florent Torchut, "Lionel Messi sur son arrivée au PSG: 'Je ne me suis pas trompé,'" *L'Equipe*, October 18, 2021.

4. Carlin, "Inside the Mind of Lionel Messi."

5. Dermot Corrigan, "Life after Messi for Barcelona: More Cuts, More Anger, More Drama," *The Athletic*, August 11, 2021.

6. Corrigan, "Life after Messi for Barcelona."
7. Goslinga, *Força Koeman,* season 2, episode 3.
8. Adam Crafton, "How Paris Saint-Germain Signed Lionel Messi," *The Athletic,* August 10, 2021.
9. Lluís Mascaró and Albert Masnou, "Messi, a SPORT: 'Me gustaría volver al Barça para ayudar, de secretario técnico,'" *Sport,* November 1, 2021.
10. "Luuk de Jong recupère le casier de Lionel Messi," *SoFoot,* September 10, 2021.
11. AP, "Barcelona's Finances Holding Up New Messi Contract," Euronews, July 1, 2021.
12. Sid Lowe, "Ferran Torres Has Joined Barcelona, but His Debut Is Unclear as Club Tries to Creatively Work Around Debt," ESPN, January 4, 2022.
13. "Barcelona Approves Debt Plan for Stadium Renovation," Reuters, December 20, 2021.

INDEX

Italicized page numbers indicate material in tables.